CW01337726

Transformations of the State

Series Editors: **Achim Hurrelmann**, Carleton University, Canada; **Stephan Leibfried**, University of Bremen, Germany; **Kerstin Martens**, University of Bremen, Germany; **Peter Mayer**, University of Bremen, Germany.

Titles include:

Steffen Schneider, Achim Hurrelmann, Zuzana Krell-Laluhová, Frank Nullmeier and Achim Wiesner
DEMOCRACY'S DEEP ROOTS
Why the Nation State Remains Legitimate

Peter Starke
RADICAL WELFARE STATE RETRENCHMENT
A Comparative Analysis

Peter Starke, Alexandra Kaasch, Franca Van Hooren (*editors*)
THE WELFARE STATE AS CRISIS MANAGER
Explaining the Diversity of Policy Responses to Economic Crisis

Silke Weinlich
THE UN SECRETARIAT'S INFLUENCE ON THE EVOLUTION OF PEACEKEEPING

Hartmut Wessler (*editor*)
PUBLIC DELIBERATION AND PUBLIC CULTURE
The Writings of Bernhard Peters, 1993–2005

Hartmut Wessler, Bernhard Peters, Michael Brüggeman, Katharina Kleinen-von Königslöw and Stefanie Sifft
TRANSNATIONALIZATION OF PUBLIC SPHERES

Jochen Zimmermann and Jörg R. Werner
REGULATING CAPITALISM?
The Evolution of Transnational Accounting Governance

Jochen Zimmerman, Jörg R. Werner and Philipp B. Volmer
GLOBAL GOVERNANCE IN ACCOUNTING
Public Power and Private Commitment

Transformations of the State
Series Standing Order ISBN   978–1–403–98544–6 (hardback)
                                 978–1–403–98545–3 (paperback)

You can receive future titles in this series as they are published by placing a standing order. Please contact your bookseller or, in case of difficulty, write to us at the address below with your name and address, the title of the series and one of the ISBNs quoted above.

Customer Services Department, Macmillan Distribution Ltd, Houndmills, Basingstoke, Hampshire RG21 6XS, England

Public Sector Employment Regimes

Transformations of the State as an Employer

Karin Gottschall
Professor of Sociology, University of Bremen, Germany

Bernhard Kittel
Professor of Economic Sociology, University of Vienna, Austria

Kendra Briken
Lecturer, University of Strathclyde, United Kingdom

Jan-Ocko Heuer
Postdoctoral Researcher, Humboldt University Berlin, Germany

Sylvia Hils
Research Assistant, University of Bremen, Germany

Sebastian Streb
Bremen, Germany

Markus Tepe
Professor of Political Science, University of Oldenburg, Germany

First published 2015 by
PALGRAVE MACMILLAN

Palgrave Macmillan in the UK is an imprint of Macmillan Publishers Limited, registered in England, company number 785998, of Houndmills, Basingstoke, Hampshire RG21 6XS.

Palgrave Macmillan in the US is a division of St Martin's Press LLC, 175 Fifth Avenue, New York, NY 10010.

Palgrave Macmillan is the global academic imprint of the above companies and has companies and representatives throughout the world.

Palgrave® and Macmillan® are registered trademarks in the United States, the United Kingdom, Europe and other countries.

ISBN: 978–0–230–33715–2

This book is printed on paper suitable for recycling and made from fully managed and sustained forest sources. Logging, pulping and manufacturing processes are expected to conform to the environmental regulations of the country of origin.

A catalogue record for this book is available from the British Library.

Library of Congress Cataloging-in-Publication Data

Gottschall, Karin.
    Public sector employment regimes : transformations of the state as an employer / Karin Gottschall, Bernhard Kittel, Kendra Briken, Jan-Ocko Heuer, Sylvia Hils, Sebastian Streb, Markus Tepe
       pages cm.—(Transfromations of the state)
    ISBN 978–0–230–33715–2 (hardback)
    1. Civil service – European Union countries. 2. Public administration – European Union countries. 3. Public-private sector cooperation – European Union countries. I. Title.

JN94.A67G67 2015
352.6094—dc23   2015020076

Contents

List of Figures

List of Tables

Series Preface

Over the past four centuries, the nation-state has emerged as the world's most effective means of organizing society, but its current status and future are decidedly uncertain. Some scholars predict the total demise of the nation-state as we know it, its powers eroded by a dynamic global economy on the one hand and by the transfer of political decision making to supranational bodies on the other. Other analysts point out the remarkable resilience of the state's core institutions and assert that even in the age of global markets and politics, the state remains the ultimate guarantor of security, democracy, welfare, and the rule of law. Does either of these interpretations describe the future of the OECD world's modern, liberal nation-state? Will the state soon be as obsolete and irrelevant as an outdated computer? Should it be scrapped for some new invention, or can it be overhauled and rejuvenated? Or is the state actually thriving and still fit to serve, just in need of a few minor reforms?

In an attempt to address these questions, the analyses in the *Transformations of the State* series separate the complex tangle of tasks and functions that comprise the state into four manageable dimensions:

- the monopolization of the means of force;
- the rule of law, as prescribed and safeguarded by the constitution;
- the guarantee of democratic self-governance; and
- the provision of welfare and the assurance of social cohesion.

In the OECD world of the 1960s and 1970s, these four dimensions formed a synergetic constellation that emerged as the central, defining characteristic of the modern state. Books in the series report the results of both empirical and theoretical studies of the transformations experienced in each of these dimensions over the past few decades.

Transformations of the State? (Stephan Leibfried and Michael Zürn (eds), Cambridge 2005), *Transforming the Golden-Age National State* (Achim Hurrelmann, Stephan Leibfried, Kerstin Martens, and Peter Mayer (eds), Basingstoke 2007), *State Transformations in OECD Countries: Dimensions, Driving Forces and Trajectories* (Heinz Rothgang and Steffen Schneider (eds), Basingstoke 2015), and *The Oxford Handbook of Transformations of the State* (Stephan Leibfried, Evelyne Huber, Matthew Lange, Jonah Levy, and Frank Nullmeier (eds), Oxford 2015) define the basic concepts of state transformation employed in all of these studies and provide an overview of the issues addressed. Written by political scientists, lawyers, economists, and sociologists, the series tracks the development of the Post-World War II OECD state. Here, at last, is an up-to-date series of reports on the state of the state and a crystal-ball glimpse into its future.

Preface

The public sector and especially the civil service were long seen as the model of protected employment in advanced welfare capitalism. Even in the normative wake of new forms of management, the public sectors of continental European countries seemed more resistant than the United Kingdom, the forerunner in addressing public deficits by privatizing public services and aligning public to private employment, which has been part of a transformation strategy known as 'New Public Management' (NPM). The focus of this book is on the effects of state transformations on change in public and civil service employment in Europe. It aims to shed light on the difficulties encountered and opportunities taken when coping with the challenges of providing public services to society. Looking back at about three decades of reforms, we hope to contribute some insights to the conditions of successfully balancing two main aims of public service provision: efficacy and efficiency.

The research on which the book is based involves both a broad analysis of change in public sector employment in all OECD countries and a deeper comparison of change in continental European states – France, Germany, and Sweden – in contrast to the United Kingdom. An important contrast between these cases is marked by the civil law tradition in many continental and Scandinavian European states versus the common law basis of public administration in the United Kingdom. The analyses find accelerated change in public employment across Europe, while the nature of reform in specific national contexts both confirms the impact of civil versus common law traditions and uncovers a number of unexpected differences between European countries with a civil law tradition.

The volume reports core results of the research project 'Transformation of the State as Employer: Public Employment Regimes between Efficiency and Effectiveness', which has been a project in the Collaborative Research Center 597 'Transformations of the State' from 2008 to 2014 at the University of Bremen, the Jacobs University Bremen, and the Carl von Ossietzky University of Oldenburg. We gratefully acknowledge the German Research Foundation's financial support and the reviewers' thorough reading of the initial proposal. We also acknowledge additional funding to Bernhard Kittel by the Ministry of Science and Culture of the State of Lower Saxony in the framework of the VW-Vorab funding facility, which allowed us to add manpower to the project at the University of Oldenburg. Furthermore, the University of Bremen supported the project with a part-time researcher position and awarded a sabbatical to Karin Gottschall to work on the project.

Many people were helpful in preparing this manuscript. In the initial stage of the project, Daniela Kroos prepared parts of the sections on France and on the police, and Julia-Carolin Brachem was engaged in the collection of aggregate data for the cross-national analyses. Several students provided support throughout the fieldwork and data analysis, namely Insa Bertram, Anna-Lena Borchert, Milena Brechenmacher, Theresa Kromer, Stephanie Lamping, Mathis Salfeld, and Hanna Schaub. Towards the end of the project, Mandi Larsen polished the manuscript's language, Jenny Hahs checked the references and supported the final editing process in various ways, Silke Birkenstock took care of the layout of the manuscript, and Julia Dorner reviewed all editorial aspects of the manuscript and in cooperation with Bernadette Rapp was in charge of the index.

Comparative analysis is a challenge, and we acknowledge the fruitful cooperation and support in the development of instruments and discussion of results with Clémence Ledoux, Benjamin Pabion, Christian Mouhanna, and Marja Lemne and her team. We also benefited from scholarly feedback as well as comments received at various conferences, in particular from Berndt Keller, Gerhard Hammerschmid, Margarita Estévez-Abe, Berthold Vogel, Wolfgang Ludwig-Mayerhofer, and Kai-Uwe Schnapp.

In particular, we thank Stephan Leibfried, speaker of the Collaborative Research Center, for motivating us to engage in this project and contribute an analysis of public employment to the second and third phases of the research centre (2007–10 and 2011–14, respectively). The most fundamental thought underlying the conception of the project – the idea of a transformation of the ideal typical 'civil servant' to the ideal typical 'public service provider' – is to be attributed to him.

The authors of the volume contributed in various ways to the overall project. Kendra Briken conducted the research for, conceptualized, and wrote large parts of the sections on France and on the police. Sylvia Hils led the research and wrote the sections on Germany and on waste collection, and Sebastian Streb those on Sweden and energy regulatory agencies. Markus Tepe was primarily responsible for drafting the sections on cross-national analysis in Chapter 4. Jan-Ocko Heuer, although joining in the final phase, was the project's invaluable firefighter and added important elements to all chapters, but in particular to the first draft of the section on the United Kingdom. Bernhard Kittel drafted Chapter 2 on theory and Chapter 3 on methods, as well as parts of the conclusion in Chapter 10. Karin Gottschall wrote the drafts of Chapters 1 and 9 and the second draft of Chapter 10. Karin Gottschall and Bernhard Kittel share responsibility for the overall project, and all authors share authorship of the volume equally. The names of the authors are differentiated according to their role in the project (principal investigator and researcher) and listed in alphabetical order within each role.

List of Abbreviations

§	section
§§	sections
2. BesVNG	Zweites Gesetz zur Vereinheitlichung und Neuregelung des Besoldungsrechts in Bund und Ländern [Second Law to Unify and Revise Pay Regulations for the Federal Government and *Länder*; Germany]
AAI	Autorité administrative indépendante [quasi-autonomous non-governmental organisation; France]
AC	Audit Commission [United Kingdom]
ADEME	Agence de l'environnement et de la maîtrise de l'énergie [French Environment and Energy Management Agency]
AIC	Akaike information criterion
Art.	article
AT	Austria
AU	Australia
BAC	baccalauréat [high school diploma; France]
BAT	Bundes-Angestelltentarifvertrag [Federal Employees' Collective Agreement; Germany]
BBC	British Broadcasting Corporation
BBesG	Bundesbesoldungsgesetz [Civil Servants' Renumeration Act; Germany]
BBG	Bundesbeamtengesetz [Federal Civil Service Act; Germany]
BDE	Bundesverband der Deutschen Entsorgungs-, Wasser- und Rohstoffwirtschaft e.V. [Federation of the German Waste, Water and Raw Materials Management Industry]
BDG	Bundesdisziplinargesetz [Federal Disciplinary Law; Germany]
BdK	Bund deutscher Kriminalbeamter [Federation of German Criminal Investigators]
BE	Belgium
BGBl.	Bundesgesetzesblatt [Federal Law Gazette; Germany]
BIC	Bayesian Information Criterion
BKrFQG	Berufskraftfahrer-Qualifikations-Gesetz [Professional Drivers' Qualification Law; Germany]
BLV	Bundeslaufbahnverordnung [Federal Career Regulation; Germany]
BMAS	Bundesministerium für Arbeit und Soziales [Federal Ministry of Labour and Social Affairs; Germany]

BMT-G	Bundesmanteltarifvertrag für Arbeiter gemeindlicher Verwaltungen und Betriebe [Federal Collective Agreement for Workers of Municipal Administrations and Companies; Germany]
BNetzA	Bundesnetzagentur für Elektrizität, Gas, Telekommunikation, Post und Eisenbahnen [Federal Network Agency for Electricity, Gas, Telecommunications, Post and Railway; Germany]
BRRG	Beamtenrechtsrahmengesetz [Civil Service Framework Act; Germany]
BSC	balanced scorecard
CA	Canada
CCNAD	Convention collective nationale des activités du déchet [National collective agreement on waste activities; France]
CCT	compulsory competitive tendering
CDG	Centre(s) de gestion de la fonction publique territoriale [Human resource coordination centres of the local authorities; France]
CH	Switzerland
CKP	Certificate in Knowledge of Policing [United Kingdom]
CNFTP	Centre national de la fonction publique territoriale [National human resource centre of the local authorities; France]
COFOG	Classification of the Functions of Government
CRE	Commission de régulation de l'énergie [Regulatory Commission of Energy; France]
CRS	Compagnies républicaines de sécurité [Republican Security Companies; France]
CS	civil servant
CSC	Civil Service Commission [United Kingdom]
CSMC	Civil Service Management Code [United Kingdom]
CTP	comité technique paritaire [joint technical committee representing the employees and the employers; France]
CVT	continual vocational training
DBB	Beamtenbund und Tarifunion (formerly: Deutscher Beamtenbund) [German Civil Service Federation]
DE	Germany
DEA	data envelopment analysis
DGB	Deutscher Gewerkschaftsbund [German Confederation of Trade Unions]
DGleiG	Gesetz zur Durchsetzung der Gleichstellung von Frauen und Männern in der Bundesverwaltung und in den Gerichten des Bundes [Act to Enforce the Equality between Men and Women in the Federal Administration and in the Federal Courts; Germany]
DIF	droit individuel à la formation [individual training right; France]

DK	Denmark
DLO	Direct Labour Organisation [United Kingdom]
DPolG	Deutsche Polizeigewerkschaft [Germany]
DSO	Direct Service Organisation [United Kingdom]
E	energy (regulatory agency/agencies)
EC	European Commission
eds.	editors
EEA	European Economic Area
EI	Energimarknadsinspektionen [Swedish Energy Markets Inspectorate]
empl.	employment
ENA	École Nationale d'Administration [National School of Administration; France]
EnWG	Energiewirtschaftsgesetz [Energy Industry Act; Germany]
EPA	Environmental Protection Act 1990 [United Kingdom]
EPA France	Établissement public à caractère administratif [Public administrative body with legal personality; France]
ERA	Employment Rights Act 1996 [United Kingdom]
ES	Spain
et al.	et alii/aliae
EU	European Union
EUGleichbUmsG	Gesetz zur Umsetzung europäischer Richtlinien zur Verwirklichung des Grundsatzes der Gleichbehandlung [Act on the Implementation of European Directives Implementing the Principle of Equal Treatment; Germany]
EUR	Euro(s)
EUROFOUND	European Foundation for the Improvement of Living and Working Conditions
exp.	expenditure
FI	Finland
FPE	fonction publique de l'Etat [State civil service; France]
FPH	fonction publique hospitalière [Hospital public service; France]
FPT	fonction publique territoriale [Territorial civil service; France]
FR	France
GBP	British Pound(s) Sterling
GdP	Gewerkschaft der Polizei [Police Trade Union; Germany]
GDP	gross domestic product
GEMA	Gas and Electricity Markets Authority [United Kingdom]

GG   Grundgesetz [Basic Law; Germany]
GNP   gross national product
gov.   government
GVBl.   Gesetz- und Verordnungsblatt [Law and Ordinance Gazette; Germany]
HM   Her/His Majesty's [United Kingdom]
HMIC   Her/His Majesty's Inspectorate of Constabulary [United Kingdom]
HÖK   Huvudöverenskommelse om lön och allmänna anställningsvillkor [Main agreement on wages and general terms of employment; Sweden]
HR   Human Resource
HRM   Human Resource Management
HSE   Health and Safety Excutive [United Kingdom]
IDS   Incomes Data Service
IE   Ireland
IEP   Instituts d'études politiques [Institutes of Political Studies; France]
IFSE   Indemnité de fonctions, de sujétions et d'expertise [wage premium related to the function exercised, the level of technicality and expertise of the job and the work's environment; France]
ILO   International Labour Organization
IMK   Innenministerkonferenz [Interior Ministers' Conference; Germany]
IPLDP   Initial Police Learning and Development Programme [United Kingdom]
IRA   independent regulatory agency
IS   Iceland
ISCO   International Standard Classification of Occupations
IT   information technology
IT   Italy
JP   Japan
KAV   Kommunaler Arbeitgeberverband [Local Employers' Association; Germany]
KFS   Kommunala företagens samorganisation [Swedish Organiation for Local Enterprises; Sweden]
KGSt   Kommunale Gemeinschaftsstelle für Verwaltungsmanagement [Municipal Community Office for Public Management; Germany]
KOM-KL   Överenskommelse om Omställningsavtal [Agreement on the Transition Agreements; Sweden]
LGA   Local Government Association [United Kingdom]
LGE   Local Government Employers [United Kingdom]
LIS   Luxembourg Income Study

LOLF	Loi organique relative aux lois de finances [Constitutional bylaw on budget acts; France]
LTC	Leadership Training Centre
MAP	Modernisation de l'action publique [Modernisation of public action; France]
MCA	multiple correspondence analysis
MPA	Metropolitan Police Authority [United Kingdom]
MPS	Metropolitan Police Service [United Kingdom]
MTArb	Manteltarifvertrag für Arbeiterinnen und Arbeiter des Bundes und der Länder [Collective Agreement for Workers of the Federal and State Governments; Germany]
n°	numéro (= number)
NBI	nouvelle bonification indiciaire [new bonification scale; France]
NCF	National Competency Framework [United Kingdom]
NHS	National Health Service [United Kingdom]
NIA	National Income Accounts
NJC	National Joint Council [United Kingdom]
NL	Netherlands
NO	Norway
NPB	National Police Board [United Kingdom]
NPIA	National Policing Improvement Agency [United Kingdom]
NPM	new public management
NSM	Neues Steuerungsmodell [New Steering Model; Germany]
NT	non-titulaire [non-permanent; France]
NWS	Neo-Weberian State
OECD	Organisation for Economic Co-operation and Development
Offer	Office of Electricity Regulation [United Kingdom]
Ofgas	Office of Gas Supply [United Kingdom]
Ofgem	Office of Gas and Electricity Markets [United Kingdom]
P	police
p	p-value, probability-test
p.	page
PACTA	Arbetsgivarförbundet för kommunalförbund och företag [Employers' Association of Municipal Associations and Companies; Sweden]
para.	paragraph
PCSO	Police Community Support Officer [United Kingdom]
PE	public employee
perc.	percentage
PNB	Police Negotiating Board [United Kingdom]
pp.	pages
PPFA	Police Performance Assessment Framework [United Kingdom]
PRP	performance-related pay
PSA	Police Superintendents' Association of England and Wales

PSC	Police Staff Council [United Kingdom]
PT	Portugal
QCF	Qualifications and Credit Framework [United Kingdom]
RALS	Ramavtal om löner inom staten [Framework agreement on wages and more for employees in the public sector agreements; Sweden]
ReföDG	Gesetz zur Reform des öffentlichen Dienstrechts (Reformgesetz) [Act to Amend the Public Service Act; Germany]
RegBl.	Regierungsblatt [Gazette; Germany]
RegTP	Regulierungsbehörde für Telekommunikation und Post [Regulatory Authority for Telecommunications and Post; Germany]
RGPP	révision générale des politiques publiques [French General Review of Public Policies]
S.	Seite (= page)
Saco	Sveriges akademikers centralorganisation [Swedish Confederation of Professional Associations]
Saco-s	Sveriges akademikers centralorganisation för statligt anställda [Swedish Confederation of Professional Associations for Public Employees]
SAGE	Swedish Agency for Government Employers [Swedish: Arbetsgivarverket]
SAP	Sveriges socialdemokratiska arbetareparti [Swedish Social Democratic Party]
SCP	Stockholm County Police [Sweden]
SCPN	Syndicat des commissaires de la Police nationale [Union of police commissioners; France]
SCS	Senior Civil Service [United Kingdom]
SE	Sweden
SEK	Swedish Krona/Kronor
Seko	Facket för service och kommunikation [Union for Service and Communications Employees; Sweden]
SFJUK	Skills for Justice UK
SGI	sustainable governance indicators
SKL	Sveriges Kommuner och Landsting [Swedish Association of Local Authorities and Regions]
SNA	United Nations System of National Accounts
SNOP-UNSA	Syndicat national des officiers de police – Union nationale des syndicats autonomes [Union of police commissioners – National union of autonomous unions; France]
SOU	Statens offentliga utredningar [Swedish Government Official Reports]

ST	Fackförbundet statsförvaltningens tjänstemannaförening [Union of Civil Servants; Sweden]
TdL	Tarifgemeinschaft deutscher Länder [Employers' Association of German *Länder*; Germany]
TQM	total quality management
TRUDI	Western nation-states after the Second World War until the 1970s, characterized by territorial unity, rule of law, legitimized by democracy and willing to intervene into market developments (Leibfried and Zürn 2005)
TULCRA	Trade Union and Labor Relations (Consolidation) Act [United Kingdom]
TUPE	Transfer of Undertakings Protection of Employment [United Kingdom]
TV-L	Tarifvertrag für den öffentlichen Dienst der Länder [Collective Agreement for the Public Service of the *Länder*; Germany]
TVöD	Tarifvertrag für den öffentlichen Dienst [Collective Agreement for the Public Service; Germany]
UK	United Kingdom of Great Britain and Northern Ireland
UN	United Nations
UNISON	Public Service Sector Union [United Kingdom]
UNSA	Union nationale des syndicats autonomes [National union of autonomous unions; France]
US	United States of America
USA	United States of America
ver.di	Vereinigte Dienstleistungsgewerkschaft [United Services Trade Union; Germany]
VKA	Verband der kommunalen Arbeitgeberverbände [Municipal Employers' Association; Germany]
VKS	Verband Kommunaler Abfallwirtschaft und Stadtreinigung [Association of Municipal Waste Management and City Cleaning; Germany]
vol.	volume(s)
vs.	versus
W	waste collection
WeGebAU	Weiterbildung Geringqualifizierter und beschäftigter Älterer in Unternehmen [Training for Low-skilled Workers and Older Workers in Companies; Germany]
WIRS92	Workplace and Industrial Relations Survey of 1992 [United Kingdom]
WIRS98	Workplace and Industrial Relations Survey of 1998 [United Kingdom]

1
Introduction

Setting the scene: public sector and state transformation

Since the 1980s, the public sector has constantly been an object of structural reforms and quantitative adjustments. In several waves, public infrastructures and services have been privatized, political power and responsibility have been decentralized and recentralized to and from the regional and local levels, and new forms of management in public administration have been implemented, thereby substantially changing the face of Western nation-states.

Driven by pressures of cost containment and a neo-liberal political agenda, many of these changes imply that the responsibility for the provision of public goods, which for a long time was linked to distinct public employment regimes, no longer lies with the state alone, but is shared with other (private) actors. Moreover, when still in charge, the state aligns its activities in the provision of services to market rules (Derlien and Peters 2008; Vaughan-Whitehead 2013).

In a broader context, these processes have been considered part of the 'unravelling' of the Western nation-state, defined as a *territorial unit (T)* which secures the *rule of law (RU)*, is legitimized by *democracy (D)*, and is willing to *intervene (I)* in market developments, summarized in the acronym TRUDI (Leibfried et al. 2015; Leibfried and Zürn 2005). The decline of TRUDI evolved in an era of accelerated economic and political globalization, in which more and more traditional state functions have been supplemented by, or handed over to, private providers or transferred to the international arena. Thereby, core attributes of the modern democratic Western state, such as sovereignty, the rule of law, and welfare provision, have been undermined (Grimm 2005; Scharpf 2000).

However, as many scholars have pointed out, the catchy narrative of nation-state decline in favour of markets is one-sided. It fails to capture the fact that market-making is also the product of state intervention. Many of the same international developments that are claimed to narrow the scope of the state, such as free capital and human resource flows, at the same time enable and call for new state activities, such as the regulation of financial markets or border controls (Levy et al. 2015). The same holds true for the privatization of public infrastructure, such as energy or telecommunication, where the newly created markets tend to be dominated by large corporations which have emanated from former state monopolies. In these fields, although the state is no longer engaged in the provision and organization of this infrastructure, it nevertheless has to take on the role of market control, which is visible in many countries in newly set-up agencies after the first waves of public infrastructure privatization (Schneider et al. 2005; Zohlnhöfer et al. 2008).

Likewise, adjustments in the volume and structure of public employment need not necessarily indicate a retreat of the state. While employment is obviously shifted from the public to the private sector by the privatization of infrastructure and the welfare state reforms privileging market provision of social services, enhanced state activities in other areas, such as public security, often imply an increase in budget and personnel (in this case, for police forces), emphasizing the provision of security as a core state function (Derlien and Peters 2008). Even personnel restructuring in public administrations and services inspired by private sector management methods may reinforce rather than weaken the role of the state. To the extent that personnel with higher qualifications becomes more important for the provision of public goods, and to the extent that public employment regimes approach private sector regimes, the openness to private labour markets imposes on the state as employer the need to be more competitive – that is, to invest in its attractiveness as an employer.

Thus, rather than addressing changes in state activities as a decline, they should be analysed as a *transformation* of states' capacities to act in changing economic, political, and social environments (Sørensen 2004; Levy 2006; Levy et al. 2015). Given the diverse facets of state activity, as well as its embeddedness in multi-level systems and national institutional orders, adequately capturing these transformations provides a challenge which can best be met by breaking down state activities into various dimensions, each of which needs to be explored (Hurrelmann et al. 2007, p. 2).

Against the background of these developments, in this volume we will address the role of the state as employer as a core element of state activity, and focus on public employment as a basic resource for the provision of a variety of normative goods in Western nation-states.[1] The main focus of the book is on changing public employment regimes, which have so far been mainly studied by scholars in public administration research. Informed by insights from both labour market sociology and political science, this book explores the role of the state as employer in a broader context. Under conditions of budget restrictions and public sector reform on the one hand and competition with the market sector on the other, how is the state shaping the employment conditions and relations of civil servants and public employees?

Change dynamics: from public sector expansion to public sector reform

Obviously, the very existence of the modern democratic nation-state rests on the existence and functioning of a public administration (Rose 1985; Derlien and Peters 2008). From the very beginning, the effectiveness and efficiency of state action has been dependent 'on the success of the state in creating bureaucratic organizations close to the Weberian ideal type' (Huber et al. 2015, p. 15). At the core of these bureaucracies is the ideal type of the *civil servant*, who trades employment security and other privileges against loyalty to the state.

While originally focused on securing safety and the rule of law, during the 'Golden Age' of the welfare state from the 1960s to the 1980s, the modern democratic state also took on the role of providing encompassing infrastructure and welfare to its citizens. Based on economic prosperity and rising state revenues in the post-war era, most Western states expanded public employment in order to provide services in a wide array of social and economic spheres, including social security, education, healthcare, labour market services, and infrastructure (Flora 1986; Kaufmann 2001). The employment conditions of the civil service included high employment security, seniority rules in pay and advancement, and prescribed career paths, which distinguished public employment from employment in the private sector. Higher standards in employment conditions were not only meant to counterbalance unilateral state power in setting employment conditions excluding or restricting the public workforce's right to strike. Rather, public employment and the state as employer also served as a role model for employment in the private sector, through high standards in work and employment and the integration of groups disadvantaged in the private labour market, such as women, disabled persons, and migrants (Bach and Kessler 2007).

Irrespective of different historical, cultural, and social traditions in the formation of the public sector and the regulation of public employment in Western states, the above-mentioned specificities and the rising share of the public sector workforce during the 'Golden Age' coined public employment as a distinct form of employment and a core element of mature welfare states.[2] This post-war 'Golden Age' set the scene for changes in the public sector and in public employment from the 1980s onwards.

Cost pressures arising from the expansion of the welfare state and inherent in the labour-intensive service sector (Baumol 1967) on the one hand and a shift from Keynesianism to monetarism in public policymaking (Pierson 2001) on the other reframed the conception of the state towards the limits of state action. This new frame challenged the traditional organization and profile of the public sector and paved the way for a marketization of public services. This trend not only induced privatization of public infrastructure and services (Schneider et al. 2005) but also instigated a process of administrative restructuring in the remaining public sector, whereby decentralization became a new imperative and, most importantly, market mechanisms and incentive schemes were introduced to replace traditional bureaucratic procedures (Hood 1991). The reform toolkits summarized under the heading of New Public Management (NPM), next to decentralization, encompass a broad spectrum of measures. These range from the introduction of performance measurement, coordination of public policy by contract instead of hierarchy, and the introduction of market-type mechanisms for the provision of public services (for example, tendering) to considering citizens as customers and using quality improvement techniques (Pollitt and Bouckaert 2011). Some of these measures either directly or indirectly impact public employment, as they seek to reduce the historical particularity of the employment conditions in the public sector. In this context, business-oriented Human Resource Management (HRM), deemed to be more efficient than traditional bureaucratic procedures, has become an important driver of reforming employment regulation and personnel politics in the public sector (Derlien and Peters 2008, pp. 5f; Bach and Bordogna 2011).

The research challenge

These public sector reforms and concurrent changes in public employment since the 1990s have been widely analysed in public administration research. However, what is missing in this field, as well as in sociology and political science, is a comparative perspective focusing on the specific role of the state as employer. Moreover, irrespective of valuable insights from this rich body of research, there are still open questions to be addressed regarding a generalization of reform paths and reform impact on employment. Moreover, there is a bias in favour of general government.

Undoubtedly, the NPM doctrine, promoted not least by the OECD and by the market-making and deficit regulation policies of the EU, has become a powerful reform influence, spreading from the Anglo-American world to countries with more entrenched bureaucracies in continental Europe, such as Germany and France. There is rich evidence that common trends of public sector reform include: privatization of public infrastructure; cost containment with respect to public sector spending; downsizing of the public sector workforce; and decentralization (Schneider et al. 2005; Pollitt and Bouckaert 2011; OECD 2009, 2011; Bach and Kessler 2007; Vaughan-Whitehead 2013). However, common trends in internal restructuring of public administrations are more difficult to identify. While the doctrine's proponents claim that the NPM orientation marks a universal shift in organizing public administration and services, the scholarly debate yields no clear results either with respect to the universality of the *reform path* or with the direction and extent of change.

Irrespective of some core elements of bureaucratic organization, such as the legal entrenchment of administration and the existence of a civil service, comparative public administration research shows that Western states differ in public administration traditions with varying levels of openness to NPM reforms (Pollitt and Bouckaert 2011). Comparative research identifies a variety of reform strategies and differences in scope and timing of reforms, suggesting that equal exposure to budgetary pressures and the availability of NPM as a powerful reform script do not necessarily generate convergence in public administration patterns, even in the longer run (Derlien and Peters 2008; Demmke and Moilanen 2010). In an attempt to typify the logic underlying the variety of administrative reform trajectories across Western countries, Pollitt and Bouckaert suggest differentiating between two ideal type models based on different principles of coordination: the *New Public Management* (NPM) model favouring market mechanisms; and the *Neo-Weberian State* (NWS) model adhering to a professionalized and consultative form of hierarchy, reaffirming strong roles of the state and administrative law, and preserving the distinct status of the public service (Pollitt and Bouckaert 2011, pp. 208f). This distinction helps to capture the openness of the common law, Anglo-American country family towards NPM, in contrast to the more hesitant and incremental reform agenda in the legally highly entrenched bureaucracy of civil law countries such as Germany and France. However, as the example of Sweden shows, this distinction might not fit for all civil law countries, since reforms of a kind that would nowadays be identified as NPM, including the abolishment of the civil servant status, were already taking place in Sweden from the 1960s onwards. Hence, there is substantial variation in administrative reform in countries qualifying as Neo-Weberian, and reference to a common civil law background might not suffice to identify specificities of reform trajectories affecting public employment. This suggests that we need to explore in more detail the reform trajectories within the NWS family.

With regard to the impact of *public sector reform on employment*, comparative and country case study research on public sector reforms in Western states throughout the last decades has provided rich insights into core features and the variety of change. Numerous studies from the 1990s onwards identified a more or less negative effect of privatization and decentralization of public services and infrastructure on the size and conditions of the public sector workforce (Farnham and Horton 1996; Rothenbacher 1997; Cusack et al. 1989; Suleiman 2003; Bach et al. 1999; OECD 2008). Similar findings result from more recent research on the impact of government austerity measures (Bach and Bordogna 2013; Vaughan-Whitehead 2013; Demmke and Moilanen 2013). However, there is also evidence that public sector reforms motivated by NPM-related ideas have more diverse outcomes, and a uniform trend of decline of public employment across the OECD, as well as a general negative effect of administrative reforms on public sector employment conditions, has been contested (Derlien and Peters 2008; OECD 2009, 2011; Pollitt and Bouckaert 2011).

Among other reasons impeding an easy settlement, a crucial problem in this debate is the assumption underlying most contributions that public management reforms more or less directly translate into changes in public sector work and employment. This assumption is, however, implausible for two reasons. First, the NPM agenda encompasses a wide spectrum of measures, of which only some directly address the size of employment and HRM: downsizing via privatization; attenuation or abolition of the civil servant status with respect to tenure, seniority, or career pathways; or the introduction of performance-related pay. Other measures refer to the governance and organization of administration and public service (that is, decentralization, coordination by contract instead of hierarchy, and market-type mechanisms for the provision of services), the impact of which is rather indirect on work and employment (Pollitt and Bouckaert 2011; Bach and Bordogna 2011).

Second, public sector reforms, as other reforms, unfold in institutional- and actor-specific contexts rather than providing a script with a uniform imprint. Whether, and to what extent, the concrete reform profile and implementation induces institutional change is an open question (Crouch 2005). Thus, the connection between public sector reform and public employment and/or public sector work might be more contingent than is often assumed (Ashworth and Entwistle 2011). Therefore, rather than postulating a relationship between administrative reform and employment, the basic underlying structures – that is, the relationship between administrative regimes and employment regimes – must be investigated in order to better understand diverse or similar outcomes of change. This will also help to answer the broader question of whether common challenges lead to similar reform trajectories and result in more homogenous public employment regimes.

In comparative public administration research, structures and changes in employment in the public sector have usually been addressed with a strong *focus on the civil service*, generating rich evidence on the specific nature, development, and variety of civil service systems throughout Europe and the OECD world (Bekke and van der Meer 2000; van der Meer 2011, Raadschelders et al. 2007; Derlien and Peters 2008; Demmke and Moilanen 2010). Inherent to this focus is a special interest in government employment and bureaucrats, strengthened not least by the NPM paradigm, which prominently features the strategic role of managers and top-level bureaucrats (Farnham et al. 1996; OECD 2010; Hammerschmid et al. 2015). However, in most countries, employment in the public sector is much broader than the civil service category suggests. It often embodies different categories of the workforce, of whom civil servants with a distinct status might represent a core but not the whole spectrum. Moreover, some aspects of the traditional civil servant status during the 'Golden Age' of the welfare state have been extended to the growing public workforce, while others were abandoned, thus creating more hybrid forms of employment than the Weberian ideal type bureaucrat suggests. As privatization, decentralization, and administrative reform show, not only are the civil service or government employees exposed to change, but so is the broader public workforce, suggesting that research should reflect the whole spectrum of the public sector workforce.

In comparative public administrative and industrial relations research, we also find two somewhat contradicting but not mutually exclusive trends. We can either assume that NPM-inspired public sector reforms and budgetary restrictions impact public employment regulation as a whole, reflecting the strategic importance, political interest, and far-reaching goals in the changes of public service management (OECD 2008; Keller 2010; Vaughan-Whitehead 2013; Bach and Bordogna 2013). Or we can observe a preference for investigating employment changes in specific public services (for example, social services) which might be especially affected by NPM reforms, since they are of specific political or budgetary interest (Farnham and Horton 1996; Bach 2004; Christensen et al. 2014). Although there are good reasons for taking both perspectives, both the *generalizing approach* and the *selective choice of units of analysis* are not satisfactory. While the latter often lacks a coherent theoretical framework, the generalizing approach tends to understate the extent to which the devolution of state responsibilities varies across different areas of public service provision in the process of public sector reforms. While some areas might be subject to privatization, others are exposed to competition between public and private provision or subject to internal marketization. These differences generate variation in public employment conditions and suggest the need for conducting a more theoretically informed area-specific analysis of public employment change.

The research question

These considerations form the background of the study that we report in this book. We will address the changing role of the state as employer and investigate how the state is shaping employment relationships of civil servants and public employees under conditions of budget restrictions and public sector reform on the one hand and competition with the market sector on the other. In order to capture the role of the state as employer, the focus will be on *public employment regimes*, encompassing the institutions regulating public employment and their distinctiveness with regard to private sector employment regulation. Assuming that during the 'Golden Age' of the welfare state a distinct public employment regime was established, generating a specific status of employment, we ask in what way this status has been affected by the pressures of cost containment and NPM ideas. More precisely, we ask to what extent core aspects of public employment have been subject to change, covering mainly the time span from the early 1980s to the early 2010s.

The study combines an *OECD-wide analysis of macro-level public employment trends* with comparative in-depth country case studies covering core sectors of state activity that have not yet been the focus of much research. Apart from identifying country trends in the size and cost of public employment, the OECD-wide analysis serves to describe institutional differences in national public employment regimes and relates these regimes to administrative regimes and their openness to NPM-inspired reforms. While this analysis helps to clarify the relationship between administrative and employment regimes, deeper and additional insights on national reforms and changes in employment systems are gained from *country case studies of Germany, France, and Sweden*, contrasting them with the United Kingdom. These countries are characterized by different civil law traditions and they are all claimed to follow a Neo-Weberian reform path, whereas the United Kingdom, a reference case of the early introduction of NPM, follows the common law tradition.

This set of countries allows us to address the question of whether the concept of the NWS sufficiently captures the common developments in countries described by this notion. Taking into account that cost containment and NPM-inspired reforms do not necessarily affect public employment in the same way across the whole spectrum of public service provision, we will focus on specific areas of the public domain, distinct in function and organization. These areas include national *energy regulatory agencies* set up after privatization of the respective public infrastructure; local *waste collection*, where public service provision is exposed to competition with private providers; and the *police* on national and regional levels, representing a core state function which is nevertheless affected by administrative reforms. In the following, we address these units of analysis as *sectors* of the public service, while the term *public sector* still refers to the whole public service in contrast to the private sector.

In order to assess changes in public employment, we make use of an ideal type (Weber 1949) construction of public employment, differentiating between a *civil servant* and a *service provider* type. While the ideal type civil servant reflects the Weberian idea of bureaucratic administration and is based on the broad literature on traditional civil service, the ideal type service provider refers to NPM-inspired ideas of alignment of public employment to the market, that is, private sector employment conditions. We argue that public employment in the 'Golden Age' has been characterized by aspects such as authoritative employment regulation, high employment security, seniority rules in pay and advancement, and prescribed career paths, which highly resonate with the ideal type civil servant. In contrast, core aspects of public employment in times of market-oriented HRM might imply labour regulation based on private law, position-based advancement, and performance-related pay and promotion. Real types of public employment regimes, which can only be identified empirically, will of course deviate from the ideal types. However, as contrasting concepts, the ideal types represent the extremities of a spectrum within which we can locate the real types.

Taken together, the case studies allow us to formulate more informed answers to the questions: To what extent have public employment regimes been subject to change? To what extent are they aligned to private sector employment conditions? And is there still such a thing as a distinct public employment regime? Results with regard to reform paths will show whether common challenges lead to similar reform trajectories by country and result in more homogenous public employment regimes. Comparing reform trajectories and employment changes by sector across countries allows us to contribute new insights into the internal heterogeneity of public employment regimes and more nuanced assessments of the effects of different extents of the devolution of state responsibilities.

Structure of the book

The book is structured in four parts. While Part I serves to introduce the research question, approach, and research design (Chapters 1, 2, and 3), main findings of cross-country analyses and of sector-specific analyses are presented in Part II (Chapters 4 and 5) and Part III (Chapters 6, 7, and 8), respectively. Finally, Part IV engages with an integrated comparison of the findings on employment change by country and sector and an outlook reflecting the more general insights gained from this study for the development of public employment regimes (Chapters 9 and 10).

In detail, the content unfolds as follows. In Chapter 2, we outline the analytical problem. We first discuss the state of the literature with respect to conceptualizations of cross-country heterogeneity according to various regime typologies and locate public employment regimes in this context. Then we focus on the main driving forces of the transformation of the state – cost pressures and the NPM ideology – and address the debate on convergence or alternative reform pathways in public administration. We finish the literature review by discussing perspectives on comparative institutional change with a special focus on typologies sensitive 'to gradual but nevertheless transformative' change (Streeck and Thelen 2005, p. 19). Second, we present our research question focusing on the transformation of distinct public employment regimes as well as the analytical framework, including expectations of employment change conditions. The framework refers to institutional and cultural factors of national public administrations as potential moderating factors in the process of public employment reform, and addresses the extent to which the state devolves responsibility to private actors as a potential factor mediating change in employment in different sectors of public service provision.

Chapter 3 introduces the research design, which encompasses three perspectives. While a cross-national statistical analysis of OECD countries explores the development of aggregate public employment figures and the timing of reform initiatives across OECD countries, comparative case studies follow a more nuanced and detailed qualitative approach to explore the extent and conditions of public employment change. Based on secondary literature and document analysis, comparative country case studies of Germany, France, and Sweden, representing variation within the Neo-Weberian reform path family in contrast to the United Kingdom, which serves as a showcase of early NPM reforms, aim to identify public employment change moderated by differences in public administration regimes. The sector case studies focusing on energy regulatory agencies, waste collection, and the police in these countries explore changes in employment regimes in the context of different modes of responsibility devolution. For these in-depth explorations in three sectors across three countries, we draw on sector-specific document analyses, small surveys, and expert interviews with Human Resource managers, and again use the United Kingdom as a reference case. Next to a comparative framework identifying administrative regimes across countries, the contrasting ideal type concepts of the civil servant and the service provider serve as analytical tools for carving out the main aspects and the extent of change in public employment across countries and sectors, taking into account central dimensions of employment regulation.

Starting the country-level comparison, Chapter 4 sets out to analyse macro-level changes in public employment regimes covering the period from 1985 to 2008. First, taking advantage of recent progress in the collection of comparative data on public administration policies in the OECD, the chapter provides a map of politico-administrative regimes in the OECD and identifies different public employment regimes. Furthermore, the analysis addresses short- and long-term trends in the size and costs of general government employment in relation to government effectiveness and the reform intensity measured by the adoption of NPM tools. The aspect of responsiveness of public employment regimes to the incorporation of NPM ideas is then refined by an analysis of the timing of the introduction of a paradigmatic NPM tool – performance-related pay – across countries. While the findings of this aggregated data analysis strongly suggest that we can discern distinct types of public administration regimes, and that inherited legal traditions and types of employment regulation impact public employment reforms, they also show the difficulty of identifying single factors for explaining long-term trends in the cost and size of public employment or timing of reforms. Moreover, this approach is unsuited for accounting for the complexity of reform processes. Also, the generalization inherent to this type of quantitative macro-comparative analysis tends to obscure both traditional and new heterogeneity in public employment regimes.

This speaks for a more in-depth analysis of country-specific change trajectories, which are addressed in Chapter 5, focusing on Germany, France, and Sweden as countries representing distinct administrative regimes within the Neo-Weberian country family. For each country, the impact of the state structure and the administrative culture on the organization of public administration and employment in the 'Golden Age', as well as the evolution of public sector reforms, are assessed. The chapter starts with the United Kingdom as a reference case in which neo-liberal ideas and NPM reforms have had the most impact on the organization of the public administration, and then proceeds with Germany, France, and Sweden. The divergent historical developments of employment regulation in the period between 1980 and the early 2010s are then summarized in terms of our analytical framework of the ideal type civil servant and the ideal type service provider.

Taking into account that public service provision is heterogeneous and that a general country trend in re-regulation of public employment, though setting a basic framework, does not necessarily apply in the same way in each country, the following three chapters engage in sector-specific analyses of employment change. This in-depth investigation focuses in Chapter 6 on energy regulatory agencies, being the most far-reaching case of unravelling state functions. With the privatization of the respective public infrastructure, the state has transferred organizational and decision-making responsibility to private actors and confines itself to market control. Untouched by administrative traditions, these newly set-up national agencies might be specifically open to HRM ideas inspired by NPM, not least in order to stay competitive with respect to the highly educated personnel which might find more attractive employment conditions in the private sector. In contrast, waste collection on the municipal level, addressed in Chapter 7, represents a case where the state retains political and decision-making power. However, the service provision is exposed to direct or indirect competition from private providers who can draw on more flexible employment contracts, which in turn may put pressure on the public sector's low wage premium. Finally, in Chapter 8, we focus on the police as a core state function, where the state is still responsible for decision making, organization, and provision of the service (that is, security as a normative good), and the resilience of the civil servant ideal type of employment will be most probable. In each chapter, the transformation of public employment regimes is assessed in a structured way, starting with an overview of the sector-specific organization and reforms of employment by country, followed by a cross-country exploration of the status and changes of core dimensions of employment regulation. A final section summarizes the extent and core aspects of the alignment to private sector employment standards, following our multidimensional analytical framework of employment regulation and highlighting both sector-specific commonalities across countries and sector-related differences within national reform trajectories.

Chapter 9 again takes a broader perspective and engages in an integrated comparison of the country and sector findings presented in the previous chapters. The comparisons show that in all countries the distinctiveness of public employment has lost ground and core aspects of public employment are aligned to rules and regulations governing employment in the private sector, though to different degrees. These commonalities emphasize the role of cost pressure and the NPM paradigm as driving forces for a common trend and direction of change. At the same time, however, the scope of change varies across sectors. Employment in the energy regulatory agencies and in waste collection, both exposed to market pressure, have approached private sector standards to a larger extent than employment in the police has. While the extent to which these changes are consistent with overall country trends varies, these findings nevertheless question the homo-geneity of national public employment regimes and the assumption of a holistic change in public employment. Pulling all of these threads together, Chapter 10 addresses the question of convergence of public employment regimes in the light of common drivers of restructuring and reform, reas-sesses the role of moderating and mediating factors for the explanation of variety of change by country and sector, and discusses the transformative character of the restructuring and reforms observed. Last but not least, the fate of the former model role of public employment, the relation and 'struc-tural fit' of public and private employment regimes, and limits to public sector alignment are addressed. Concluding remarks refer to the need for further research.

Part I
Approach and Research Design

2
The Analytical Problem

We start the first section by briefly summarizing important research traditions from which we draw insights for our own analysis of public employment regimes. The first subsection situates classifications of public employment regimes within the wider context of welfare regimes, capitalist systems, and public administration regimes. We then discuss existing conceptualizations of public employment regimes and civil service systems.

These two subsections set the scene for the ensuing discussion of what we consider to be the main driving forces of change in public employment regimes: cost pressures and the ideology of New Public Management. Together, both driving forces arguably lead to a convergence of institutional regimes: cost pressures close off alternative trajectories, while New Public Management postulates that it offers a seemingly easy solution to maximizing both effectiveness and efficiency of public services. However, a second literature suggests that existing institutions limit the room to move, and reforms that may have been inspired by New Public Management in various countries take different trajectories, which have been summarized by the concept of the *Neo-Weberian State*. We close the section by exploring the literature on institutional change, which will serve as a conceptual reference point for the empirical analyses in later chapters.

In the second section, we present the research question which, metaphorically speaking, asks whether the 'traditional' civil servant has been replaced by the 'modern' public service provider. Our explanatory strategy distinguishes between two types of factors which we expect to deter the driving forces from producing a process of convergence. We argue that the effect of these forces is moderated by institutional and cultural conditions which predominantly vary across countries, and is mediated by functional exigencies which vary across sectors.

State of the art review

Public administration regimes in context

One of the major shifts in the literature on public administration since the 1980s is the acknowledgement of the existence of a variety of different administrative regimes in the Organisation for Economic Co-operation and Development (OECD) world. This shift follows similar developments in two neighbouring fields of research. On the one hand, in the field of welfare state research, scholars have identified different 'welfare regimes' exhibiting similar institutional structures of societal redistribution (Esping-Andersen 1990) or 'families of nations' implementing similar policies for solving welfare problems (Castles 1993). On the other hand, in the field of political economy, scholars have distinguished between 'varieties of capitalism' that differ in their mode of regulating and organizing societal production (Hall and Soskice 2001).

In his analysis of the 'three worlds of welfare', Esping-Andersen (1990) differentiated between conservative or *corporative* state-dominated insurance systems with marginal private markets and pronounced occupational (especially civil servant) segregation, social democratic or *universalistic* state-dominated systems where universal social rights eradicate both status privilege and markets, and liberal or *residualist* systems strongly dominated by private markets. In the two decades spanning Esping-Andersen's (1990) initial analysis and its most recent re-evaluation by Scruggs and Allan (2008), a large number of scholars have debated the existence of distinct welfare regimes and the different principles and (re)distributive logics on which they are based.[1] The original distinction between liberal, social democratic and conservative 'worlds of welfare' has given rise to a large number of alternative classifications and typologies, which have predominantly been spurred by the inclusion of more countries into the original set of countries (Arts and Gelissen 2002; Obinger and Wagschal 2010). Nevertheless, the ideal-typical conceptualization underlying the 'three worlds' seems to have weathered all conceptual and empirical scrutiny and still dominates the discussion (Ferragina and Seeleib-Kaiser 2011; Kasza 2002). Empirically, findings suggest that, overall, Esping-Andersen's three-world typology 'neither passes the empirical tests with flying colours, nor dismally fails them' (Arts and Gelissen 2002, p. 153).

In a partially connected, parallel literature on 'varieties of capitalism', discussions have revolved around the notions of 'liberal' and 'coordinated' market economies as distinct societal modes of production (Crouch 2009; Hall and Soskice 2001). The main argument is that different patterns of institutional complementarities in the relations between firms and other agents in an economy result in a varying ability of nation-states to cope with economic challenges and to foster growth (Allen 2004; Hall and Gingerich 2009). However, the supposed positive effect of institutional coherence on economic performance remains disputed (Kenworthy 2006). Nevertheless, by extending the idea of complementarity to the interrelations between a country's production regime and distribution regime, scholars have argued that the structural affinities between these two regimes stabilize a society (Crouch 2010; Schröder 2013; Thelen 2012).

The term 'regime' is employed in a rather vague way in this literature and typically refers to 'principles, norms, rules, and decision-making procedures around which actor expectations converge in a given issue-area' (Krasner 1982, p. 185). In a comparative perspective, the complementarity of these principles, norms, and procedures ('elective affinities') is considered a prerequisite for the longer-term stability that is required for the qualification of institutional constellations as regimes (Crouch 2010). Thus, in this context the term 'regime' refers to a coherent set of institutions. Regime typologies are a first step in abstracting from the description of national differences to conceptualizing them by theoretical constructs. Typologies as such, however, are auxiliary notions developed to represent a reality that cannot yet be described by laws (Arts and Gelissen 2002, p. 138).

Attempts to structure the national diversity of administrative patterns have resulted in various country typologies of administrative systems. Page (1995), for example, distinguishes between six administrative traditions. The German Continental administration is characterized by a federalist structure based on Roman law and a strong emphasis on ministerial autonomy (*Ressorts*). The French Continental administration is defined by its unpoliticized professionalism. The Southern European administration is characterized by its politically weak status and patronage. The Scandinavian administration is defined by its professionalism, fragmented character, and tradition of corporatist cooperation. The British-Irish administration is defined by its neutrality. Finally, an Eastern European administration is characterized by its communist legacies (see also, Lodge 2009, p. 294).

Knill (1999) and Hood (2000) suggest alternative strategies to structure the national diversity of administrative patterns by focusing on how administrative systems respond to political demand for change. In this respect, Knill (1999) distinguishes between 'autonomous' and 'instrumental' bureaucracies. While the former are characterized by strategies of self-adaptation to reform pressures in the context of weak leadership, the latter are characterized by a limited ability to influence the process of policy formulation. Hood (2000) uses the term 'public sector bargain' to characterize the relationship between politics and administration, and distinguishes between two types, or modes, of interaction between the administrative and the political system. In the 'trustee' mode, the civil services take a quasi-autonomous position, which makes it a broader part of the institutional arrangement, whereas in the 'agency' mode, contracts establish a principal-agent type relationship between the political and administrative systems. Both Knill (1999) and Hood (2000) not only provide a framework for comparing administrative

Table 2.1   Varieties of capitalism, welfare regimes, and public administration regimes

	Public administration regime			
	Anglo-American	**Napoleonic**	**Germanic**	**Scandinavian**
Type of market economy				
Liberal	Australia, Canada, Ireland, New Zealand, UK, US			
Coordinated		Belgium, Italy, France, Netherlands, Portugal, Spain	Austria, Germany, Japan, Switzerland	Norway, Denmark, Finland, Sweden
Welfare regime				
English	US, Canada, Australia, UK, Ireland, Netherlands			
Southern		Italy, Spain, Portugal	Japan	
Continental		Belgium, France	Germany, Austria	
Nordic				Denmark, Norway, Sweden, Finland

Sources: Obinger and Wagschal (2010), Hall and Gingerich (2009), and Tepe et al. (2010).

patterns in different countries but also suggest that administrative systems respond differently to similar reform pressures and reform ideas, such as New Public Management.

Although national systems of public administration in OECD countries have undergone a variety of reforms and changes, observers discern a 'persistence of patterns of administrative thought and practice' (Painter and Peters 2010, p. 3). Embedded in specific political institutions and state structures, national systems of public administration vary substantially. Any attempt to identify administrative patterns in comparative perspective needs to take into account the country-specific foundation and organization of the relationship between politics and administration (Lodge 2009, p. 285), as well as the difficulties in differentiating between the two, since administrative and political functions often overlap.

The empirical cross-classification of the type of market economy and the type of public administration regime shown in the upper panel of Table 2.1

reveals that the distinctive nature of liberal market economies is fully congruent with the Anglo-American public administration regime, whereas coordinated market economies can be observed in countries characterized by the other three types of public administration regimes. Similarly, the cross-classification of welfare regimes and public administration regimes in the lower panel of Table 2.1 reveals an almost equally clear congruence of regime types. These observations suggest that the idea of 'families of nations' extends beyond public policies in the welfare state (Castles 1993; Castles and Obinger 2008) to a broader conception that includes the structure of market economies as well as the organization of public administration (Tepe et al. 2010).

Before we seek to identify public employment regimes and describe the reforms that have taken place within these regimes, we outline the stylized framework introduced by Pollitt and Bouckaert (2011), which is based on the previously discussed conceptualizations and captures structural differences in the politico-administrative systems. Understanding these differences is important for two reasons. First, the politico-administrative system sets the basic parameters for public employment regimes, in particular with respect to the relationship between the political and administrative elites. Second, the political rules and institutions that constitute a politico-administrative system, in the sense of Pollitt and Bouckaert (2011), are inherently linked to the capacity and resources to reform the administrative systems, including its public workforce. More specifically, the institutionalized arrangement of competences between the political and administrative elites has been considered an important factor shaping New Public Management reforms (Dahlström and Lapuente 2010).

According to Pollitt and Bouckaert (2011, p. 47), any comparative analysis of public management reforms needs to consider characteristics of the existing political and administrative system in shaping or contextualizing such reforms. To capture these aspects, they use the term 'politico-administrative regimes', which provides a refinement of previous typologies by focusing on the constitutional, functional, and cultural elements of public administration systems. Their framework identifies five politico-administrative dimensions that are claimed to constitute the terrain for public employment regimes. The first two dimensions refer to basic characteristics of the constitution. First, the 'state structure' captures the most relevant constitutional differences among countries. Referring to the division of state authority on different levels of government, this dimension measures the horizontal and vertical separation of governmental powers. According to Huber and Shipan (2002), these structural conditions lead to an either more or less discretionary bureaucracy. Comparing various countries, these authors find a positive relationship between the density of administrative regulations and the extent to which the state is structured in a system of federal units. The second dimension, somewhat confusingly named 'executive government', refers to the type of democracy. In line with the literature, two basic types of democratic systems are distinguished: majoritarian and consensual democracies. Majoritarian democracies are characterized by a two-party system with majority voting, one-party governments, executive dominance over the legislature, and a pluralistic representation of interests. Consensual democracies, by contrast, tend to have a proportional voting system, multiple-party coalitions, a relative balance between the executive and legislative branches, and a corporatist representation of interests.

The third dimension of Pollitt and Bouckaert's framework deals with the relationship between the political and the administrative elites. This dimension, which they call 'minister/mandarin relations', concerns the influence of top-ranking officials on political decisions and the relationship between the bureaucracy and the government in general. We can observe two 'ideal' functionally equivalent modes of arranging the relationship between political and bureaucratic actors, both of which can be traced back to the delegation problem in hierarchical organizations. If it is costly for a political principal to oversee the behaviour of its bureaucratic agent, the bureaucratic agent faces a systematic incentive to deviate from the political order. The rational solution to this delegation problem lies in *ex ante* oversight, which should incentivize agents to provide high effort in implementing the given political order, and to establish a pay scheme that makes the agents' payoff highly dependent on the outcome of his or her behaviour (Miller 2005). The alternative approach would be to give political principals the opportunity to hire those bureaucratic agents who support their political goals and to fire those who do not. Giving political principals the opportunity to choose bureaucrats according to their partisan preferences has been considered a distinguishing feature of parliamentary democracies (Strøm et al. 2003), while the reliance on *ex ante* oversight to prevent bureaucrats from shirking has been considered to be the prominent approach to the delegation problem in presidential systems (Kiwiet and McCubbins 1991). The institutionalized relationship between political and administrative executives – integrated or separated – is likely to be an essential factor in public management reforms (Dahlström and Lapuente 2010). To what extent 'deals' between the two elites can be negotiated depends in particular on the administrative executives and the extent to which they are entrenched within the political elite and engaged in partisan politics.

The role of legal traditions and historical legacies in the development of administrative systems might be crucial for understanding contemporary administrative systems and their inherent reform logics (Painter and Peters 2010, p. 4). The fourth dimension, therefore, aims to describe differences in administrative traditions. Pollitt and Bouckaert (2011) differentiate between public management regimes with a 'public interest' orientation and those with a legalistic 'constitutional state' orientation. As mentioned above, regarding the legal basis of administrative systems, two main legal traditions can be distinguished: 'common law' on the one hand and 'civil law' with a French, a German, and a Scandinavian variant on the other (La Porta et al. 1998; La Porta et al. 2008). Various scholars agree that the legal origin of a country can be assumed to find an expression in its administrative tradition (Rugge 2007; Zweigert and Kötz 1998).

The last dimension of Pollitt and Bouckaert's (2011) framework refers to the diversity of the key sources of advice to ministers on public management reform issues. Theoretically, ministers might take advice from their political party, mandarins, lobbyists, or academia. The wider the range of customary sources of advice, the more likely it is that new ideas from outside the public sector will gain influence.

Table 2.2 summarizes the dimensions of Pollitt and Bouckaert's (2011) framework for the analysis of politico-administrative regimes and the operationalization of this framework with comparative indicators for 19 OECD countries. We regroup the five variables and order the countries according

Table 2.2 Politico-administrative regimes

Country	Legal tradition[a]	State structure[b]	Executive government[b]	Minister/ mandarin relations[c]	Diversity of policy advice[d]
United Kingdom	Common	Unitary	Majoritarian	Separate	Medium
Ireland	Common	Unitary	Majoritarian	Separate	Low
Australia	Common	Federal	Majoritarian	Separate	Medium
United States	Common	Federal	Majoritarian	Separate	High
Canada	Common	Federal	Majoritarian	Separate	High
Germany	Civil (Ger.)	Federal	Mixed	Separate	Low
Austria	Civil (Ger.)	Federal	Mixed	Integrated	Low
Switzerland	Civil (Ger.)	Federal	Consensual	Separate	Low
Japan	Civil (Ger.)	Mixed	Mixed	Integrated	Low
Italy	Civil (Fra.)	Mixed	Consensual	Integrated	Low
Spain	Civil (Fra.)	Mixed	Majoritarian	Integrated	Low
Netherlands	Civil (Fra.)	Mixed	Consensual	Separate	Medium
Belgium	Civil (Fra.)	Mixed	Consensual	Integrated	Low
Portugal	Civil (Fra.)	Unitary	Mixed	Integrated	Low
France	Civil (Fra.)	Unitary	Majoritarian	Integrated	Low
Denmark	Civil (Scan.)	Mixed	Consensual	Separate	High
Norway	Civil (Scan.)	Unitary	Mixed	Separate	High
Finland	Civil (Scan.)	Unitary	Consensual	Separate	Low
Sweden	Civil (Scan.)	Unitary	Mixed	Separate	High

Note: a = La Porta et al. (1998), b = Lijphart (1999), c = Dahlström and Lapuente (2010, p. 588), Switzerland code by the authors, d = Bertelsmann Stiftung (2009) (M1.3 Scholarly Advice). Metric variables transformed into terciles, with the middle tercile representing mixed systems (for state structure and executive government) or a medium level (for diversity of policy advice).

to the legal tradition as the most fundamental criterion because it defines the basic constitutional principles of state action (Raadschelders and Rutgers 1999; Painter and Peters 2010; La Porta et al. 2008). One main insight is that 'common law' countries tend to combine separate minister/mandarin relations with a majoritarian type of executive government and medium/high diversity of policy advice, whereas countries with a Scandinavian civil law tradition combine separate minister/mandarin relations with a unitary state structure and a high level of external policy advice. In contrast, countries with a French or German civil law tradition share a low level of external policy advice.

Civil service systems and public employment regimes

During the 'Golden Age' of the nation-state, representing the period between the end of the Second World War and the 1970s, public sector employment was distinct from employment in the private sector in various respects. In fact, this distinction is as old as the state itself, because the trade of employment guarantees and other privileges against the loyalty of the rulers' servants was the very fundament of its power maintenance. The state was characterized in that period by being a *territorial unit* which secures the *rule of law*, legitimized by *democracy* and willing to *intervene* into market developments, summarized in the acronym TRUDI (Leibfried et al. 2015; Leibfried and Zürn 2005). The expansion of the state's role beyond safety and rule of law to the democratic and interventionist state resulting in TRUDI went hand in hand with a vast extension in the number of public employees. Some countries extended the employment conditions of the traditional civil service to these new functions, while others made differentiations. In particular, the Germanic and French administrative traditions relying on the civil service conception were extended to a wider set of employees. Most fundamentally, in procedural terms, the state acted as a sovereign employer in control of personnel policies by rule of law. In substantive terms, the state aimed at being a model employer for the private sector, typically by setting higher standards of employment in terms of working conditions, and by integrating disadvantaged groups such as women, disabled persons, and migrants (Bach and Kessler 2007; Beaumont 1992). Because of the public, tax-based funding of employment, special exigencies on accountability and transparency apply. These limit the discretion of personnel management in the public sector, particularly with respect to pay determination, which was typically centralized and authoritatively implemented by law. In their literature review on Human Resource Management in the public sector, Bach and Kessler (2007, p. 472) identify several dimensions in which the structure of public employment in the 'Golden Age' of TRUDI has been distinctive from labour markets in the private sector. They observe that public services are highly labour-intensive, that the proportion of well-qualified, professional personnel is comparatively high, and that public services require a strong commitment to the public interest on the part of employees. Moreover, they point out that the proportions of female labour and of part-time workers are comparatively high and are increasing.

This list highlights some aspects of the specificity of the public labour force. However, the differences are more institutionally entrenched than such a mere phenomenological summary suggests. Rule-based, bureaucratic procedures intended to ensure public accountability show elective affinities with specific types of employment practices which differentiate public employment regimes from the private sector: 'Elaborate internal labour markets, high levels of job security, and career progression based primarily on length of service and initial qualifications ensured stability and conformance to explicit procedures' (Bach and Kessler 2007, p. 474).

While public employment regimes are embedded in the more general public administration regimes, little is known about the systematic variety of these regimes. The comparative literature closest to the notion of public employment has revolved around the narrower concept of civil service system, which is broadly defined as 'the whole of mediating institutions that mobilise human resources in the service of the affairs of the state' (Morgan and Perry 1988, cited in Bekke and van der Meer 2000, p. 3). In its operationalization, however, the concept is restricted to a literal reading of 'service' in the sense of a public law status of officials appointed by the state through formal procedures. Demmke and Moilanen (2010, pp. 51–52) cite four criteria used by the World Bank to distinguish the civil servant status from ordinary employment:

- appointment by an authorized public institution;
- strong constraints on dismissal to balance responsiveness to the government with the respect of state institutions;
- special constitutional and legal constraints on actions; and
- employment within civilian government.

By contrast, Bezès and Lodge (2007, pp. 123–26) argue that civil service systems can be described in terms of the specific constellation of five components: legal entrenchment, pervasiveness, political-administrative nexus, career, and rewards. Reforms in public administration will touch upon any or all of these components. There is a wide consensus in the literature that national civil service systems vary considerably across countries. Bekke and van der Meer conclude their comparative analysis of civil service systems by pointing out the complexity of similarities and differences between countries:

Despite the...Western European tradition and history of the countries...there are many differences that can be attributed to particular social and cultural circumstances and traditions. But there are as many similarities which are caused by common backgrounds, political and cultural interrelations and – not least – a shared classical Greek-Roman origin which means that many institutional arrangements are grounded in the political philosophy of Greek-Roman ancestors. (Bekke and van der Meer 2000, p. 288)

In the same vein, in their encompassing overview of civil service systems in the European Union, Demmke and Moilanen conclude:

[I]t becomes increasingly difficult to classify the Member States into country traditions, geographical or civil service clusters. In fact, similarities exist only with regard to some institutional and structural issues. (Demmke and Moilanen 2010, p. 245)

Restricting the analysis to the civil service, however, does not take into account the fact that one of the major implications of the extension of state responsibilities during the 'Golden Age' was to substantially increase and differentiate the public workforce. This extension of public employment did not, however, necessarily imply an increase in the number of civil servants, but resulted in a change of the composition of the public workforce. In some countries, the category of public employees in a contractual relationship to the state was extended; in other countries, the status of civil servants remained restricted to a more narrow set of occupations. In order to include this category of employees and to analyze shifts between the two categories, we will use the wider concept of *public employment regimes*.

Currently, there is no generally accepted conceptualization of public employment regimes available in the literature. However, on the basis of the literature on 'varieties of capitalism' and 'production regimes', attempts have been made to measure and compare the quality of employment in general. Comparing employment conditions in the private sector in five European countries, differences in the skill structure have been shown to co-vary with the production regime (Gallie 2007a). Yet, in other dimensions such as task discretion, job variety, and opportunities for self-development, the Scandinavian countries are set apart from the other countries, thus suggesting a dimension of variation cutting across production regimes. More specifically, Gallie (2007b) distinguishes between an 'inclusive', a 'dualist', and a 'market' employment regime. Viewed from the perspective of the role of labour in employment policy and regulation, the inclusive regime, in which labour participation in policymaking is strongly institutionalized, 'minimizes differentials between different types of employee and provides a strong safety net for weaker categories of employee' (Gallie 2007b, p. 18). In dualist regimes, in contrast, the involvement of organized labour in political decisions is of a more consultative nature, and the 'nature of employment regulation will tend to reflect this [by] providing strong employment protection, good employment conditions, and generous welfare support for the core workforce, but much poorer conditions for those on non-standard contracts' (Gallie 2007b, p. 19, amendment in square brackets by the authors). In market employment regimes, labour tends to be excluded from policymaking and employment is assumed to be governed by market principles (Gallie 2007b, p. 19).

This typology illuminates differences in private sector employment conditions and the principles underlying the regime-specific ideas of employment in general. The distinction between an equalizing, a status-differentiating, and a market-driven conceptualization is useful to guide expectations about the principles underlying public sector employment regimes and its potential change. However, focusing on private sector employment regimes also leaves aside important differences between the public and the private sector.

A core insight from work in the tradition of labour market segmentation theory (Doeringer and Piore 1971; Piore and Berger 1980) is that there are huge differences in work conditions (for example, pay level, duration of contracts, extensiveness of social security, and quality of work) between the primary and secondary segments (Kalleberg and Sørensen 1979). Public employment was typically located in the core of the primary segment of the labour market, especially given that the civil servant status served as a template for contractual employees. As a result, public employment obtained a distinct set of characteristics, making it legitimate to speak of a distinct public employment regime.

This public employment regime has at least three defining characteristics. First, an important feature is the extraordinary level of employment security and employee-friendly work conditions, such as strong dismissal protection and internal labour markets marked by a career system and connected to a specialized internal system for continuing education.

Second, employment conditions in the public sector have been explicitly conceptualized as a showcase model for the private sector. Given their dependence on political actors, public employers are expected to act in accordance with the political agenda. Both in line with social democratic ideas of employee empowerment and as the result of the dependence of political parties on the satisfaction of their constituency – among which the fraction of public employees increased substantially during the 'Golden Age' of TRUDI – employee-friendly regulations were typically introduced in the public sector at an early stage.

Third, the combination of equal opportunity legislation, employee-friendly working conditions, and the specific focus of public services – with large portions of the workforce being employed in the education and health sectors – provided employment opportunities for population groups typically marginalized in the private sector, such as women, migrants, and physically impaired persons (Kroos and Gottschall 2012).

There is no doubt that civil servants in Anglo-American countries differ from *fonctionnaires* in France or *Beamte* in Germany (Wise 1996; van der Meer et al. 2007). The analysis of the politico-administrative systems has already shown that constitutional decisions – such as whether the relationship between the political and administrative elites should be integrated or separated – distinguishes countries with a German or French civil law tradition from those with a common law tradition. On the one hand, these differences have implications for the design of employment contracts concerning aspects such as tenure or fixed wages; on the other hand, such politico-administrative features set the framework for public sector reforms.

The embeddedness of public employment regimes in the broader context of elective affinities between domains of state-society relations has been further explored by Tepe et al. (2010, pp. 670–72). By means of a multiple correspondence analysis, they map the characteristics of public administration regimes in a two-dimensional space and show that the Anglo-American, Scandinavian, and Continental public employment regimes are clearly separate, while the two variants of the Continental type, the French and the Germanic, are much closer but still distinct. They also show that this mapping is congruent with the differentiation in different variants of capitalist systems when it comes to distinguishing the Anglo-American regime from other regimes. However, the divide between the Continental and the Scandinavian types of public employment regimes does not follow the varieties of capitalism. While both country groups are characterized by highly coordinated versions of capitalism, they differ with respect to their public employment regimes, and this separation is in line with the welfare regime.

These interrelations between the public employment regime and the welfare regime might be understood as follows. On the one hand, the universalistic welfare state, which relies on a large public labour force, is combined with a close alignment of public and private employment conditions, with the public employment regime setting the standards for private employment. On the other hand, the conservative welfare regime is based on the idea of status preservation, which is also the main driving force behind the divide between public and private employment conditions. Thus, we observe a rather complex setting of country clusters, which are internally fairly homogeneous, but which exhibit different profiles of capitalist organization, welfare regimes, public administration traditions, and public employment regimes. Although this does not imply that the interrelations within these profiles can be causally interpreted, there seems to be a structural 'fit' between the different dimensions of the institutional structure of 'families of nations' that produce internally relatively coherent systems (Tepe et al. 2010).

The driving forces of change: cost pressures and new public management

Since the 1970s, major transformations have been observed in the conception of the state and public policymaking in the OECD area. The origin of these changes has been traced to two mutually connected developments. On the one hand, the expansion of the welfare state (Nullmeier and Kaufmann 2010) and the cost pressures inherent in the labour-intensive service sector (Baumol 1967; Baumol and Bowen 1965) caused public expenditures to gradually become a major element of the gross national product in OECD countries. This expansion, in turn, stirred a debate about the limits of welfare growth (Flora 1986). On the other hand, the replacement of Keynesianism with monetarism as the dominant paradigm of economic policymaking over the course of the 1970s and early 1980s (Hall 1986) instigated the juxtaposition of the liberal and the coordinated types of market economy as a core element of public policy. Within a few years after this paradigmatic change, retrenchment policies were initiated in the welfare states of most OECD countries (Obinger et al. 2010; Pierson 2001).

Thus, traditional public administration regimes were challenged from two sides: the cost pressures pushing welfare state retrenchment did not only call the size and content of welfare programmes into question but also questioned the organizational format of welfare provision, which was and is predominantly part of the public sector in most OECD states. The welfare state itself typically accounts for about one-fifth to one-third of public expenditures (Kittel and Obinger 2003). Within our sample of 19 OECD nations, the average government expenditure on government employees' compensation (averaged over 1995 and 2008) amounts to 24.2 per cent of total government expenditure and 11.6 per cent per GDP (averaging Columns 3 and 4, and 5 and 6, respectively, in Table 4.2). Two general trends accelerating the upward movement in the costs of the public workforce became apparent in the 1990s (Rothenbacher 1998). First, a gradual shift in the composition of the public workforce towards more qualified occupations amplified the competitive pressure in the higher echelons of the labour market requiring public employers to reduce the public-private wage gap. According to recent statistical studies, the 2000s witnessed an overall wage premium for the public sector, which particular holds for women, low-pay scales, and the education and administration sectors (Giordano et al. 2011; Rubery 2014). A more detailed study using quantile regression suggests that there is a clear premium for low-wage jobs, while for the higher echelons – which are more abundant in the public sector – the private sector tends to offer higher earnings (Tepe et al. 2015). Second, the generous pension schemes for civil servants, established after the Second World War in many countries and initially meant to compensate for the earnings gap with respect to the private sector, became effective at a wider scale as a consequence of the expansion of the public sector during the 'Golden Age' of TRUDI. Thus, in times of fiscal austerity, it does not come as a surprise that downsizing government employment and containing personnel costs have become core issues on the public policy reform agenda (for example, Economist 2010). Given the large share of personnel costs in total public expenditures, the public employment regime is a natural candidate for reform attempts in the public sector, aiming at cutting costs and increasing both efficiency and effectiveness.

The second driving force – neo-liberal ideology based on the monetarist paradigm – did not only constitute an attack on elements of state-led market coordination in the private sector, such as corporatist arrangements (Molina and Rhodes 2002), but also called for the marketization of public services. This strategy involved two elements. First, the privatization of public infrastructure and state-owned industries became a core objective of government strategies across the OECD. The privatization of public services is not only an important element of a cost-cutting strategy but is also purported to increase efficiency through the introduction of market forces in the public services (Schneider et al. 2005; Zohlnhöfer et al. 2008). Privatization tends to result in less advantageous employment conditions, in particular in labour-intensive sectors (Hermann and Flecker 2012). Typically, employees in privatized administrative units or enterprises are offered private contracts, which is one of the major elements of a cost-cutting strategy. For those employees with a special status, such as the German or Austrian *Beamte*, contract clauses maintain on an individual basis some or all of the privileges which they enjoyed as public employees (Atzmüller and Hermann 2004). Given that our study focuses on public employment regimes, we do not discuss this privatization strategy and its implications in more detail.

Second, market institutions and incentive schemes were introduced to replace bureaucratic procedures in those public services that remained part of the public infrastructure. New Public Management became the dominant doctrine of public sector reform in the 1990s, including the claim to universal applicability (Hood 1991). In a best-selling popular science book, American management consultants Osborne and Gaebler (1991) put together a set of principles underlying 'entrepreneurial government'. These authors claim to observe and advocate shifts that:

- introduce stronger leadership in government;
- empower citizens;
- increase competition in service delivery;
- transform rule-driven into mission-driven organizations;
- strengthen outcome-oriented policies;
- meet the needs of customers instead of bureaucrats;
- emphasize earnings instead of spending;
- focus on prevention rather than cure;

- decentralize power; and
- replace command mechanisms with market mechanisms.

Although the approach built upon concepts developed much earlier (Page 2005), the new element was the joint and concerted application of a whole set of reform measures in the context of a policy of state retrenchment. Summarizing the transformations in New Zealand, the country which most radically implemented New Public Management reforms, Donald Kettl, a leading proponent of the paradigm, remarked:

> The driving idea behind this broad array of reforms has been 'managerialism'. The approach argues that traditional bureaucratic hierarchy had become unresponsive. Reformers sought to replace authority and rigidity with flexibility; the traditional preoccupation with structure with improvements to process; and the comfortable stability of government agencies and budgets with market-style competition. (Kettl 1997, p. 447)

In a nutshell, the doctrine advocates (Pollitt and Bouckaert 2011, p. 10):

- the reorganization of public administration into disaggregated and decentralized structures;
- the introduction of performance measurement;
- coordination of public policies by contract instead of hierarchy;
- market-type mechanisms for the provision of public services, such as competitive tendering, benchmarking, leagues, and so on;
- considering citizens as customers; and
- using quality improvement techniques.

The proponents of reform also claim that these shifts do not only characterize developments in the Anglo-American family of countries, but are an inevitable, global process (Kettl 2000). New Public Management became the dominant doctrine among OECD consultants, and various OECD reports developed benchmarking systems comparing the extent to which countries have attained the goal of 'reinventing government' (see, for example, OECD 2013).

With respect to the public employment regime, New Public Management reforms sought to challenge the fundamental differences in private sector employment conditions. Bach and Bordogna (2011, p. 2285) summarize these policies as follows (see also, OECD 2008):

- a decrease in the number of public sector employees as a result of outsourcing and privatization;
- a decrease in the number of public sector employees with prerogative employment status;

- a reduction in the scope and intensity of prerogatives for those employees in privileged positions;
- a replacement of unilateral regulation by collective bargaining;
- a decentralization of collective bargaining;
- a replacement of seniority-based career trajectories by more differentiated, flexible, and individualized mechanisms; and
- a reduction in state support for trade unions and a strengthening of managerial prerogatives.

Convergence or alternative reform pathways in public administration?

In both the comparative public administration literature (Pollitt and Bouckaert 2011; Rothenbacher 1998; Suleiman 2003) and public debates about the long-term development of public employment in affluent democracies, the reform debate circles around the concepts of 'convergence' and 'divergence'. In theoretical terms, the focus of analysis has shifted from questions like 'are there distinct public employment regimes?' and 'what is the correct number of regimes?' towards the question of whether the long- and short-term adjustments in the development of government employment show patterns of change and adjustment that are specific to certain public employment regimes. Confronted with similar reform pressures, such as increasing budgetary problems, one might expect governments to take similar steps towards reform, causing public employment regimes across the OECD to converge ('convergence thesis'). According to Knill (2005, p. 768) such 'policy convergence can be defined as any increase in the similarity between one or more characteristics of a certain policy (for example, policy objectives, policy instruments, policy settings) across a given set of political jurisdictions (supranational institutions, states, regions, local authorities) over a given period of time'.

Even though the potential similarity of reform pressures and a tendency towards legal harmonization across EU and OECD nations might be important driving forces behind convergence of public employment regimes, there are also equally plausible factors that suggest the persistence of differences between, or even divergence of, national systems of public employment ('divergence thesis'). Rather than assuming a uniform set of New Public Management reforms across the OECD, one might need to acknowledge that different policies are implemented in different configurations. With respect to welfare state reforms, Steinmo (2010, p. 5), uses the term 'evolutionary narratives' to describe such long-term reform patterns. In a similar vein, a 'divergence thesis' of public employment regimes does not at all expect stasis; instead, it expects that reforms are not explained by a singular determinant or set of determinants that exert the same effect on public employment regimes across all OECD countries. The 'divergence thesis' is linked to the idea that different variables matter in different contexts (Steinmo 2010, p. 11). The politico-administrative context, in particular, can be assumed to mediate reform pressures. Following this account, equal reform pressures might be translated into very different reform steps.

A third and intermediate position suggests that countries belonging to the same public employment regime might take similar steps towards reform ('regime-specific gradual reform'). This view strengthens the idea that countries deliberately choose reform instruments in a way that ensures their fit with the specific public employment regime. Thus, contrary to the adoption of a homogenous New Public Management reform model as indicated by the 'convergence thesis', countries belonging to the same public employment regime are expected to choose similar reform strategies. This view would imply that administrative systems – and in particular the rules and Human Resource Management techniques that apply to government employees – become more similar among countries belonging to the same public employment regime, while differences between dissimilar public employment regimes persist. Such reform dynamics might also be coined as 'bounded change', whereby the boundaries of change are set through a country's regime affiliation, which predetermines its menu of applicable reform instruments. The three possible developments – convergence, divergence, and regime-specific gradual reform – will serve as a frame of reference for evaluating the long-term trend in government employment in Chapter 4.

Also with respect to the second driving force of change, New Public Management, observers do not agree on a common interpretation of developments. Given the variety of public administration traditions discussed above, it does not come as a surprise that scholars have questioned the validity of the claim that administrative systems across countries will converge towards the principles and practices advertised by the proponents of New Public Management (Hood 1995; Pollitt 2001, 2002). Critical scholars have argued that it is empirically implausible that one strategy will resonate with all regimes and that one strategy will have identical outcomes in different regimes. The adoption of New Public Management reforms in the 1980s and early 1990s varied considerably across countries, and the reluctance in adhering to the new paradigm suggested, already at that stage, that the observed differences are not an issue of early and late adoption in a seminal process of convergence, but rather point towards divergence.

From the fragmentary literature on public management reform over the 1980s the high NPM group in the OECD countries would be likely to include Sweden, Canada, New Zealand, Australia and the UK with France, Denmark, the Netherlands, Norway and Ireland also showing a number of marked shifts in the direction of NPM. At the other end, the low NPM group would be likely to include Germany, Greece, Spain, Switzerland, Japan and Turkey. (Hood 1995, p. 99)

Despite various policy shifts in the context of a general trend towards experimentation with structural reforms, this early pattern has turned out to be rather persistent over the years (Demmke and Moilanen 2010; OECD 2008, 2013). Following a distinction introduced by Brunnson (1989), Pollitt (2007) argues that convergence may be observed at different levels. 'Discursive convergence' refers to the usage of the same vocabulary in public discourse, which, on the one hand, may or may not refer to the same practices, and, on the other hand, may or may not be accompanied by actual convergence of practices. 'Decisional convergence' implies that certain policies are identical across countries, without actually being implemented in the same way. 'Operational convergence' means that actual practices follow the same principles, although the outcome may still vary widely across countries. Finally, and extending the scheme proposed by Brunnson, Pollitt adds 'results convergence' as a fourth level, which points to identical outcomes measured in terms of efficiency or effectiveness, without necessarily resulting from the same practices. This ambivalence in the meaning of convergence, besides invalidating any sweeping claims about the impact of New Public Management, calls for a more detailed and contextualized analysis of reform trajectories. Pollitt assumes a clear hierarchy in the extent to which convergence can be expected: '[T]here may be a considerable convergence of discourse and/or of decisions, without anything like the same degree of convergence of practice (and still less of results)' (Pollitt 2002, p. 487).

Demmke and Moilanen (2010, p. 21) observe a general shift from the traditional bureaucratic role models towards 'post-bureaucratic differentiation'. In the former, 'a hierarchical and formalised organisational structure, clear and rigid career paths, life-time tenure, full-time employment, seniority, advantageous pension systems and rigid remuneration systems were introduced in order to reduce as far as possible the risk of too much political influence, corruption, misconduct, the exercise of private interests and instability of government' (Demmke and Moilanen 2010, p. 25). In contrast, the term 'post-bureaucratic' is deliberatively chosen to reflect the only vaguely circumscribed shift away from the bureaucratic model: 'post-modern administrations tend to be much more diverse, less hierarchical, more flexible, diverse (sic!), representative and less separated from the citizenry. Whereas the term "bureaucracy" represents clear values (such as hierarchy, formalism, standardisation, rationality, or obedience), the term "postmodernism" implies conflicting values and value dilemmas' (Demmke and Moilanen 2010, p. 28). Thus, different views on the hierarchical structure of public administration, the level of formalization, standardization, and rationality, and on the extent to which obedience is required, are claimed to undermine the societal consensus of the 'Golden Age' on the organization of public employment.

Demmke and Moilanen (2010, p. 188) summarize their extensive analysis of dimensions of civil service systems in a continuum ranging from traditional bureaucracy to post-bureaucracy, and position the 27 EU countries on that scale. They then show that the countries within the Continental, Mediterranean, Scandinavian, and South-Eastern European administrative traditions tend to cluster either higher or lower along the bureaucracy continuum, while the Anglo-American and Eastern European traditions reveal a wider variety of positions (Demmke and Moilanen 2010, p. 245).

However, the variation in reform trajectories is too large and the outcomes are too diverse to warrant their interpretation as variants leading, or lagging in, the implementation of a common model (Bach and Bordogna 2011, p. 2290). Pollitt and Bouckaert (2011) propose a distinction between two ideal type models underlying reform efforts in the OECD world. For the first ideal type, they use the concept of *New Public Management* (NPM), which dominates public political discourse about reforms in public administration. Thereby, the concept is transferred from the discursive level to the analytical level, denoting the concrete and literal implementation of the measures highlighted as beneficial for the efficiency and effectiveness of public services. The other ideal type, the *Neo-Weberian State* (NWS), according to Pollitt and Bouckaert, characterizes the way in which the ideas discussed under the heading of New Public Management are actually implemented in states that depart from a one-to-one translation of ideas into rules and practices. Each concept expresses 'different principles of coordination – NPM favours market mechanisms designed and guided to yield outcomes which are in the public interest; NWS displays a professionalized and consultative form of hierarchy...' (Pollitt and Bouckaert 2011, p. 208).[2] Thus, according to this reading, *New Public Management* and the *Neo-Weberian State* are analytical categories, which differentiate two pathways of public administration reform in the OECD world. Pollitt and Bouckaert (2011, p. 117) identify the United Kingdom, Australia, New Zealand, and, with some hesitation, the United States, as the '*core New Public Management group*'. In contrast, they present Germany, France, the Netherlands, and Sweden, as the most pronounced examples of the *Neo-Weberian State* and claim that these countries follow 'a defensive strategy... to try to protect the "European Social Model" and the "European administrative space" from the depradations of globalized neo-liberalism' (Pollitt and Bouckaert 2011, p. 120).

Neo-Weberian reform trajectories are characterized by the reaffirmation of a strong state role legitimized by representative democratic institutions, a reaffirmation of the importance of administrative law in preserving basic principles of public administration such as equality before the law and legal security, and the preservation of a distinctive status of public service (Pollitt and Bouckaert 2011, p. 118). The distinct status is characterized by the maintenance of employment security and decent working conditions as major employment principles of the public sector, and an emphasis on the negotiation of reforms with strong trade unions. Based on these principles, Neo-Weberian reforms furthermore entail a focus on meeting citizens' needs and wishes instead of strict rule following, an increased role of consultation with citizens' views, a shift towards more emphasis on outcomes rather than procedures, and the introduction of professional management replacing bureaucratic procedures (Pollitt and Bouckaert 2011, pp. 118–19).

Moreover, trends do not seem to be unidirectional, as some of the early New Public Management reforms have been abandoned. This partial countermovement makes the picture even more complex. In order to include these processes, the concept of Post-New Public Management reforms has been introduced to label processes of recentralization and renewed coordination. It also speaks to shifts back towards public provision of services that have been observed in those countries which proceeded the furthest in implementing New Public Management reforms (Chapman and Duncan 2007; Christensen 2012). These reforms, which partially overturn New Public Management reforms, are usually intended to correct for negative externalities generated by the previous reforms (Bach and Bordogna 2011, p. 2286).

Recent studies have highlighted the increasing differentiation of employment conditions and social welfare in Continental European employment regimes. These studies show that status differences are gaining prominence. On the one hand, the core workforce is shielded against market fluctuations and deteriorating employment conditions. On the other hand, an increasing number of workers are marginalized, being employed on temporary contracts with less compensation and only restricted access to social security (Emmenegger et al. 2012). This process has not halted before the public sector. Summarizing detailed country-specific case studies, Vaughan-Whitehead (2013) identifies four structural reform processes in the public sector: decentralization of responsibilities, intensification of Human Resource Management, downsizing of public operations, and privatization of infrastructure and services. The remaining workforce is confronted with decreasing pay levels and employment security, increasing work pressure, and rising inequalities between core and marginal employees.

Perspectives on institutional change

The hypothesis underlying the present project, that the state as an employer is in a process of transformation, implies that the institutions characterizing public employment regimes are changing. However, a core defining property of an institution is its robustness to change over time. For this reason, institutional change has only recently become an object of systematic comparative inquiry (Streeck and Thelen 2005a). In early contributions, institutional change has been conceptualized in terms of long phases of stable equilibrium punctuated by ruptures, 'critical junctures', in which the institutional setup of a political arena is reordered (Baumgartner and Jones 1993; Jones and Baumgartner 2012; Pierson 2004). This view has been challenged by the literature on comparative institutional analysis, which emphasizes the incremental nature of institutional change (Campbell 2009, pp. 92–106; Lindner 2003). The main difficulty with the punctuated equilibrium approach is identifying and circumscribing junctures by defining the beginning and end of the critical phase separating two stable periods of institutional equilibrium.

Several theoretical traditions in comparative institutional analysis have contributed to the study of institutional change. According to the oldest, functionalist perspective, institutional change is a consequence of technical change and adaptation to contextual exigencies. Organizational structures of firms continuously adjust to changes in market size that are related to communication and transportation technologies. In search of efficiency, organizational forms are chosen that minimize transaction costs (Williamson 1981). Although much criticism has been levied against the automatism implied in the functionalist approach – for example, neglecting variation in cultural and political contexts – the need to adjust organizational forms to changing contexts is a powerful driving force behind institutional change. Against the automatism of the functionalist perspective, diffusion theory suggests that institutional change can be effectuated by deliberate choice by institutional agents. Organizations observe the performance of other, comparable organizations and establish common rules and practices by imitation, learning, codification, or benchmarking (DiMaggio 1997; Powell and DiMaggio 1991). Another twist to this idea is added by a view pointing at conflict and power struggles: the institutional structures are shaped by those agents who were able to obtain the power to adjust the rules to their interests, thereby using examples of other institutions as blueprints (Amable 2003, 2009). Finally, an integrative approach suggests that these power struggles only partly generate coherent institutional structures. Instead, institutional principles and practices may be recombined and rearranged in a piecemeal way (bricolage), or elements taken from elsewhere may be modified and blended together with existing institutions (translation) (Crouch 2005).

All these approaches highlight specific conditions which may either stabilize institutions or trigger structural changes in institutions. A focus on the presence or absence of specific conditions, however, does not capture the actual complexity of real institutions. None of the regime types identified in Chapter 2 is present in a pure form in real political economies. Instead, a large variety of hybrid constellations is observed. In each political economy, a specific constellation of interconnected institutions is in operation at different levels of a political system, and the meaning of institutions is ambiguous and can be interpreted in various ways depending on the context (Campbell 2009, pp. 102–105).

These caveats require exploring the dynamics and mechanisms of institutional change in more detail. According to perhaps the most influential approach to studying institutional continuity and change in comparative political economy (Hall and Thelen 2009; Mahoney and Thelen 2010; Streeck and Thelen 2005a), four modes of 'gradual but nevertheless transformative' change (Streeck and Thelen 2005b, p. 19) can be distinguished: displacement, layering, drift, and conversion.[3] The distinction in these four modes is the result of the combined effect of the possibility to interpret rules at the discretion of agents within an institution, and the number of veto possibilities for institutional change by other agents in an institution's political context. Table 2.3 presents a cross-tabulation of a dichotomous operationalization of the two dimensions and the associated mode of change.

Change under the condition of a high rigidity of rules requires formal decisions to apply new rules. Layering is a process by which existing rules are amended by new rules. Strong veto possibilities imply that the political context is in favour of agents resisting change in existing institutions. In such circumstances, a negotiated compromise is likely to produce additional rules which result in a gradual shift in the operation of an institution. If resistance to change cannot generate barriers against the abolishment of existing rules, institutional change is the result of replacing existing rules with new, but possibly also hitherto subordinate or dormant, ones. This has been termed 'displacement of institutions' (Mahoney and Thelen 2010, p. 16).

If an institution has more discretion over the interpretation of rules, the mode of institutional change depends on the amount of external resistance

Table 2.3   Contextual and institutional sources of institutional change

	Characteristics of targeted institution	
	Low level of discretion in interpretation/ enforcement	High level of discretion in interpretation/ enforcement
Characteristics of political context		
Strong veto possibilities	Layering (existing rules amended by new rules)	Drift (decay and implicit redefinition of existing rules)
Weak veto possibilities	Displacement (existing rules replaced by new or dormant rules)	Conversion (redeployment of rules for other purposes)

Sources: Mahoney and Thelen (2010, p. 28) and Van der Heijden (2010, p. 237).

confronted by proponents of change. If weak external veto possibilities give much leeway to institutional agents, they can enact existing rules according to their own interpretation and use ambiguities and loopholes to convert rules and redeploy institutions to other purposes. If, however, strong external veto possibilities limit the possibilities for overt internal reorganization, neglect of adaptation to changing circumstances can let an institution decay and thereby implicitly alter the outcome of institutional activity. Hence, the institution drifts in a new direction (Mahoney and Thelen 2010, p. 17).

This typology is certainly a useful grid for conceptualizing empirical studies of institutional change. The devil, however, is in the details. In particular, two problems have been highlighted. Firstly, the abstract classification does not specify what exactly is meant by an institution and a change in an institution (Capano 2009). The classification of a change in institutional structure depends on the time horizon, on the level of analysis, or on the perspective. For example, institutional drift may be embedded in a process of layering, or displacement may be preceded by conversion. One and the same observed institutional change may be interpreted in terms of different modes of change, depending on the exact focus of the research question and the context considered for comparison. Different frames of references may thus yield very different conclusions about what has actually happened (Kickert and Van der Meer 2011; Van der Heijden 2012). Secondly, the fact that institutional change occurs within a constellation of institutions occupied by agents with heterogeneous interests suggests that institutional change is contested and conflictual. This implies that it can be expected to be piecemeal, following 'an incremental path-dependent process, not deviating radically from the past', whereby '[a]ctors may seek institutional and functional equivalents to pre-existing forms of coordination' (Campbell 2009, p. 102). Thus, all processes of institutional change will, at some point, entail some bricolage with formal rules.

The most promising, and also most widely studied, mode of institutional change is considered to be institutional layering (Van der Heijden 2011). Layering is the result of a tug-of-war between the proponents of continuity and those of change when an institution's outcomes do not match its intentions, and each group has sufficient power to veto decisions (Campbell 2009; Van der Heijden 2011). As such, layering is a hybrid outcome, a momentary state resulting from a series of institutional adaptations (Mahoney and Thelen 2010). It is a patchwork of different rules that may have been inserted at different points in time by different actors with different aims. The proponents of continuity are sufficiently powerful to defend the existing institution, but insufficiently so to prevent the addition of new elements. In turn, the proponents of change are sufficiently powerful to add new elements, but insufficiently so to abolish existing ones. By highlighting the political context, the characteristics of the institution, and the actors' stance towards an institution, the concept allows for a more nuanced appraisal of institutional change which potentially bridges prior approaches (Van der Heijden 2011, pp. 12, 16).

These provisos are particularly salient in reforms of public employment regimes. The importance of the concept of layering is apparent in the description by Christensen and Lægreid (2011) of the process of public administration reform in terms of increasing complexity and hybridity of the public sector:

> [Complexity] has a structural dimension addressing vertical and horizontal specialization and a cultural dimension addressing the variety of informal norms and values. [Hybridity] addressing (sic!) the potential tension or inconsistency between diverse structural and cultural elements in government. Hybrid organizations are multifunctional entities combining different tasks, values and organizational forms. They are composite and compounded arrangements that are combining partly inconsistent considerations producing difficult and unstable trade-offs and lasting tensions. (Christensen and Lægreid 2011, p. 410)

In this vein, speaking of civil service systems, Bezès and Lodge (2007) argue that the stronger the legal entrenchment, the more likely it is that

> any 'new' types of ideas – such as those supposedly managerial ideas associated with the 'new public management' movement – will be filtered in the light of legal coherence and standard operating procedures, both cognitively as well as structurally through the existence of judicial institutions that further raise potentially 'reversal' costs that are involved in any proposal for change. (Bezès and Lodge 2007, p. 124)

The degree of pervasiveness of the civil service system referring to administrative centralization influences the extent to which decentralization of administrative duties and the introduction of autonomous agencies can be enforced. The prior existence of decentralized structures and agencies fosters administrative reforms in this direction, while integrated government structures and strong local units hinder reforms (Bezès and Lodge 2007, p. 124). The political-administrative nexus refers to the relationship between politicians and top administrators. Ideas stemming from New Public Management are expected to obtain more resonance among '"instrumental" bureaucracies where public servants loyalty is directed towards their political masters instead of something more abstract, such as a constitution' (Bezès and Lodge 2007, p. 125). The career component captures the openness of the public service labour market and distinguishes between a job-based and a career-based recruitment and promotion system (Bezès and Lodge 2007, p. 125). Finally, the reward component refers to the differentiation between fixed salary scales and the introduction of private sector elements into the public service, such as performance-related pay, reduced pension rights, and a more flexible and open labour market (Bezès and Lodge 2007, p. 126).

Proponents of New Public Management can be expected to push forward in all these dimensions. At the same time, resistance will vary across the policy areas, thereby most likely generating a process that can be described from a bird's-eye perspective as incremental change. Any particular institution, rule, or operating procedure, if observed in isolation, may be subject to drift, displacement, conversion, or even exhaustion. However, the identification of the general pattern will be less straightforward and will also be characterized by differences in the direction of change, the speed of adjustment, and the scope of reform. As stated above, these developments are summarized by the concept of layering. In consequence, layering should have a different epistemological status than the other three or four proposed patterns of institutional change (Mahoney and Thelen 2010; Streeck and Thelen 2005b), as it suggests that the outcome of change is more complex and may actually encompass the other patterns as part of the process (Barzelay and Gallego 2006; MacCarthaigh and Roness 2012).

Research question, analytical framework, and expectations

Transformations of public employment regimes: the research question

The literature on public administration systems and institutional change has yielded many insights into the variation across countries and generally supports the idea that countries cluster into families of nations, which, despite all differences and nuances in detail, exhibit similar and internally rather coherent constellations of institutions. Within this context, civil service systems exhibit specific traits, being characterized by particularly high employment security and comparatively employee-friendly working conditions, and being consistently embedded in the wider public administration systems. We have also noted the common challenges to public services stemming from cost pressures and the ideological turn towards New Public Management, with its emphasis on cost containment and efficiency. One of the major consequences of administrative reform was the widespread privatization and outsourcing of public services to private service providers.

Much less is known, however, about the effects of the two driving forces on the employment regimes in those public services that remained in the public sector. In what way has the distinctive status of public employment been affected by the pressures generated by cost containment and New Public Management? How did different public employment regimes respond to largely similar pressures? Does the concept of the *Neo-Weberian State* sufficiently capture the common developments in countries described by this notion? How are changes in the administration systems reflected in the parameters of the public employment regime? In which way have reforms inspired by New Public Management been introduced, and how did they fare in the context of the Neo-Weberian State? Starting from heterogeneous initial conditions, did the common challenges lead to similar reform trajectories and result in more homogeneous public employment regimes? Or have the structural differences been stronger than the driving forces, thereby producing path-dependent trajectories of change with differing outcomes?

Currently, we have to conclude that there is no consensus about an analytic framework for studying change in public sector organizations in general, and public employment regimes in particular. Building on the considerations outlined above, we will explore changes in the specificity and privileged nature of public employment.

Our starting point is the ideal type of the 'civil servant', which Max Weber describes as follows:

> That the office is a 'vocation' (*Beruf*) finds expression, first, in the requirement of a prescribed course of training, which demands the entire working capacity for a long period of time, and in generally prescribed special examinations as prerequisites of employment. Furthermore, it finds expression in that the position of the official is in the nature of a 'duty' (*Pflicht*). This determines the character of his relations in the following manner: Legally and actually, office holding is not considered ownership of a source of income, to be exploited for rents or emoluments in exchange for the rendering of certain services..., nor is office holding considered a common exchange of services, as in the case of free employment contracts. Rather, entrance into an office, including one in the private economy, is considered an acceptance of a specific duty of fealty to the purpose of the office (*Amtstreue*) in return for the grant of a secure existence. It is decisive for the modern loyalty to an office that, in the pure type, it does not establish a relationship to a person, like the vassals or disciple's faith under feudal or patrimonial authority, but rather is devoted to impersonal and functional purposes. (Weber 1968, pp. 958–59)

The image of the public employee held by proponents of New Public Management is diametrically opposed to this view. Inspired by principal-agent theory, the picture sketched by this perspective is one of an egoistic utility-maximizing bureaucrat, whose utility function is solely determined by the size of the budget for which he is responsible (Niskanen 1971, p. 38). In contrast to the Weberian conception, this bureaucrat is neither motivated by duty to the state nor by service to the citizen. From the perspective of New Public Management, the public employee can only be motivated to provide the best possible service to the public, instead of focusing on budget maximization, by offering her or him private incentives to perform according to some externally defined criteria. We call this ideal type the 'service provider'.

Until the 'Golden Age' of TRUDI, the Weberian ideal type has been the dominating vision of public administration in many Western, in particular European, countries, although countries have approached the ideal type to different degrees in the institutionalization of their public employment regimes. The conception of the budget-maximizing bureaucrat has taken over a similar role in the perspective heralded by New Public Management. We thus contend that the institutions established in a societal field depend, at least to some degree, on the underlying assumptions about the motivations and incentives of employees.

We differentiate the specificity and privileged nature of public employment into two main dimensions, which both focus on employer behaviour (Bach and Bordogna 2011; Gallie 2007a, 2007b; Hermann and Flecker 2012). On the one hand, employment regulation refers to the institutional framework of employment in the public sector. On the other hand, personnel policies address more or less standardized practices. The core criteria of employment regulation are the legal status of employment (civil servant status vs. employee), the mode of regulation of employment conditions (authoritative vs. contractual), and the available strategies in the case of employment-related conflict (loyalty requirements vs. right to strike). With respect to personnel policies, we focus on entry requirements and recruitment strategies, personnel management (personnel deployment, incentives, and evaluation), and personnel development (further education and career paths).

While personnel policies in the traditional, bureaucratic public employment regime were determined by the career model with little to no discretion on the part of superiors, efficiency-oriented reforms in the spirit of New Public Management have questioned the preponderance and appropriateness of these traditional characteristics of public employment (Bach and Della Rocca 2000; Kißler et al. 2006). From a cross-country comparative perspective, the initial situation at the point of departure of this study can be expected to vary considerably (Bordogna 2007). The extent to which employment regimes are responsive to changes depends on their openness at the outset of a reform trajectory.

In this vein, this study asks, what has happened to those employees who remain in the public service? Did the rhetoric of New Public Management, which can be observed all over the world, result in significant changes in actual employment conditions? Does the legal and contractual status of public employees converge towards the private sector conditions or does the public sector maintain special arrangements? In which ways does the state diverge from private enterprises in the perception of the role as an employer? In what ways do reforms vary across countries and across administrative sectors?

In addition, we will explore the implications of the paradigmatic shifts in the public services on the integrative potential of public employment with respect to women and marginalized groups (Kroos and Gottschall 2012; Rubery 2014), and on the ambition of public employment regimes with respect to the establishment of exemplary working conditions (Briken et al. 2014; Vaughan-Whitehead 2013).

Analytical framework: moderating and mediating factors

Being part of the administrative regime of a country, institutional change in the public employment regime is embedded in a wider process of transformation of the state (Leibfried et al. 2015; Leibfried and Zürn 2005). Acknowledging that particular functions of the state can be represented and fulfilled by different but functionally equivalent institutional forms, Leibfried and Zürn define a transformation as an epidemic change of institutional forms across states. However, they immediately ask: 'But just how much change must be observed?' (Leibfried and Zürn 2005, p. 16), and specify that the 'corridor of variation', which refers to minor variation within a particular paradigmatic structure, itself must change in size or shape.

The two major driving factors of reform in the public sector face a variety of issues potentially deflecting the thrust of the instigated process, or, as Leibfried and Zürn (2005, p. 16) put it, contribute to an 'unravelling' of the very fabric of the institutional structure. The term 'unravelling' refers to a set of changes which do not simply 'crease' the 'tightly woven fabric' of TRUDI, nor will this fabric be 'mended or rewoven', but rather 'separate and follow individual fates in post-modern fashion' (Leibfried and Zürn 2005, p. 3).

In this vein, we will explore to what extent the traditional concept of public employees as 'state servants' unravels into a multitude of 'public service providers' with varying status and tasks. We will argue that two sets of factors interfere with the reform trajectories of public employment regimes instigated by cost pressures and the new ideological paradigm of New Public Management: one set which moderates the effect of the driving forces across countries, and another set which mediates the effect of the driving forces within countries but across sectors. Moderators influence the strength and direction of the effect, mediators explain the relationship between the driving force and the outcome (Baron and Kenny 1986). In a nutshell, the structure of our argument is as follows. Firstly, in line with the literature on alternative reform pathways in public administration, we expect the purportedly worldwide, unidirectional trend towards New Public Management to be differentiated into country-specific trajectories by the moderating force of institutional and cultural conditions. Secondly, we argue that the scope of reform is mediated by the extent of the state's responsibility devolution to the private sector, which varies across sectors. In this way, we expect that public employment regimes 'unravel' across both nations and sectors.

Moderating factors: conditions of public employment reform

We have outlined the variety of administrative traditions and systems across European countries in which the cost-cutting strategies and New Public Management reforms have been discussed and initiated, and the differentiated trajectories of reform. Thus, the process of unravelling state responsibilities described above takes place in different administrative contexts and is subject to different dynamics. In view of the arguments developed in the previous subsections, we should expect both cross-national and cross-sectoral variation in reform strategies, reform pathways, and reform outcomes. These differences may be partly related to the functional exigencies of specific sectors, partly be the consequence of specific traits of the administrative culture, and partly even be the idiosyncratic results of individual actions.

We now elaborate upon how institutional and cultural factors may deflect the trajectory of reforms of public administration regimes in general. According to Horton and Farnham (2000), a variety of factors explain cross-national variation in Human Resource Management in the public sector across nation-states. They mention the perception of the state in society, the constitution, the political system and the political culture, administrative traditions and the role of administrative law, the structure of the public sector, the industrial relations system, the influence of trade unions and other associations, as well as the political leadership. Further factors typically mentioned in the literature are: the legal status of public employees, the influence of public employees on political decisions, both in terms of direct influence of top administrators on policy making and in terms of the electoral force of public employees, the joint identity of public employees and their strong organization in trade unions, and limits to the discretion of government (Pierson 1994; Pollitt and Bouckaert 2011; Tsebelis 2002). In view of the theoretical argument on the diversity of developments described by the concept of institutional layering, and the variety of factors claimed to influence changes in employment regimes, we should expect to actually find a variety of developments.

However, this list of factors is too large and too unstructured to guide an analysis. We first turn to the institutional context of administrative reform. According to Pollitt and Bouckaert (2011), the constitutional complexion of the state and the administrative culture are the core factors separating the New Public Management from the Neo-Weberian reform path of European administrative regimes.

The constitutional complexion is basically composed of two facets: the structure of the state, and the nature of executive government. The structure of the state determines the extent to which institutional barriers limit the discretion of government activity and refers to the 'vertical dispersion of authority' and the 'degree of horizontal coordination within central government' (Pollitt and Bouckaert 2011, pp. 49, 53). At the constitutional level, unitary constitutions are differentiated from federalist ones (Lijphart 1999; Obinger et al. 2005). In practical terms, though, the unitary constitution is not a sufficient condition for government discretion. In addition, the level of centralization of decision-making must be taken into account. A low level of centralization is regarded as the functional equivalent to a federalist constitution. It is expected that 'reforms in highly decentralized states (whether they be unitary or federal) are likely to be less broad in scope and less uniform in practice than in centralized states' (Pollitt and Bouckaert 2011, p. 51). This is because with increasing autonomy, decentralized units are able to explore different directions of change. An important example of the immobilizing effect of vertically layered authority is the 'Joint-Decision Trap' diagnosed for federal systems in which different levels of government can block each others' decisions (Scharpf 1988, 2006). In turn, unitary, centralized states can overrule any local policies considered aberrations from the centrally chosen course of action. In the horizontal dimension, the leeway of cabinet ministers to initiate reforms in their policy areas depends on the internal structure of the government, that is the extent to which single agents like the prime minister or the finance minister have authority over the decisions of other ministers (Laver and Shepsle 1994). The more ministerial freedom, the less unitary the reforms will be and the less powerful the central government will be in relation to lower levels of government (Pollitt and Bouckaert 2011, p. 53). Thus, the scope of reform is affected by the structure of the state.

The nature of executive government is reflected in the number of parties necessary for making political decisions (Laver and Schofield 1998). The electoral system strongly influences the number of competing parties with prospects for obtaining seats in parliament (Duverger 1951) and, partly as a consequence, the number of parties needed for a majority. Majoritarian systems result by definition in one-party governments, while this is just one possible outcome in plurality systems which often result in coalition governments (Ahmed 2013; Katz 1980). The more parties are needed for obtaining a majority for a reform initiative, the more diverse opinions have to be considered, and the more likely a compromise will be reached which limits the speed and severity of reform.

Together, the two facets determine the extent to which government decisions can be blocked by other agents holding constitutionally guaranteed veto power (Tsebelis 2000). The more centralized the state's structure and the stronger the majoritarian traits of executive government are, the faster, more radical, and more encompassing the reforms in public management, including the employment regime, will be. Conversely, the more decentralized the authority and the more consensual the executive government, the slower, more incremental, and more restricted the reforms will be.

The cultural context is much more fluid and ambiguous. According to Pollitt and Bouckaert (2011), three facets of the administrative culture have an impact on managerial reform in the public sector: the relationship between ministers and top-level administrators ('mandarins'), the philosophy and culture of governance, and the diversity of policy advice. Senior administrators are brokers between the political aims of the ministers and the standard operating procedures of the ministries and operational administrative units. The balance of power between the minister and senior administrators is a crucial factor for the success of reform initiatives in public administration. This relationship is mediated by the politicization of senior administrative positions, hence the extent to which they are protected against displacement, and the ideological congruence between the ministers and the senior officers. The stronger the tenure of senior administrators and the wider the ideological distance between the minister and the senior administrators, the larger the potential for resistance against reforms will be. Powerful mandarins can immobilize ministers.

Regarding the philosophy and culture of governance, we have discussed variation in administrative culture across European states and the broad distinction between the principles of rule of law and of public interest. Pollitt and Bouckaert (2011, pp. 62–3, emphasis in original) argue that '*Rechtsstaat* systems would be "stickier" and slower to reform than public interest regimes. This is because management change would always require changes in the law and, culturally, because senior civil servants who are highly trained in administrative law may find it more difficult than generalists to shift to a "managerial" or "performance-oriented" perspective.'

Finally, the diversity of sources of advice used by ministers may also affect the choice of reform pathways. Pollitt and Bouckaert (2011, p. 66) suggest: 'The basic proposition here is that the wider the range of customary sources of advice, the more likely it is that new ideas – especially those from outside the public sector – will reach ministers' ears in persuasive and influential forms.'

These cultural elements are much more open to the discretion of the agents of change, and resistance in reform processes, than the institutional structure. Senior administrators may be more or less loyal to a minister. Thus, they may either use their power or not when they are in the position to support or obstruct reform initiatives. The philosophy dominating an administrative culture may be taken as a guideline of action or may be combatted by senior administrators. Moreover, different ministers and senior administrators will vary in the extent to which they are willing to look for external sources of advice. All of these facets will vary within one and the same administrative system, and depend much more on the specific administrative culture that has evolved at a particular level, or in a particular section of the administration of public services, than on the national culture.

Mediating factors: modes of responsibility devolution

Throughout the literature discussed so far, changes in public administration regimes, civil service systems, and public employment regimes are conceptualized in a holistic way. Arguments refer to whole nation-states and treat public employment as an internally undifferentiated regime. To some extent, this approach is supported by the fact that the state is a largely unitary employer with the special prerogative to unilaterally dictate conditions by legal act (Traxler 1999). Many regulations hold across the whole public sector of a country, but vary across countries.

However, such an approach rests on the assumption that the driving forces affect all sectors of public services in the same way. This view, in turn, assumes that all sectors are actually exposed to the driving forces to the same extent. Our main contention is that this is unlikely to be the case because the process of unravelling state functions has generated variation across sectors in the extent to which they are exposed to the market. During the 'Golden Age' of TRUDI, responsibility for the production of normative goods such as legitimacy, rule of law, security, or welfare was concentrated in the nation-state (Leibfried and Zürn 2005). The state can take responsibility at three levels:

- *Political responsibility*: At the most general level, the parliament decides on the rules of the game and the principles to be applied to policies, and the state is responsible for the supervision of developments in the policy area;
- *Decision-making responsibility*: The state is responsible for the definition of services provided and for defining and maintaining concrete standards of service provision;
- *Organizational responsibility*: The state is responsible for the actual provision of services.

The neo-liberal paradigm underlying New Public Management reforms challenged the concentration of responsibility in the nation-state by claiming that the public services producing these normative goods can be organized at lower costs, more efficiently, and at the same time more effectively, by separating the different levels of responsibility and transferring as much responsibility as possible to the private sector (Suleiman 2003). In the context of cost pressures in public budgets, privatization of public services has been one main consequence of the empowerment of this ideology.

Indeed, one of the core observations related to recent transformations of the state in general (Leibfried et al. 2015; Leibfried and Zürn 2005) is that the three levels of responsibility for the production of normative goods unravel. However, in different countries and different areas of state activity, the political responsibility, the decision-making responsibility, and the organizational responsibility drift in different directions. The three types of responsibility are nested. The state holds organizational responsibility for a subset of instances for which it holds decision-making responsibility. In turn, the state holds decision-making responsibility for a subset of those instances for which it holds political responsibility. Actually, giving up political responsibility implies that the state would entirely withdraw from a particular policy area. Such a radical abolishment of state power is not part of even the most extreme neo-liberal programme of state retraction because markets need at the very least institutions ascertaining the rule of law and the preservation of competition (North 1990). Consequently, political responsibility cannot be withdrawn without also giving up the claim of societal order. Disregarding such a case of complete surrender of a policy area to the market, we can distinguish three modes of reform according to the extent to which responsibility is devolved to private actors.

The most far-reaching devolution of state responsibility occurs if *both organizational and decision-making responsibilities* are transferred to private agents. This setting is attained by privatizing public enterprises and administrative units, and opening up competitive markets of public services. The services are specified and offered by private firms operating on a competitive market. Given the severe imbalances in size and market power between incumbents, which were government agencies or ministerial departments before the privatization, and private newcomers, such markets are typically considered in need of strict market regulation in order to prevent monopolies, collusions, and other market failures undermining the core aims of cost reduction and improvement of efficiency and effectiveness. Consequently, privatization not only transfers public employees to the private sector, but also requires the state to employ personnel in charge of supervision tasks in regulatory agencies. Given that such agencies are usually established in response to the privatization of a sector, they provide a rare opportunity for governments and top administrations to design administrative units rather unhindered by existing arrangements, traditions, and power structures. Ideas inspired by New Public Management should thus be easier to implement in such agencies than in well-established units. As most likely cases for reform, these agencies are crucial observations for testing the implementation of New Public Management. The less the employment regime governing these agencies is influenced by New Public Management, the less this perspective is expected to impact on the public employment regime in general.

The second mode is that the state only devolves the organizational responsibility, but retains both the political and the decision-making responsibility. While such moves typically aim at cost containment and a reduction in the number of public employees, they are often accompanied by market creation measures, such as compulsory competitive tendering. Service provision is exposed to market pressures intended to increase efficiency, but the kind of services provided is still defined by the state. Examples of such arrangements are the outsourcing of certain tasks to private firms partly owned by public authorities, the conversion of administrative units into private legal entities, or public-private partnerships. This setting involves a range of organizations with different ownership structures in close competition with each other. Reforms of public employment regimes can thus be studied under pressure from a market for services. Adjustments will be less at the discretion of the state as an employer, as is the case for newly established regulatory agencies. Instead, concerns over cost competitiveness with respect to private firms offering the same services will drive reforms in the employment regime.

The third mode is the preservation of all three types of responsibility under control of the state. Changes to the employment regime will then not be triggered by environmental changes, such as the need for new regulatory agencies or competitive pressure, but instead will follow the pathway and logic of administrative reform. The chance of radical shifts is minor due to a large potential for resistance from employees who are traditionally well-organized in the public sector and represent a substantial group of voters in national elections that can become dangerous for the re-election of government (Goodin 1996; Pierson 1994). In contrast to newly established agencies, this mode is the least likely case for reform. If substantial reforms are observed under these circumstances, the state's role as employer can be considered subject to substantial change in a country.

Comparing the three modes of responsibility devolution, we can expect that in new agencies established to keep under control oligopolistic markets resulting from the surrender of both decision-making and organizational responsibility for providing the normative good to the private sector, the government's current view on the organization of the public employment regime should be expressed most clearly. In contrast, devolution of organizational responsibility should generate competition between private and public providers of services, and cost reduction will be the dominant motive of reform in the employment regime. Finally, adjusting employment regimes in long-standing public administration contexts will confront well-organized vested interests, potentially resulting in reluctant and piecemeal changes at the margins.

3
Research Design and Methods

General approach

In the introduction and in Chapter 2, we have discussed the shift from the traditional paradigm of the public employee as a civil servant to an emerging paradigm of the public employee as a provider of public services. In this vein, our core research question is: To what extent have European countries preserved a distinct status of public employees? The theoretical perspective outlined in Chapter 2 suggests that the expected variation in reforms of public employment regimes, triggered by cost concerns and New Public Management ideology, is moderated by the institutional and cultural framework on the one hand and mediated by the extent of devolution of the state's responsibility for normative goods to private service providers on the other hand. An empirical investigation of this general hypothesis requires different types of information.

As we have argued in Chapter 2, deviations from New Public Management strategies observed in Western European countries have been summarized by the notion of a Neo-Weberian reform trajectory. This trajectory is characterized by the reaffirmation of a strong state legitimated by representative democratic institutions, a reaffirmation of the importance of administrative law in preserving basic principles of public administration such as equality before the law and legal security, and the preservation of a distinctive status of public service. These conditions restrict the scope of reform. While they differentiate reforms in the Continental and Nordic European countries from the Anglo-American pattern, the fact that almost all European states are characterized as Neo-Weberian implies a large amount of homogeneity across European countries. But why should we expect countries with such diverse public administration traditions as described in Chapter 2 to follow the same reform trajectory if their major commonality is to deviate from New Public Management recommendations? The analytical problem evoked by the homogenizing assumptions underlying typologies, which tend to sweep variation within and between countries under the rug, has been succinctly summarized with respect to welfare regimes:

[C]ountries are not likely to possess coherent welfare regimes because (1) each welfare policy tends to change incrementally over many years; (2) different welfare policies in the same country typically have different histories; (3) discrete sets of policy actors are involved in the various fields of welfare policy; (4) variations in the policy-making process affect the substance of policy; and (5) borrowing from foreign models introduces diverse practical and normative elements into each country's welfare package. For these reasons we should expect to find considerable incoherence in any country's welfare policies, and that incoherence should increase with the age and size of each country's welfare programmes. (Kasza 2002, p. 282)

In order to address general trends of cost containment and policy reform, the moderating effect of institutions and culture, and the mediating effect of functional requirements, we need to combine three different perspectives, each focusing on a specific aspect of Neo-Weberian reform trajectories and using a different methodological approach. To understand the general trends and dynamics of reforms, we need to explore the development of aggregate public employment figures and the timing of reform initiatives across OECD countries. While the moderators tend to vary across countries, the mediators are conditioned both on government policies, also resulting in variation across countries, and on the more functional requirements and possibilities in different economic sectors. We thus expect, on top of cross-country variation, cross-sectoral variation in outcomes within countries. Each of the three perspectives – the broad cross-national comparisons, the detailed case studies of country systems, and the longitudinal analysis of processes of change in sectors – provides evidence for answering different questions, which jointly contribute to resolving the puzzle underlying the research question.

Although we collect data and information from a variety of sources, we do not claim to follow a multi- or mixed-methods approach, nor do we employ triangulation (Bergman 2008; Tashakkori and Teddlie 2002). Such an approach would require that we access one research question from various perspectives using different methods for answering this single research question. At best, we can make such a claim at a very abstract and superficial level only. It is more appropriate, in our view, to speak of an approach using complementary methods in which each method contributes different pieces of information for solving the puzzle of changes in public employment regimes.

By combining the macro-quantitative comparison across OECD countries, the focused comparison of country-specific developments, and the comparison of the sector-specific changes, we intend to strike a balance between the ambition to generalize and the reflection on case-specific idiosyncrasies. For scholars working along a strictly hypothetico-deductive approach to science, this approach may generate insufficiently generalizable observations, whereas for scholars adhering to the interpretative paradigm, still too little attention may be given to the fine details and nuances of the cases analysed. We intend to strike a middle ground between these extreme views and, although perhaps impossible from a philosophy of social science perspective (Rosenberg 2012), we contend that this approach yields results that are both sufficiently nuanced and sufficiently general to warrant informed guesses about possible trajectories which may even be relevant reference points for other countries and sectors.

Cross-national comparisons: statistical analyses

We employ a macro-comparative quantitative design for analysing the two core driving forces of reform and their effects on public employment regimes at a general level. In Chapter 4 we will explore several aspects of reform in public employment regimes. We start with an overall assessment of differences between public administration and public employment regimes based on more recent data than previous studies have used. Then we analyse longer-term trends in public employment as a major driving force of public expenditures. While studies have predominantly addressed the determinants of costs and expenditures directly, we will focus on numerical changes in employment and ask to what extent they can be attributed to cost pressures and New Public Management reforms. By studying the size of the public workforce, we assess the extent to which reforms have actually been effective in reducing public employment. We also consider the overall effectiveness of government in relation to the size of the workforce. Finally, we focus on a core dimension of New Public Management – the introduction of elements of performance-related pay into public sector remuneration schemes – in order to capture qualitative changes in the design of public employment regimes.

While public sector reform is certainly a worldwide challenge, we restrict the scope of this study of reform in public employment regimes to rich, industrialized Western countries which are members of the Organization for Economic Co-operation and Development (OECD). The problems faced by governments and public administrations in this set of countries differ too much from the problems dominating reform attempts in developing countries to include emerging economies into the analyses as well. Unfortunately, relevant data are not available for all 34 OECD member states (let alone other parts of the world), resulting in a smaller set of 19 countries included in this study. The selection bias resulting from these restrictions implies that the set of countries is not more than a convenience sample and findings may be considered relevant, though not representative in the statistical sense, for Western Europe and the Anglo-American family of nations, but not beyond (Ebbinghaus 2005).

In contrast to common practice in quantitative macro-comparative political economy (Beck and Katz 2011), we do not use pooled time-series cross-section analysis as a default method. Since we explore cross-country differences and long-term trends in slow-moving and institutional variables, studying annual data does not add inferential leverage to most of the questions addressed in this analysis. Instead, it would introduce much unnecessary noise and time-series problems, such as autocorrelation in the residuals and non-stationarity (Jackman 1985; Kittel 2008).

We employ a larger set of tools for describing patterns in the data which do not emphasize the statistical significance of effects but support finding 'unobvious regularities' (Hoover 2002, p. 173) in the data. Specifically, Chapter 4 consists of three empirical sections. First, it focuses on the politico-administrative context that is expected to shape a country's capacity to conduct administrative reforms. By taking advantage of recent progress in the collection of comparative data on public administration policies, it provides a map of politico-administrative regimes in the OECD. In the next step, the exploration moves forward towards the conceptualization and identification of distinct public employment regimes within the OECD by means of a multiple correspondence analysis (MCA). For the exploration of public employment regimes, we particularly focus on national differences in the implementation of New Public Management instruments.

Second, Chapter 4 examines the long- and short-term trends in the size and costs of general government employment. In particular, it explores the association of these trends with the resources of national systems of administration, the output of these systems in terms of government effectiveness, and the reform intensity measured by the adoption of NPM tools. In each instance, we discuss systematic differences in these relationships across and within public employment regimes.

Finally, Chapter 4 explores the responsiveness of public employment regimes towards the incorporation of NPM ideas. Focusing only on quantitative changes in the size and costs of government employment neglects the possibility that countries may adopt similar reform measures at different points in time. In order to identify the 'early birds' and 'latecomers' in NPM with respect to Human Resource Management (HRM), the third section explores the timing of the introduction of performance-related pay (PRP). PRP is certainly only a single element in the NPM agenda, but as we will see, it represents a particular paradigmatic change or 'structural break' in the traditional seniority-based remuneration scheme in public administrations. The chapter concludes with a summary of empirical findings and discusses their implications for the in-depth country- and sector-specific analyses.

Comparing countries: comparative case studies

Much of the previous comparative work on public employment regimes has been designed as compilations of single-case studies linked by a common list of aspects described in country chapters. In contrast to this literature, however, the case descriptions in our study are guided by an integrated theoretical argument focusing on the systematic relationships between state structures, public administration, and public employment regimes.

At a superficial level, setting up a study of Neo-Weberian reform trajectories of public employment regimes comes close to selecting on the outcome, an approach that has been widely criticized by scholars working from the template of the quantitative paradigm (Geddes 1991; King et al. 1994). This charge, however, would imply a misunderstanding of the aim of this study, which is not to explain the Neo-Weberian reform path as such, but to explore variation *within* the set of countries qualified as Neo-Weberian (Collier et al. 2004). The focus on this particular set of countries simply restricts the scope of possible outcomes, which helps to highlight nuance and ambivalence within this set that is otherwise buried under the rough generalizations of 'big structures, large processes, [and] huge comparisons' (Tilly 1984), of which the term 'Neo-Weberian' is an almost prototypical example.

In order to identify the location of these hypothesized variants of the Neo-Weberian reform trajectory in the larger conceptual space of public employment regimes, and to appreciate the effects of the moderating variables, we include the United Kingdom – and thus a *non*-Neo-Weberian public administration regime – as a reference point for the comparisons. As a showcase of far-reaching reforms inspired by New Public Management, the United Kingdom offers an impression of the extent to which the public administration, including public employment, can be reorganized by a radical government under rather favourable conditions, although it has become clear that the reform process has not fully reached the initial goals (Pierson 1994).

Besides contrasting the Neo-Weberian trajectories to the path taken in the United Kingdom, we attempt to maximize variation on the hypothesized moderating variables in order to deviate the thrust of the driving forces into alternative trajectories within this set of countries. In Chapter 2, we have discussed variations in the institutional structure of the state and its administrative culture across European countries. We have also highlighted the exemplary roles assigned in the literature to Germany, France, and Sweden for different, internally consistent conceptions of the state structure and the administrative culture, which have turned out to be close to the ideal-typical representation of four administrative traditions and public employment regimes (Tepe et al. 2010). These differences are perfectly predestined to serve as the starting point of a simple and uncontroversial method of case selection labelled the 'diverse case' strategy (Gerring 2007, pp. 97–101;

Rohlfing 2012). The aim of this strategy is to maximize variation on crucial explanatory variables in order to maximize the differentiating potential of the analysis.

This strategy can be traced back as far as the 'method of difference' (Mill 1882, p. 452). This method stipulates that if two cases differ on the dependent variable and 'have every circumstance in common save one', that one circumstance must be considered the cause of the differences between the two cases with respect to the dependent variable (Blatter and Haverland 2012; George and Bennett 2005). This matching technique translates the design of experimental studies to that of case studies, which cannot approximate experimental conditions by means of statistical control (Lijphart 1971, 1975). For practical research, however, this approach is far from exact for two reasons. First, given the open nature of societal systems and the impossibility of a fully specified model, the number of potentially influential variables is indefinite. Hence, we cannot decide which factors must be held constant. Second, even if we can make a reasonable guess about the relevant variables, due to the small number of observational units in cross-country comparative research, the probability of finding two countries that satisfy Mill's requirement is miniscule, because countries simply differ on too many factors. We can thus merely factor in the most prominent variables at a fairly abstract level of conceptualization. Nevertheless, we attempt to maximize inferential leverage by carefully pitching countries according to the core explanatory variables. In addition, we are not exploring uncharted territory and, consequently, we cannot seriously observe the methodological requirement of complete ignorance about the likely conditions of the dependent variable in the different countries. We can, however, reasonably elaborate upon our motivation of case selection by referring only to the countries' profiles on the main purported causal factors. With respect to the state structure, the horizontal and vertical *organization of government* as defined by the constitution separates the Anglo-American and Napoleonic from the Germanic and Scandinavian traditions. In the former two traditions, the state is unitary and centralized, with the British version of unitary government including some aspects of local self-government (Kingdom 2014), whereas the Napoleonic tradition is strictly hierarchically organized (Charlot 1994). In stark contrast to these traditions, the Germanic and Scandinavian traditions are much more decentralized, and local authorities have considerable leeway for their own policies. The German tradition involves an integrated, 'organic' system which, on the one hand, enforces co-operation among the *Länder*[1] and between the central government and the *Länder*, with a strong veto position of the latter in the second chamber of parliament, the *Bundesrat*. On the other hand, important public functions are delegated to non-state corporations with public legal status, which organize policy areas, such as sickness insurance, by self-government (Rudzio 2011). The Swedish tradition is built on a decentralized administration with ample freedom at the local level (Häggroth et al. 1996). The differences with respect to the organization of government have been summarized as follows:

> During the 19th century and well into the 20th century, England was the European 'mother country' of classical, multi-functional local government, and, since the late 1970s, has seen the political and functional status of its local government structures severely reduced. Historically until well into the 1970s, France was an example of a unitary, centralist country in which local government played only a marginal role. Since the 1980s, however, the country has embarked on decentralization, devolving major functions to local government. Sweden is a unitary country with traditionally decentralized and strong local government structures, which, since the 1990s, has further decentralised political and administrative structures. Germany finally is a federal country with traditionally decentralised and strong local government. While political and administrative functions have been further strengthened, elements of local administration have continued to be 'integrated' into federal and state government administration. (Kersting et al. 2009, p. 36)

Turning to the public administration regimes, three aspects have been highlighted (Lodge 2009; Page 1995). First, as emphasized in Chapter 2, important differences can be traced back to the historical development of the *legal system*. English common law developed as aristocratic landowners and merchants desired a legal system that protected their property against the Crown, whereas French law developed in the wake of the French revolution (Mahoney 2001, pp. 504–505). Napoleon wished a legal system that enabled

Table 3.1 Comparative framework for country case studies

	Germany (DE)	France (FR)	Sweden (SE)	United Kingdom (UK)
State structure	Federalist, coordinated	Unitarian, centralized	Unitarian, decentralized	Unitarian, centralized-coordinated
Comparisons	DE vs. FR + SE + UK; FR vs. SE			
Legal system and administrative culture	'Prussian' rule of law	'Napoleonic' rule of law	Constitutional state, less formalization, 'Active state'	Common law, 'Public interest' culture
Comparisons	DE + FR vs. SE + UK; DE vs. FR; SE vs. UK			
Reform path	Neo-Weberian	Neo-Weberian	Neo-Weberian	New Public Management
Comparisons	DE + FR + SE vs. UK; DE vs. FR vs. SE			

the state to alter property rights and limit the influence of judges. Similar to French civil law, German civil law also has its roots in ancient Roman legislation and shares many procedural characteristics with French civil law. However, the fundament of modern German private law – the *Bürgerliches Gesetzbuch* – did not come into effect until 1900. Compared to the French legal system, it assigns a larger role to judicial lawmaking (La Porta et al. 2008, p. 290). Scandinavian law is considered to be less a derivative of Roman law than the French and the German legal traditions are. Gomard (1961) sees a distinctive feature of the Scandinavian legal tradition in its rather limited formal and procedural requirements, which he attributes to the homogeneity of Scandinavian societies.

Secondly, the conception of the *relationship between the state and society* determines the general perspective on public administration (Raadschelders and Rutgers 1999). In the absolutist era, the Continental European states were legitimized by reference to a divine mandate of the emperor. The state was considered an entity rooted in, but distinct from, society. Inhabitants were not regarded as citizens, but were subjects without political rights. In the German version, the nation-state evolving in the 19th century was conceptualized as the organic synthesis of the social and system dimensions of society, in the Hegelian parlance of the family and civil society. In the French version, the state claimed to represent the *volonté generale* and thus to know what was best for society. Both versions imply the view that the state possesses a higher level of rationality than citizens do, who are subjected to the will of the state, from which the entitlement to authoritatively implement acts of sovereignty has been derived. A further distinction has to be made between the Continental and the Scandinavian traditions. Although the Scandinavian countries have adopted the organic conception of the German state tradition, this conception is not translated into a hierarchical relationship between the sovereign and the subject, but is couched in an older, strongly communitarian tradition based on local self-government. In contrast, the power of the British Crown was limited by fundamental political freedom rights of the nobility codified in the Magna Charta of 1215, which was gradually extended to wider population groups. By implication, sovereign acts of government agencies were considered a consequence of a free agreement by the citizens of the United Kingdom, as exemplified in Hobbes' contract theory of the state. The state was thus considered the locus of public affairs in which a plurality of interests among the citizens is articulated and channelled into a political decision, which is then implemented in the name of the citizens. Public administration is thus embedded in very different conceptions of the relationship between the state and society.

Finally, a third dimension of variation relates to the *civil service*. The importance of legality in the Continental tradition implies a Weberian conception of the civil service as the 'limbs' of the state that impartially execute the legal order. The German *Beamte* and the French *fonctionnaires* have a high status and privileged employment conditions in return for a full commitment to the state based upon an oath of office. A contrary conception dominates the Anglo-American and Scandinavian traditions, as terms and conditions of public employment are rather similar to those in the private sector. We will discuss this dimension in more detail in later chapters. Here, it has a special status since it actually refers to an important element of the public employment regime and is thus susceptible to the allegation of selecting on the dependent variable. However, given our focus on changes in public employment regimes, the state of the civil service refers to the historically established system and thus to the starting point of change. Although we may expect a large amount of resilience to change, which is in line with the path-dependency argument, such a critique misses the point because it does not predetermine change.

In sum, in contrast to the Anglo-American administrative tradition, the Napoleonic, Germanic, and Scandinavian administrative traditions have many commonalities, such as the legal tradition of the state, the legal accountability mechanisms, the civil law tradition, and the special role of the civil service. Another distinctive characteristic is the dichotomy between the rule of law (*Rechtsstaat*) and the public interest administrative culture of public administration. While the Napoleonic, Germanic, and Scandinavian traditions are subcategories of the legalistically oriented rule of law culture, the Anglo-American tradition is characterized by a public interest culture.

The variation with respect to the three dimensions generates specific profiles of public administration regimes with high internal coherence. The emphasis on the rule of law is congruent with the conception of a strong state as an agent in its own right, both distinct from and superior to society. Moreover, the conception of the civil service is in line with these traits. Given the transcendental derivation of the state as the sovereign, to which the population is subjected, bureaucratic action is justified by reference to the rule of law. The Anglo-American conception, rooted in the contract theory of the state, considers citizens as the sovereign and public administration as a service to citizens, which implies that civil servants are simple employees entrusted with a case-oriented delivery of the service. The conceptions underlying both the Anglo-American public administration regime and the liberal market economy stem from the same understanding of the role of the state in society as a guardian of peace and safety in the name of citizens. Beyond these minimal guarantees, the state should not interfere in the autonomous organization of society. In turn, the more interventionist role of the state in coordinated market economies has an elective affinity to a more patronizing role of the state and the ensuing legalistic and hierarchical conception of public administration regimes.

The comparison of public employment regimes, as well as the reforms initiated and implemented in these four countries, represents the scope of variation in modes of public employment regulation and the general direction of change across countries.

Comparing public administration sectors

In Chapter 2 we discussed the reform potential of three modes of organizing public responsibility for normative goods. We proposed the hypothesis that the scope of reform in a public employment regime depends on the devolution of public responsibility: the more extensively that responsibilities are transferred to the private sector, the more the public employment regime is exposed to competition from the private market, albeit in different ways depending on the market domain to which it applies. In particular, two markets are relevant here, although with different implications. With respect to the product market, the establishment of a market for public services through the state's withdrawal from organizational responsibility exposed state organizations and public agencies, which had previously offered such services as a monopoly, to direct private competition, which is typically characterized by more flexible employment contracts and less employee-friendly employment conditions. The full privatization of service provision as a consequence of the state's withdrawal from both organizational and decision-making responsibility often created a highly unbalanced market, either dominated by the former public enterprise or with a strong oligopolistic tendency because of high market entrance barriers. In order to generate and maintain competition, such markets need strong regulation by a public agency.

With respect to the labour market, the two modes in which product market exposure becomes relevant for public employment regimes have different implications. The direct competition for the provision of services predominantly affects the lower-paid echelons of employees actually providing the service. According to previous findings (Tepe et al. 2015), employment conditions, in particular wages and salaries and employment security, are more advantageous for public employees at income levels associated with these lower echelons. In contrast, market regulation is a highly specialized task requiring high education levels. These tasks are typically located in higher wage brackets. At this level, the premium on public employment disappears or is even reversed into a public sector penalty. Under this condition, the public sector does not compete on the product market with private firms for the provision of services, but rather competes for qualified employees on the labour market.

Different sectors are thus exposed to different pressures. These differences should be reflected in the potential and scope of reform of public employment regimes. We select one sector for each of the three modes of responsibility devolution (see Figure 3.1).

We will study the effects of the devolution of both organizational and decision-making responsibility to the private sector on public employment regimes in *energy regulation agencies*. Mandated by European Union directives, all European member states have established independent regulatory agencies (IRAs) for the supervision of markets for services in former public utilities. In the United Kingdom, the Office of Gas and Electricity Markets (Ofgem) was established in 2000 as a result of a merger between the agencies for gas and electricity regulation that had been created in the late 1980s. France and Sweden have special agencies for energy market regulation, the *Commission de regulation de l'energie* (CRE), established in 2000, and the *Energimarknadsinspektionen* (EI), set up in 2005. Also in 2005, Germany mandated the agency for the regulation of telecommunications and postal services, dating back to 1998, to regulate the energy markets (electricity and gas) as well. In 2006, after integration of the railway system, this agency was named *Bundesnetzagentur für Elektrizität, Gas, Telekommunikation, Post und Eisenbahnen* (BNetzA). These agencies employ from a few hundred to more than 2,400 mostly highly qualified specialists.

The devolution of only organizational responsibility will be examined in the *waste collection sector*. While waste collection was considered a public task, predominantly in the hands of municipalities until the end of the 'Golden Age', this sector was one of the major targets of market building under the influence of New Public Management. As a result, a variety of constellations of private firms, publicly owned enterprises, and public

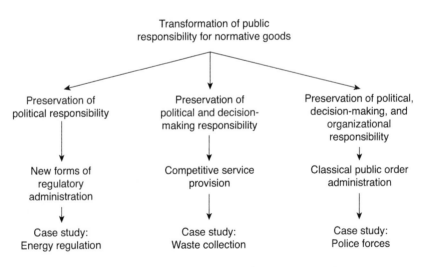

Figure 3.1 Types of state responsibility and cases for sector comparison

organizations have emerged. In many countries, recycling processes have largely been transferred to private firms, while household waste remained a responsibility of the municipalities, which could, however, transfer the task to private firms. As a result, the sector is now characterized by complex market structures in which municipal and private firms compete in different ways.

Finally, the *police forces* represent a sector in which the state maintains political, decision-making, and organizational responsibility. Public safety has remained a core task of the state in all European countries, but the location of responsibility varies across countries. In the United Kingdom, Sweden, and Germany, large segments of the police forces are organized at sub-national levels, while France maintains three functionally separate authorities, two of which are attached to the central state. All four countries, however, witnessed reorganizations of the police forces resulting in changing working conditions and a differentiation of the workforce, for example, due to the establishment of new job categories of less-protected civilian employees.

By exploring the transformations in public employment regimes in these sectors over time, we attempt to carve out in detail the sector-related differences within national trajectories, and to identify the scope of variation within countries. In methodological terms, this part of the study is informed by the emerging literature on process tracing (Beach and Pedersen 2013; Hall 2008; Mahoney and Rueschemeyer 2003). We reconstruct the historical sequences of events marking important changes in the layout of public employment regimes.

The selection of the three sectors is motivated by their characteristics with respect to the extent of responsibility devolution. In contrast to the country comparisons outlined above, much less information is available about the outcome, because practically all existing studies dealing in some way with public employment regimes focus on the general traits at the level of central government, not on the details of specific sectors. Hence, a large part of the sector chapters in this study is devoted to a narrative description of historical events based on a reading of the specialized literature, the analysis of policy documents, and interviews conducted at various stages of the research process with both academic and administrative experts of the three sectors. Reviews of secondary literature on existing empirical research on the terms and conditions of sector-specific employment were supplemented by a comprehensive document analysis covering the evaluation of laws, administrative regulations, and sector-specific national stakeholder documents (see Appendix A.1 for a list of statutory regulations). While these analyses served to assess the institutional frameworks and content of employment regulation relevant for the sector, information on actual practice were gained from expert interviews with practitioners involved in Human Resource Management. All in all, 40 interviews were conducted.

Experts addressed were Human Resource managers, equal opportunity officers, and union representatives (see overview in Appendix A.2). Based on a common interview guideline, these interviews aimed at addressing the status quo of employment conditions, personnel systems and management, as well as the perceptions of employment reforms and the course of their implementation. The recorded interviews lasted between one and two hours and were studied by means of a content analysis after transcription.[2] Further insights were gained from bilateral and workshop-based exchanges with academic experts in the field from the countries involved in order to contextualize the results.

After reconstructing the 'facts' using the evidence excavated from these sources, we take inspiration from the process-tracing approach for interpreting the findings in view of the theoretical expectations. Beach and Pedersen (2013) distinguish three purposes of the process-tracing approach: theory testing, theory building, and explaining outcomes. While all three variants presuppose that both the potential causal factors and the outcomes have been identified, they vary in their status relative to theoretical arguments. Theory testing needs a set of specified hypotheses that suggest the working of certain mechanisms in general. Theory building aims at generalizing inferences beyond a single case, but no hypotheses have been spelled out at the time of data collection and analysis. Explaining outcomes focuses on the case investigated and attempts to identify the causal mechanisms leading to the particular outcome in that instance. Among these three purposes, our study's design comes closest to the theory testing approach, given that we are working from the set of guiding hypotheses outlined in Chapter 2.

Dimensions of public employment regimes

Having clarified the three perspectives integrated into our approach to studying public employment regimes, we now need to shed some more light on what exactly we mean by employment regimes and their changes. We have stated in Chapter 2 that this study conceptualizes public employment along three dimensions. First and foremost, we focus on employment regulations. Second, we address the integration of disadvantaged groups into the workforce. Third, we take into account the objective of the state being an exemplary employer setting standards for the private sector.

Table 3.2 summarizes our conceptualization. We distinguish two ideal-typical public employees, the civil servant – the epitomization of the Weberian idea of a 'modern bureaucracy' – and the service provider – its contemporary successor according to the vision of New Public Management. We group the dimensions to be studied in detail into four analytical categories and one summary assessment relating public employment to private sector employment.

Table 3.2 Dimensions and characteristics of public employment regulation

Dimensions and characteristics	Ideal type of employment	
	Civil servant	Service provider
1. Regulation of employment conditions		
Legal status	Civil servant or equivalent privileges and duties	Employee
Collective regulations	Authoritative/unilateral	Collective agreement
Regulation of labour conflicts	Disciplinary law, no right to strike	Right to strike
2. Personnel system		
Mode of Advancement	Career-based	Position-based
Openness	Low	High
3. Personnel management		
Entry requirements	Formalized, high	Non-formalized, high
Recruitment	Special public service training pathways	General qualification
Pay structure	Determined by law	Negotiation-based
Evaluation and assessment	Seniority rules	Performance-based
Performance incentives	No	Yes
Opportunities for promotion	Seniority-based	Performance-based
Further education	Legally determined	Flexible
4. Integration function of public employment regime		
Payment, social security	High	Low
Employment security	High	Low
Equal opportunity and treatment at the workplace	High	Low
5. Specificity of public employment regime		
Difference as compared to private sector employment regime	Large	Small

The first category summarizes different aspects of the regulation of employment conditions. The *legal status* of public employees may be constituted either by public law or by private contract. This distinction, however, should not be taken literally because contracts may define privileged employment conditions for contractual employees which are similar to those of civil servants. We thus have to assess the contractual employment practices in more detail. *Collective* employment *regulations* such as pay or working time may be set unilaterally, by authoritative rule, or by collective agreement. Moreover, the arsenal of public employees in conflicts with respect to such regulations may either exclude or include the *right to strike*. The former conditions in these three aspects refer to the ideal-type characterization of the civil servant; the latter are associated with the service provider.

The second category zeroes in on aspects of the personnel system. The *mode of advancement* may be based on career trajectories within specific service classes or it may entail the definition of positions to which employees can apply. In that sense, the *openness* of the personnel system is either low, which is indicative of a closed personnel system with in-house recruitment characterized by little exchange with the private sector, or high in the sense of permeable to outsiders. Again, the former conditions are characteristic of the idea of a civil servant system, while the latter are typical for the notion of a service provider.

Even more specific aspects of the public employment regime are collected in the third category, which addresses several details of the personnel management system. *Entry requirements* may include formal qualifications, and placements may need to follow a strictly regulated procedure, or requirements and procedures may be less formalized. *Recruitment* thereby requires either diplomas obtained by following specialized public service training pathways or general qualifications. In line with the general regulation of employment conditions, the *pay structure* is either rigidly determined by law or negotiable. Tools such as *evaluation, assessment,* and *performance incentives* are either non-existent because of a system of strictly seniority-based career trajectories or form a parameter of Human Resource Management. Consequently, *opportunities for promotion* are either rigidly defined in seniority-based career trajectories or based on a positive record with respect to the above-mentioned Human Resource Management practices. Likewise, and in line with the recruitment systems, *further education* may be either legally determined – for example, by requiring certain additional specific diplomas for the advancement to a higher service class – or flexibly adjustable to the specific requirements of positions. As before, the former conditions represent the ideal type of the civil servant, while the latter characterize the service provider.

Turning to the integration function of public employment regimes as a fourth category, we will explore three aspects: *payment* and *social security, employment security,* and *equal opportunity and equal treatment at the workplace* for disadvantaged groups on the labour market, such as women, handicapped people, or minorities. With respect to these aspects, the state may choose either a high road by setting higher standards than the private economy in order to present a showcase for integration, or a low road, which follows or even undercuts practices in the private sector. The former is associated with the civil servant, the latter with the service provider.

Finally, the *difference from the private sector employment regime* may be either large or small. The public employment regime may constitute a separate world of employment, entailing large differences as compared to the private employment regime, or such differences may be minor or even absent. Jointly, the profiles exhibited by the country- and sector-specific case studies with respect to the four categories and their constitutive aspects, and the shifts from one ideal type to the other, characterize shifts in the nature of public employment regimes. In Chapters 5 to 8, we will extensively elaborate on the extent to which actual employment regimes come close to one or the other of the two ideal types, and come back to the overall assessment of actual changes in Chapter 9.

Part II
Cross-Country Analysis

4
Public Employment Regimes in OECD Countries

Introduction

The term *public employment* refers to a large and heterogeneous group of employees who are directly or indirectly involved in the production and provision of publicly financed goods and services. This conceptual imprecision has made the term popular in political debates, but it limits its usefulness in analytical and scientific discourses. Thus, before we embark on a study of the functional and institutional differentiation of public employment in particular sectors, this chapter gives a broad, comparative overview of government employment in general. Following an OECD definition, *general government employment* denotes public employees in all levels of government (central, state, regional, and local), who are working in ministries, agencies, departments, and non-profit organizations that are controlled and mainly financed by public authorities (OECD 2011, p. 102). This definition excludes employees in *public corporations*, which are legal units mainly owned or controlled by the government, producing goods and services for sale on the market (OECD 2011, p. 102). In conceptual terms, the notion of 'general government employment' refers to the 'core' of the public workforce. These employees implement the sovereign functions of the state, such as public administration, law enforcement, or education, and enjoy the greatest independence from private sector pressures. For these reasons, it can be assumed that deviations from working conditions in the private sector are particularly pronounced, and structural resistances towards the transferability of New Public Management instruments are the strongest in this particular segment of the public workforce. Hence, if there are persistent differences in country-specific regulations and reform trajectories of public employment regimes, general government employment is the first segment of public employment to examine.

The primary endeavour of this chapter is not just to describe the institutional differences in national systems of public employment in terms of regimes but also to relate regimes to the implementation of reforms inspired by NPM. Based on the presumption that public employment regimes correspond with distinct reform trajectories, we will explore long-term trends in public employment and the timing of performance-related pay (PRP) reforms as a showcase instrument from the NPM agenda.

The chapter consists of three empirical sections. First, we focus on the politico-administrative context that is expected to shape a country's capacity to conduct administrative reforms. By taking advantage of recent progress in the collection of comparative data on public administration policies in the OECD, the first section provides a map of politico-administrative regimes in the OECD. Next, the exploration moves forward towards the conceptualization and identification of distinct public employment regimes within the OECD by using multiple correspondence analysis (MCA). For the exploration of public employment regimes, national differences in the implementation of NPM instruments are particularly interesting.

The second section examines the long- and short-term trends in the size and costs of general government employment. In particular, we analyse how these trends relate to the resources of national systems of administration, the output of these systems in terms of government effectiveness, and the reform intensity measured by the adoption of NPM tools. In each instance, we discuss the extent to which these relationships differ systematically across and within public employment regimes.

The third section of this chapter explores the responsiveness of public employment regimes towards the incorporation of NPM ideas. Quantitative changes in the size and cost of government employment neglect the possibility that countries may adopt similar reform measures at different points in time. In order to identify the 'early birds' and 'latecomers' in NPM with respect to Human Resource Management, the third section explores the timing of the introduction of PRP. PRP is certainly just a single element in the NPM agenda, but it represents a particular paradigmatic change or a 'structural break', so to speak, with the traditional seniority-based remuneration scheme in public administration. The chapter concludes with a summary of empirical findings and discusses their implications for the in-depth country- and sector-specific analyses.

Public administration and public employment regimes

As mentioned in Chapter 2, we utilize the five politico-administrative dimensions suggested by Pollitt and Bouckaert (2011) to empirically identify structural differences and similarities between national systems of public administration. The five dimensions have been operationalized as follows (see also Table 2.2 in Chapter 2):

1. *State structure*: Pollitt and Bouckaert (2011, pp. 50, 55) use a loosely adapted version of Lijphart's (1999) federal/unitary index to measure differences

in state structures. Following this approach, we also use Lijphart's (1999) federal/unitary index, but we prefer using the original version contained in the *Comparative Political Data Set I* (Armingeon et al. 2012).

2. *Executive government*: Following Pollitt and Bouckaert's (2011, p. 50) suggestion, executive government structure is captured by means of Lijphart's (1999) executive government index, which distinguishes between consensual and majoritarian democracies.

3. *Minister/mandarin relations*: The measure for the integration or separation of the minister/mandarin relations is taken from Dahlström and Lapuente (2010, p. 588).

4. *Administrative tradition*: Painter and Peters (2010) use the term 'administrative tradition' to describe the relationship between the state and civil society. According to their conceptualization, the administrative tradition 'reflects the logic of the emergence of the state historically and patterns of political thought' that were central for the formation of the state (Painter and Peters 2010, p. 6). Since the essential rules of the relationship between the state and civil society are codified by law, Painter and Peters's (2010, p. 19) empirical classification of administrative tradition is largely identical with La Porta et al.'s (1998, 2008) classification of legal traditions, which we will use in this analysis because of the wider set of countries included in their data.[1]

5. *Diversity of policy advice:* Due to the limited availability of comparative data on this dimension, we have to rely on a single indicator taken from the Sustainable Governance Indicators (SGI 2009). In this study, country experts have been asked: 'How influential are non-governmental academic experts for government decision-making?' Given that academic experts are more likely to develop independent, unbiased ideas than experts employed by interest groups, their integration into policy-making is a useful proxy for the diversity of policy advice.

In order to reduce the dimensionality, we implement a multiple correspondence analysis (Clausen 1998; Blasius and Greenacre 2006). The basic idea of this method is to reduce a complex data matrix into a limited number of dimensions without losing essential information. To this end, MCA represents the association between two or more categorical variables by locating the categories of the variables as points in a two- or multidimensional space (Clausen 1998, p. 2). Categories with similar distributions are represented as points that are close to each other, while categories that are very dissimilar in their distribution will be positioned far apart (Clausen 1998, p. 10). The resulting dimensions are evaluated on the basis of their contribution to capturing total variance. If there are distinct public administration regimes among our 19 OECD nations, we expect to find certain clusters of points.[2]

Figure 4.1 shows the results of the MCA based on the variables from Table 2.2 in Chapter 2. The two axes of the two-dimensional diagram

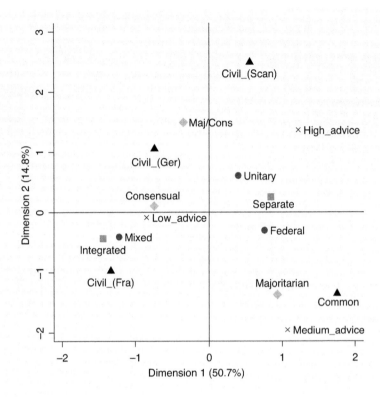

Figure 4.1 Mapping politico-administrative regimes in OECD countries

Note: Variables in the MCA: State structure (Federal, Mixed, Unitary), Executive government (Consensual, Majoritarian/Consensual, Majoritarian), Minister/Mandarin relationship (Separate, Integrated), Administrative tradition (Common law, Civil law (Germany), Civil law (France), Civil law (Scandinavian), Diversity of policy advice (Low advice, Medium advice, High advice).

Countries: United Kingdom, Ireland, Australia, United States, Canada, Germany, Austria, Switzerland, Japan, Italy, Spain, Netherlands, Belgium, Portugal, France, Denmark, Norway, Finland, Sweden.

account for 50.71 and 14.78 per cent of total variance, hence about two-thirds of the variation jointly. These two dimensions are used to plot the conceptual landscape of politico-administrative regimes.[3] We can identify several clusters of points. The points representing a common law legal tradition are associated with a majoritarian executive government, a medium level of diversity of policy advice, and a federal state structure. The points representing a French civil law tradition are associated with a mixed state structure and an integrated minister/mandarin relationship.[4] The points representing a Scandinavian civil law legal tradition are associated with a majoritarian/consensual executive government and a high level of diversity of policy advice. The points representing a German civil law tradition are associated with a consensual executive government, a low level of diversity of policy advice, and a mixed state structure. These clusters resonate well with the descriptions of the four prototypical countries (see Chapter 3) and suggest that the selected countries can indeed be regarded as representative of certain clusters of countries with distinct legal traditions.

The three civil law traditions and the common law tradition each lie in a different quadrant of the two-dimensional space, suggesting that they are described by different combinations of high and low values on the two dimensions. Figure 4.1 thus suggests that, contrary to a simple civil/common law dichotomy, there are relevant differences within the group of countries in the civil law tradition. Since the legal tradition goes hand in hand with other aspects of the politico-administrative regime, such as the type of government and policy advice, it may serve as a particularly important proxy for politico-administrative regimes. This pattern has also been observed by Tepe et al. (2010), examining the relationship between politico-administrative regimes and market economy models (Hall and Soskice 2001).[5]

The second step of the empirical exploration of structural similarities and differences between national systems of public administration is to move beyond the five dimensions of politico-administrative regimes suggested by Pollitt and Bouckaert (2011) and to more specifically address the legal rules and structural features applying to national systems of public employment. In particular, we explore public employment regimes using three indicators, namely *work security, performance assessment,* and *PRP.* This selection of indicators aims to capture two potentially independent dimensions of a public employment regime. The alleged privileges of public sector employment (higher levels of work security), on the one hand, and the exposure to Human Resource Management tools inspired by the NPM agenda (performance assessment and PRP), on the other. Specifically, these two dimensions are operationalized as follows:

1. *Administrative tradition*: Similar to the conceptualization of politico-administrative regimes, La Porta et al.'s (1998, 2008) classification of legal traditions is used to account for different administrative traditions.
2. *Work security*: We measure the possibility of dismissing employees with open-term contracts when a ministry or agency seeks to restructure or decrease the number of its employees (OECD 2012, pp. 62–63). In some countries, public employees can be dismissed under these circumstances and the employees receive an allowance, while in several other OECD countries, this option does not exist.
3. *Performance assessment*: The proxy indicator for the extent of the implementation of performance assessment practices in national public

administrations is taken from the OECD's Government at a Glance (2011, p. 129).

4. *Performance-related pay*: In order to measure the extent to which PRP systems are implemented in the public sector, we rely on a composite index generated by the OECD (2011). This index has been transformed into three equally large percentiles in order to integrate it into the MCA as an ordinal measure.

Table 4.1 summarizes the four dimensions capturing the different aspects of public employment regimes and the operationalization of these dimensions with comparative indicators. Whereas the indicator on dismissal

Table 4.1   Public employment regimes

Country	Legal tradition[a]	Possibility of dismissing employees with open-term contracts[b]	Extent of the use of performance assessments in HR decisions in central government[c]	Extent of the use of PRP in central government[d]
United Kingdom	Common	Yes	High	High
Ireland	Common	No	Medium	Low
Australia	Common	Yes	High	Medium
United States	Common	Yes	Medium	Medium
Canada	Common	Yes	Medium	Medium
Germany	Civil (German)	No	Medium	Low
Austria	Civil (German)	Yes	Low	Low
Switzerland	Civil (German)	Yes	Low	High
Japan	Civil (German)	No	High	High
Italy	Civil (French)	No	Medium	Medium
Spain	Civil (French)	No	Low	Low
Netherlands	Civil (French)	No	Low	Low
Belgium	Civil (French)	No	Low	
Portugal	Civil (French)	Yes	High	Low
France	Civil (French)	No	High	Medium
Denmark	Civil (Scandinavian)	Yes	High	High
Norway	Civil (Scandinavian)	Yes	Low	Medium
Finland	Civil (Scandinavian)	Yes	Low	High
Sweden	Civil (Scandinavian)	Yes	Medium	Medium

Note: a = La Porta et al. (1998); b = OECD (2012, pp. 62–63): Yes, and the employee receives an allowance; c = OECD (2011, p. 129, Fig. 31.1); d = OECD (2011, p. 129, Fig. 31.2), metric variables have been transformed into terciles (low, medium, high).

policies refers to core public employment regulations, the third and fourth dimensions – performance assessment and PRP – can be directly related to the reform agenda of NPM. If common law countries are perceived as the forerunners of NPM, one can expect that these countries score particularly high on these indicators. In this respect, Table 4.1 indicates that German and French civil law countries might share low levels of performance assessment and PRP, while Scandinavian civil law and common law countries show some remarkable commonalities in these areas of public sector Human Resource Management. In order to identify systematic associations between these variables, we conduct a second MCA.

Table 4.1 already suggests that we can expect certain overlaps in the configuration of politico-administrative rules and the corresponding public employment regime. The question is, whether a comparative analysis focusing on public employment regulation rather than politico-administrative rules and institutions can identify 'distinct' public employment regimes. The next step of the analysis, therefore, is to move beyond the description of politico-administrative regimes towards a more focused conceptualization of public employment regimes.

In doing so, the variable capturing the legal tradition will now enter the MCA as a passive (sometimes also called supplementary) variable. The categories of the passive variable are also mapped into the MCA solution space, but they do not affect the location of the active variables' points (Greenacre 2006) because they are included as points without mass, implying that they do not contribute to the explained variance. However, since we are able to calculate the Chi-square distances for these passive points, they can be located in MCA solution space (Clausen 1998, p. 21).

Figure 4.2 shows the results of the MCA based on the variables from Table 4.2. Jointly, both axes of the two-dimensional diagram account for 76.9 per cent of total variance. Again, the two dimensions can be used to define the landscape of public employment regimes. As before, the four regimes can be clearly distinguished and they are located in different quadrants of the grid. The horizontal dimension appears to separate high performance assessment and PRP, combined with the absence of tenure, from lower values on these scales. The vertical dimension seems to differentiate medium levels of performance assessment and PRP from low values on these variables, with the widespread existence of tenure being placed near the latter. As a result, the four legal traditions, though entered without mass, are placed in a compelling pattern. The two Continental civil law traditions are placed at the top, clearly contrasted with the common law tradition at the bottom. The Scandinavian tradition is placed in an intermediate location somewhat off to the left of the imaginative line connecting the three other traditions, but closer to the common law tradition. These patterns suggest a differentiation of the countries into three major clusters, separating the Scandinavian civil law and the common law countries

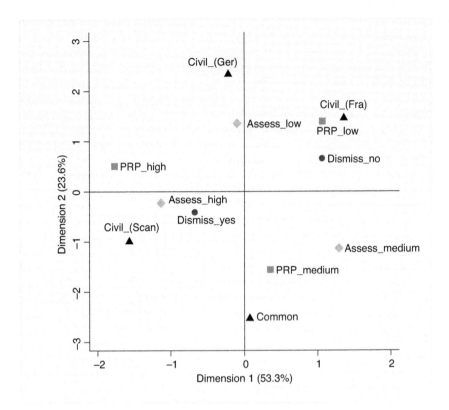

Figure 4.2   Mapping public employment regimes in OECD countries

Note: Active variables in the MCA: Possibility of dismissing employees with open-term contracts, Extent of the use of performance assessments in HR decisions in central government, Extent of the use of PRP in central government; Passive variable in the MCA: Legal tradition.

Countries: United Kingdom, Ireland, Australia, United States, Canada, Germany, Austria, Switzerland, Japan, Italy, Spain, Netherlands, Portugal, Belgium, France, Denmark, Norway, Finland, Sweden.

from the Continental civil law countries, which, however, are grouped into two neighbouring but still distinct clusters by the scope of tenure and the severity of resistance to performance assessment and PRP. Countries in the German civil law tradition appear to be somewhat less reluctant to integrate elements of NPM into their public employment regimes than those in the French tradition.

In sum, using Pollitt and Bouckaert's (2011) framework to analyse differences in national politico-administrative systems reveals four clusters of politico-administrative regimes. If we refine this approach in order to identify public employment regimes, the empirical analysis also reveals the existence of four distinct public employment regimes, namely French and

German civil law clusters, a Scandinavian civil law cluster, and a common law cluster. These public employment regimes are largely congruent with their politico-administrative counterparts. From this congruence one might conclude that distinct public employment regimes are born out of distinct politico-administrative configurations – a conclusion that will be subject to further empirical investigation.

Most notably, there are substantive differences within the group of civil law countries with respect to the adoption of NPM ideas in Human Resource Management. These differences are particularly strong if countries with a Scandinavian legal tradition are compared to countries with a French or German civil law tradition. In addition, there are also systematic differences between countries with a French or German civil law tradition. These findings support Pollitt and Bouckaert's (2011, p. 3) observation that many continental European countries that have previously resisted a wide-scale implementation of NPM cannot generally be characterized by high rigidity and encompassing resistance to reform. Instead, they seem to pursue their own models of modernizing public employment. Pollitt and Bouckaert (2011) distinguish between countries proactively following the agenda of NPM, which mainly applies to Anglo-American countries or countries with a common law tradition, and continental European countries or countries with a civil law tradition, labelled as Neo-Weberian States (NWS). Whereas in the NPM path, bureaucratic mechanisms are replaced by market mechanisms, in the Neo-Weberian path, the classic role of the state, representative democracy, and bureaucratic administration is in a dialectical sense abolished and politico-administrative action is supplemented rather than replaced by new managerial elements (Schnapp 2004, p. 343). Findings from the identification of public employment regimes indicate that the dichotomy of NPM versus NWS needs to be refined by separating the Scandinavian pathway from the French and German reform paths.

The notion of public employment 'regimes' emphasizes that nations differ in their historical trajectories of the public employment system.[6] Historical developments enshrine early institutional differences of differentiating and sharing responsibilities between the state and the market. These differences might be enhanced through the logic of institutional path dependency (Pierson 2000, 2004; Thelen 2003). Drawing on these mechanisms, we assume that the affiliation of a country to a specific public employment regime might limit the scope of public employment reforms. This does not imply that certain regimes inhibit changes in public employment regimes. In contrast, these findings suggest that public employment reforms take place in all regimes, but the intensity, pace, and selection of reform instruments is constrained by the institutional design of public employment regimes. The identification of public employment regimes on the basis of indicators measuring the extent to which countries have adopted certain Human Resource Management tools from the NPM agenda, such as performance assessment and PRP, have revealed systematic variation across public employment regimes. This provides some preliminary evidence of regime-specific rigidities in public employment regimes when confronted with NPM. In the next section we, therefore, explore whether such regime-specific reform paths can also be observed in the development of the size and cost of government employment.

Long-term trends in public employment

Even though public employment is a key resource of modern statehood, there has been little effort to explain change in the size or costs of public employment across countries. Exceptions include the work of Rose (1985), who have most extensively studied public employment in Western countries; Cusack et al. (1989) in collecting comparative public employment data; and more recent attempts by Parry (2007) using disaggregated government expenditures.

Disputes over changes in public employment are often dominated by extreme views. One perspective, which may be labelled as the 'personnel cut' thesis, defends the thesis that drastic cuts in public personnel have undermined the capabilities of the public sector (Suleiman 2003). The other perspective, the 'cost explosion' thesis, issues increasingly urgent claims that the compensation costs of public personnel are growing beyond control (Baumol and Bowen 1966). Depending on whether the protagonists argue for either maintaining public employment or for the austerity of public budgets, they are likely to refer to the personnel cut or cost explosion thesis in one way or another. Assessing the empirical validity of these theses is at the centre of this section. Specifically, we contrast the personnel cut thesis and the cost explosion thesis against empirical evidence on the long-term trends in public employment. We explore the variation of these developments across public employment regimes and ask whether we can speak of regime-specific dynamics of change.

Prior studies exploring the development of overall public sector employment between the 1970s and mid-1990s indicate that the size of the public workforce has been reduced (Suleiman 2003, p. 115; Cusack et al. 1989; Rothenbacher 1998). From the investigation of long-term trends in public employment in Belgium, Germany, France, Sweden, and the United Kingdom, Rothenbacher (1997) concludes that the main development that characterizes public sector employment is a decline after a long growth period. The reduction of public employment has been perceived as a consequence of the privatization of public services and public infrastructure. Even though privatization may require setting up new regulatory agencies that demand new public servants, the gross effect of privatizing public services on public employment is supposed to be negative.

Another process hypothesized to have affected the size of public employment is the reform of the welfare state. With increasing budgetary pressure from demographic change and new labour market trends, many OECD countries attempted to improve the fiscal sustainability of their welfare system by demanding more private responsibility. Even though the extent to which public provision has been substituted by private provision of welfare, such as in public health, education, or old-age security, varies across countries, we cannot exclude the possibility that these changes have also affected the level of government employment (Rothenbacher 1998).

Public sector reforms motivated by NPM-related ideas have also been hypothesized to accelerate the retrenchment of public employment (OECD 2004, 2005, 2007). These ideas are compelling to policymakers with scarce fiscal resources, as NPM suggests improving the efficiency of public service provision without demanding more financial resources. The basic idea is to impose private sector steering mechanisms – including Human Resource Management policies – on hitherto bureaucratic administrations. In contrast to the privatization of public service or welfare services, these reforms are aimed directly at government employees.

While these developments seem to have resulted in a substantial decrease in government employment in some countries, it is still questionable whether the reduction of the public workforce is a general trend across all OECD countries. Since the ability to reduce government employment is likely to depend on various aspects, such as the current employment level or the reform capabilities of the politico-administrative system, one may also expect that the extent of public employment downsizing varies across countries. According to this argument, a uniform decline in public employment across countries appears rather unlikely.

The second expectation about change in public employment may be described rather gloomily by 'exploding' costs of public employment compensation. The political debate about the 'right' size of public employment is often deeply rooted in fiscal considerations. In this context, the seminal work of Baumol and Bowen (1966) has become a modern classic in the public administration literature, even though the concept as such does not exclusively apply to the public sector. If wages rise according to overall rather than sector-specific productivity growth, the wages of service sector employees grow faster than their productivity. The services that are affected by the so-called Baumol cost disease are those that require personal interaction, such as social care, education, and public administration. Baumol (1993) argues that productivity growth of these services lags behind the manufacturing sector because personal services are mostly inconsistent with any standardization, and because the quality of these services is inevitably linked to the amount of human labour. According to Baumol and Bowen (1966) and Baumol (1993), this cost disease mechanism is expected to be particularly strong in the public sector, as this sector is primarily concerned with the production of personal services. Advocates of a smaller state frequently refer to this argument in order to claim a reduction of public spending, whereas, on the other hand, there is no doubt that technological progress has led to dramatic improvements in public administration employees' productivity, for example via telecommunications and other internet-based technologies.

Empirical evidence on Baumol's cost disease in public administration is still scarce. Although we might know the costs of production inputs (such as personnel, facilities, or information technology), there is neither a coherent concept nor appropriate data to capture the output of a bureaucracy and thereby the productivity of its personnel. Due to these empirical limitations, we explore a simpler argument derived from the cost disease hypothesis: if personnel costs are inherently growing, we expect that the share of government expenditure for employees' compensation, measured by the share of overall government expenditure in GDP, must also grow in comparison to non-personnel expenditures.

In order to assess the cost explosion argument, we need appropriate indicators and time-series data on government employment. We use the OECD's general government employment figures (OECD 2009b, 2011) and the figures on the costs of government employment (OECD 2009a). Following Parry (2007), we measure the costs of employee compensation as a share of GDP. Additionally, we measure the costs of employee compensation as a share of total government expenditure. Whereas the first measure provides an overall indicator for the proportion of public resources devoted to government employment, the latter captures the relative importance of employees' compensation expenditure in the governments' budget (for details, see Appendix A.3).

As the mid-1990s have been characterized as the 'high times of public sector reform' (Pollitt and Bouckaert 2011) and growing fiscal pressure on government budgets (such as the Maastricht criteria), we expect that observing this decade is particularly relevant for an exploration of the statistical relationship between the size and costs of public employment. Table 4.2 tabulates the raw data for the size and costs of public employment across 19 OECD countries. The countries are arranged according to legal tradition in order to locate countries on the map of public employment regimes. The measure for the size of public employment indicates that Scandinavian civil law countries have the largest public workforce (about one-quarter of the total labour force), followed by French civil law and common law countries, which have almost equally large public employment sectors (about 15 per cent of the total labour force). Countries belonging to the German civil law tradition appear to have rather small public workforces. From the public employment regime perspective, German civil law countries tend to have the lowest level of general government employment (roughly 10 per cent of the total labour force).

Turning to the cost perspective, we find that these regime-specific differences become less prominent when measured by public employment compensation as a share of GDP. Apart from the Scandinavian countries,

Table 4.2 Quantitative changes in the size and costs of public employment

	Employment in general government as a percentage of the labour force[a]		Employment compensation expenditure (per GDP)[b]		Employment compensation expenditure as a percentage of total government expenditure[b]	
	1995	2008	1995	2008	1995	2008
Common law						
Australia	13.9	15.6	na	na	na	na
Canada	17.9	16.5	13.7	na	28.2	na
Ireland	15.9	14.8	10.1	11.3	24.6	26.5
United Kingdom	na	17.4	10.6	11.1	24.1	23.3
United States	na	14.6	10.5	10.4	28.2	26.8
Average	**15.9**	**15.8**	**11.2**	**10.9**	**26.3**	**25.5**
Civil law German						
Austria	11.8	11.4	12.6	9.2	22.4	18.8
Germany	12.2	9.6	8.7	6.9	16.0	15.7
Japan	na	6.7	6.3	6.1	17.1	16.4
Switzerland	7.2	9.7	na	7.7	na	24
Average	**10.4**	**9.4**	**9.2**	**7.5**	**18.5**	**18.7**
Civil law French						
Belgium	16.9	17.1	11.9	12.1	22.8	24.0
France	21.6	21.9	13.6	12.8	25.0	24.0
Italy	14.2	14.3	11.0	10.8	20.9	22.2
Netherlands	13.1	12	10.6	9.2	18.8	19.9
Portugal	13.0	12.1	12.5	11.8	30.1	27.0
Spain	11.5	12.3	11.2	10.9	25.2	26.4
Average	**15.1**	**15.0**	**11.8**	**11.3**	**23.8**	**23.9**
Civil law Scandinavian						
Denmark	na	28.7	17.2	17.2	28.9	33.1
Finland	21.0	22.9	15.2	13.4	24.7	27.1
Norway	na	29.3	14	12.2	27.5	29.9
Sweden	29.8	26.2	16.3	14.8	25.2	28.6
Average	**25.4**	**26.8**	**15.7**	**14.4**	**26.6**	**29.7**

Note: na = data not available; a = OECD Government at Glance 2009 and 2011; b = OECD (2009a), COFOG Database.

which stand out in terms of government employment compensation expenditures (15 per cent of GDP), the three other regimes spend about 10 per cent of their GDP on compensation of government employees. In this respect, it is remarkable that countries like France, with a large share of government employment (21.9 per cent of the total labour force in 2008), still manage to spend only 12.8 per cent of GDP on government employees' compensation.

This observation might point to country-specific patterns in the occupational composition of the public workforce. For example, a country with a small and effective administrative elite may attempt to provide more low-skill public service jobs than a country with a rather expensive and inefficient administrative elite. As a result, countries may end up spending the same amount of their fiscal resources on government employment, but in doing so they pay for very different public sector jobs and services.

A look at government employment compensation expenditure as a share of total government expenditure further refines the picture. This indicator aims to take into account that countries inherit very different spending levels, and rather than altering the total amount of government spending, political conflicts may focus on the reallocation of scarce government resources. In the Scandinavian and French civil law countries with high and medium levels of government employment, compensation expenditure accounts for 23 to 29 per cent of total government expenditure. This is not surprising given their large shares of public employment measured as a percentage of the total labour force. Similarly, we find that the German civil law countries spend only 18 per cent of total government expenditure on government employees' compensation. It is remarkable, however, that the common law countries, which tend to have only a small government workforce, spend one-quarter of total government expenditure on government employees' compensation. Even though this figure does not come as a surprise with respect to small-sized governments in this regime, it indicates the political pressure and attractiveness of this policy domain for fiscal consolidation plans.

In order to explore the macro-trends in the development of the size and costs of public employment, Figure 4.3 presents two scatterplots. The first scatterplot shows the relationship between general government employment and public employees' compensation costs measured as a share of GDP. The second scatterplot shows the relationship between general public employment and public employees' compensation costs measured as a share of total government expenditure.

The clustering of countries in the two scatterplots suggests that the Scandinavian and German civil law countries use different combinations of the size and costs of public employment. The cloud of points in the middle of the scatterplots refers to French civil law and common law countries. The pairwise correlation between the size of public employment and its cost measured as a share of GDP grew slightly from 0.81 in 1995 to 0.87 in 2008 (for both, $p < 0.01$). In contrast, the pairwise correlation between the size of public employment and its cost measured as a share of total government expenditure increased from a statistically insignificant 0.30 in 1995 to 0.77 ($p < 0.01$) in 2008. Thus, while the relationship between general government employment and its relative costs as a share of GDP remained almost

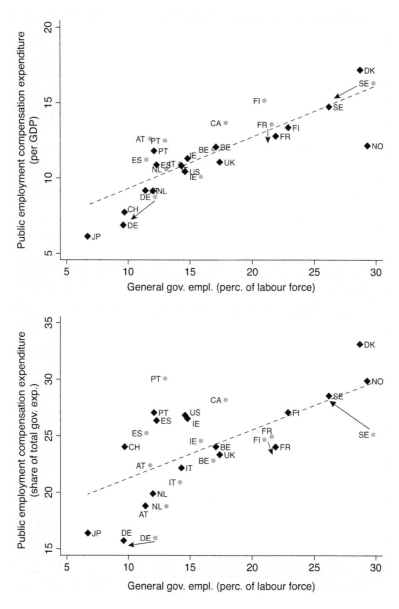

Figure 4.3 Trends in the size and costs of government employment, 1995 and 2008

Note: Grey circles refer to 1995; black diamonds refer to 2008; United Kingdom 1995 not included due to missing data (see Table 4.2).

unchanged, the relationship between general government employment and its relative costs as a share of total government expenditure grew.

Comparing the two points in time (1995 and 2008) provides an opportunity to describe changes in the relative position of public employment regimes. These changes are visualized by arrows in Figure 4.3. Concerning the first scatterplot, the pattern of change is the same in Sweden and Germany: both countries reduced the size and costs of government employment compensation (per GDP). In France, the size of the public workforce barely changed while the compensation costs were slightly reduced. If we look at the second scatterplot measuring the costs of public employment relative to total government outlays, the pattern of change remains the same in Germany and France. In Sweden, however, the reduction in the size of government employment seemed to be achieved at the expense of increasing government employees' compensation costs relative to total government outlays. This pattern may also apply to other Scandinavian countries where the size of general government employment remained almost unchanged while the fiscal burdens of financing these employees grew from year to year. For example, the alignment of public and private employment regimes in Sweden, which we will discuss in more detail in Chapter 5, implies that productivity-driven pay raises in the private sector directly affect the public sector, in contrast to separated employment regimes in other countries. Furthermore, accrued pension liabilities add to the burden.

In order to elaborate on the argument that similar levels of government expenditure on public employees' compensation can be accompanied by different sizes of the public workforce, Table 4.3 explores the occupational composition of government employment in more detail. Since such exploration requires comparative micro-level data on government employees' occupations, we use data from various waves of the Luxembourg Income Study

Table 4.3 Occupational composition of public sector workforce (in percentage points)

		Managers and professionals (ISCO 1 & 2)	Other skilled workers (ISCO 3–8, 10)	Labourers and elementary (ISCO 9)
Germany	1994	29.5	63.4	7.1
	2004	29.6	63.3	7.1
	Change	**0.1**	**–0.1**	**0.0**
France	1994	39.0	57.8	3.2
	2005	33.0	64.6	2.4
	Change	**–6.0**	**6.8**	**–0.8**
Sweden	1995	56.6	39.7	3.7
	2005	56.0	29.8	14.2
	Change	**–0.6**	**–9.9**	**10.5**

Source: Luxembourg Income Study (various waves, own calculations, weighted).

(LIS). The LIS contains information on the respondent's occupation and sector of employment. We use this information to look at the distribution of occupations of respondents stating that they work for the federal, state, or local government. The occupation is measured with a simplification of the ISCO88, namely with the three categories: *managers and professionals* (ISCO 1–2), *other skilled workers* (ISCO 3–8, 10), and *labourers and elementary workers* (ISCO 9) (Tepe et al. 2015). Given the limited availability of this information for all OECD countries, Table 4.3 presents the distribution of occupations (in percentage points) for two points in time (1994/95 and 2004/05) for the countries which will be discussed in detail in subsequent chapters.[7]

In Germany, about 30 per cent of government employees are working in management and professional jobs, whereas the large majority (60 per cent) are other skilled workers. The French public service has a similar distribution, apart from the fact that the share of government employees in management and professional jobs has been reduced relative to other occupational skill levels between the mid-1990s and the mid-2000s. The distribution of government employees' occupations in Sweden reveals a different pattern. About 55 per cent of government employees are working in management and professional jobs, whereas only 39 per cent are other skilled workers. Looking at the relative changes in the distribution of government employees' occupations, we find that the two patterns (France and Germany versus Sweden) have been fairly stable between 1994/95 and 2004/05. Only Sweden has experienced a slight reallocation of about 10 percentage points from other skilled workers (ISCO 3–8, 10) to labourers and elementary workers (ISCO 9).

Exploring the size and costs of general government employment indicates that there is no empirical evidence at the aggregate level which clearly supports either the 'cost explosion' or the 'personnel cut' arguments. In the observed period, there has been no sharp upward trend in compensation cost for government employees (*cost explosion thesis*). Nor do we find that the size of government employment has been rapidly or radically cut in OECD countries over the observed decade (*personnel cut thesis*). The multiple trajectories of general government employment in terms of size and compensation expenditure summarized in Tables 4.2 and 4.3 and Figure 4.3 indicate that OECD countries might have taken different pathways with respect to public employment. This overall picture is generally more consistent with the idea of regime-specific reforms trajectories in which different variables matter in different contexts.

Given that employment protection rules in the public sector are rather strict as compared to their private sector counterparts (Vaughan-Whitehead 2013), reforms, even if consisting of sharp reductions in the size or costs of public employment, will not only need time to materialize but also will depend on the current level of government employment. Hence, the political room to move and alter general government employment is likely to be at least partially determined by the level of government employment.

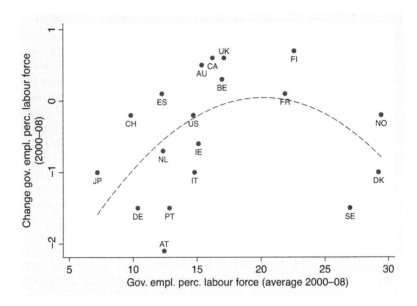

Figure 4.4   Level and change in size of government employment
Note: Dashed line represents quadratic prediction.

The association between levels and changes in general government employment is summarized in Figure 4.4. The x-axis represents the average size of general government employment as a share of the total labour force from 2000 to 2008, while the y-axis reports changes in general government employment as a share of the total labour force in this period.[8] This plot shows that instead of a linear relationship, there is a 'hump'-shaped relationship between the level and change in general government employment. In fact, countries with a low level of general government employment (in particular Japan, Switzerland, Germany, and Austria) and those with a high level of general government employment (in particular Sweden, Denmark, and Norway) experienced reductions in general government employment. In contrast, countries with a medium level of general government employment (in particular Australia, Canada, and the United Kingdom, but also France) experienced a further increase in general government employment over this period. The three Anglo-American countries are known to be front runners of NPM. Yet, in terms of these highly aggregated figures, we do not observe substantial cutbacks in government employment in these countries.[9]

This observation further strengthens the view that the mere size of the public workforce is not a sufficient indicator for a country's effort to transform its public employment regime. In addition, the comparison of levels and changes indicates that the German civil law and Scandinavian civil law public employment regimes may have adopted similar reform strategies, leading to a reduction of public employment for different reasons. The personnel cost pressure argument in the vein of Baumol and Bowen (1966) is more likely to apply to the case of Scandinavian countries with a large government workforce. Similar reductions in general government employment can be found in countries belonging to the German civil law regime. Note also that countries with a similar moderate level of general government employment (such as Austria and Spain) can vary considerably with respect to the change in general government employment over time. Austria reduced the public workforce by 2 percentage points, while Spain witnessed a slight increase of 0.2 percentage points. Nevertheless, in general, these appear to be small changes.

In order to understand these diverse changes, we take a closer look at the longer-term macroeconomic pressures that might trigger or hamper adjustments in general government employment. Thus, we consider the resources available to bear the fiscal, political, and societal costs of public sector reforms. Instead of being attributed to efforts at cost reduction or NPM ideas, observed changes may also, and perhaps better, be explained by fiscal pressures stemming from general government debt in combination with low economic growth rates.

Table 4.4 lists several important socioeconomic variables which are standard predictors in comparative political economy. A functionalist view suggests that the size of government employment depends on the resources available for public production. Thus, we will look at debt levels, GDP growth, and unemployment rates as basic indicators capturing the *general state of the economy*. Prior studies exploring determinants of public employment (Cusack et al. 1989; Pennings 1999) considered public debt as an important determinant of the reduction of the size and costs of public employment. In the aftermath of the oil shock, the shift towards the service economy, and difficulties in financing welfare services in ageing societies, public employment policies take place in the context of fiscal austerity. One could, therefore, expect that higher levels of debt are associated with a reduction of public employment (Cusack et al. 1989). As shown in Table 4.5, none of these indicators (debt levels, GDP growth, and unemployment rates) is strongly correlated with general government employment measured as a share of total employment. This should not be misinterpreted in the sense that the state of the economy is irrelevant for government employment policies. It only implies that levels of public employment are persistent over the long term. A straightforward positive relationship can be observed between the size of the *welfare state* and the size of general government employment (Table 4.5). Social expenditure as a share of GDP is by far the most frequently used indicator to measure the size of a country's welfare system (Kittel and Obinger 2003).

Table 4.4 Long-term association between government employment and macro-socioeconomic variables, 2000–08

	General government employment as percentage of labour force[a]	Gross government debt (financial liabilities) as percentage of GDP[b]	Unemployment rate as percentage of civilian labour force[b]	Growth of real GDP, percentage change from previous year[b]	Total public social expenditure as percentage of GDP[c]	Government outsourcing as percentage of GDP[d]	Left-party cabinet share[e]	Union density[e]
Common law								
Australia	15.4	18.6	5.5	3.1	17.0	6.6	12.0	22.3
Canada	16.2	74.5	6.9	2.6	17.0	9.3	0.0	29.9
Ireland	15.1	35.3	4.4	5.0	15.9	5.5	2.3	38.2
United Kingdom	17.1	45.2	5.1	2.5	20.0	11.4	100.0	29.5
United States	14.7	60.1	5.1	2.4	15.9	8.0	0.0	12.2
Average	**15.7**	**46.7**	**5.4**	**3.1**	**17.2**	**8.1**	**22.9**	**26.4**
Civil law German								
Austria	12.5	69.4	4.3	2.3	26.9	4.9	11.5	34.4
Germany	10.4	65.6	9.1	1.7	26.6	4.3	82.8	22.4
Japan	7.2	160.2	4.6	1.5	18.0	3.4	0.0	19.8
Switzerland	9.8	52.6	3.5	2.1	19.1	3.9	28.6	20.0
Average	**10.0**	**86.9**	**5.4**	**1.9**	**22.7**	**4.1**	**30.7**	**24.1**
Civil law French								
Belgium	17.0	100.6	7.7	2.0	26.2	3.6	50.2	52.1
France	21.9	70.5	8.3	1.9	29.6	5.3	27.4	8.1
Italy	14.8	117.6	8.2	1.4	24.4	5.6	27.8	33.8
Netherlands	12.4	60.2	3.4	2.2	20.8	7.4	19.1	21.9
Portugal	12.9	69.3	6.4	1.5	21.6	4.5	39.5	18.9
Spain	12.3	53.7	10.7	3.3	20.9	5.1	52.3	15.6
Average	**15.2**	**78.6**	**7.4**	**2.0**	**23.9**	**5.2**	**36.1**	**25.1**
Civil law Scandinavian								
Denmark	29.2	47.0	4.7	1.6	27.2	9.1	16.1	71.8
Finland	22.6	47.8	8.4	3.1	25.3	9.6	40.0	73.0
Norway	29.4	48.3	3.7	2.4	21.9	6.8	45.8	54.7
Sweden	27.0	57.6	6.2	2.6	28.7	9.4	75.1	76.9
Average	**27.0**	**50.2**	**5.7**	**2.4**	**25.8**	**8.7**	**44.3**	**69.1**

Note: a = OECD (2009, 2011); b = Armingeon et al. (2012); c = OECD Social Expenditure Database (SOCX) (2012); d = OECD (2011, p. 169) only goods and services used by general government; e = Armingeon at al. (2012): Union density = Net union membership as a proportion of wage and salary earners in employment.

Table 4.5 Pairwise correlations between government employment and macro-socioeconomic determinants, 2000–08

	Government employment	Debt	Unemploy-ment	GDP growth	Social expenditure	Out-sourcing	Left-cabinet share
Debt	−0.37						
	(0.12)						
Unemployment	−0.04	0.13					
	(0.87)	(0.59)					
GDP growth	0.06	−0.57	−0.04				
	(0.80)	(0.01)	(0.88)				
Social expenditure	0.46	0.10	0.37	−0.42			
	(0.05)	(0.70)	(0.12)	(0.08)			
Outsourcing	0.57	−0.45	−0.12	0.21	−0.02		
	(0.01)	(0.05)	(0.64)	(0.40)	(0.92)		
Left-cabinet share	0.20	−0.18	0.36	−0.12	0.43	0.21	
	(0.42)	(0.47)	(0.13)	(0.62)	(0.07)	(0.38)	
Union density	0.74	−0.16	−0.06	0.12	0.45	0.45	0.22
	(0.00)	(0.51)	(0.81)	(0.64)	(0.05)	(0.05)	(0.36)

Note: For source and definition of variables, see Table 4.4, p-value in parentheses.

With respect to general government employment, we see that countries belonging to the liberal welfare regime do have a smaller government workforce, and that those countries considered to belong to the social democratic welfare regime have a larger government workforce. These results are generally in line with comparative welfare state research drawing on different types of welfare regimes. Following Esping-Andersen (1990), countries belonging to the social democratic type consist of a large public sector due to a generous state-run provision of social services. In countries belonging to the conservative type, welfare provisions are rather medium in size and rather consist of cash benefits than public services, with the latter being provided by a mixture of non-profit organizations (*dt. Parafiskus*) and state services.

There are, however, interesting differences within the group of Continental welfare states, in particular between France and Germany, as these two tend to have an almost equally large share of welfare state spending but different sizes of general government employment. One interpretation of this pattern is that the legal tradition of public employment regimes characterizes differences within the conservative welfare state regime. A fundamental mechanism that may underlie these differences, and which may also affect the general capacity to reform public employment, could be the extent to which the French and German public administrations are considered to be politicized. The German civil law tradition puts greater emphasis on the separation of the political and bureaucratic spheres and may therefore be associated with a less-politicized public administration as compared to the French civil law tradition.

Thus far, we have focused on the size and costs of government employment, along with government production. This view neglected the fact that since the mid-1980s, governments have turned to outsourcing as a way of accessing external expertise and delivering more cost-effective services (OECD 2011, p. 168). In fiscal terms, outsourcing is the result of a reconsideration of the assumption that public financing of goods and services is necessarily coupled with public production of these goods and services. Thus, governments choose between *public and private sector production*. Contracting private companies to provide public goods and services allows, on the one hand, to exploit economies of scale, while on the other hand it requires tools to supervise contractors and to evaluate the quality of the goods and services. The OECD (2011, p. 168) measures government outsourcing as the size of expenditures in relation to the goods and services purchased by central, state, and local governments.

In this vein, one can argue that governments that decide to employ private companies require fewer public employees. Table 4.5, however, indicates that the level of government outsourcing is positively, rather than negatively, associated with general government employment. One way to interpret this positive relationship is to consider outsourcing as an attempt by the government to respond to high levels of government employment. This interpretation, however, would only apply to countries with a Scandinavian legal tradition that combines high levels of government employment and high levels of government outsourcing. However, the common law countries, which are also characterized by high levels of government outsourcing, have a rather small government workforce. Hence, a merely functionalistic view that interprets outsourcing as a tool to reduce government employment does not seem to help in solving the empirical puzzle. Instead, the association between outsourcing and the size of government employment indicates that countries end up choosing similar reform paths for different reasons.

The reduction in the size and costs of public employment could be considered an ideological programme. This puts the *political power resources* available to policymakers to implement NPM measures at centre stage. Standard accounts of partisanship in public policies would suggest that social democratic parties are generally more willing to finance a larger public sector (Tufte 1978). Hence, a larger share of ministers from left-wing parties in the cabinet should be associated with a larger public workforce and higher costs of public employment. This standard account, however, might have changed in an era of fiscal austerity (Pierson 2001). Social democratic parties have been responsible for the implementation of various public sector reforms aimed at the reduction of the public workforce (Suleiman 2003). Hence, whether conservative governments are more likely to retrench public employment while left-wing governments are more reluctant to implement such reforms becomes an empirical question.

Given the constant decline of union density in affluent democracies, the partnership between left parties and trade unions in representing labour might have vanished in recent decades (Ebbinghaus and Visser 1999, 2000; Bryson et al. 2011). Therefore, trade unions need to be considered as an independent collective interest group pushing for a strong public sector. This hypothesis is based on the idea that the industrial sector and the public service sector are traditional strongholds of trade unions. In order to account for the strength of organized labour in determining the size and payroll costs of government employment, we use overall trade union density, as measured by Armingeon et al. (2012), and expect that this measure is positively correlated with public sector trade union density, which is not available.

Table 4.5 shows that government employment, measured as a share of total employment, is uncorrelated with the share of left-wing cabinet seats, but highly correlated with trade union density. This association is even stronger than the association between government employment and welfare state spending. Hence, a larger share of general government employees goes hand in hand with stronger trade union density and more resources devoted to the welfare state.

Another way to think of the 'right' size of general government employment is to consider the output of government policies relative to the resources invested. From this perspective, public employees are the single most important input factor in the production of government services. If two countries use the same proportion of government employees (input) to realize different amounts of government services (output), we can conclude that, *ceteris paribus*, one country uses its public employees ('human resources') more efficiently than the other does. In order to answer questions on the efficiency of certain input/output relationships, scholars in operational research have developed a statistical tool called Data Envelopment Analysis (DEA). Afonso et al. (2005, p. 322) compiled data on various public expenditure categories and socioeconomic variables, reflecting the outputs, or outcomes, of government policies in 23 OECD countries. The efficiency of the public sector for each country is measured by a non-parametric production frontier technique. The challenge of such an approach clearly lies in the difficulty of specifying the 'production function' of a government. For the purpose of this chapter, we will simply compare the share of general government employment and the effectiveness of government.[10]

According to the World Bank's (2011) Worldwide Governance Indicators, government effectiveness is broadly defined to capture perceptions of the quality of public services, the quality of the civil service, the degree of its independence from political pressures, the quality of policy formulation and implementation, and the credibility of the government's commitment to such policies (World Bank 2011). A measure of government effectiveness that is more specific in terms of capturing the quality of public administration is a composite sub-indicator from the Economist Intelligence Unit

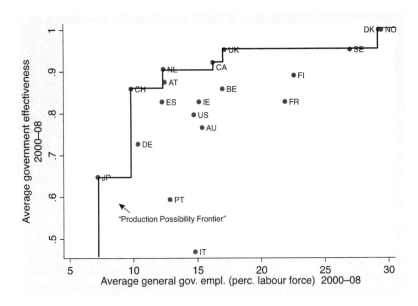

Figure 4.5   Level of government employment and effectiveness of government, 2000–08

Note: Economist Intelligence Unit (EIU) Country RiskWire Service Expert Assessment Democracy Index; the full EIU dataset is commercially available. The indicators range from 1 (good) through 4 (bad). Only the averages of sub-indicators are publicly available in this spreadsheet.

RiskWire Service & Democracy Index, namely 'Quality of bureaucracy / institutional effectiveness' and 'Excessive bureaucracy / red tape'.

Figure 4.5 shows the existence of a positive long-term relationship between the size of general government employment, measured as a share of total employment, and government effectiveness. Assuming a production-function-like relationship between government employment and government effectiveness, we can draw a line between those countries that achieve the highest level of government effectiveness for each level of government employment. Government effectiveness in Japan, for example, is almost as low as in Portugal. However, Japan achieves its 'low' level of government effectiveness with a 'low' level of government employment, whereas Portugal needs 'more' government employees to achieve a similar level of government effectiveness. Thus, if we compare these outcomes relative to the resources employed, we see that Japan lies on the 'production frontier', indicating that – at least when it comes to these two input/output factors – it is more efficient. Using this logic, we find that Scandinavian civil law countries with high levels of government employment can be considered as relatively efficient since these countries also realize high levels of government effectiveness. The United Kingdom, Canada, the Netherlands, and Switzerland combine moderate levels of government employment with moderate levels of government effectiveness. The United States, Belgium, and France do not lie on the 'production frontier', indicating a less efficient use of government employment if government output is measured in terms of effectiveness.

The ultimate conclusion from this comparison is that a larger government workforce by no means serves as a sufficient indicator for government inefficiency. As we have seen, countries with different legal traditions and public employment regime affiliations can be found on the 'production frontier'. This fuels our doubt that there is a single equilibrium in resources devoted to governments that guarantees an efficient output of state activity. It remains a political decision which services should be delivered by the state, and whether more services require, *ceteris paribus*, more employees.

Trends towards NPM Reforms

We now explore to which extent the use of Human Resource Management policies may reflect a political response to a growing public workforce. Figure 4.6 shows how changes in general government employment between 2000 and 2008 relate to the intensity of PRP policies in central government (upper panel), and how changes in general government employment in the same period relate to intensity of performance assessment in human resource decisions (lower panel).

The upper panel of Figure 4.6 indicates a positive association between the use of PRP and the change in general government employment. This relationship is not overwhelmingly strong, since various countries making rather frequent use of PRP, such as Denmark and Japan, experienced a decrease in general government employment. Apart from Spain, all countries that experienced an increase in general government employment tend to be in the upper segment of the scale of PRP. The lower panel of Figure 4.6, which shows the relationship between performance assessment policies and changes in general government employment, does not indicate any association.

This analysis – which is certainly limited by the rough measurement of PRP – has two major implications. First, in line with the mapping of public employment regimes, the analysis of long-term trends in government employment confirms that there are substantive differences within the group of countries characterized by a civil law tradition, which highlights that the Neo-Weberian reform path needs further differentiation. Second, exploring the relationship between resources devoted to government employment and the output of government employment indicates the existence of divergent reform paths in terms of the chosen tools of Human Resource Management, as well as in terms of the depth of implementation.

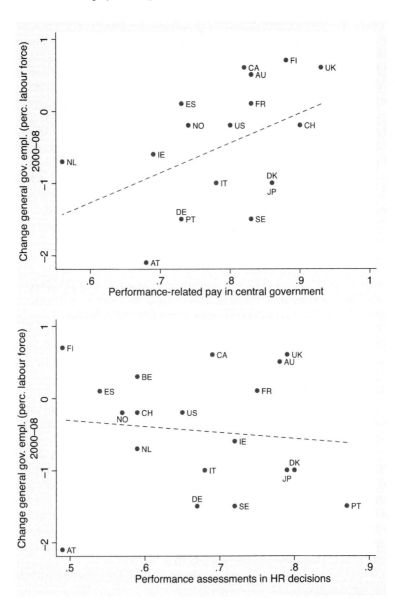

Figure 4.6 Change in the size of government employment and NPM reform measures

In addition, these scatterplots indicate that PRP policies might represent a particularly interesting showcase reform to explore the degree to which OECD countries try to adopt NPM policies.

The introduction of PRP policies is usually considered a watershed in public sector modernization, as it challenges a central element of traditional public employment: career-based payment schemes designed to maximize the loyalty of public servants. Since gratification and promotion are independent from individual work performance, career-based payment schemes are assumed to lead to the self-sorting of certain motivational types into the public sector, typically characterized by either a preference for employment security or a high public service motivation (Vandenabeele 2008; Dahlström and Lapuente 2010; Tepe 2015). Performance-related schemes, in contrast, build on a position-based system, which replaces the expectation of intrinsic motivation and loyalty of public staff by the assumption that public and private sector employees are guided by the same extrinsic motivations (Miller 1992). For these reasons, an exploration of the timing of PRP policies should provide particularly valuable insights into the dynamics of public employment reforms.

In view of the rather limited numerical changes in the size and scope of government employment, we thus consider more subtle organization reforms which introduce monetary incentives to government employees. Here, subtle should not be misunderstood as less consequential. As we will argue, transferring managerial Human Resource Management instruments such as PRP onto government employees might have little immediate effect on the number of government employees, but it can have a substantial effect on the nature of differences between the public and the private sector. A particular prominent thesis in this context is that PRP schemes 'crowd out' government employees' cooperative work motivation. Miller and Whitford (2002, p. 253) suspect that performance-based pay, which is based on the principle of 'quid pro quo', eliminates the character of a 'gift-exchange' between a political principal and an administrative agent, and thereby causes a reduction in government employees' work effort (also see Georgellis et al. 2011). Although the validity of this argument remains an open empirical question that we cannot address in this chapter, the debate certainly highlights the relevance of PRP in the NPM debate.

This section will focus on the reform dynamics and factors that shape the implementation of PRP policies. Compared to private sector contracts, government employment tends to be based on long-term contracts. Hence, short-term cuts in public personnel are rather constrained by the nature of employment contracts. Moreover, drastic cuts of public employment threaten the re-election chances of incumbent governments (Weaver 1986; Pierson 2001). On the other hand, we know from individual-level analysis (Tepe 2012) that government employees, particularly those involved in the production of public goods and services, still have rather strong political ties with left-wing parties. For this reason, drastic cuts in government employment should be a politically risky endeavour, in particular for left-wing incumbents.

Scholars in comparative welfare research have found that governments seeking re-election, when faced with the need for unpopular cutbacks, have developed various strategies for sharing and avoiding blame for these reforms (see, for example, Weaver 1986; Giger and Nelson 2011). We assume that such tactics of blame avoidance are also likely to apply to other policy domains, such as government employment. A strategy to establish Human Resource Management reforms in the public sector without risking resistance from the government workforce might be to restrict new rules, such as PRP, to new employees. Hence, the established workforce is not affected by these reforms. Such strategies, however, have some important implications for what we can expect to find in the long-term trends in government employment. First, the strategic timing of Human Resource Management reforms makes drastic and short-term changes in the size or costs of government employment unlikely, because the budget-restricting effect of such reforms unfolds rather gradually over longer periods. Second, if such reforms are costly or politically risky, for example because of protests from civil service trade unions, the timing of the implementation of PRP may be subject to strategic considerations.

PRP implies a shift from 'low-powered' incentives such as flat salaries and seniority-based advancement to 'high-powered' ones. Rewards may be awarded to individuals or groups of employees. When PRP is designed as a zero-sum game, where bonuses for high performers are financed by wage cuts of low performers, it will be controversial among policymakers and the public workforce alike. In this context, not only the institutional design but also the timing of reform becomes politically relevant.

Prior research in the field of comparative welfare state and industrial relations exploring the role of temporality and sequence in political processes was mainly concerned with the timing of macroeconomic and macro-fiscal reforms (Tepe and Vanhuysse 2010; Ebbinghaus and Kittel 2005; Hicks and Zorn 2005). Alesina et al. (2006), for example, show that mounting crisis often contributes to the acceleration of reforms, such as the adjustment of budget deficits, inflation, or debt. Thus, we now address the determinants of the timing of reforms introducing PRP in the comparative framework of the OECD countries.

Despite the popularity of PRP among policymakers and public managers, only a few studies directly address the explanation of cross-country variations in PRP reforms (Christensen and Lægreid 2001; Peters and Pierre 2001; Pollitt and Bouckaert 2011). The comparative public administration literature has focused more generally on theoretical explanations of NPM and has stressed the role of the administrative tradition. According to these ideas,

NPM is presented as a natural consequence of the Anglo-Saxon administrative tradition (Castles and Merrill 1989, p. 181; Pollitt 1990). Others have argued that NPM is a preferred policy of right-wing parties gaining political control in the mid-1980s. These conservative governments were inspired by the ideas of neo-liberal economists and ideologically predisposed to cut back the state, including the public bureaucracy. According to this approach, NPM is associated with right-wing governments (Bach 1999; Barlow et al. 1996). Others have stressed the role of economic and fiscal pressures resulting from economic globalization. According to this view, even governments that did not follow the neo-liberal reform agenda were forced to cut public spending, which also involved measures to improve the efficiency of public Human Resource Management (Keller 1999; Thompson 2007).

In contrast to these general accounts on the causes of NPM, Dahlström and Lapuente (2010) explored the causes of PRP reforms across countries. They argue that PRP is more likely to be implemented in administrations in which there is a relative separation between those who benefit from PRP (for example politicians) and those who manage the incentive system (that is, senior civil servants). In countries where the interests of both groups overlap (for example, the careers of senior officials and politicians are intertwined), the implementation of encompassing PRP reforms is less likely. Drawing on cross-sectional regression analyses for 25 OECD countries, they find that PRP is significantly more often initiated in contexts with clear separation of interests between politicians and senior civil servants.

Apart from blame avoidance tactics, the particular timing of unpopular or risky policy reforms may be used by incumbents to survive unpopular policies in times of fiscal austerity. Tepe and Vanhuysse (2010) argue that policymakers have a strong incentive to strategically manipulate the timing of cutbacks in social expenditure. With respect to the timing of PRP policies, it remains an open question whether those factors that are associated with the configuration of public employment regimes, especially the scope of government employment, also help to explain whether a country belongs to the 'early birds' or 'latecomers' in implementing PRP. In the following, we consider three explanatory factors:

1. *Legal tradition*: We can extend Dahlström and Lapuente's (2010) argument, cited above, about the timing of PRP reforms. In general, we expect performance assessment and performance-based pay to be more reconcilable with the common law tradition, since in this context there is a clearer separation of interests between politicians and senior civil servants (Dahlström and Lapuente 2010, p. 577).

In empirical terms, common law countries generally have been 'early birds' in implementing NPM instruments (Pollitt and Bouckaert 2011). Yet, it remains to be explored whether differences exist within the group of civil law countries in the timing of PRP reforms. If anything, Scandinavian civil law countries have been faster in learning from the developments in the Anglo-American countries. In some respects, these countries have even been more proactive, for example in the equalization of employment rules in the public and private sector. In terms of implementing PRP instruments, we therefore expect that Scandinavian civil law countries adopted PRP earlier than German and French civil law countries, while we remain doubtful about the relationship in the timing of PRP between Scandinavian civil law and common law countries.

2. *Political parties and left-wing power resources*: According to the Bureaucratic Voting Model (BVM), left-wing governments are expected to expand public services and thereby secure public sector employment (Garand et al. 1991). Survey research confirms that public sector employees in affluent democracies are more supportive of bigger governments and are slightly more likely to vote for left-wing parties (Tepe 2012). Building on these micro-level observations, it appears plausible that PRP schemes should be less likely to be implemented by left-wing governments.

From a public policy perspective, however, it remains questionable whether a left-wing government – elected with or without the support of public employees – will or will not consider NPM as a means to transform the public workforce. The ideological re-orientation of social democratic parties in affluent democracies in the 1990s, frequently labelled as a *Third Way* (Giddens 1994), altered traditional ties between unionized public sector employees and left-wing governments. In this respect, the hypothesis that left-wing governments eschew the implementation of NPM in general, and PRP in particular, needs empirical scrutiny.

Regardless of the relationship between political parties and unions, stronger and more aggressive trade unions can be expected to delay the implementation of PRP. Drawing on similar theoretical considerations as those used to describe the relationship between left-wing governments and the timing of PRP reforms, countries with strong public sector trade union representation are less likely to implement such reforms.

3. *Macroeconomic conditions*: In order to make sure that the legal tradition argument is not confounded by the macroeconomic conditions, the statistical analysis controls for debt, GDP growth, and unemployment. In particular, debt decreases policymakers' fiscal room to move, and therefore might increase fiscal pressures to implement zero-sum PRP schemes. Growing fiscal debt indicates growing fiscal constraints. Debt is therefore expected to foster early implementation of PRP reforms.

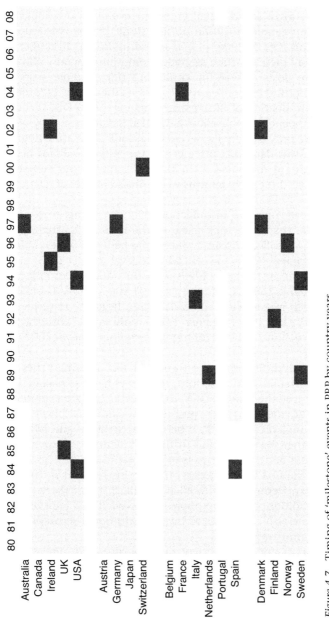

Figure 4.7 Timing of 'milestone' events in PRP by country-years

Note: See Appendix A.4. Dark grey indicates 'milestone' events in the introduction of PRP in the public sector. Light grey indicates the period used in the event analysis. The period actually included in the statistical analysis deviates from the observation period due to missing data in the independent variables.

A specific difficulty in testing the potential determinants of the timing in PRP reforms is to find concise measures for such events. For the purpose of this study, we focus on so-called milestone events in the implementation of PRP. The operationalization of 'milestone' events is based on the OECD's definition (OECD 2005, p. 27), according to which, PRP excludes any automatic pay increase (such as grade promotion) and any allowances based on certain posts or working conditions (for example, working in particular geographical areas). Figure 4.7 presents the timing of 'milestone' events in the introduction of PRP instruments for the 19 OECD countries in our sample. Appendix A.4 provides a detailed list of the coding of 'milestone' events. We only explore PRP events that took place after 1980, since reforms prior to this date took place before the NPM paradigm began its rise into a dominant discourse, even though some of the motives that might have caused these early reforms were consistent with the latter NPM framework.

Figure 4.7 shows that the introduction of PRP reforms took place in three waves. The first wave took place in the mid-1980s. Denmark, the Netherlands, New Zealand, Spain, Sweden, the United Kingdom, and the United States adopted PRP at the central state level (OECD 2005, p. 29). A second wave started in the early 1990s with the adoption of PRP policies in Australia, Finland, Ireland, and Italy (OECD 2005, p. 29). German civil law countries such as Germany and Switzerland began to implement PRP instruments in the late 1990s, whereas France only started with the partial introduction of such instruments for top-level civil servants in 2004 (OECD 2005, pp. 29–30).

Figure 4.7 also indicates that the timing of PRP reforms varies across countries with different legal traditions. In line with our expectations, the United Kingdom and the United States – both of which share a common law legal tradition – are the 'early birds', and civil law countries appear to be the 'latecomers' in implementing PRP. Whereas the political and administrative elites are rather separate groups in the common law context, an integrated relationship between the two is more likely in the civil law context. Moreover, after the first experiences with these instruments in the Anglo-American context, Denmark and Sweden – both of which share a distinct civil law legal tradition – began to implement explicit PRP reforms as well. Both countries are also characterized by an institutional separation of the political and administrative elites.

Yet, the picture is not that clear-cut since we also find some cases that deviate from the legal tradition pattern. On the one hand, Spain adopted some PRP measures already in the early 1980s, but no Spanish government since then continued on this pathway. On the other hand, the Netherlands implemented PRP instruments in the 1990s. The Netherlands are an exception to the group of German and French civil law countries, as they have turned out to be the 'front runners' in public sector modernization in continental Europe (Pollitt and Bouckaert 2011). From a historical perspective, one can show how the 'Tilburg Model of Public Sector Modernization', developed by public administration research in the Netherlands, has initiated the German debate on the reform of the municipal administration with the use of managerial steering techniques (Jann 2011).

Using multivariate analysis, we explore the extent to which the timing of PRP reforms has been determined by the legal tradition, the political factors, and the economic conditions. 'Milestone' events are operationalized as binary variables, which take the value of one for country-years in which a PRP reform in the public sector has been implemented and the value of zero otherwise. Following Beck et al.'s (1998) non-parametric approach, we started with a logit specification including a series of dummy variables. These dummies refer to the number of periods since the previous occurrence of a 'milestone' event or, by default, the first year in the dataset (Beck et al. 1998, p. 1261). Auxiliary tests, however, have shown that the inclusion of two splines instead of the full set of temporal dummies (see Beck et al. 1998) provides a better model fit. Thus, we discuss the spline specification. In order to deal with multiple 'milestone' events within one country, a variable counting the number of previous events in a country is included in the model.

The analysis of the timing of 'milestone' events in the introduction of PRP is presented in Table 4.6. Models 1 and 2 explore whether we can consider the administration as a dichotomous measure or whether there are relevant differences in the legal tradition within the civil law group of countries. Models 3 and 4 include both sets of time-varying controls. Before we describe the theoretically substantive results, we look at the variables accounting for the temporal dynamics. The variable 'Duration since last event' counts the number of years since the previous reform on PRP within a single country. The positive and statistically significant coefficient indicates that further PRP reforms become more likely once a country has implemented an initial reform. In this respect, PRP reforms can be viewed as a gradual learning process. The variable 'Previous failures' fails to exert a statistically significant effect on the likelihood of a reform.

A comparison of Models 1 and 2 shows that the structural differences within the group of civil law countries must be accounted for, since the simple administrative tradition dummy fails to exert an effect on the likelihood of PRP reforms, whereas the set of dummies for legal tradition does. In line with the findings from Figure 4.4, German and French civil law countries are the 'latecomers' in implementing PRP reforms as compared to common law countries. In substantive terms, Model 2 indicates that the likelihood of a reform decreases by 1.68 percentage points in German civil law countries as compared to common law countries.[11] The corresponding decrease in the likelihood of such events in French civil law countries is 1.54 percentage points.

Table 4.6 Likelihood of 'milestone' events in performance-related pay (PRP)

	Milestone event in PRP			
	Model 1	Model 2	Model 3	Model 4
Civil law	−0.704			
	[0.55]			
German civil law		−1.573**	−1.647	−1.607
		[0.75]	[1.00]	[1.10]
French civil law		−1.183*	−1.346*	−0.850
		[0.63]	[0.71]	[0.80]
Scandinavian civil law		0.437	0.389	1.653
		[0.66]	[0.69]	[1.56]
GDP growth			0.106	0.130
			[0.19]	[0.18]
Debt			0.001	−0.001
			[0.01]	[0.01]
Unemployment			−0.037	−0.0524
			[0.08]	[0.08]
Left-cabinet share				−0.024***
				[0.01]
Union density				−0.010
				[0.03]
Duration since last event	1.973***	1.890***	1.912***	2.105***
	[0.42]	[0.40]	[0.50]	[0.62]
Previous failures	−0.121	−0.346	−0.337	−0.273
	[0.35]	[0.30]	[0.28]	[0.38]
First spline	0.055***	0.051***	0.050***	0.054***
	[0.01]	[0.01]	[0.02]	[0.02]
Second spline	−0.023***	−0.022***	−0.021***	−0.022**
	[0.01]	[0.01]	[0.01]	[0.01]
Observations	522	522	478	449
Pseudo R-squared	0.077	0.119	0.136	0.184
AIC	168.6	165.6	160.1	154.4
BIC	194.2	199.6	206.0	207.8

Note: Constant included but not reported; standard errors in brackets; ***p < 0.01; **p < 0.05; *p < 0.1.

Countries: United Kingdom, Ireland, Australia, United States, Canada, Germany, Austria, Switzerland, Japan, Italy, Spain, Netherlands, Belgium, Portugal, France, Denmark, Norway, Finland, Sweden.

None of the macroeconomic control variables exerts a substantively and statistically significant effect on the timing of PRP reforms (Model 3). Of the two left-wing political power measures, however, the share of left-wing cabinet seats significantly delays PRP reforms. In substantive terms, Model 4 indicates that the likelihood of a PRP event decreases by 1.94 percentage points if the share of left-wing cabinet seats increases by 1 percentage point.

In substantive terms, the effect of a country's legal tradition on the timing of PRP reforms appears to be rather small. However, this result needs to be qualified in view of the finding that the duration between two reforms, and the duration between the first year in the dataset and the first reform, explain the majority of variance in the probability of a 'milestone' event in PRP policy. Compared to the substantive effect of political determinants (in particular, left-wing cabinet power), the legal tradition still has a moderate impact. This assessment, however, should not obscure the fact that using macro proxy measures for the statistical analysis of the timing of PRP reforms can only provide superficial insights into the multiple factors in the political process that eventually caused the implementation of PRP policies.

Conclusions

Focusing on government employment as the core of the public workforce, this chapter provided a map of public employment regimes, described the long-term trends in the size and compensation cost expenditure on government employment, and explored the timing of NPM reforms. The multiple empirical findings can be condensed into three main results.

First, the analysis of the political and institutional foundations of government employment indicates the presence of four politico-administrative regimes in the OECD. The constitution of these regimes is centred on three legal traditions, namely common law, Scandinavian civil law, and Continental civil law with French and German variants. In this respect, the legal tradition serves as a proxy to differentiate politico-administrative regimes. Moreover, the legal tradition, which is largely congruent with previous analyses of structural differences between administrative systems in comparative public administration research, is also congruent with four public employment regimes. The first regime includes only Anglo-American countries, the second only Scandinavian countries, and the third and fourth regimes consist of continental and Mediterranean European countries in the French and German traditions. One interpretation of this relationship is that the legal tradition captures institutional features that predetermine the selection of certain modes of public employment regulation. This interpretation is supported by a more specific look at the adoption of NPM tools. The extent to which countries have adopted such tools in their national systems of administration appears to be particularly helpful for discriminating between different configurations of public employment regimes.

Second, the exploration of changes in the size and costs of government employment across countries reveals large variation within the group of civil law countries. This variation indicates that the distinction by Pollitt and Bouckaert (2011) between a reform path inspired by NPM and a second Neo-Weberian reform path seems to be an oversimplification with respect to countries with a civil law tradition. Although government employees' compensation expenditure appears to demand a growing fraction of government budgets in some countries, supporting Baumol's cost disease hypothesis, the majority of countries managed to contain or even reduce absolute government personnel expenditure.

Third, the timing of 'milestone' events in Human Resource Management reforms, namely the introduction of PRP schemes, systematically varies across public employment regimes. The descriptive and multivariate analyses indicate that whether a country belongs to the 'early birds' or 'latecomers' in implementing PRP is associated with the country's legal tradition, which is largely congruent with the public employment regime. The United Kingdom and the United States are clearly the 'early birds' in the implementation of PRP policies, while German civil law countries are more likely to be 'latecomers'. This observation needs to be refined, since Denmark and Sweden, both of which are also civil law countries, were among the 'early birds' in implementing PRP policies.

In this context, there are also signs that the timing of PRP reforms is subject to electoral and strategic concerns, as the partisan orientation of the government is associated with the speed of these reforms. The substantive interpretation of the timing of implementation of PRP, however, is limited by the fact that the measure of 'milestone' events does not account for potential differences in the scope of PRP reforms. Moreover, the substantive interpretation of these effects needs to be qualified in view of the overall performance of the statistical model, which is largely determined by the duration since the last event (which in some countries is simply the first year in the dataset) and the second spline. Both are variables that are of little theoretical interest. Nevertheless, these analyses indicate that the responsiveness of countries towards the incorporation of NPM ideas into their public sector Human Resource Management practices varies across public employment regimes.

Moving towards a more detailed analysis of public employment reform paths within countries, Table 4.7 summarizes the main findings from this chapter with respect to the selection of our reference country and three primary country cases (United Kingdom, Germany, France, and Sweden). What are the implications of this chapter for the comparative case analyses?

First, our results strongly suggest that the country selection described in Chapter 3 – that is, including countries from four different legal traditions rather than relying on a dichotomy of common and civil law – indeed has some representative potential. Since the three primary countries (France, Germany, and Sweden) and the reference country (United Kingdom) represent different legal traditions, the macro-comparative analysis strengthens our confidence that the country selection contains substantial variation. The empirical analysis presented in this chapter strongly suggests that the

Table 4.7 Summary of empirical findings for the United Kingdom, France, Germany, and Sweden

	United Kingdom	France	Germany	Sweden
Mapping public employment				
Politico-administrative regime	Unitary state structure with separate minister/mandarin relations	Unitary state structure with integrated minister/mandarin relations	Federal state structure with separate minister/mandarin relations	Unitary state structure with separate minister/mandarin relations
Public employment regime	Common law / NPM openness	Civil law / no NPM openness	Civil law / limited NPM openness	Civil law / NPM openness
Long-term trends				
Government employment	Increase at a medium level	Increase at a high level	Decrease at a low level	Decrease at a high level
Resources / embeddedness	Outsourcing	Fiscal pressure / civil service unionism	Fiscal pressure	Outsourcing / welfarism
Efficient use of general government employment	Efficient	Inefficient	Efficient	Efficient
Timing of reform				
Timing of PRP reforms	Early bird	Delayed	Latecomer	Early bird

inherited legal traditions, and the practical interpretation of these traditions with respect to public employment regulation, are major conditions of any reform in public employment regimes.

Second, the exploration of levels and changes in general government employment shows that the changes in public employment regimes are embedded in evolving institutional systems, in which different variables matter in different contexts at different times. Furthermore, the limited ability to identify a single factor explaining long-term developments in the cost and size of government employment across different countries speaks in favour of a qualitative, in-depth exploration of the sequential combination of factors and components that led either to the reduction or the reconfiguration of government employment in individual countries.

Finally, the generalizations inherent in macro-comparative quantitative analyses ignored country-specific configurations of sectors and branches of public employment. The cross-country comparison presented in this chapter reveals the limitations of comparing 'the public employees'. Public employment is a large and heterogeneous workforce. A cross-country comparative perspective inevitably ignores sector-specific formal and informal rules that shape NPM reforms.

This chapter has shown that changes in government employment will hardly take place on the highly aggregated macro-level, such as the size and costs of public employment, but will take more subtle forms, such as organizational changes which unfold over time and which require in-depth case studies focusing on reforms in employment regimes.

5
A Comparison of Public Employment Regimes in Germany, France, Sweden, and the United Kingdom

Introduction

The overview of quantitative developments and 'milestone' events in Chapter 4 has suggested that the general picture of public sector employment is one of rather rigid structures, slow processes, and contradictory trends. This conclusion, however, is the result of limited and incomplete aggregate-level data, which precludes a closer look into the processes themselves. In this chapter, we therefore explore the development of public employment regimes regarding regulations at the national level, which concern all layers of public administration. We trace nationwide changes and adaptations of the public employment regimes in the four countries representative of the different ideal types of public administration. The United Kingdom serves as a reference case in which neo-liberal ideas and New Public Management (NPM) reforms have had the most impact on the organization of public administration. Then we discuss the public employment regimes in Germany, France, and Sweden. These studies are intended to assess the impact of the constitutional structure of the state and the administrative culture on nationwide trends in the organization of public administration regimes, and to outline the framework for the detailed sector studies in the following chapters.

While we used the common framework outlined in Chapter 3 and Table 3.2 to analyse the systems and changes, we will present the process of public sector reforms for each country in its historical evolution in order to show the internal logic of each national reform trajectory. However, in order to integrate the divergent historical developments into our analytical framework, the final section of this chapter will summarize the changes in the nationwide public employment regimes of the four countries by characterizing the elements of Table 3.2 for the period prior to 1980 and for the early 2010s.

The United Kingdom as a forerunner of public sector reforms

In the present study, the United Kingdom serves as a reference point for the analysis of changes in public employment regimes in the other three countries. The United Kingdom is useful as a foil for comparison because it shows to which extent the public sector, including the public employment regime, can be reorganized under conditions that are favourable to reform. In fact, within Europe the United Kingdom is arguably the country that has made the most substantial reforms of its public sector in the last decades, and it is no coincidence that Hood's seminal text on NPM (Hood 1991) is primarily based on the UK experience. The United Kingdom played a pivotal role in the development of the NPM paradigm and is frequently referred to as NPM's 'birthplace' (McLaughlin and Osborne 2002, p. 1), as well as its 'textbook case' (Wegrich 2009, p. 137). Moreover, the United Kingdom – as well as Sweden, which began reforming its public sector and public employment regime as early as the 1960s – has not only been a forerunner of public sector reforms but is also a potential role model. When NPM became one of the dominant paradigms of public sector reform in the 1990s and was advocated by international organizations such as the OECD and the World Bank, the UK experience became a prominent example for reforms in other countries. It is thus useful to outline the characteristics and trajectories of the UK public sector and public employment regime as a baseline for the analysis of reforms in other public employment regimes.

State structure, political system, and administrative culture

The United Kingdom is a unitary and centralized state under a constitutional monarchy (see, for example, Leyland 2012). Noteworthy is that the constitution of the United Kingdom is not codified in a single legal document which sets out the state structure and the distribution of powers between different institutions and the state and its citizens. Instead, the constitution consists of an array of sources, such as approximately two dozen statutes, judge-made case law, international treaties, and informal conventions. Moreover, the UK has a majoritarian and adversarial political system, with a first-past-the-post electoral basis. The UK parliamentary system is the prototypical 'Westminster model' with a bicameral parliament: an elected lower house (House of Commons) and an appointed upper house (House of Lords). Due to the far-reaching powers of the sovereign Parliament and the tight party discipline in the House of Commons, the executive is very powerful and 'in normal times it can almost always get its legislation through' (Pollitt and Bouckaert 2011, p. 314). The House of Lords has only the power to delay, but not reject, government legislation. The administrative culture follows the 'public interest'-tradition, which 'accords the state a less extensive or dominant role within society' and where 'civil servants are regarded as simply citizens who work for government organizations, not some kind of special caste or cadre with a higher mission to represent "the state"' (Pollitt and Bouckaert 2011, p. 62). Last but not least, the structure of the public sector and the Civil Service are not regulated at the level of the constitution, and sometimes are not even regulated by law at all (Wegrich 2009, p. 140).

This institutional set-up provides excellent conditions for far-reaching reforms of the public sector and public employment. The unitary and centralized state structure allows nationwide changes through legislation by the central government,[1] and the lack of a single written constitution allows constitutional changes to be adopted through simple Acts of Parliament. The majority voting system, the majoritarian government, and the powerful executive allow the adoption of changes without much resistance by 'veto players'. Finally, the pragmatic, instrumental, and flexible administrative culture, as well as the lack of constitutional regulation of the public sector and the Civil Service, allow far-reaching changes regarding public services and the status of public servants. In short, 'the UK's institutional setting enables a determined elected government to implement public management reforms so extensive as to change the constitutional arrangement itself' (Wegrich 2009, p. 140).

The history and characteristics of public sector employment in the UK

The British Civil Service developed over the course of the 19th century (Parry 2011, p. 348), with the most important event being the publication of the Northcote-Trevelyan Report in 1854. This report established the guiding principles of the Civil Service, including competitive merit-based entry, political neutrality, a generalist tradition, lifelong career paths, and a strong policy advisory role (Page 2010). This so-called 'Whitehall model' (named after the London street in which most central government buildings are located) was maintained until the 1980s and 1990s in a highly centralized model of governance (Jarvis 2002, p. 43). The core Civil Service is surrounded by other forms of public employment which emerged and evolved in conjunction with the general development of the public sector. In the early 20th century, a shift from Victorian 'anti-state' values towards Fabianism already involved the recognition of the limitations of the philanthropic sector and a growing importance of the public sector (Osborne and McLaughlin 2008, p. 73). The main shift in public sector development, however, occurred in the immediate aftermath of the Second World War, when many industries were nationalized and the reform of health, education, and social service provisions established the basis of a substantial welfare state (Winchester and Bach 1999, p. 22).

With the rise of the welfare state, public employment grew considerably. The Labour government elected in 1945 already added 2 million workers to the public workforce in the major transport and extractive industries (Parry 1985, p. 54). Subsequently, public sector employment increased continuously until the early 1980s, when it reached more than 7 million employees, nearly 30 per cent of the employed labour force (Winchester and Bach 1999, p. 22). The common distinction in the public sector is between three subsectors (see Winchester and Bach 1999, p. 23). First, the term 'central government' refers to all organizations for whose activities a government minister is responsible to Parliament, including the Civil Service, the armed services, and publicly constituted bodies funded by the central government. Second, organizations with some degree of financial independence from the central government are referred to as 'public corporations' and included the nationalized industries in telecommunications, air transport, gas, electricity, water, and railways until their privatization in the 1980s, and today mainly the National Health Service (NHS). Finally, 'local authorities', which have the duty to provide a broad range of services and the power to raise taxes and levies, employ a large share of the public sector workforce (see Table 5.1).

While the Civil Service comprised only a small share of the public workforce, it served as a role model for public employment. On all levels of public administration, a distinct approach to personnel management evolved, characterized by special institutions and practices, such as an administrative personnel management function, a paternalistic style of management, standardized employment practices, and collectivist patterns of industrial relations (Farnham and Horton 1996, pp. 43–89). Overall, public employment regulation was highly centralized, as policies on recruitment procedures, pay, and conditions of service were decided at the top and little discretion was left to line managers and personnel administrators (Burnham and Horton 2013, p. 200).

Public employment was significant not only due to its sheer size and specific characteristics but also because the state was supposed to be a 'good practice' and 'model' employer in three respects. First, many public service employees had a greater degree of job security, more clearly defined career prospects, and generally better pensions, sickness pay, and other

Table 5.1   United Kingdom: public sector employment 1979–2014 (selected years)

	Central government (in 1,000s)	Local government (in 1,000s)	Public corporations (in 1,000s)	Total (in 1,000s)	Belonging to Civil Service (in 1,000s)
1979	2,387	2,997	2,065	7,449	739
1999	2,346	2,739	361	5,446	504
2004	2,808	2,921	386	6,115	571
2009	2,852	2,908	570*	6,330	527
2014	2,883	2,352	184	5,419	442

Note: Mid-year headcount figures, including casual staff; * = Growth mainly due to transfers of failed private banks into the public corporation sector.

Source: Burnham/Horton 2013, p. 50; Office for National Statistics (2014).

benefits than their private sector counterparts (Winchester and Bach 1999, p. 26). Second, the composition of the workforce in the public sector differed markedly from the private sector, with higher shares of women, part-time workers, ethnic minorities, and persons identifying themselves as 'disabled'. In other words, the state pursued equal opportunity policies and had an integration function for disadvantaged groups on the labour market (Farnham and Horton 1996). Third, employment relations and the regulation of pay, recruitment, training, and work conditions in the public sector were supposed to serve as a role model for employment regulation and industrial relations in the private sector (Boyne et al. 1999; Morgan and Allington 2003). This exemplary function of the public employment regime for employment in the private sector was eased by the fact that they had always been closer together than in many other countries due to the absence of a fundamental division between public and private sector employment legislation (Winchester and Bach 1999, pp. 22–26).

Changes in public sector employment in the UK since the 1980s

Far-reaching changes in the UK's public sector and public employment regime began with Prime Minister Margaret Thatcher's first term as leader of the incoming Conservative government in 1979. After Thatcher's prime ministership (1979–90), the changes continued under her Conservative successor John Major (1990–97) and, with a different emphasis, under the 'New Labour' governments of Tony Blair (1997–2007) and Gordon Brown (2007–10), as well as under the current Conservative-Liberal coalition government under David Cameron (since 2010). In other words, since the 1980s, the UK public sector and public employment regime have undergone a series of reforms in various areas over an extended period of time, with differing aims, and with an 'increasing speed of "policy succession" and "reversals", i.e. the application of contrasting if not contradictory solutions to recurring issues of governing public services' (Wegrich 2009, p. 149). In sum, these reforms have turned the UK public and Civil Service into the 'prototypical example of [a] managerial, client-oriented, competitive public service' (Kickert 1997, p. 20).[2]

With good reason, the UK is commonly viewed as a prime example of the NPM paradigm and its effects on public employment. The basic doctrine of Thatcher's Conservative government was that markets are inherently more efficient than other institutional forms of service provision or coordination. Accordingly, market principles should be used whenever possible, and market mechanisms should be used when a market as an institution is not feasible (Wegrich 2009, p. 139). The public sector was viewed as 'overstaffed, inefficient, supplier-led and unresponsive to public needs or demands while the trade unions and professional associations were blamed for the rises in public expenditure' (Burnham and Horton 2013, p. 201). Thus, the successive Conservative governments under Thatcher and Major pursued a series of reforms in the public sector with privatization as the top priority, followed by the exposition of public services to market competition via compulsory competitive tendering or 'market testing' and contracting out; the establishment of 'quasi-markets' based on the split of purchaser and provider roles; and the promotion of private sector management styles and recruitment of staff from the private sector (Wegrich 2009, p. 139).

The main reforms under Thatcher began with the 'Rayner scrutinies' (1979), which were supposed to detect organizational slack and to prepare workforce reductions in central government. Subsequently, a variety of policy instruments were introduced. On the one hand, most public corporations were privatized, including air transportation (1981), telecommunications (1984), gas (1986), electricity (1987), water (1989–91), and railways (1993–94). On the other hand, public service delivery was fundamentally reorganized. This included compulsory competitive tendering for service provision by local authorities (1980–88) and the Financial Management Initiative (1982), which established output measures for all central government departments and delegated financial and personnel responsibility to line managers, as well as the introduction of PRP in central government (1985–87). Moreover, the creation of more than 100 executive agencies in central government under the 'Next Steps' programme (1988) resulted in a decentralization of the central government level and facilitated the adoption of private sector management styles (see Wegrich 2009, p. 142; Pollitt and Bouckaert 2011, pp. 316–17). Under Prime Minister Major, the rapid pace of marketization of the public sector continued, primarily with the 'Citizen's Charter' (1991), which extended performance assessments and was supposed to foster customer orientation. The introduction of 'market testing' for central government and the resulting contracting out (1991), the Private Finance Initiative (1994) which reformed public investment, the implementation of new standards of accounting (1994), and the creation of a Senior Civil Service (1994–96) were intended to ensure continuity in light of decentralization and the creation of executive agencies on the central government level (see Wegrich 2009, pp. 142–43; Pollitt and Bouckaert 2011, p. 317).

Under the 'New Labour' governments of 1997 to 2010, 'the urge to privatize disappeared, but there was no countervailing desire to take organizations or functions back into public ownership' (Pollitt and Bouckaert 2011, pp. 315–16). In fact, most reform measures were accepted or slightly modified, such as the replacement of compulsory competitive tendering for local authorities by a 'Best Value' regime, and the rebranding of the 'Citizen's Charter' programme as the 'Service First' initiative. Among numerous public sector reforms, three main priorities can be identified: a strong emphasis on performance management; the promotion of 'joint-up government', which views the private sector as a partner in service provision; and an emphasis on 'user choice' in public service delivery (Pollitt and Bouckaert 2011, pp. 317–18). Generally, from 1979 onwards, the public sector in the UK was fundamentally reformed on all levels, and the current Conservative-Liberal coalition government, partly driven by the financial crisis, continues the trend of downward adjustment and redesign or elimination of service provision by the public sector (Grimshaw 2013).

The effects of these public sector reforms on public employment were three-fold. One major effect was a massive reduction of the public workforce. Under the successive Conservative governments (1979–97), the public workforce was reduced from more than 7 million employees to roughly 5.5 million. This was the result of the privatization of public corporations, which created a major loss of personnel in this subsector. It also resulted from 'market testing' and contracting out on the central government level, leading to a substantial decrease in Civil Service employment (from 739,000 in 1979 to 516,000 in 1997). In contrast, aggregate employment in the NHS and in local authorities remained relatively stable.[3] Under the 'New Labour' governments, the decline of public sector employment was initially partly reversed, but in 2004 another round of workforce reduction began (Wegrich 2009, p. 149). In 2009, the public sector workforce grew considerably, but this was due to the financial crisis and the transfer of failed banks in the public corporations subsector. The current Conservative-Liberal government continues the overarching trend of public workforce reduction (Grimshaw 2013).

The second major effect was a decentralization, flexibilization, and individualization of public employment regulation. Reform measures such as the Financial Management Initiative, performance management, agencification, contractorization and the quality movement, as well as new private sector management styles have fundamentally changed all aspects of public employment, including employment relations, recruitment, pay, career advancement, and staff training. These changes have been most pronounced in the Civil Service and the new executive agencies, but have had an impact on all levels of the public sector, including the NHS, public corporations, and local authorities (Burnham and Horton 2013, pp. 202–22). On the level of central government, the Cabinet Office has overall responsibility for personnel management, but since 1996 this function is highly decentralized, and all departments and agencies have obtained delegated authority to manage their own staff. Only three unifying factors remain, namely national human rights, employment, and health and safety rules which apply to all public and private employment. The changes have been codified in the Civil Service Management Code (1996), which lays down some general principles regarding working conditions in the Civil Service, and the Civil Service Recruitment Principles, which are formulated and controlled by the Civil Service Commission, a public body sponsored by the Cabinet Office that was established in 1855 and has a statutory basis since 2010 (Burnham and Horton 2013, pp. 205–15).

Regarding public sector employment relations, the main changes since the 1980s are the weakening of trade unions (although trade union membership in the public sector is still considerably higher than in the private sector) and the decline of collective bargaining, due to decentralization, the establishment of agencies, contracting out, and the rise of PRP and individualized contracts. However, it is argued that 'public sector employment relations continue to be distinctive' (Prowse and Prowse 2007, p. 58), as managers continue to consult and involve unions, even though 'that involvement is more de-centralized and uneven at times' (Prowse and Prowse 2007, p. 58). In personnel recruitment, there has been a shift from centrally organized competitions run by the Civil Service Commission towards highly decentralized procedures at the level of departments and agencies. All procedures are nevertheless bound by the principles of fairness, openness, equal opportunities, and merit-based selection as outlined in the Civil Service Recruitment Principles (Burnham and Horton 2013, p. 209). With respect to pay, a shift has taken place from national pay structures with long incremental scales and automatic progression, towards the delegation of pay arrangements to departments and agencies for all staff below the Senior Civil Service. This measure has often resulted in a combination of base salaries and bonuses through decentralized collective bargaining and the near-universal application of PRP (OECD 2012, p. 3). Finally, career advancement for civil servants has undergone a shift from a career-based system to a position-based (or hybrid) type. This change is characterized by a much higher turnover of staff and individuals no longer staying in the service 'for life', but also because specific jobs are now advertised and people are appointed to a post, often for a specific period of time (Burnham and Horton 2013, p. 209).

The third and final effect was a departure from the presumption that the public sector should be a 'good employer' and 'model employer'. This presumption was explicitly denied by the Conservative governments, which basically reversed the direction of policy learning, as the public sector was supposed to learn from the private sector. The resulting changes eroded many of the previous differences from private sector labour markets and resulted in 'downward harmonization', 'with many employees in the public services facing the same degree of job insecurity, work intensification and limited promotion prospects as their private sector equivalents' (Winchester and Bach 1999, p. 26). However, the composition of the public sector workforce still differs markedly from the private sector: 'The civil service already does much better on diversity than the private sector with three times as many women in senior positions and continually improving ratios of ethnic minorities and disabled persons at every level' (Burnham and Horton 2013, p. 224). In sum, we can observe some continuity with respect to advantages of the public sector for employees, in particular in view of the widespread deterioration of private sector employment conditions. While it is debatable whether the public sector in the UK is still a 'good' employer, it is certainly not a 'model' employer any longer.

Germany

The three core elements of the German public service have not changed over the last 30 years. First, the system is characterized by a dualism between civil servants (*Beamte*) whose rights and duties are unilaterally regulated by the employer, and public employees (*Angestellte*) with collectively negotiated contracts. Second, public authorities at the three administrative levels – central government, federal states (*Länder*), and local authorities – are traditionally independent employers. Third, despite these fragmentations by status groups and by levels of administration, employment regulation is horizontally and vertically coordinated. Regulations for both status groups (*Beamte* and *Angestellte*) are similar throughout the three administrative levels. Due to the stability of the system, Germany has been considered a latecomer in public sector reform, and transformations are regarded as rather incremental (Ferner 1994; Knill 1999; Pollitt and Bouckaert 2011; Röber and Löffler 2000). However, since the 2000s, public sector reforms affecting the system's institutional structure have begun to challenge the German public service in its traditional form. In view of the extent of public sector reforms in other countries, these developments are neither new nor notably radical. Nevertheless, for Germany they are considered to constitute 'the end of an era' (Keller 2006).

In the following, we describe the main characteristics of public employment in Germany, most notably its derivation from the concept of the *Rechtsstaat* (rule of law) and its distinctive administrative system. We argue that, on the one hand, the unilateral regulation of civil service employment warranted by the German constitution (*Grundgesetz*, GG, Basic Law) and the vertically and horizontally highly coordinated system have been a hindrance to encompassing public sector transformations. On the other hand, the comparatively small size and the decentralized organization of the German public sector already contained elements that are core targets of NPM in other countries. Moreover, in the absence of comprehensive public sector reforms, changes in the institutional context had a major impact on the German public employment regime. While public employment still entails many characteristics of the bureaucratic civil servant model, the end of coordination between administrative levels and status groups marks a strong trend towards the diversification of the public employment regime. This trend includes the alignment with private sector employment regulations for some segments of public employment.

Rule of law and federal administration

In Germany the formation and development of a professional civil service with a distinctive status was the result of the establishment of the Prussian central government in the 17th and 18th centuries, which was enforced against the interest of the estates, especially the clergy and the nobility

(Mayntz 1985, pp. 23f.). This process was accompanied and enabled by the establishment of a public workforce that obtained specific rights and duties in exchange for loyalty to the Prussian king: the civil service. Legal regulation of civil service rights and duties was already set in 1794 in the Prussian General Land Law (*Preußische Landordnung von 1794*), which defined the official status, tenure, pension, and recruitment for a specific career as its main features (Mayntz 1985, p. 138). Workers who were contracted for manual tasks were in a stark minority and did not enjoy the specific status and privileges of civil servants (Mayntz 1985, p. 138). Salaried employees (*Angestellte*) were a rather new form of public employment established only at the beginning of the 20th century, but with ever increasing shares (Derlien 2008, pp. 183–84). A consequence of the state's demand for full and unconditional devotion of the workforce to their profession was that the civil service was, in its beginnings, exclusively reserved for men. As di Luzio (2002) shows, characteristics of civil service employment that excluded women were not only influential for the whole public sector but also corresponded to and strengthened a new form of family with the husband providing a stable income and the wife being concerned with childcare and housekeeping.

After the Second World War, the German Federal Parliament *(Bundestag)* regarded the dualism of civil servants and a contracted workforce as best suited for different tasks. While civil servants with their distinctive loyal relationship towards the state, based on specific rights and duties, would best meet the requirements of sovereign tasks (Günther 2010, p. 8), employment based on private labour law would suffice for other tasks and services. Public employment followed the ideal type of male standard employment. Women gained full access to the (West) German civil service only during the 'Golden Age' of the welfare state in the expanding sectors of education, social services, and health, where they formed the vast majority of the workforce. However, irrespective of the high and still rising share of women in public employment and the importance of the state as employer for women, gender segmentation has persisted. Indicative of this observation are lower shares of women in the civil service as compared to contracted employment and a concentration of women in part-time employment and lower ranks (Gottschall 2009). From 1991 to 2011, the share of women in public employment rose from 47 per cent to 54 per cent, not least due to an expansion of part-time work (Statistisches Bundesamt 2000, 2012). Only since the 1980s has the aim of equal participation of women in public employment begun to receive more attention, and changes in the formerly exclusionary structures have only been on the agenda since the 1990s (di Luzio 2002, pp. 201ff.).

The notion of the *Rechtsstaat* 'describes the type of state architecture and political order system in which all publicly applied power is created by the law, is obliged to its regulations, and underlies numerous fragmentations of power and control mechanisms' (Koetter 2010, p. 1). The Basic Law demands that 'the legislature shall be bound by the constitutional order, the executive and the judiciary by law and justice' (GG Art. 20 Para. 3). It regulates the structure of the state and of the public administration according to three major principles. First, the concept of federalism conveys that the states (*Länder*) retain sovereign powers of their own despite their membership in the Federation (GG Art. 30). Second, local self-government guarantees local authorities a high degree of administrative autonomy in local matters (GG Art. 28 Para. 2). Third, the separation of powers between the legislative, executive, and judicial branches implies that each task is allocated to a separate institution. As a result, the structure of the German administration consists of three independent levels: the federation, the 16 *Länder*, and the administration of the local authorities, which are made up of 3,104 autonomous authorities, including 412 districts and non-county municipalities (Siewert and Wendler 2005, p. 889). In principle, each of these administrative levels has its defined functions and holds sovereignty over personnel decisions, being granted the right to select, engage, promote, and dismiss staff (Civil Service Framework Act, *Beamtenrechtsrahmengesetz*, BRRG, Art. 122).

The Basic Law entails the so-called *Funktionsvorbehalt* (caveat for public functions), which demands the entrustment of the exercise of sovereign authority only to members of the civil service (GG Art. 33 Para. 4). Accordingly, tasks that require particular reliability, continuity, and rule of law must be carried out by civil servants whose rights and duties are legally defined and follow the 'traditional principles of the civil service' (GG Art. 33 Para. 5). These principles are abstract legal concepts that date back to the Prussian General Land Law and the Weimar Constitution of 1919. Even though no exact definition of the elements that constitute these principles exists, characteristic elements are considered to be: loyalty, political neutrality, dedication to the public service, unilateral legal regulation, lifetime occupation, a career system, and appropriate pay and pension according to the respective status (Derlien 2005, p. 104; Goetz 2000, p. 65). The *Funktionsvorbehalt* is regarded as a constitutional guarantee of the professional civil service (Günther 2010, p. 12) and as a 'constitutional life insurance for civil servants' (Lecheler 2007, p. 19), because a two-thirds majority in both the *Bundestag* (German Federal Parliament) and the *Bundesrat* (German Federal Council) would be required to change this fundamental rule. However, the *Funktionsvorbehalt* does not mean that civil servants may not be employed for other executive tasks (Günther 2010, p. 11). In practice, the rules for staffing with civil servants or public employees are unclear in some fields, and in some cases public employees and civil servants do the same job (for example, in various administrative tasks) (Hebeler 2008, p. 86–87; Innenministerium des Landes Nordrhein-Westfalen 2003, p. 60). For this reason, the distinction has not been left undisputed, although the concerns raised have not had an impact on the system (Bull 2006; Innenministerium des Landes Nordrhein-Westfalen 2003; Studienkommission 1973).

In order to execute their tasks, all levels of the state employ their own workforce consisting of both civil servants and public employees. The allocation of tasks to the three governmental levels is mirrored both by the quantitative distribution of the public workforce among the three levels and by the status structure of employment. With a share of about 11 per cent of the total labour force, the German public service is relatively small in comparison to other countries (OECD 2011, p. 103). This is due both to the decentralized German state structure and to the principle of subsidiarity.[4] In contrast to other countries, health services are not only provided by the state but organized in a tripartite system of public, non-profit, and private institutions (Schmidt and Rose 1985, p. 135).

The central government is responsible for tasks which are mandated to be uniformly regulated, but in many instances it relies on the *Länder* for the execution of federal policies. As Table 5.2 and Figure 5.1 show, central government accounts for the smallest share of the public workforce, consisting mostly of civil servants. The *Länder*, being responsible for secondary and tertiary education, the police forces, and the judicial system, along with their own general and financial administration, employ by far the largest share of the public workforce. As most of these occupations are regarded as sovereign tasks, civil service dominates the workforce at the *Länder* level. The municipal level is also large, accounting for about one-third of total public employment, but in contrast to the *Länder*, municipalities are responsible for many operative tasks and thus the workforce consists mainly of contracted staff. Local authorities have autonomy in regulating local affairs (local administration and public services, such as waste collection). In addition, local authorities implement government and *Land* policies in their respective

Table 5.2   Germany: distribution of public workforce, 30 June 2013

Type of employment	Total (in 1,000s)	Civil service (in 1,000s)	Military service (in 1,000s)	Contractual employment (in 1,000s)
Central government	503.9	180.3	174.2	149.4
Länder	2,353.7	1,293.8	–	1,059.9
Local level	1,406.4	186.5	–	1,219.9
Social insurance	371.3	33.9	–	337.4
Total	4,635.2	1,694.5	174.2	2,766.6

Source: Destatis (2015).

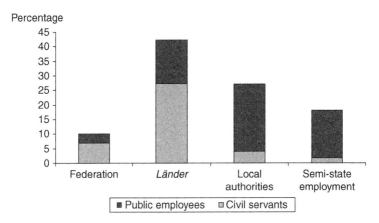

Figure 5.1   Shares of public employment by administrative levels and status groups
Source: Statistisches Bundesamt (2010), illustration by authors.

areas. Furthermore, a further category of so-called semi-state employment exists in self-governing public organizations, such as public
pension and health funds.[5]

The state as employer: coordinated and harmonized employment

Even though the three governmental levels differ with regard to the
composition of the public workforce, and irrespective of the fact that
the three administrative levels held sovereignty over personnel decisions, personnel policies across the levels were more or less aligned until
the first decade of the 21st century. A high level of coordination in the
German federal system (Benz 1994) allowed a harmonized regulation of
the civil service, and joint collective bargaining throughout all levels of
government led to similar collective agreements for the entire contracted
workforce (Keller 2010, p. 11). Furthermore, civil service employment
conditions and the collective agreements of the contracted workforce
became closely aligned.

For the group of civil servants, the former uniformity was the result of the
federal government's extensive use of its right to determine the legal status
of all civil servants according to Basic Law (GG Art. 75 Para. 1 and BRRG).
Until 2006, the federal government also made use of its competency and
unilaterally defined major regulations on pay and pensions (GG Art. 74a
Para. 1 and *Bundesbesoldungsgesetz*, BBesG). This uniform civil service regulation was enacted in order to avoid competition between administrative
levels (Kuhlmann and Röber 2004, p. 3) and was widely accepted until the
end of the 1990s (Günther 2010, p. 14). For all civil servants, the 'traditional

principles' of the Weberian ideal typical bureaucrat constituted the distinctive civil service status:

- the guarantee of the institution of the civil service as such;
- unilateral regulation of status and salary by law, as well as appointment by authoritative act instead of a contract;
- a ban on strikes by civil servants according to prevailing case law;
- a duty of loyalty to the constitution and the obligation to devote the full work capacity to the state;
- protection and support of the civil servant by the state; and
- a career system with lifelong tenure, professional training, and promotion, as well as automatic pay progression.

Traditionally, the career system of civil servants has been differentiated into four service classes with distinctive regulations for recruitment, career advancement, and pay. Entry requirements were legally regulated and based on formal education levels (*Bundeslaufbahnverordnung*, BLV). For example, entrance to the higher service required a university degree or equivalent. Civil servants generally entered their service class in the lowest grade (that is, the entry level). As the state had its own system of staff training, civil servants generally started their employment with an apprenticeship, the length of which depended on the respective service class. After the apprenticeship and a period of probation, varying in length for different service classes, civil servants were appointed for life. The typical career path consisted of sequential steps within the service class depending on time of service (Mayntz 1985, p. 145). Advancement to a higher service class was possible in principle and legally regulated. However, in practice, such advancement to a higher service class was relatively rare (Mayntz 1985, p. 145). Remuneration is based on the 'alimentation principle' (*Alimentationsprinzip*), according to which remuneration and pensions must ensure that both the civil servant and their family are provided with a means for a living in accordance with the rank, importance, and responsibility of their office (*amtsangemessener Unterhalt*).

The alimentation principle has been traditionally justified by the argument that it enables civil servants to fully devote themselves to their duty because of their economic independence. Remuneration consequently consisted of several components: the basic salary determined by pay grade and 'service age' (dependent on age, age at entry, and length of service); a family supplement for married civil servants and civil servants with children; an annual supplement paid in December; and an annual holiday payment (Second Law to Unify and Revise Pay Regulations for the Federal Government and *Länder*, *Zweites Gesetz zur Vereinheitlichung und Neuregelung des Besoldungsrechts in Bund und Ländern*, 2. BesVNG). The alimentation principle reflects the strong male breadwinner model dominant in West

Germany until the late 1970s. In combination with the duty of loyalty, both rules reassured male dominance in the civil service, which only gradually eroded over time (Gottschall 2009).

In contrast to the civil service, public employees' terms and conditions of employment were set in collective agreements based on private labour law.[6] The traditional principles that apply to civil servants did not apply to public employees. While civil servants were recruited for a specific service class without detailed job descriptions, recruitment of public employees was based on their qualification for a concrete position. Detailed job characteristics in collective agreements determined the classification of employees into wage groups. A system of automatic promotion (*Bewährungsaufstieg*) defined seniority as the main factor of advancement. Like in the civil service, salaries depended on the length of service and were amended by non-work-related supplements such as family allowances (Brandes and Buttler 1990, pp. 85ff., 96ff.). Collective bargaining was centralized, primarily in order to maintain the uniformity of employment conditions (Keller 2006, p. 83). Even though separate collective agreements existed for salaried employees and workers until 2005 (BAT for salaried employees, MTArb and BMT-G for workers), collective bargaining took place for both groups jointly most of the time, and thus collective agreements were very similar (Brandes and Buttler 1990, pp. 85, 96). Furthermore, in practice, the regulations of the civil service explicitly served as a role model for collective agreements. Thus, in spite of the fact that employment regulations were based on private labour law specified in collective agreements, employment conditions for contracted staff resembled those of civil servants. High work security and the structure of pay differentiate contractual public employment from private sector employment (Hils and Streb 2010, p. 10). In the opposite direction, employee-friendly elements of collective agreements (for example, concerning working hours or pay raises) were often transferred into legal regulation for civil servants (Keller 2006, p. 80). This alignment was enabled not only by the willingness of public employers to set high employment standards but also by strong public sector unions.

Reforms, transformations, and the public service

Key aspects of a reform initiative in the early 1970s were dissatisfaction with the efficiency and effectiveness of the public administration in general and with the dualism of civil service and contracted workforce in particular (Jörges-Süß 2007, pp. 116, 155–56). The governing coalition of Social Democrats and Liberals established a 'Study Commission for the Reform of Public Service Law' (*Studienkommission für die Reform des öffentlichen Dienstrechts*), which was composed of representatives of all relevant actors and stakeholders. The commission elaborated ambitious and far-reaching proposals aiming at radically changing the traditional system of public employment. The main suggestions were: the replacement of dualism by a single regulatory framework for the whole public workforce; the replacement of status-based differentiation with functional differentiation; and the introduction of performance-based elements in pay schedules and career progression rules (Studienkommission 1973, pp. 104, 272).

Due to a lack of political consensus and strong reservations and resistance against any substantial change by many civil servants and their unions, only the commission's minor recommendations were implemented (Goetz 2000). The term 'civil service reform' itself became discredited because it was associated with expectations of a profound transformation of public employment (Jörges-Süß 2007, p. 148). Whereas other countries, in particular the UK and Sweden, have experienced comprehensive administrative and civil service reforms since the 1980s or earlier (Demmke 2011), after the attempt of a comprehensive public sector reform had failed in the 1970s, administrative and public employment reforms were not on the agenda in Germany again until the 1990s (Derlien 2008, p. 171). A few reform efforts in the 1980s and 1990s were rather isolated approaches without a comprehensive concept (Czerwick 2007, p. 187; Lorse 2007, p. 24). This reflects the high legal barriers to changing the constitutive elements of the German civil service mentioned above. An effective coalition for change is difficult to achieve since the responsibility for managing the civil service is institutionally dispersed over the three levels of government, and civil service unions are strong. Moreover, many German executive politicians and members of parliament have a civil service employment background (Ferner 1994, pp. 72–73; Goetz 2000, pp. 83–84; Günther 2010, p. 8).

Thus, personnel policies were comparatively stable, and the size of public employment in Germany rose continuously until 1990 (Kuhlmann and Röber 2004, p. 11). In the 1990s, after reunification, the public workforce grew rapidly by 1.8 million, mostly due to the high level of public employment in the newly formed German states that made up the former German Democratic Republic. The increasing costs made downsizing the public sector an important point on the political agenda (Schröter 2001, p. 67). A major concept was the so-called New Steering Model (*Neues Steuerungsmodell, NSM*) established by the local governments' 'Joint Agency for Municipal Management' (*Kommunale Gemeinschaftsstelle für Verwaltungsmanagement, KGSt*). The NSM is regarded as the 'German version of New Public Management' (Kuhlmann et al. 2008, p. 851) and was mainly inspired by local government modernization in the Netherlands. Focusing on competition and performance, the model entailed a promise of more efficiency, effectiveness, and customer orientation.

In the absence of a general concept for public sector 'modernization', the NSM has become a major template for local government reforms and also had an impact on the other administrative levels. Thus, contrary to other European countries, public management reform in Germany is interpreted as a bottom-up movement (Kuhlmann et al. 2008, p. 851). Even though the

NSM comprised elements of Human Resource Management such as PRP, its impact on public personnel policies was limited. Rather, it provided a toolkit for privatization and outsourcing, and in response to tight budgets, total public sector employment was reduced from 1991 to 2004 by 31.5 per cent (32.5 per cent in municipalities) (Czerwick 2007, pp. 74–75). The reduction affected the status groups to varying degrees, leading to a change in the composition of the workforce. This is most evident in the *Länder*, where the proportion of civil servants rose from 41.7 per cent in 1991 to 59.8 per cent in 2004 due to the cutbacks among employees (Czerwick 2007, p. 77).

In the context of NPM discourses, the debate about civil service reforms evolved in the mid-1990s. Public employment regulation was criticized as rigid and as a hindrance to sustainable modernization. Fundamental reforms were demanded, such as the abolition of the civil service or the formal redefinition of its traditional principles (Naschold 1996, Wollmann 1996, Koch 2008). In 1997, a civil service reform was initiated (*Gesetz zur Reform des öffentlichen Dienstrechts, Reformgesetz*, ReföDG, BGBl. I 1997, pp. 322–47), which contained extended opportunities for part-time work, the facilitation of secondment of civil servants to other departments, and the introduction of performance-based bonuses. Although the civil service reform entailed some changes in the traditional status of civil servants (Günther 2010, p. 14), it cannot be considered a fundamental transformation, but rather a series of incremental changes concentrated on singular interventions (Lorig 2011, p. 182).

Eventually, it was a structural reform of the federal system that spurred reforms in the organization of civil service employment. In 2006, a new law regarding the federalist system came into force (*Föderalismusreform*, BGBl. I 2006, pp. 2034–38). Regarding the civil service, the federal government's competencies in regulating matters for the entire civil service were restricted, while the independence of the *Länder* and the federal government as employers was strengthened. In contrast to the former all-encompassing regulation by the federal government, comprised of detailed regulations for the service classes, career advancement, pay, and pensions (BRRG, BBesG and *Bundesbeamtengesetz*, BBG), the new regulations only allow the federal government to define the general status rights and obligations of all civil servants.[7] The Basic Law still provides the institutional guarantee for civil service employment for sovereign tasks (*Funktionsvorbehalt*, GG Art. 33 Para. 4) and confines the legislators to the 'traditional principles'. However, within this framework, the federal government and the 16 *Länder* are independent in their regulation of civil servants' salaries and pensions, the system of service classes, and career advancement rules. Furthermore, since the reform in 2006, *Länder* and the federal government are not only required to 'regulate' civil service employment as before, but 'the law governing the public service shall be regulated and *developed* with due regard to the traditional principles of the professional civil service' (GG Art. 33 Para. 5; emphasis added by the authors). Thus, through the decentralization of regulative competencies, the 17 employers have not only gained more flexibility to regulate civil service employment; they are also admonished to actually make use of it. Especially with respect to the career system and the pay schedule, the legislators implemented a variety of service classes and pay systems across the 17 public employers. Table 5.3 illustrates the diversity of employment regimes introduced after the 2006 reform.

The comparison of actual pay levels of civil servants in Table 5.4 reveals further differences. Pay is particularly low in the state of Hesse, where civil servants in the lowest pay grade receive less than all of their colleagues in Germany, with the largest difference (EUR 194 per month) being in contrast to the federal government. In this context, it should be added that working time also differs depending on the public employer: the regular weekly working time ranges from 40 to 42 hours.[8] However, as the examples of Hesse and Thuringia show, differences in pay are not linked to working time. As a result, the changes initiated by the 2006 reform in the structure

Table 5.3   Germany: service classes and pay grades (in pay grade A) across *Länder*

	Number of service classes (*Laufbahngruppen*)	Number of pay grades (*Besoldungsgruppen*)	Number of steps (Automatic pay progression) (*Erfahrungsstufen*)
Federal government	4	15	8
Baden-Württemberg	3	12	12
Bavaria	1	14	11
Berlin	2	12	8
Brandenburg	4	15	12
Bremen	2	15	12
Hamburg	2	12	8
Hesse	4*	15	12
Lower Saxony	2	15	12
Mecklenburg-Western Pomerania	2	15	12
North Rhine-Westphalia	4*	15	12
Rhineland-Palatinate	1	15	12
Saarland	4	15	12
Saxony	4*	15	12
Saxony-Anhalt	2	12	8
Schleswig-Holstein	2	15	12
Thuringia	4*	14	12

Notes: * a reduction of the number of service classes is discussed.

Sources: DBB 2013; Besoldungsordnungen von Bund und Ländern 2013 (DBB 2015); compilation by the authors.

Table 5.4 Germany: range of pay levels of public employers

	Lowest pay bracket			Highest pay bracket		
	Entrance level in EUR	Highest level in EUR	Difference in EUR (%)	Entrance level in EUR	Highest level in EUR	Difference in EUR (in %)
Federal government	1,703	1,941	238 (14.0)	4,837	6,136	1,299 (26.9)
Baden-Württemberg	1,605	1,834	229 (14.3)	4,651	5,906	1,255 (27.0)
Bavaria	1,732	2,057	325 (18.8)	4,671	5,926	1,255 (26.9)
Berlin	1,627	1,925	298 (18.3)	4,464	5,674	1,210 (27.1)
Brandenburg	1,652	1,886	234 (14.2)	4,757	6,036	1,279 (26.9)
Bremen	1,693	1,941	248 (14.6)	4,715	5,988	1,272 (27.0)
Hamburg	1,762	1,995	233 (13.2)	4,761	5,863	1,101 (23.1)
Hesse	1,583	1,813	229 (14.5)	4,629	5,884	1,255 (27.1)
Lower Saxony	1,628	1,861	233 (14.3)	4,720	5,993	1,274 (27.0)
Mecklenburg-Western Pomerania	1,627	1,859	233 (14.3)	4,715	5,988	1,272 (27.0)
North Rhine-Westphalia	1,627	1,859	233 (14.3)	4,715	5,988	1,272 (27.0)
Rhineland-Palatinate	1,749	1,994	245 (13.3)	4,842	6,143	1,301 (26.9)
Saarland	1,754	1,988	234 (13.3)	4,824	6,101	1,367 (26.5)
Saxony	1,722	1,951	229 (16.6)	4,734	5,987	1,254 (26.5)
Saxony-Anhalt	1,753	2,044	291 (14.1)	4,736	6,009	1,272 (26.9)
Schleswig-Holstein	1,648	1,880	233 (14.4)	4,736	6,009	1,272 (26.9)
Thuringia	1,777	2,034	257 (14.5)	4,788	6,074	1,286 (26.5)

Note: Solid underline = highest pay level or difference in category; dashed underline = lowest pay level or difference in category.

Source: Besoldungsordnungen von Bund und Ländern DBB (2015); own compilation.

of service classes, pay levels, and statutory working time have generated substantial variation in the conditions of public employment across the German *Länder*.

The collective agreements of public employees based on private labour law were also subject to significant changes. Here especially, the breaking up of the centrally coordinated negotiations by the *Länder* had major effects on collective agreements (Keller 2006). Since the end of joint negotiations, two major collective agreements were concluded: the *Tarifvertrag für den öffentlichen Dienst* (TVöD), regulating pay and employment conditions for public employees of the federal government and the municipalities; and the *Tarifvertrag für den öffentlichen Dienst der Länder* (TV-L 2006), entailing regulations for employees on the *Länder* level.[9] The implementation of the TVöD in 2005 and the abolishment of former status differences between salaried employees and workers (*Bundes-Angestelltentarifvertrag* BAT for salaried employees and the *Manteltarifvertrag* BMT-G and MTArb for wage earners) were regarded by the social partners as the 'reform of the century' (*Jahrhundertreform*) and as a first step toward a profound modernization of public employment (Keller 2008).[10] Besides the abolishment of the former distinction between white-collar and blue-collar staff, the contract contained regulations increasing the flexibility of working time and introduced a new low-wage bracket, which has since then gained importance (Keller and Seifert 2014). Furthermore, pay grades and pay systems were restructured. Family-related salary components and seniority-related pay progression were abolished, and performance-based salary components and experience-related pay progression were established. The collective agreement for the public employees of the *Länder* (TV-L, for all *Länder* with the exception of Berlin and Hesse) took effect in 2006. The agreement was largely based on the provisions of the TVöD, with a substantial difference in terms of working hours since the TV-L provides specific regulations for the *Länder*. PRP components were introduced in the TV-L in 2006, but abolished three years later due to resistance from the trade unions (Mehde 2011, p. 141).

Summary

Despite the fragmented system of two status groups and independent employers at the three levels of administration, public employment in Germany was highly coordinated until the mid-2000s. Corresponding to the constitutional structure of Germany, the core elements of the German public service included harmonized regulation of the civil service and coordinated collective bargaining throughout all levels of government (Keller 2010, p. 11). Furthermore, civil service employment and collective agreements of the contracted workforce were closely aligned. The uniform civil service regulation was enacted to avoid competition between administrative levels and was widely accepted until the end of the 1990s (Günther 2010, p. 14). As a result, public employment in Germany resembled to a large degree the ideal type of the – originally male – public servant. Personnel policies were characterized by lifetime employment or very high work security, and career progression was based on seniority. Pay was determined according to rank, importance, and responsibility, but also with an eye towards covering the costs of maintaining a certain lifestyle for the civil servant and their family. While the civil service opened up for women and abolished discriminating regulations in the early 1980s, the principle of the rule of law, the federalist administrative system, the coordinated system of employment regulation, and the strong public sector unions were strong barriers against comprehensive reforms.

Nevertheless, transformations starting in the mid-2000s have left their traces on the public employment regime. The formerly close connection between the two status groups (civil servants and public employees) has eroded, and decentralization and fragmentation of employment regulations posing new challenges to the still strong public sector unions (Briken et al. 2014) had major effects. Regulations for civil servants were affected by the federalism reform in 2006, and the breakup of the joint negotiations by the public employers initiated a divergence of employment terms and conditions for public employees. Even though these changes are rather piecemeal and concern neither the entire public sector nor one of the two status groups in its entirety, their impact should not be underestimated because they set in motion a process of small changes and adjustments and eventually led to a transformation of the whole public sector. In fact, a broad divergence of personnel policies can be observed: between public employees and civil servants; within the status groups based on the financial situation of the respective *Länder* or municipalities (Wolff 2009, p. 73); and within public organizations between staff with vested rights and younger cohorts that are affected by more unfavourable regulations. Due to the breakup of the former close connections, equal pay is thus no longer aimed at in German public service. Forty years after the first attempts to restructure the public employment regime, Germany can no longer be regarded as 'a solid rock in rough seas' (Schröter 2001).

France

The French political system is state-centred and based on a semi-presidential government structure. This system was stabilized by a broad consensus that France should be a centralized nation, as laid down in the French Constitution's 20th Article stating that the central government decides and directs the nation's policy. In line with the Napoleonic tradition, the French state is equated with the general interest and, as such, is seen as the driving force of societal integration. This notion is of substantial relevance for the conception of public administration and its role in society (Peters 2008, p. 121). As Cole (1999, p. 168) notes, the 'mobilising myth of social progress through public service has come to form part of modern French political culture.' Since the 1980s, *la république une et indivisible* ('the one and indivisible Republic') experienced a sequence of reforms. However, these initiatives cannot be regarded as a general shift to NPM, but rather as a regrouping of the *mille-feuille administrative* ('puff pastry administration') focusing on two broad themes, namely decentralization and modernization. With regard to public employment (*fonction publique*), the public employment system has remained relatively resistant to NPM ideology, and the overall workforce has constantly increased (Kroos 2010).

Today, the core specifics of the French civil service are as follows: the entry requirements, recruitment, and pay are centralized and highly standardized for the whole civil service (Auer et al. 1996, p. 40). However, the French system cannot be described as a homogenous model. Three different civil services exist, namely the Central Government Public Service (*fonction publique de l'Etat*, FPE), the Sub-Central Government Public Service (*fonction publique territoriale*, FPT), and the Public Health Sector (*fonction publique hospitaliere*, FPH).[11] Policies on the number of staff and personnel management are decided within each branch of the public service. Within each service, a multitude of different career paths and posts (*corps*) exists. Furthermore, a specific elitist group (*grand corps de l'Etat*) has direct access to the most prestigious and influential posts.

During the rise of the welfare state, the number of public servants increased from about 2 million in the 1960s to currently over 5 million public employees. Today, more than 40 per cent work in the central government, about 35 per cent at the regional or local level, and more than 20 per cent in the health sector (see Table 5.5).

In the following, we first outline relevant aspects of the French political system and its administrative structures which frame the determinants of public employment. Then we focus on the French civil servant tradition and early reforms, followed by a closer look at events since the 1980s. The remainder of the chapter considers current and ongoing reforms of, and challenges facing, the public employment system in France.

Table 5.5   France: public employment, 31 December 2012

	All			Full-time equivalent in 1,000s
	Number, in 1,000s	Percentage	Percentage part-time	
Fonction publique de l'État	2,373	44.2	15.7	2,257
Fonction publique territoriale	1,862	34.7	26.6	1,685
Fonction publique hospitalière	1,137	21.2	22.8	1,052
Total	5,373	100	20.9	4,995

Source: Ministère de la décentralization et de la fonction publique (2014, p. 92, figure V1–2).

The French state: political system and administrative structure

The characterization of France as a nation-state with a particular emphasis on national independence and a preoccupation with its history and superiority is commonplace. It is captured in the notion of 'French exceptionalism' (Godin and Chafer 2005; Meunier 2000). The predominant conceptualization of this exceptionalism derived from a specific understanding of French republicanism, focusing on the more or less universalistic exemplary nature of the French egalitarian and democratic principles, legitimizing at the same time an activist role for the state. France can be characterized as a strong state driven by dirigisme, centralization, and uniformity, acting with 'visible hands' in a coordinated manner of policymaking (Lovecy 1999, pp. 206–07). The revolutionary myth plays an important role and finds it expression in notions like Jacobinism, Napoleonic tradition, and republicanism.

The French political system is based on a 'semi-presidential government' (Duverger 1974).[12] The nature of the French semi-presidential system is such that the president cannot exercise power without the support, admittance, or sufferance of the prime minister, and vice versa. Thus both political actors form a twin-headed executive or diarchy. However, the president remains the highest authority, such that the diarchy is embedded in a hierarchical structure. As these two individuals are not necessarily members of the same political party or stem from the same part of the political spectrum, their relationship is critical. When they are of different political persuasions (as was the case in 1986, 1993, and 1997), commentators speak of a period of 'cohabitation'.

The conception of the French state dates back to the French Revolution. The feudal system, relying on aristocracy via birthright and thus forming the ruling class, was abolished and substituted by an 'enlightened' new class of nobility. The *citoyen* was integrated into society not by local belonging, but by identifying as a French citizen. Indeed, already over the course of the 18th century, the old world of nobility began to recede and bureaucrats became more important, signalling a decisive turn in the evolution of the administration towards a modern form of organization.[13] In stark contrast to English-style liberalism entailing representative and intermediary bodies and a mixed government consisting of the House of Lords, the House of Commons, and the monarch, the French state was marked by rationalism, with a preference for technocratic administration of the nation (Rosanvallon 1990, p. 129). In this administrative structure, two conflicting ideas were merged: the Napoleonic 'will to power' and the Jacobean 'will of the people', both influencing the relationship between the state and society and the configuration of the mediating institutional bodies. The elected national and subnational governments are to carry out 'the will of the people' directly, without mediation by other group-specific interests.

The rearrangement of the French territory in 1790 followed the idea of destroying the spirit of the pre-revolutionary feudal provinces (*esprit de province*) by organizing the French state into 83 departments, all equal in the size of territory, though not in the number of inhabitants. From the capital down to local governments, a rigidly centralized administrative system was installed, cascading from the prime minister in Paris down to the prefect in the departments and to the subprefect in the *arrondissements*.[14] The regional level, at this point, delivered encompassing services, while the central government kept the inherited control over, and responsibility for, the service delivery. Today, the French state is structured into three administrative levels: over 36,000 cities and communities (*communes*), 101 departments (*départements*), and until 2015 26 semi-autonomous regions (*régions*).

Parallel to the formal system of centralization, a system of negotiations between the state and locally elected politicians played an important role (Négrier 1999, p. 120), which can be interpreted as *jacobisme approvoisé* according to Grémion (1976).[15] Even though the state and particularly the prefect played a central role in the social and political domains, and held the key instruments of political action, it was the 'territorial feasibility' (Négrier 1999, p. 120) that was decisive for the acceptance of political decisions on the local level.

French subnational governance consists of a complex network of actors, and policy is managed by a plurality of actors with overlapping responsibilities at several levels. These systems produce interdependent relationships rather than clear-cut lines of responsibility (Cole 2006, p. 35). These interdependencies are maintained by a system known as accumulation of mandates (*cumul des mandates*) within which elected officials hold a number of different offices at different administrative levels, thus binding together all government levels. In this way, the centre directs local policies, but local interests direct the policies of the central government as well. The dominance of the regions via the central government is also tamed by the fact that the ministries in Paris do not dispose of the human resources necessary to appropriately coordinate the multitude of local authorities appropriately (Edwards and Hupe 2000, p. 135). It was only in 2014 that the French Parliament adopted two laws placing limits on the ability of politicians to hold multiple concurrent political offices.[16]

An important facet of the French conception of the state is its role as a frame for social cohesion and integration (Rosanvallon 1990, p. 91). In line with this tradition, civil servants occupy an important position in the French system of governance. The idea that public sector employment is not comparable to that in the private sector dates back to the absolutist Bourbon Monarchy. This idea was reaffirmed by the French Revolution and the ensuing regimes, and has grown even stronger since.

The French public service is constructed around the idea of being an independent entity. The civil servants (*fonctionnaires*) have to work independently from any political interest other than the 'will of the people.' The civil service follows the idea of a technocratic but dignified personification of the state and the people. In accordance with the Rousseauist principle, the state resisted the presence of any intermediary agent seeking to serve as a bridge between the state and its citizens. This statist tradition is in stark contrast to the Anglo-Saxon predominance of individual responsibility, as well as to the principle of subsidiarity that is so important in the German tradition (Archambault et al. 1999, p. 82).

Although Napoléon successfully initiated the installation of an administrative elite (*grands corps de l'État*), he did so with the chief purpose of creating strong political and social forces acting by order of the state. The establishment of the French civil service system was not based on a specific profession; instead, candidates were primarily selected from the military or technical professions. In other professions, a number of initiatives to establish *Grand Écoles* following the example of the technical and military elite schools failed.[17] The main reason for this is again to be found in revolutionary philosophy and the direct representation of the general interest by the state: the civil service, as soon as it would be too strongly organized and thus given the opportunity to build an interest group on its own, was regarded as a threat to the Republican model.

The role of collective bodies, such as political parties and unions, is to be understood in this context. In contrast to the bargaining processes in the private sector, French governments usually have dealt with a small number of core associations (big employers, big unions) rather than being open for a wider range of interest or issue groups, thus establishing a strong sectoral corporatism within the public service (Pollitt and Bouckaert 2011, p. 272).

The post-war constellation

The regulation of employment relationships in the French administrative system is based on the principle of rule of law (Pollitt and Bouckaert 2011). On 19 October 1946, the status of civil servants was laid down, defining the basic principles of civil servant employment (Bodiguel 1978; Pochard 2011, p. 10; Rouban 2007, p. 480). The public service officials are placed in a legal context fully separated from private law, and a specific framework of guarantees and obligations is applicable to the so-called 'civil servant citoyen' (*fonctionnaire citoyen*). The regulation of employment terms and conditions is unilateral, and the codified core values and obligations are fairly close to the Weberian bureaucratic ideal type, entailing loyalty, impartiality, neutrality, integrity, and legality. Even though the Statute of 1946 contains the right to build unions (Art. 6: '*Le droit syndical est reconnu aux fonctionnaires*'), a positive right to strike had not been formulated at that time. The French civil service policy is founded in the meritocratic ideal, and irrespective of social background, every French citizen is eligible to become a civil servant.[18] With the regulation of 9 October 1945 given the *'priorité absolue ... au problème général de la formation et du recrutement des fonctionnaires'* (the absolute priority on the training and recruitment of civil servants),[19] the *École Nationale d'Administration* (ENA) as well as the *Instituts d'études politiques* (IEP, SciencesPo), the Office of the Comptroller-General (*Direction de la fonction publique*), and the Body of Civil Administration (*corps unique des administrateurs civils*) were created. However, it is important to note that the civil servant status was restricted to the central state functions within the realm of the central government administration (ministries) and the national public administrative establishments under public labour law (except hospitals).

One general characteristic of the French administrative structure due to its military and technical roots is that of the civil servant as a 'technocrat', characterized by following orders and by a strong division of tasks. Since 1945, the whole civil service is organized along the lines of so-called *corps*, each offering specific career paths within ministries as well as criteria of professional excellence.[20] Furthermore, there are three hierarchical categories from A to C in decreasing order of educational knowledge required. Civil servants in *Catégorie A* occupy highly skilled or managerial positions and have a higher education degree. *Catégorie B* comprises agents in mid-level management tasks and requires a *baccalauréat* (secondary school degree). *Catégorie C* includes personnel dedicated to daily administrative tasks.

Within each category, every civil servant belongs to a *corps*. On the one hand, this system implies very restricted, if not nearly impossible, horizontal mobility. Promotion is essentially based on the seniority principle (*ancienneté*) and pay scales are based on job classifications (grades). On the other hand, within the state civil service (with tenure), *corps*, grading, and hierarchy are precisely defined and strengthen the *esprit de corps*, and contract employees belong to another social culture. This led to a specific 'Republican elitism' (Tümmers 2006, p. 196), as the structure of the French civil service is characterized by social fragmentation, and the career system is based on the distinction between grade and employment (*grade et emploi*), making it impossible to change from one *corps* to another.

The French civil service personnel system is considered a closed-shop system (Auer et al. 1996). The selection and recruitment process is highly segmented due to the *corps* and elite training system. Access routes into the national civil service and those into the local service are separated. The postgraduate training for the higher civil service is accomplished by the *École Nationale d'Administration* (ENA) in Strasbourg and – for lower-ranking executives – by the *Institute Régional d'Administration* which comprises five regional locations. The key institution for education and training of local administrative staff in France comprises 1,700 employees working in the 'National Centre for Territorial Administration Ministry' (*Centre National de la Fonction Publique Territoriale*, CNFPT) headquartered in Paris and 28 regional outposts (*Délégation régionales*) in the provinces. Thus, in the French case, the idea of corporatism refers more to the internal competition of *corps* within the civil service in order to protect and defend their professional field, and to maintain the social hierarchy among the various *corps*. The result is a hierarchy produced and reproduced by competitive exams and the system of *Grandes Écoles*. The status of higher civil servants being employed by a *grand corps de l' État,* especially graduates of ENA, is an indisputable sign of social achievement and access to power. Working as a higher civil servant in this regard is closer to politics and sustaining powerful networks than to serving the general interest (Bourdieu 1989).

When it comes to the integration of women into the public employment labour market, employment in the public sector was already a preferred option for French women in the 1960s (Vimont and Gotier 1965, p. 34). Even today, women constitute the majority of public service employees (Table 5.6), perhaps influenced by the extensive set of options for reconciling career and family in the overall French employment system (for example, through part-time work). However, in the French case, two differences set it apart from other countries and necessitate mention. First, women are not underrepresented in full-time employment in France. Second, the hiring process may encourage the recruitment of women, since the risk of gender discrimination in hiring is attenuated by a high degree of formalization and depersonalization of the recruitment process, in particular through formal exams.

However, the public service remains segregated across occupations and hierarchies. While the overall distribution of sexes among the three categories of civil servants is roughly equal, the majority of women are working in typically female occupations (Rouban 2008b, p. 244). This leads to a misinterpretation of the rather equal share in *Catégorie A* (see Table 5.6): if

Table 5.6   France: gender distribution in the public sector

	Men	Women
Catégorie A	37.2	62.8
Catégorie B	44.2	55.8
Catégorie C	37.6	62.4
All	38.8	61.2

Note: Row percentages.

Source: Ministère de la décentralisation et de la fonction publique (2014, p. 92, figure V1–14).

education is excluded, the proportion of women in *Catégorie A* decreases to around 33 per cent. Or, as Rouban (2008b, pp. 244–45) pointed out, whereas 'women constitute more than 59 per cent of secondary school teachers, only 40 per cent of line managers and 19 per cent of top level managers are women.'

The years 1981–90: modernization, extension, and incremental reforms

Even though around 420 decrees have been issued by the central government in Paris since the 1950s to modernize administrative procedures (Thoenig 2005, p. 686), the core elements – a Weberian state bureaucracy, a highly centralized structure, a specific and strong employment status, and a specific public service identity and self-understanding – of the French public employment system remained relatively stable over the long term. For a long period, growth in the public sector was basically due to the post-war educational and administrative expansion (Béduwé and Planas 2002, pp. 116–18). It was only under the first Socialist government in 1981 that a major shift in the basic organizational principles took place. The rather homogenous central civil service was extended to the public health sector and to workers providing public services on the local level (for example, waste collection). While the workforce on the municipal level and in the public health system had been employed under a variety of different employment conditions until the 1980s (Mossé and Tchobanian 1999, p. 133), workers on the local level now became part of the *fonction publique territoriale,* and thus civil servants with the enactment of the threefold system of the French public sector in 1983.[21] At the same time, the right to strike became an active right for all civil servants.

The enactment of this system generated more homogenous public employment relations. Pay for all civil servants became the object of legal regulation.[22] The Law of 13 July 1983 set remuneration for the three different levels of public employment under uniform regulation and formalized the right of trade unions to negotiate with the government over remuneration. As bargaining is centralized for the whole public sector, bargaining on the local level is not relevant (Burnham 2000, p. 109). As a result, 'France has probably the most centralized wage-setting system of all 27 EU Member States' (EUROFOUND 2007, p. 29). While the 1983 law has been considered, on the one hand, a 'milestone in the convergence of private and public sector employment relations, ... on the other hand, it can be seen as no more than a political sop to the unions – recognizing their legitimacy but without giving them any substantial new power' (Mossé and Tchobanian 1999, p. 143). Collective agreements have no legal status and they do not override the government's unilateral power for decision-making. Moreover, the government decides when pay negotiations take place and defines strict parameters of negotiation. Nevertheless, as it is the outcome of a political compromise, all players, including the government, adhere to it.

Remuneration comprises a base wage and job-related supplements, as well as non-work-related supplements (such as housing and family allowances, both calculated from a system of index points). In addition, premiums exist for certain functions. A specific index point is defined for all grades and levels of employment. Depending on the level of technical expertise or responsibility attached to certain jobs or functions, further index points based on the NBI (*novelle bonification indiciaire*) are added. The value of 100 index points is determined in annual pay negotiations (Burnham 2000, p. 110). In principle, wages are centrally negotiated through collective bargaining between social partners as established in 1983, and should at least reflect changes in the cost of living, but the outcome of the bargaining process is not legally binding for the government. Unlike in the United Kingdom, wages in the public sector are not settled in reference to private sector pay. In practice, the level of the multiplier applied to the pay indices on the single integrated pay structure is still decided unilaterally by governments. Public pay levels thus signify policy orientations, public budgetary conditions, and, to some extent, political business cycles (Bargain and Melly 2008, pp. 5–6). Due to strong labour regulations in the private sector (minimum wage, working duration, unemployment benefits, job protection), the public sector wage gap is smaller in France than in liberal market economies (Lucifora and Meurs 2006, p. 54). The bargaining process may only influence compensation through changes in bonuses and premiums, or through upgrades in the pay ladder of a given occupation. Apart from that, union representation plays a key role in the consultative committees (*comités techniques*) within the different administrations and the different *corps*. Union representatives here participate in fixing the individual career patterns (that is, job assignments and promotions) (Audier et al. 2012, p. 9).

Civil servants start at the lowest index point for their grade and, providing their performance is satisfactory, move upwards through the scales. Supplements are fixed amounts. Four different hierarchical levels entailing different salary scales are differentiated. Progression within these levels reflects work experience in the specific job. As a result, pay is uniform for the same occupations throughout the whole public sector in France. Pay components include basic pay and allowances, complemented with lifelong employment and special pension schemes. While it is common in the top positions of the civil service to change from public to private organizations through the so-called *pantouflage* (revolving doors), in general, personnel transitions within the public service as well as between public and private sectors are difficult because of the highly specialized *corps* system.

The extension of the civil service status homogenized the legal status of public service employees. At the same time, it multiplied the number of *corps* and their specific training and career paths. Following the technocratic tradition of the French civil service, each *corps* refers to a job family and qualification, and has to be understood as an internal sub-labour market with its own recruitment and selection procedures. Mobility between *corps* was, until recently, limited. Seniority plays the main role in all the *corps* when it comes to career advancement, with split grades, each composed of different levels. Many bonuses also depend on the *corps*, thus they play a crucial role in the pay system. Progression inside a given grade through the levels is mainly based on seniority within the grade. Specialization grew since there are a large number of specific and specialized hiring bodies (for example, ministries, local governments, health facilities, branch offices, *établissements publics*) in each of the three different sections of civil service (state, local governments, health). By the end of the 1980s, about 1,800 different *corps* existed and were managed and promoted according to the same particular statute supplementing the general statutory rules, such as the *corps* of tax inspectors and the *corps* of police officers. Due to the missing horizontal and restricted vertical mobility (only by internal exams), the French public service became a massive and inflexible construction. Furthermore, with the decentralization of fiscal and administrative rights to the local level,[23] the sub-central level from now on was able to decide on the number of public servants needed, leading to a veritable 'hiring boom'. Between 1982 and 1985, while the government was still steering at a distance, local government employment increased by 16 per cent compared to only 1.4 per cent on the central level (Rouban 2008b; Silicani 2008, p. 19; for more recent developments, see Kroos 2010). The methods of selecting, training, and paying employees of local authorities – whether city managers or street cleaners – remained defined by (national) law (Thoenig 2005, p. 688). In sharp contrast to the British pattern, the core *fonctionnaires citoyen* saw a strengthening of their role in both qualitative and quantitative terms since the 1980s. Neither market institutions nor incentive schemes were introduced to replace bureaucratic procedures. The neo-liberal discourse remained focused on the privatization of state-owned enterprises, which peaked during the period when the Socialist Party and their allies ruled France from 1981 to 1986.

The years 1990–2000: reform without doctrine

In 1989, a new policy entitled Public Service Renewal, initiated by Prime Minister Michel Rocard (1988–91), was launched. This agenda centred on a managerialist philosophy, the spread of centres of responsibility and performance contracting within ministries, and a change in career structures to facilitate upward mobility. The modernization programme valued service quality and user orientation. It was an internal organizational approach employing quality circles with strong participation of public servants and controlled through mutuality. The reform claimed an explicit link to public service values of public servants (Jeannot 2006). Experiments and learning processes were favoured as the dominant style of reform. In a context of major social unrest within the public sector in 1988–89, the 'Renewal' programme (*Le renouveau du service public*, February 1989) offered an acceptable trade-off by enhancing the participation of civil service unions and the social dialogue while introducing principles of HRM and techniques such as a policy evaluation programmes. It also experimented with forms of contracts between ministries (Jeannot 2003; Bezès 2009, p. 357): incremental budgetary micro-changes were adopted, like the 'aggregated headings', intended to give ministerial managers latitude in how to (re)allocate appropriations; contracting between central administrations, state local units, and the Budget Directorate was tested; and more control over spending at the territorial level was adopted. Ideas, policy instruments, goals, and the scope of reform were largely redesigned by the mid-1990s, and the NPM 'tool-kit' gradually became the dominant inspiration in administrative reform policies (Bezès 2009, pp. 341–413). These were mainly adopted by top bureaucrats from the French *grands corps* through repeated state reform committees and reports (Bezès 2009, pp. 372–87).

However, despite the ambitious rhetoric of a 'watershed reform', the Public Service Renewal Programme only left a 'faint footprint' (Bezès 2001, p. 124) on the public service. The public employment regime remained relatively stable, if not stuck on the values of a strong administrative state still responsible for the planned provision of public services. In particular, centralized control of personnel was still in place, and no reforms aimed at bringing budgeting, accounting, and performance measurement into a single, compatible framework were established. Obviously, in the different units and departments, the higher *corps* reinterpreted the reform along established lines of corporatism (Cole and Jones 2005). Furthermore, the conflicting interpretations of the logic of reorganization between different ministries led to a heterogeneous implementation practice (Bezès 2009, pp. 371ff.). In sum, the reform programme was unsuccessful either in shifting the public service towards efficiency or in promoting the idea of cutting costs (Cole 2010, p. 346). To the contrary, the reforms did not succeed in clearly separating competences and authority, but instead mostly doubled them. The administrative interweaving (*enchevetrement*) and the institutional competition intensified (Kuhlmann 2011). The central state hereby rather enforced the *mille-feuille administrative* and even allowed for the extension of the public service (Kroos 2010). Nevertheless, the reform emphasized the need for a more user-friendly administration, as some reform aspects focused on a more equal access to public services for 'excluded' citizens, such as the creation of 'One Stop Shops' in rural and poor urban areas (Clark 2002, p. 32; Chevallier 1996, pp. 190–91).

The years 2001–14: top-down changes

In the 2000s, the desire to rehabilitate the state apparatus was widely shared among French elites (Pollitt and Bouckaert 2011) and the public deficits and debts inspired NPM reforms in 2002. The re-election of President Jacques Chirac and the election of Prime Minister Jean-Pierre Raffarin indicated a renewed interest in liberal reforms (Rouban 2007). The ongoing determination to modernize the state was manifested in the establishment of a new directorate of state modernization *(Direction générale de la modernisation de l'État)* in 2005 (Bordogna and Neri 2011).

In this period, reforms inspired by NPM ideas were initiated on four levels. First, the budget reform *Loi organique relative aux lois de finances* (LOLF)[24] was enacted in 2001. Its intention was to decrease the budget deficit, which had doubled from 1991 to 1995, and to increase budgetary control of the parliament. In brief, it consisted of budgeting and performance measurement and was directed at increasing executives' accountability for budgets. Planning became strategic, containing annual performance plans, target formulation, and evaluation. Before the LOLF, deputies voted on the budgetary plans of all ministries at once. Evaluation of policy objectives and expenditures was not envisaged, and parliament lacked budgetary oversight. Furthermore, the transfer of funds across budgets was limited. The LOLF allocated the budget according to programmes which were defined much more broadly than the old budgetary chapters were. Moreover, it enabled the transfer of funds across expenditure categories within programmes. As staff cuts could be spent on non-staff items, whereas the reverse was not possible, the LOLF produced one-sided incentives to reduce staff costs. The new flexibility in budget allocation also allowed for shifting jobs between *corps*. Furthermore, the LOLF introduced a budgetary requirement formulating objectives of each programme, as well as a set of performance indicators (Cole 2010). The implementation of the LOLF from 2006 onwards served as a vehicle for internal changes, like the increased use of HRM techniques, accelerating the whole reform process. The power of managers was devolved and performance-related bonuses and pay for high level bureaucrats were introduced (Bordogna and Neri 2011; Pollitt and Bouckaert 2011; Rouban 2008a).

Second, and even more important, this new legal order required public servants to take a 'pro-active role that clarifies their responsibility' (Corbett 2010, p. 226). The reform process was paralleled by the transition from a resource-based to a result-based approach in order to create greater flexibility, particularly in terms of pay. Increases in salary are now based on employees' performance evaluated during previous employment periods (Forest 2008, p. 326). With the introduction of individual PRP in 2008, a structure was established to remunerate individual performance for the first time.[25]

Third, the management of the public service focused on a so-called internal externalization (Audier et al. 2012, p. 10) that refers to efforts to *increase flexibility* within the public service. This had important effects for employment status. Due to the pressure to cut costs, especially the local governments make greater use of the recruitment of non-civil servant employees, which has increased in recent years despite strong opposition from trade unions. In 2012, the government under the conservative President Nicolas Sarkozy enacted a law that aimed to reduce the number of fixed-term contracts. Although it improved temporary workers' access to permanent contracts, it did not go so far as to offer them civil servant status.[26] Furthermore, the career system became leaner. The reduction of *corps* from 685 in 2007 to 380 in 2009 explicitly aimed at an increase in interdepartmental mobility and flexibility (Audier et al. 2012, p. 12).[27]

However, while the local governments were not subject to the two principal NPM approaches adopted – the budgetary law (LOLF) and the General Policy Review (RGPP) – they also had to face cost cuts. In response, the sub-central government public service increased the number of *non-titulaires* to meet the objectives to a much higher degree than the other public functions (Kroos 2010, p. 18). For example, in 2006, 42 per cent of all new recruits in the FPT were hired as *non-titulaire* (Ministère du Budget, des Comptes Publics et de la Fonction Publique 2008, p. 43). Even though the percentage of *non-titulaires* decreased in terms of full-time equivalents, the annual rise between 2002 and 2012 is 4 per cent in the FPT, as opposed to only 0.6 per cent in the FPE and 2.8 per cent in the FPH. This can be explained by different recruitment strategies, since the majority of *non-titulaire* in the FPT is employed on a part-time contract (Kroos 2010, p. 17).

Table 5.7 France: distribution of public employment, according to *fonction publique*, 2002 and 2012

	Catégorie A		Catégorie B		Catégorie C	
	2002	2012	2002	2012	2002	2012
Fonction publique de l'État (ministères et Épa)	44.3	54.6	24.5	25.2	31.2	20.1
Fonction publique territoriale	7.8	9.2	13.6	13.6	78.7	77.1
Fonction publique hospitalière	13.7	30.2	36.9	20.4	49.4	49.4
Total	27.4	33.8	23.6	20.2	49.0	46.0
Belonging to non-educational civil service	13.7	20.2	23.4	22.0	62.8	57.8

Note: Entries in percentages, row sums per year.

Source: Ministère de la décentralisation et de la fonction publique (2014, p. 92, figure V1–9).

Table 5.7 summarizes the general distribution of the three categories for the three types of civil servants in 2002 and 2012. Both in general government and in the health sector, the share of *Catégorie* A has increased substantially, at the expense of *Catégorie* C and *Catégorie* B, respectively. The number of public sector employees with prerogative employment status increased in particular in the public health sector and in education (Gautié 2013, pp. 112–13).

Last but not least, on the *fourth* level, pay in the civil service was targeted to cut costs. The first pay measure introduced by Nicolas Sarkozy's government was a freeze on the point value of civil service pay from 2010.[28] Point value grew by 2.8 per cent over the 2008–11 period, at a time when inflation was 4.4 per cent, bringing a real-terms salary cut of 1.6 per cent. A second austerity measure was to reduce the number of civil servants and conduct corresponding reorganizations. The measure was embodied in the non-replacement of half of retiring civil servants. In this sense, cutting government service jobs was effective: 75,000 jobs were cut in 2008, and a further 45,000 were cut in 2009, which represents 5 per cent of government jobs over those two years.

Summary and outlook

In France, the first reforms took place from the early 1980s through the early 1990s and concerned decentralization and devolution of authority, followed by privatization. The second wave covered the 1990s and led to budget reform and the introduction of performance management in 2001. The third wave began in the early 2000s and contained a 'qualitative shift', with strong cutbacks and intensified performance management. The official objective was not to retrench public service activity, but instead to increase its productivity and quality by 'doing better with less'. However, the outsourcing of support activities to the private sector was encouraged, and a significant downsizing of jobs in central government public administration induced *de facto* withdrawal of some public service activities.

Compared to the key NPM policies described by Bach and Bordogna (2011, p. 2285), the French case still lacks much of a NPM model both in quantitative and qualitative terms. The number of public sector employees decreased only slowly, and no relevant reduction in the scope and intensity of prerogatives for employees in privileged positions can be observed (Bezès and Jeannot 2013). The replacement of seniority-based career trajectories by more differentiated, flexible, and individualized mechanisms is limited and most often introduced at the group level rather than at the individual level. The unilateral regulation remains stable, and there is no formal change in the public employment relations or a strengthening of managerial prerogatives. To the contrary, up until now, the French government set in place rather traditional cost-cutting strategies such as wage freezes and delayed or non-replacement of staff.

However, most reforms have been steered without any reference to social dialogue, and in the eyes of many public servants and the unions, the state as employer acted 'worse in term of social dialogue and accompanying measures than many large private companies' (Gautié 2013, p. 113). Since the presidency of Francois Hollande in 2012, the precarious working conditions of the *non-titulaire* have somewhat improved. Moreover, Hollande launched his own socialist version of a state reform programme entitled the 'Public Policy Modernization Programme' (*Modernisation de l'Action publique*, MAP). It shows important differences from the General Review of Public Policies (RGPP) implemented under Nicolas Sarkozy (2007–12). The MAP encompasses state ministries, local government, the welfare system, and public agencies and relies on policy evaluations rather than fixed targets to be applied indiscriminate of sector. Unlike the NPM approach, targets would be determined at the end of a process of negotiation with the social partners rather than in accordance with a budgetary template (Cole 2014, p. 117). Consequently, in 2013, the individual PRP was abolished and replaced by a competence-oriented model called IFSE (*Indemnité de fonctions, de sujétions et d'expertise*).[29] This new system can be understood as a clear break with the management-by-objectives approach set up under the Sarkozy government, which only merits individual flexibility and change. Instead, recent performance, professional experience, and structural effects like overtime and work intensification are merited on the basis of the work performed.

Sweden

The Swedish public employment regime inherited from the 19th century state originally exhibited the characteristics of a career-based system. In the wake of incremental reforms that started as early as the mid-1960s, the current public employment regime is largely harmonized with employment in the private sector. Principally, the same general labour law applies to the public sector as well as to all the other sectors of the labour market. Except for a few positions (such as judges), there is no lifelong employment guarantee for Swedish central government employees, and the rules on job security as set out in the 1982 Employment Protection Act (*Lag (1982:80) om anställningsskydd*) apply to almost all employees with permanent contracts, both in the public and private sectors. While a few advantages for central government employees remain, these are not determined unilaterally, but rather benefits are generally determined through collective agreements.

The Swedish public administration system is marked by two interrelated elements: a far-reaching delegation of employer responsibilities on all administrative levels; and the use of multi-tiered collective agreements instead of laws for establishing pay and other employment conditions. This decentralized system is regulated by different control mechanisms, including the principle of public access to official documents (*offentlighetsprincipen*), strong union involvement, and new forms of accountability to the central government. The following section will show that the changes in the Swedish public employment regime are linked to both the historically expanding state and administrative structure, and to the establishment and evolution of the 'Swedish Model'.[30]

The traditional administration and the expansion of the welfare state

Sweden is a constitutional monarchy with a representative and parliamentary government, as well as constitutionally stipulated local self-government. This construction has been characterized as a decentralized unitary state (Kersting et al. 2009, p. 42). A key feature of the Swedish state structure is the considerable degree of autonomy at all three administrative levels (that is, central government, counties, and municipalities). This autonomy is expressed in a high degree of self-government, independent elections, and the right to levy taxes (Von Otter 1996, p. 102; Wilks 1996, p. 23). At the central government level, there is a separation between relatively small ministries (*departement*) that are responsible for policymaking and the agencies (*statliga förvaltningsmyndigheter*) that are largely independent organizations for policy implementation.

The government issues general instructions on the agencies' policies and activities, but otherwise they have a high degree of autonomy given the absence of ministerial rule and a prohibition of direct government interference into the agencies' exercise of public tasks. This peculiar construction dates back to the 17th century when agencies were set up as a counterweight against the power of the king (Wollmann 2008, p. 269). Currently, the vast majority of the approximately 237,000 central government employees (Statistiska centralbyrån 2014) work in approximately 250 agencies; only about 2 per cent work in the Swedish Government Office (*Regeringskansliet*), a single formal organization headed by the prime minister in which the ministries are jointly organized (Jacobsson and Sundström 2009, p. 104).[31] Following mergers, closings, and corporatization, the number of government agencies has declined over the past two decades. In the beginning, this process was accompanied by a sharp reduction in the workforce at the central government level: from 1992 to 2001, the number of employees declined from 326,400 to 202,100. However, in the last decade the number rose again to 237,300 employees (Statistiska centralbyrån 2014). The agencies cover a wide range of responsibilities, including: infrastructure, work life, care and education, tax administration and customs, culture, development, supervision and evaluation of public services, environment and technology, courts, police and prosecution authorities, defence, higher education and research, and commission-based activities. Each university and college can be considered a government authority of its own (Statistics Sweden 2008, pp. 83–85, 89). Taken together, universities and colleges constitute the largest area within central government, accounting for about 29 per cent of all central government employees in 2010. This is followed by the Swedish Police Service, accounting for about 13 per cent, and defence, accounting for circa 10 per cent of central government employees (Statistiska centralbyrån 2011).[32] Depending on their specific function, agencies vary considerably in size, the largest being those that require local offices across Sweden in order to fulfil their tasks.[33]

The Swedish subnational level comprises two tiers: counties (*landsting*) and municipalities (*kommuner*). Sweden has a strong tradition of local self-government, and the independence of counties and municipalities is primarily reflected in their considerable fiscal and budgetary autonomy. A large part of their expenditures are covered by personal income tax. The currently 20 counties (including the regions of Gotland, Halland, Skåne, and Västra Götaland) are primarily responsible for the management of the health care system.[34] In 2013, about 236,000 individuals were working for the counties (Statistiska centralbyrån 2014). The 290 municipalities have a wider range of functions, which primarily relate to the autonomous planning, organization, and provision of social welfare services.[35] This multitude of tasks is also reflected in the number of employees, which amounts to 790,000 (Statistiska centralbyrån 2014).

The development of this decentralized administrative structure was not only backed by a perception of the state as a benevolent actor and source of solidarity – reflected not least in a linguistic assimilation of 'state' and 'society' common to all Nordic languages (Kananen 2014, p. 78) – but it was also, to a considerable extent, shaped by and geared towards the establishment and expansion of the Swedish welfare state between the 1950s and 1970s. While on the central level the dominant Swedish Social Democratic Workers' Party (*Sveriges socialdemokratiska arbetareparti*, SAP[36]) formulated policies, 'local government was given the task of implementing and, to a significant extent, financing the unprecedented growth of Sweden's welfare state…– which in many regards can be called a *local* welfare state' (Wollmann 2008, p. 263). In other words, while the building of the social democratic welfare state required a considerable centralization of political and administrative decision-making, '[t]he sheer size and the complexity of the huge welfare commitment required considerable delegation and decentralization of operative and production tasks' (Premfors 1998, p. 158). As a consequence, the public sector grew both in terms of public employment and public expenditure. Between 1950 and 1980, the share of public sector personnel in total employment more than doubled from 15.2 per cent to 38.2 per cent (Peters 1985, pp. 270–71), the most rapid expansion taking place during the 1970s. While in 1960, the ratio of public expenditure to GNP was still close to the OECD average at about 30 per cent, by 1980, it exceeded 60 per cent, far above the OECD average of about 40 per cent (Wollmann 2008, p. 264). For society as a whole, the establishment of the welfare state created wealth for vulnerable groups and reduced the differences between social classes by providing the entire population with the same standards of health care, education, and childcare. It also decreased the unpaid reproductive work mostly done by women by providing them with jobs in an expansive service sector (Von Otter 1999, pp. 87–92).[37] The concept and the quantitative expansion of the universal Swedish welfare state also contributed to the development of a specific administrative culture which has been described as 'cooperative, consensus-seeking, problem oriented and pragmatic [and is] characterized by a high degree of informality, bridging organizational borders and hierarchical levels' (Hustedt and Tiessen 2006, p. 38). This 'cooperative contact culture' (Jann 2000, p. 341) or 'collegial administration' (Lehmbruch 1991, p. 144) is combined with a traditionally 'very strong credo in *Rechtsstaat* ideals and values guiding the public bureaucracy' (Pierre 2003, p. 184).

Public employment before 1980: public servant tradition and early reforms

Distinct forms of employment at the Swedish central government level date back to the early 17th century. In contrast, the rural local level was dominated by voluntary and lay administrations until the 1950s, which was only replaced by full-time professional administrative personnel as a consequence of growing tasks and the enlargement of municipalities following territorial reforms (Häggroth et al. 1999, p. 15; Kuhlmann and Wollmann 2010, p. 65).[38] The longer tradition of central government employment, together with the higher degree of centralization as compared to the local level, might explain the imbalance in both the academic literature and in official documents on public employment in Sweden. While central government employment is comparatively well documented, the quantitatively larger subnational employment is mostly mentioned from a functional perspective, that is, concerning its outstanding importance for the provision of social services. Consequently, the following description focuses primarily on developments at the central government level. However, what holds for the Swedish central government 'also applies to other areas of the public sector, although trends there have either sped ahead or lagged behind those at the centre' (Murray 2000, p. 169).

From the early 17th century until the mid-1960s, the Swedish central government administration was characterized by a public servant system. Agencies were staffed by merit-based career civil servants (*ämbetsmanna*), whose core values were independence, objectivity, integrity, and adherence to the law (Ehn 2011, p. 18; Premfors 1998, p. 156; Wollmann 2008, p. 271). Central government employees enjoyed constitutionally guaranteed tenure, which should ensure administrative integrity and independence from government (Murray 2000, p. 175). In contrast to the private sector, where working conditions and terms of employment were subjected to strongly centralized collective bargaining since the end of the Second World War, the working conditions and terms of employment of central government employees were unilaterally defined by the government. This was primarily justified with the argument of sovereignty, that is, the importance of the preservation of democratic government and the state's responsibility for the effective delivery of services. In this regard, 'conflicts between employers and employees could not be allowed to have an influence on the performance of public sector services and their quality [and] [t]he civil service was felt to require specific loyalty and obedience' (Gustafsson and Svensson 1999, pp. 119–20).

The unilaterally determined pay system was extremely rigid. Every position was ranked within a uniform grade system and pay was set according to the grade. Agencies were not entitled to create positions and define their grading, but this was a prerogative of the government or the Swedish Parliament (*Riksdag*). The only avenue of pay advancement for a public employee was the application and appointment to a position with a higher grade. In this context, the criterion for promotion had a rather formal character and was primarily based on the number of years of service (Andersson and Schager 1999, p. 244). Although there has never been a special examination or recruitment test (Murray 2000, p. 174), '[t]he natural educational route to the traditional civil service posts was through legal studies [and] [f]or many years lawyers were the dominant profession in the Swedish administration' (Petersson 1994, p. 105). This dominance of the legal profession gradually eroded from the second half of the 19th century onwards as a result of a shift towards professional knowledge over the course of industrialization as more and more engineers and economists started working for the central government (Ehn 2011, p. 19). From 61 per cent in 1917, the share of public employees with an education in law dropped to 29 per cent in 1971 and 21 per cent in 1990 (Ehn et al. 2003, p. 437).

Based on the principle of equality as a cornerstone of the Swedish Model, starting in the mid-1960s, political elites and trade unions actively promoted the harmonization of the traditionally diverging working conditions and terms of employment between the public (especially central government administration) and the private sector. Among a series of bigger and smaller reforms, two major milestones have been the introduction of collective bargaining for central government employees in 1965 and the reform of labour legislation since the early 1970s (Ehn 2011, p. 20; Gustafsson and Svensson 1999, pp. 117, 120).

In 1965, the unilateral determination of employment conditions was abolished. The trade unions in the central government sector were given the legal right to negotiate collective agreements with the central government and were also granted the right to strike.[39] A newly established agency, the National Collective Bargaining Office, was delegated the task of negotiating for the government as an employer (Andersson and Schager 1999, pp. 244–45). Apart from equality considerations, negotiations were regarded to be more effective for regulating the employment conditions of public employees since they allowed different interests to adjust to each other (Gustafsson and Svensson 1999, p. 120).

Although the bargaining system was aligned to the conditions in the private sector, 'the rigid structure of pay coupled to positions and grades remained unaltered [and] [c]ollective agreements on changes in the level and structure of pay had to work within this framework' (Andersson and Schager 1999, p. 246). Moreover, the autonomy of the new agency as an employer representative was restricted by the provision that all collective agreements had to be submitted to the government for final approval. In this regard, the high costs of pay increases 'prompted the Cabinet to intervene more vigorously in the pay-bargaining process' (Murray 2000, p. 172).

Apart from the introduction of collective bargaining, major efforts have been made to make the general labour legislation commonly applicable to both the private and the public labour market. Among these activities were the 1974 Employment Protection Act (*Lag (1974:12) om anställningsskydd*) and the 1974 Trade Union Representatives Act (*Lag (1974:358) om facklig förtroendemans ställning på arbetsplatsen*) (Ministry of the Budget 1978, p. 12). In addition, the *Riksdag* enacted the 1976 Co-Determination in the Workplace Act (*Lag (1976:580) om medbestämmande i arbetslivet*), which applied to both the private and the public sector, and the 1976 Public Employment Act (*Lag (1976:600) om offentlig anställning*), which was restricted to state employees.

The 1976 Co-Determination in the Workplace Act reshaped the Swedish labour law in many respects. It is the final and most important piece of labour legislation that resulted from the trade unions' efforts for industrial democracy (that is, efforts to increase employee participation in the decision-making process in companies) (Åsard 1986; Haug 2004). The law, which has been supplemented by special co-determination agreements, guarantees employees the right of information and sets out rules for joint decision-making between the employer and employee organizations on matters connected with terms of employment, as well as for the management and the distribution of work and general business activities. Although the employer is legally admonished to negotiate with employees prior to making any changes, if no agreement can be reached, the employer can decide unilaterally (Ministry of the Budget 1978, p. 20; Petersson 1994, p. 159). Even though public employees were formally granted the same right of co-determination as private sector employees, there existed self-imposed restrictions. While it was commonly acknowledged that public employees should have a considerable degree of influence on their working conditions, both public employers at the central and local levels and the main trade unions agreed that public employees' influence on the activities of public authorities was constrained by the 'sovereignty of political democracy' (Ministry of the Budget 1978, p. 15).

> All enfranchised persons – public employees included – are able by their votes to influence decisions concerning the activities to be conducted by national and local authorities…. It would be contrary to the established democratic order in Sweden – as expressed above all in the 1974 Instrument of Government and the 1977 Local Government Act – to allow public employees to obtain through the medium of collective agreements another, more direct form of influence than is exerted by other citizens on decisions about the *aims* (goals), *direction*, *scale* and *quality* of the activities of public authorities. (Ministry of the Budget 1978, p. 24)

In contrast to the Co-Determination in the Workplace Act, the 1976 Public Employment Act did not apply to the whole labour market, but exclusively to state employees. It contained rules and provisions for central government employees, for example on the filling of appointments, the right to accept extra employment, the termination of employment, and dismissal on grounds of redundancy. Besides this, it also contained several provisions on disciplinary liability, dismissal, suspension, and compulsory medical examination, as well as rules of procedure, for example on the authority to decide on various personnel issues (Ministry of the Budget 1978, pp. 14–15). For employees at the local level, the law only covered industrial disputes, whereas the 'employment and working conditions of these employees are regulated by other means' (Ministry of the Budget 1978, p. 14).

The introduction of collective bargaining into the public sector and the establishment of an almost completely common labour legislation led to an approximate equalization of the working conditions and terms of employment between the public and the private sector. This provided a solid foundation for intensified reforms of public employment in the 1980s and 1990s.

Public employment reforms since 1980: decentralization as a path-dependent reform strategy

The reforms of public employment mainly took place between the early 1980s and mid-1990s, and have been part of the more general restructuring of the Swedish public sector. In this regard, the Swedish case indicates that public sector reforms are interdependent and that public personnel policies cannot be analysed in isolation from broader organizational structures and the budget system (Smith and Lidbury 1996, p. 261).

In the early 1980s, the public sector's established model was faced with two challenges, namely a leftist claim for more participation and a rightist claim for more efficiency (Premfors 1991, pp. 85ff.). Since the early 1970s, critics from the left increasingly complained about 'professional paternalism' (Von Otter 1994, p. 258), referring to oversized and rigid public bureaucracies, and called for more direct influence of individual consumers on public and social services (Burkitt and Whyman 1994, p. 280; Yates 2000, p. 166). The challenge from the right, in contrast, emanated from a budget deficit growing at an alarming rate since the late 1970s (with a peak of 13 per cent of GDP in 1982), which contributed to a change in the political climate. Previously, a strong cross-party consensus regarded state intervention and public spending as 'solutions', but after the early 1980s, government in general and public spending in particular were increasingly perceived of as major 'problems' (Premfors 1991, p. 86). The reforms that took place from 1982 onwards can roughly be divided into two major phases (1982–88 and 1988–2000) during which, depending on the politico-economic context and the dominant reform ideology, the challenges were approached with differing prioritization. Although the reforms focused on different priorities, observers speak of a 'path-dependent administrative reform strategy' (Pierre 2001, p. 133) that revolved around an extensive decentralization of the Swedish public sector. From the early 2000s onwards, however, Swedish public sector reforms took another turn and focused again on the recreation of a strong centre (Pierre 2010, p. 198).

The reforms between 1982 and 1988 focused on tackling the challenge from the left in the sense of a 'decentralization-cum-participation' (Premfors 1991, p. 92). Although the SAP that returned to power in 1982 took some measures to reduce the budget deficit, the reforms were primarily geared towards participation and decentralization in order to 'make the state machine more responsive and accessible to the ordinary citizen' (Pollitt and Bouckaert 2011, p. 308). Based on the *Leitmotif* 'from authority culture to service culture' (quoted after Premfors 1991, p. 88), the emphasis lay on the decentralization of activities from the centre to the subnational levels, as well as providing counties and municipalities with greater autonomy, thus enabling them to adapt their decisions and measures to local conditions and needs (Wilks 1996, p. 37). The overall conception of the reforms during this first phase was a '[p]olitical and administrative decentralization of a radical nature but within the context of a public sector essentially unchanged in scope, structure and commitments' (Premfors 1998, p. 150).

The mounting dissatisfaction with both Bo Holmberg (known as the 'decentralizer'), who had been at the top of the Ministry of Public Administration (*civildepartementet*) since its establishment in 1983, and his replacement following the general election in autumn 1988, marked the beginning of a second period of reforms.[40] At the end of the 1980s, the Swedish electorate made an unprecedented swing to the right and signs of a resurging economic crisis loomed large.[41] As a result, the 'economizers' within the Social Democratic Party gained the upper hand in the debates about public sector reform. When Sweden was hit by a severe financial crisis in the early 1990s with unemployment rising from 3–4 per cent to 11–12 per cent and a soaring budget deficit, '[e]fficiency and cost-cutting became the *Leitmotif* of the public sector' (Pierre 2010, p. 195). This meant a retreat from the traditional principles of Swedish social democracy with its focus on public sector expansion for solving both social and macroeconomic problems (Pontusson 1992; Premfors 1991, pp. 86–87). In contrast to its previous position, the Social Democratic government now generally advocated complementary private alternatives in service provision on the county and municipal levels. On the central government level, the most important measure was the implementation of a system of frame appropriations and 'management by results' for agencies.

> The basic rationale was that agencies should be given clear and concise goals by the department for their activities but that there should be only a minimum of interference in the agencies' pursuit of these goals. ... The reform aimed at according agencies even greater autonomy than usual in the process of cutbacks and restructuring, the philosophy being that agencies themselves were the best judges of where reductions should be implemented. (Pierre 2001, p. 135)

The reform agenda was radicalized towards a decidedly neo-liberal direction when in 1991, for the first time since 1930, a conservative-led government came into office. Even though this government had to compromise on its original plans in the face of the deepest economic crisis since the 1930s, the Swedish public sector underwent fundamental changes between 1991 and 1994 (Premfors 1998, pp. 150ff.). The slogans 'A free choice revolution in local government' and 'Dissolve the public monopolies' (Von Otter 1996, p. 105) stand for a period that, apart from massive cutbacks in all public expenditure, saw an expansion of private elements in the provision of social services and the formal privatization of public service utilities (Schalauske and Streb 2008). The autonomy of municipalities was further strengthened through a new system of central government grants which included fewer detailed regulations from the centre. As with the central government agencies, this was also primarily a means to limit public expenditure since it 'also permitted central government to fix tight frame budgets and leave the local authorities to sort out how they would allocate their circumscribed allocations' (Pollitt and Bouckaert 2011, p. 309). As a result, the total public employment was reduced from 1,640,700 to 1,368,200 between 1991 and 1995 (Ekonomifakta 2014). When the Social Democrats returned to government in 1994, public sector reforms lost their neo-liberal ideological note. Even so, although the pace of privatization and marketization in the public sector slowed down, it was not brought to a complete halt (Premfors 1998, p. 152).

From the early 2000s onwards, public sector reforms began to depart from the principle of decentralization. Given a certain inefficiency of the hitherto established control mechanisms and facing demographic and ongoing financial challenges, reforms have been characterized by a strategy of reducing the institutional autonomy of local authorities and agencies in order to ensure more compliance with government policies (Pierre 2010, pp. 196–98).

Apart from the above-named effects on the size of public employment, employment regulations and conditions were also subject to changes. With respect to pay regulations, public employment reforms were influenced by the developments in the Swedish private sector labour market in the early 1980s. Despite early reforms, the public sector pay and bargaining system differed considerably from the determination of pay in the private sector because of the unaltered rigid pay structure and political intervention. Until the early 1980s, the central government (especially when social democratic) pursued social redistributive goals connected with the principle of equality and worked towards agreements that reduced the dispersion of pay in the central government sector (Andersson and Schager 1999, p. 246; Gustafsson and Svensson 1999, p. 122). In a letter of intent produced during the first salary negotiations under the new rules in 1966, it is noted that 'in the distribution of salary raises the main emphasis should be put on an increase of the low income earners' salaries' (quoted after Gustafsson and Svensson 1999, p. 122).

This ideal eroded in the late 1970s when the private sector was confronted with difficulties in recruiting and retaining employees, forcing employers to offer wages above the levels agreed to in the central agreements. The erosion of centralized bargaining and the resulting wage drift led to a pay gap between the central government and the private sector (Andersson and Schager 1999, p. 246; Wise 1993, p. 79), which has been referred to as the 'double imbalance'. While the central government sector often paid low-skilled employees remarkably more than the private sector did (for example, a driver at the post office could earn 20 per cent more than the private counterpart), the salaries for highly skilled employees were 20 or 30 per cent below those in the private sector (Gustafsson and Svensson 1999, p. 122). Since the Swedish economy was characterized by a labour shortage in the 1980s, the central government had difficulties recruiting highly qualified staff such as IT experts, lawyers, and economists (Murray 2000, p. 173). This resulted in considerable tensions between the two sectors (Bender and Elliott 2003, p. 85), and it became evident in the early 1980s that the 'double imbalance' was unsustainable.

Reactions against the pay policy emanated from both public utilities and central government agencies which competed for labour with the private sector, and from 'those subsectors of central government in which competition for qualified labour was of a more long-run character and worked through the choice of careers by young people with higher education' (Andersson and Schager 1999, p. 246). The growing dissatisfaction of individual authorities with this competitive disadvantage contributed to 'the gradual erosion of the system of pay in the central government sector' (Andersson and Schager 1999, p. 246). Thus, personnel management and especially pay policy were decentralized and made more flexible in order to enable the central government sector to recruit and retain the required personnel.

Although a first step towards the decentralization of the pay system was taken in 1978,[42] the crucial break only occurred in 1985 with the adoption of the Government's Personnel Policy Bill, which made clear that pay policy and other employer policies should first and foremost be geared towards the fulfilment of agencies' activities (Andersson and Schager 1999, p. 247). It stated that '[t]he state's position in wage negotiations must be more securely based on the objective of achieving effectiveness and an appropriate supply of personnel' (quoted after Swedish Ministry of Finance 1995, p. 20). Furthermore, the bill postulated that 'substantial wage differentials should be avoided as regards employees with similar work in different labour market sectors' (quoted after Swedish Ministry of Finance 1995, p. 20). Thus, 'more market-oriented setting of pay was explicitly identified as desirable' (Andersson and Schager 1999, p. 247). The Government's Personnel Policy Bill has been considered the start of a new employer policy (Swedish Ministry of Finance 1995, p. 20). From that point onwards, the central government's traditionally emphasized egalitarian motives in pay setting had been 'replaced by a pragmatic personnel management philosophy', and wage-setting was 'moved out of its social, democratic context and into administrative renewal policy' (Gustafsson and Svensson 1999, p. 123).

The universal system of pay grades was formally abolished in 1989 when a framework agreement between the National Collective Bargaining Office and the trade unions replaced it with a system of individual and differentiated pay similar to the private sector (Andersson and Schager 1999, 247; OECD 2005, p. 153). Local governments experienced the same reforms during that period and made perhaps even greater progress in installing individualized pay systems (Wise 1993, p. 80).

In 1994, the Swedish government accomplished the final step in delegating HRM responsibility from the central level to the agency level (Gustafsson and Svensson 1999, p. 117; OECD 2005, p. 153). This was achieved by two measures. First, the government replaced the National Collective Bargaining Office in 1994 with the newly created independent Swedish Agency for Government Employers (*Arbetsgivarverket*). *Arbetsgivarverket* differs from other central government agencies in that it is a member organization which is completely run and funded by its members (that is, government agencies and other employers that are connected to the government sector). Its primary function is the negotiation of central agreements with the trade unions. Moreover, it develops employer policies for the central government sector and supports and advises its members in all aspects of employer policies (Arbetsgivarverket 2009b). The establishment of *Arbetsgivarverket* disconnected collective bargaining in the public sector from political influence.

> The principle behind the move is simply that as each agency is given responsibility for HRM, including pay, those employers should also have the corresponding freedom to determine the form and contact of relations and negotiations with the unions involved in those matters. (Smith and Lidbury 1996, p. 247)

Second, a flexible budget system with frame appropriations and 'management by results' was introduced with the aim of cutting costs. The reform of the Swedish budget process had been on the political agenda since the mid-1980s and resulted in the introduction of a more flexible budget system. Detailed annual appropriations containing specifications of different items were replaced by three-year frame budgets covering an agency's total administrative costs, including wage increases resulting from central and local pay negotiations. This was combined with stronger monitoring and evaluation of the agencies' outputs (OECD 2005, p. 153; Swedish Ministry of Finance 1995, pp. 14–15, 18; Wilks 1996, pp. 43–44).

In times of economic recession, the new budget system intended to ensure better longer-term control of public sector expenditures. Moreover, it required the agencies to improve the quality of their accounting systems. Among other reforms, the reform of the budget system was thus a 'response to the recession of the early 1990s, when the general government budget deficit underwent an acute deterioration' (Yates 2000, p. 162). In the old budget system, agencies were fully compensated for increases in labour costs that followed from central agreements between the National Collective Bargaining Office and the trade unions (that is, appropriations were adjusted on a flat-rate basis after each round of negotiations).

Given the guaranteed funding, unlike private employers, central government agencies were eager to accept high pay increases for their employees, as it made their pay level more competitive (Andersson and Schager 1999, p. 253; Swedish Ministry of Finance 1995, p. 18). Irrespective of their political colour, 'governments have been increasingly aware that the automatic funding of any cost increase that follows from the central agreements has perverse effects on the cost incentives of central government agencies' (Andersson and Schager 1999, p. 253). By introducing frame appropriations with cash limits, central government employers were exposed to the same incentives as private employers to keep the costs in the central agreements low. Consequently, there was no more need for government and parliament to approve central agreements because of budgetary considerations, and the respective rule in the Swedish Constitution was abolished in 1994

(Andersson and Schager 1999, p. 255). Apart from the economic point of view, the new budget system with unspecified frame appropriations was 'essential to enable the Government to delegate its employer responsibility entirely to the agencies under the new arrangements for state employers' (Swedish Ministry of Finance 1995, p. 18). Agencies now were – albeit within certain budgetary limits – fully independent in deciding the size and structure of workforce and wages (Gustafsson and Svensson 1999, p. 128).

As a consequence of the outlined reforms, since the mid-1990s central government agencies are almost completely autonomous with regard to their policies, as employers decide (or negotiate) on pay, promotion, recruitment, dismissals, and so on. This applies analogously to the subnational level, where as a result of decentralization, managers also gained increasing control over personnel policy, internal organization, and decision-making. Individual counties and municipalities have even 'taken on a far greater responsibility for all aspects of personnel policy in institutions such as schools, hospitals and prisons' (Wilks 1996, p. 32).

Since 2001, there are two possibilities for negotiating pay at the agency level (Arbetsgivarpolitikutredningen 2002, pp. 95–96): the older system of negotiations between the agency and the local unions, and a pay-setting dialogue between individual employees and their line managers (the so-called *lönesättande samtal*). Agencies and local union representatives have to agree on using the individual pay-setting dialogue (Bodiguel 1978).

On the subnational level, the equivalent to *Arbetsgivarverket* as an employer organization is the Swedish Association of Local Authorities and Regions (*Sveriges Kommuner och Landsting*, SKL). Although its organizational form and financing principally correspond to *Arbetsgivarverket*, it is different in that membership is voluntary. Nevertheless, all municipalities, county councils, and regions are currently members of SKL (SALAR 2009, p. 7; SKL 2015). The autonomy is limited by governmental monitoring of the local employer policy, and agencies report annually on their competence planning, pay level development, age structure, and staff turnover. Nevertheless, the decentralization of decision-making has resulted in considerable variation in employment conditions across local governments.

Summary: the characteristics of public employment in Sweden

Swedish central government employment was characterized by core elements of a civil servant system for a long time. Following a series of piecemeal and incremental changes that took place from the mid-1960s onwards, public employment in Sweden has become barely distinguishable from private sector employment since the mid-1990s. Specific legislation on public employment gradually became thinner, and specific allowances and benefits of public employees became more and more similar to those of the private sector. Perhaps even more important, employer responsibilities were delegated to authorities on all administrative levels, and highly decentralized collective bargaining became the established form of regulating employment conditions (Gustafsson and Svensson 1999, p. 136). While job security and pensions are set in national collective agreements between *Arbetsgivarverket* or SKL and the unions, working conditions and pay are established in collective or individual agreements at the authority level.

In the second half of the 1990s, official evaluations came to different conclusions on the delegation of employer responsibilities in central government. While the Government Commission of Inquiry on the Delegation of Employer Responsibility concluded that delegation generally had worked out well (*Sverige Kommittén angående den arbetsgivarpolitiska delegeringen* 1997), other reports issued concerns about increasing fragmentation of HRM in the central government (*Förvaltningspolitiska kommissionen* 1997; Parliamentary Auditors 1995). These concerns made some commentators – for example, Murray (2000, p. 188) – predict a re-centralization of HRM in order to constrain the staffing and pay flexibilities of agencies.

So far, the most recent encompassing official evaluation of the 1994 reforms, however, concluded that the delegation of employer responsibilities has generally been successful and explicitly did not suggest a more centralized approach to HRM (*Arbetsgivarpolitikutredningen* 2002). As a consequence, no efforts have been made to re-centralize the personnel policy. In contrast, with the introduction of pay-setting dialogues (*lönesättande samtal*) between individual employees and their line managers in 2001, the personnel system has obtained an even more decentralized character. However, the decentralized system of HRM is accompanied by different control mechanisms, including both traditional correctives, such as the principle of public access to official documents (*offentlighetsprincipen*) and strong union involvement, as well as new forms of accountability to the central government.

Comparative assessment of national public employment regimes

The narratives of the changes in the general, nationwide frameworks of public employment regimes reveal a variety of trajectories, according to which each country seems to follow its own, idiosyncratic path. While we will postpone a more detailed interpretation of the observed processes until Chapter 9, we pause for a moment to summarize the developments in view of the conceptualization of public employment regimes outlined in Chapter 3 (Table 3.2) by comparing the dominant traits before the 1980s to those present in the early 2010s. Tables 5.8 to 5.11 list brief characterizations of the public employment regimes for these two periods. These entries necessarily abstract from the details described in the country sections, and they oversimplify regulations and constellations that are much more complex in reality. Nevertheless, they give a bird's-eye view of the general trends.

Table 5.8   United Kingdom: dimensions and characteristics of public employment regulation

Dimensions and characteristics	Pre-1980s	Early 2010s
1. Regulation of employment conditions		
Legal status	Core civil service, increasing number of contractual employees	Declining number of civil service positions
Collective regulations	Authoritative and unilateral, highly centralized	Authoritative and unilateral, decentralized
Regulation of labour conflicts	Confrontative, including strikes	Unilateral decisions based on limited consultation with trade unions
2. Personnel system		
Mode of advancement	Career-based	Position-based (or mixed)
Openness	Low	High
3. Personnel management		
Entry requirements	Formalized	Less formalized and decentralized, discretion by agencies and departments
Recruitment	Centrally organized competitions	Autonomy of departments and agencies
Pay structure	Uniform national system	Core civil service, autonomy of departments and agencies
Evaluation and assessment	Predominantly seniority rules	Performance-based
Performance incentives	No	Encompassing system of incentives
Opportunities for promotion	Seniority-based	Performance-based
Further education	Flexible	Flexible
4. Integration function of public employment regime		
Payment, social security	High	Low
Employment security	High	Medium
Equal opportunity and treatment at the workplace	High	Medium to low
5. Specificity of public employment regime		
Difference as compared to private sector employment regime	High	Low, downward adjustment of conditions

Table 5.9 Germany: dimensions and characteristics of public employment regulation

Dimensions and characteristics	Pre-1980s	Early 2010s
1. Regulation of employment conditions		
Legal status	CS: Civil servant PE: Public employees (two status groups)	CS: Civil servant PE: Public employee (one status group)
Collective regulations	CS: Authoritative/ unilateral (federal law) PE: Collective agreement (one bargaining round)	CS: Authoritative/unilateral (federal law and *Länder* law) PE: Collective agreement (separate bargaining for employees of the *Länder* and the federal state together with the municipalities)
Regulation of labour conflicts	CS: Disciplinary law, no right to strike PE: Positive right to strike	CS: Disciplinary law, no right to strike PE: Positive right to strike
2. Personnel system		
Mode of advancement	CS: Career-based PE: Position-based	CS: Career-based PE: Position-based
Openness	CS: Low PE: Medium	CS: Low PE: Medium to high
3. Personnel management		
Entry requirements	CS: Formalized, high PE: Less formalized	CS: Formalized, high PE: Less formalized
Recruitment	CS: Special public service training pathways PE: General qualification	CS: Special public service training pathways (easier external entry) PE: General qualification
Pay structure	CS: Determined by law (federal states) PE: Negotiation-based	CS: Determined by law (federal/ *Länder*) PE: Negotiation-based
Evaluation and assessment	CS: Seniority rules PE: Seniority rules and performance-based	CS: Seniority and performance-based PE: Performance-based
Performance incentives	CS: No PE: No	CS: Yes, but very low PE: *Länder*: No; Municipalities and the federal state: Yes, but very low
Opportunities for promotion	CS: Seniority-based PE: Seniority-based and performance-based	CS: Seniority-based and performance-based PE: Performance-based
Further education	CS: Legally determined PE: Flexible	CS: Legally determined PE: Flexible

Continued

Table 5.9   Continued

Dimensions and characteristics	Pre-1980s	Early 2010s
4. Integration function of public employment regime		
Payment, social security	CS: Social security: very high PE: Comparatively high	CS: Social security: very high PE: Broad variety
Employment security	CS: Very high PE: Very high	CS: Very high PE: Broad variety, but still high
Equal opportunity and treatment at the workplace	CS: High PE: High	CS: High PE: high
5. Specificity of public employment regime		
Difference as compared to private sector employment regime	CS: High PE: High	CS: High PE: Broad variety, lower

Table 5.10   France: dimensions and characteristics of public employment regulation

Dimensions and characteristics	Pre-1980s	Early 2010s
1. Regulation of employment conditions		
Legal status	CS: Civil servant, small portion of *non-titulaire* (NT)	CS: Civil servant, growing number of *non-titulaire* (NT)
Collective regulations	CS: Authoritative/unilateral NT: Collective agreement	CS: Authoritative/unilateral NT: Collective agreement
Regulation of labour conflicts	CS: Disciplinary law, no right to strike NT: Positive right to strike	CS: Disciplinary law, right to strike, but 'minimal service' agreement, and no right to strike for police NT: Positive right to strike
2. Personnel system		
Mode of advancement	CS: Career-based NT: Position-based	CS: Career-based NT: Position-based
Openness	CS: Low NT: High	CS: Low NT: High

Continued

Table 5.10   Continued

Dimensions and characteristics	Pre-1980s	Early 2010s
3. Personnel management		
Entry requirements	CS: Formalized, high NT: Less formalized	CS: Formalized, medium NT: Less formalized
Recruitment	CS: Special public service training pathways NT: General qualification	CS: Special public service training pathways (internal flexibilization) NT: General qualification
Pay structure	CS: Determined by law NT: Negotiation-based	CS: Connected to general economic performance (index points)
Evaluation and assessment	CS: Seniority rules NT: Depending on hiring body	CS: Seniority-based and performance-based NT: Depending on hiring body
Performance incentives	CS: Yes, but informal, depending on hiring body NT: Informal	CS: Yes, very low NT: Yes, very low
Opportunities for promotion	CS: Seniority-based NT: None (temporary contracts)	CS: Seniority-based and performance-based NT: Low
Further education	CS: Legally determined NT: Flexible	CS: Legally determined NT: Flexible
4. Integration function of public employment regime		
Payment, social security	CS: Social security: very high NT: Comparatively high	CS: Social security: very high NT: Boad variety
Employment security	CS: Very high NT: High	CS: Very high NT: Medium
Equal opportunity and treatment at the workplace	CS: High NT: High	CS: High NT: High
5. Specificity of public employment regime		
Difference as compared to private sector employment regime	CS: High NT: Low	CS: High NT: Low

Table 5.11 Sweden: dimensions and characteristics of public employment regulation

Dimensions and characteristics	Pre-1980s	Early 2010s
1. Regulation of employment conditions		
Legal status	Public servant (until mid-1960s)	Employee
Collective regulations	Authoritative/unilateral (until mid-1960s); collective agreements (since mid-1960s)	Collective agreements
Regulation of labour conflicts	No right to strike (until mid-1960s); right to strike (since mid-1960s)	Right to strike
2. Personnel system		
Mode of advancement	Career-based	Position-based
Openness	Low	High
3. Personnel management		
Entry requirements	Low formalization	Non-formalized
Recruitment	General qualification	General qualification
Pay structure	Determined by law (until mid-1960s); negotiation-based	Negotiation-based
Evaluation and assessment	Seniority rules (until mid-1960s)	Performance-based
Performance incentives	No	Yes
Opportunities for promotion		
Further education		Flexible; decentralized
4. Integration function of public employment regime		
Payment, social security	High	High
Employment security	High (until mid-1960s)	High; 'permanent contracts'
Equal opportunity and treatment at the workplace	High	No special obligations for public employer, but generally high
5. Specificity of public employment regime		
Difference as compared to private sector employment regime	High (until mid-1960s)	Low

In the United Kingdom, the clear trend from the originally dominating ideal type of the Weberian civil servant toward NPM's ideal type of the service provider (Table 5.8) in practically all dimensions of the public employment regime reflects the fact that the neo-liberal ideology underlying the Thatcherite reforms has thoroughly altered the public employment regime. However, the extent of downward adjustment of public employment standards in line with similar or even more encompassing developments in the private economy is still striking and indicative of an impressive downward adjustment of employment conditions in the United Kingdom in general.

Compared to this sweeping transformation in the United Kingdom, the reorientation of the German public employment regime (Table 5.9) is modest at most. Instead of an alignment with the private sector, we observe an ongoing sharp distinction between a core public employment regime in which the civil servant status is maintained for large segments of the public workforce. Despite some scattered explorations with elements of performance evaluation and incentives, almost no aspects of the ideal type of the 'service provider' have been introduced at a wider scale, in part because the civil servants' prerogatives are constitutionally guaranteed. Nevertheless, two observations testify that the system is less immobile than this depiction would suggest. On the one hand, the traditional unified structure of employment regulation for civil servants is unravelling along territorial borders within Germany, which generates a growing diversity of employment conditions in the public sector. On the other hand, while maintaining the employment conditions for the core workforce, the state has become a major employer of marginalized labour, with increasing segments of the workforce being employed on temporary and part-time contracts with low pay (Keller and Seifert 2014).

France has taken a similar pathway. Resistance against major changes in the fundamental structure of the public employment regime has been fierce and no reforms in the spirit of NPM have been introduced on a wider scale. Nevertheless, the French administration has also been confronted with cost pressures, which have been dealt with by traditional cost-cutting strategies but without fundamental adjustments to the public employment regime. Instead, similar to Germany, marginalized employment has been created to some extent.

Quite the contrary has happened in Sweden. With the public servant status for almost all professions in the public service abolished in the mid-1960s, constitutional rigidity in the public employment regime is not an issue. In line with the hegemonic social democratic worldview, the alignment of the public and private sectors implied the extension of the public sector's employment to the private sector. However, along with the increasing cost pressures from the 1990s onwards went a piecemeal adoption of reforms which could be labelled as 'left-wing NPM' in contrast to the United Kingdom (Hood 1995). Hence, most public employees work under the conditions of a position-based career trajectory, internal and external flexibility, negotiated salaries, and routine performance evaluation.

All four countries have been core players in the European political game of the absolutist era and beyond. In that era, the monarchs established civil services which eventually evolved into 'modern' bureaucracies in the Weberian sense. Hence, in all four countries, the prototypical public employee was a civil servant. From this starting point, however, pathways forked in different directions. Viewed in retrospect, the major distinction separates the United Kingdom and Sweden as cases of far-reaching reforms towards the ideal type of the service provider from Germany and France as cases which maintained the fundamental traits of the Weberian ideal civil servant. Hence, discussing developments in these countries under the heading of the NWS is certainly a useful conceptual starting point. However, the substantial deviation from the ideal type of the civil servant suggests that a more nuanced assessment of the group labelled as Neo-Weberian is necessary.

The two countries which are nowadays close to the ideal type of the service provider followed very different trajectories to reach that point. Sweden's decision to abolish the traditional concept of the civil servant in an affluent period facilitated its choice for an encompassing and economy-wide upgrade of employment conditions. The United Kingdom's decision to abolish public employment prerogatives in a period of austerity, on the other hand, mandated a reverse alignment, resulting in a general down-grading of employment conditions. In that sense, Sweden and the United Kingdom represent a 'high road' and a 'low road', respectively, from the civil servant to the service provider.

Although both Germany and France have maintained the fundamental elements of the civil servant, their reform trajectories have taken different pathways as well. A major distinction is due to the state structure. Cost pressures have eventually caused Germany's federalist system to unravel the hitherto unified public employment regime into 17 separate regulation systems, which are gradually moving in different directions. In contrast, France undertakes its attempts to cope with the cost pressures in the context of its strictly vertically and horizontally layered system of the *fonction publique*. With an eye on those differences in approach, we can speak of a 'bottom-up' and a 'top-down' design of the Neo-Weberian path from the civil servant to the service provider. It is still up for debate, however, whether these countries will ever, in their totality, end up near the latter ideal type.

Implications for the analysis of sectoral developments – outlook on the next chapters

As we have seen in this chapter, public employment regulation is subject to change in all countries, but the extent to which traditional civil service employment features are altered varies considerably.

We will now shift the focus from the country level to the change of employment regulation by sector, taking into account that public service provision is heterogeneous and that a general country trend in re-regulation of public employment, though setting a basic framework, need not apply in the same way across the board. Rather, we assume that depending on the extent of devolution of state responsibility in different public sectors, the shift towards a more service provider-like employment type is more or less likely.

As argued in Chapter 2, we can discern three levels of unravelling of state functions, of which privatization of public infrastructure represents the most far-reaching case. Here the state transfers organizational and decision-making responsibility to private actors and, in turn, sets up regulatory agencies for market control. *Energy regulatory agencies* are an example of these newly founded national agencies, which provide a rare occasion for governments and top administrations to design these units unhindered by existing administrative traditions and employment regulations, and thus might be specifically open to NPM ideas. At the same time, the specialized task of market control requires highly educated personnel and confronts the state as employer with competition on the labour market due to the traditional public sector wage penalty in the higher wage brackets.

Instead of a complete transferral of organizational and decision-making responsibility, the state might also only devolve organizational responsibility and retain both the political and decision-making power. This is often the case with *waste collection* on the municipal level. Here, the delivery of the respective services becomes competitive and the state as employer competes with private providers who can draw on more flexible employment contracts. In turn, this might put pressure on the relatively advantageous public employment conditions, including a low-wage premium.

In contrast to these constellations, core state functions such as public safety represent a case where the state retains all three modes of responsibility. In the *police,* changes to the employment regime thus will not be triggered by environmental changes, such as the need for new administrative units or competitive pressure, but rather follow the pathway and logic of administrative reform. Radical changes might be less probable, not least due to a homogeneous and well-organized workforce vested with the civil servant status, and the importance of this group as voters.

In the following three chapters, we map the transformations of public employment regulation in energy regulatory agencies (Chapter 6), waste collection (Chapter 7), and the police (Chapter 8) in Germany, France, and Sweden. Again, the UK will serve as a reference case of extensive and early NPM-oriented public employment reforms. Starting with the functional specificities of the respective public good, each case study gives an overview of the sector-specific organization and reforms of employment by country. This will be followed by a comparative cross-country exploration of the employment regulations covering entry requirements and recruitment, pay, career advancement and further training, job security, and equal opportunity policies. Finally, sector-specific summaries highlight the extent and core features of alignment of public employment to private sector standards, recap sector-specific commonalities across countries, and indicate sector-related differences within national trajectories.

Part III
Sector Studies

6
Energy Regulatory Agencies

Introduction

From an economic perspective, the network-based energy sector has traditionally been conceived of as a natural monopoly (Cameron 2007, pp. 21ff.). From a political perspective, after the Second World War, most OECD countries developed specific concepts of gas and electricity as public services that are essential for the well-being of society and the economy and thus 'should be regulated in the public interest in terms of price quality, security and access' (Genoud and Finger 2004, p. 32). In most Western European countries, these economic and political considerations motivated the exclusion of electricity and gas supply from economic competition. Instead, the distribution of these resources was organized as vertically and horizontally integrated public monopolies. In spite of national differences in the institutional designs of the energy sector – for example, with regard to ownership structures and the scope of monopoly rights (Eberlein 2005, p. 43; McGowan 1996; Cross 1996) – a safe, comprehensive, and stable provision at reasonable prices was supposed to be guaranteed by non-commercial or semi-commercial publicly owned companies and ministerial steering.

Thus, the modern nation-state – characterized by territorial unity, rule of law, democracy, and market intervention (TRUDI) – made use of publicly owned companies and political steering to provide gas and electricity as a public good. However, the global wave of liberalization and deregulation policies since the late 1980s has fundamentally transformed this sector. While in the 'Golden Age' of the welfare state, the state had the political, decision-making, and organizational responsibility for the production, transmission, and distribution of gas and electricity, by the early 2000s, in most OECD countries, only the political responsibility has remained with the state, whereas decision-making and organizational responsibilities have been delegated to private actors (Schneider et al. 2005; Zohlnhöfer et al. 2008). This, in turn, 'gives rise to a two-fold need for re-regulation: firstly, in order to make markets work and to prevent market dominance from becoming concentrated in the hands of a few actors, and, secondly, to correct the outcome of market processes so that social and political goals may be met' (Héritier 2001, p. 828). Thus, in contrast to TRUDI, the regulatory state (Grande 1997; Grande and Eberlein 2000; Majone 1994, 1996, 1997; Moran 2002) is no longer the sole provider of gas and electricity, but a regulator of market processes.

This regulatory challenge in the aftermath of liberalization caused an extensive process of institution building and re-building across countries, with independent regulatory agencies (IRAs) as the most notable institutional innovation. The emergence of IRAs can be put in the context of a more general 'agency fever' (Pollitt et al. 2001), which refers to the transfer of government activities to authorities operating 'at arm's length' from the government. Accordingly, agency-type organizations are not restricted to regulatory tasks, but perform a wide range of functions. In order to be considered as an IRA, an agency must (1) have its own powers and responsibilities under public law; (2) be organizationally separated from ministries; and (3) not be managed by elected officials (Thatcher 2002, p. 127).

IRAs in the utility sector are empowered to regulate certain aspects of an industry in order to create and maintain fair competition and, thereby, to benefit consumers.[1] Their functions include the regulation of network access and pricing and end-user tariffs. In addition, regulatory agencies might possess judicial or quasi-judicial authority to set fines and penalties or act as arbitrators in conflicts between industry participants (International Energy Agency 2001, p. 14). The novel public task of creating and maintaining competition in a technically highly complex area such as the energy sector is considered very demanding. In contrast to the traditional state-owned monopoly which did not require any regulatory expertise, in the new regulatory state, 'effective regulation in electricity requires not just substantial numbers of staff, it requires substantial numbers of staff *with particular and scarce specialist skills* e.g. economists, lawyers, accountants, financial analysts as well as engineers' (Stern 2000, p. 136, original emphasis).

From a labour market perspective, difficulties in recruiting and retaining personnel most often concern specialists because their supply generally tends to be smaller than demand. As a consequence, the public and private sectors compete for personnel (OECD 2001). The prevailing opinion in the literature on Human Resource Management is that in order to be competitive in the contest for specialists, organizations 'have to sharpen up their recruitment and selection processes, reconsider their salary policies, and focus extra attention on methods of retaining skilled categories of staff' (Cole 2002, p. 14). In order to empower public departments and agencies for the competition for employees, during the last decades, governments have reformed their employment policies and increasingly delegated authority over HRM responsibilities to departments and agencies (OECD 2008, pp. 33–43). According to the OECD, the 'fact that managerial discretion and adaptation to business needs tends to lead to employment conditions closer to private sector rules ... reflects the market forces on a more open, cohesive and competitive labour market' (OECD 2008, p. 22).

If this were the case, especially in IRAs, one would expect to observe an alignment with private sector HRM practices because of their specific functional requirements. However, the approximation of public and private employment conditions is likely to be restricted by institutional constraints. Departments and agencies continue to be subject to country-specific institutional frameworks for public employment. These frameworks vary strongly between countries and comprise centrally defined and often formally codified rules and regulations on employment conditions, and HRM as well as regulations on the organizations' budgets. Even though IRAs have no power to change these centrally defined institutional frameworks, they may allow for different applications and interpretations through departments and agencies, making the concrete design of their HRM a result of 'compliance' with the established rules (Mahoney and Thelen 2010, pp. 10–14).

The following analysis refers to the energy regulatory agencies in the United Kingdom, Germany, France, and Sweden established from the late 1990s onwards. Apart from an analysis of agency-specific documents on employment regulation, the chapter is based on a small exploratory survey gathering information on size, organization, and HRM guidelines, as well as four expert interviews with the heads of the HRM departments of the respective agencies. Since HRM is of high importance in this sector, in the following account, ample room is given to the HR managers' perception of strategies for recruiting and retaining highly qualified personnel.[2]

The establishment of regulatory agencies in the energy sector

In Europe, the opening of the energy markets to competition was an integral part of the EU's internal market programme and was primarily driven by the European Commission. Although the first attempts at liberalization were controversial and caused opposition from most member states (for details, see Schmidt 1998; Eising 2000; Eising, 2002; Héritier 2001), countries gradually accepted the necessity of EU legislation for the creation of an energy market open to competition. The EU legislation that was passed from the mid-1990s onwards ended the member states' rights to keep up monopolies, insisted on separation of electricity generation from its transmission, and introduced rules for ensuring 'fair and effective' competition (Thatcher 2007, p. 208). While the first EU electricity and gas directives from 1996 and 1998 did not require the member states to establish IRAs, the directives from the early 2000s onwards for the internal market in electricity (Directive 2003/54/EC) and gas (Directive 2003/55/EC) explicitly prescribed the existence of national independent regulatory agencies and set out 'minimum requirements for the functions and competences of sector regulatory bodies charged by the Member States with supervising the electricity and gas sectors' (Cameron 2007, p. 98). Most importantly, it was required that the new regulatory authorities 'shall be wholly independent from the interests of the electricity industry. They shall ... at least be responsible for ensuring non-discrimination, effective competition and the efficient functioning of the market ... ' (Directive 2003/54/EC, Art. 23 (1)).

Apart from these requirements, no EU-level prescriptions exist on the formal organization of energy regulatory agencies, and member states have discretion over the choice of a competent body and its legal status (Cameron 2007, pp. 97f.). As a result, the organizational structures of the energy regulatory agencies of the United Kingdom, Germany, France, and Sweden are expected to reflect country-specific differences on the one hand and functionally motivated similarities on the other.

United Kingdom: Office of Gas and Electricity Markets (Ofgem)

The Gas Act 1986 and the Electricity Act 1989 constitute the first steps in the United Kingdom in the establishment of separate and independent regulatory agencies for the energy market: the Office of Gas Supply (Ofgas) and the Office of Electricity Regulation (Offer). Their creation was a central element of Thatcher's industrial policy, which aimed at 'transforming the former monopolistic public sector gas and electricity industries into competitive private sector industries and protecting the interests of consumers in terms of security and supply and controlling prices while that was achieved' (Bower 2003, p. 1). With the Utilities Act 2000, the gas and electricity regulators were merged into the Office of Gas and Electricity Markets (Ofgem). Ofgem has the status of a non-ministerial government department.[3] These are formally independent from the government and carry out executive functions as stipulated by legislature.[4] They are accountable to parliament and courts but not to the government. In line with this administrative status, Ofgem is exclusively staffed with members of the Civil Service, and in 2009 it counted 327 employees (Ofgem 2010a).[5] Its personnel policies are subject to the Civil Service Management Code (CSMC), first issued in 1996, which sets out regulations and instructions to departments and agencies on the terms and conditions of service of civil servants. The CSMC provides departments and agencies with far-reaching autonomy and, in a way, is characterized as a manifesto of delegation of HR responsibilities. Among other things, the code enables departments and agencies to determine staff numbers, recruit staff, decide on promotion, training, and development, and determine an appropriate pay and grading structure.[6]

Germany: Bundesnetzagentur (BNetzA)

The German Federal Network Agency (*Bundesnetzagentur*, BNetzA) was established on 1 January 1998 under the name Regulatory Authority for Telecommunications and Post (*Regulierungsbehörde für Telekommunikation und Post*, RegTP)[7] as a Higher Federal Authority (*Höhere Bundesbehörde*) within the scope of business of the Federal Ministry of Economics and Technology (Bundesnetzagentur 2009, p. 192). Higher Federal Authorities belong to the direct federal administration (*unmittelbare Bundesverwaltung*). This status guarantees the agency certain independence with regard to personnel, organizational, and financial matters (Schmidt 2005, p. 1027). In 2005–06, the RegTP was assigned the functions from the new Energy Act (*Energiewirtschaftsgesetz*) and the amended General Railway Act (*Allgemeines Eisenbahngesetz*) and renamed as the Federal Agency for Electricity, Gas, Telecommunications, Post, and Railway (Bundesnetzagentur 2009, p. 192). Since 2005, the agency is responsible for the regulation of the energy market.[8]

Hence, in contrast to the British, French, and Swedish energy regulatory agencies, the BNetzA is a cross-sectoral regulatory agency. In addition, apart from promoting competition and ensuring the appropriate provision of services in the different sectors through regulation, the BNetzA performs various other technical functions. Its tasks 'range from cases addressed in quasi-judicial proceedings in economic regulation areas right down to its nationwide presence for technical trouble-shooting' (Bundesnetzagentur 2009, p. 192). This variety of tasks is the reason for both the comparatively large size of the BNetzA and its heterogeneous workforce, consisting mainly of lawyers, economists, and engineers for regulatory tasks in the headquarters, and technical staff in numerous regional offices. As a Higher Federal Authority, the BNetzA's workforce reflects the dual system of legal employment statuses that is characteristic for all administrative levels in Germany. In June 2010, the German regulatory agency employed 2,197 civil servants (*Beamte*) subject to civil service law and 281 public employees (*Angestellte*) subject to the collective agreement TVöD. Of the total group, 172 were working in the division of energy regulation.[9] Due to the numerical dominance of civil servants, the dual system of legal employment statuses has no noteworthy effects on the HRM practices of the BNetzA, and civil service law is dominant.

France: Commission de Régulation de l'Énergie (CRE)

The French energy regulatory agency was established in March 2000 as the regulator of the electricity sector. In 2003, its competencies were expanded to the gas market and the agency was renamed from *Commission de Régulation de l'Électricité* to *Commission de Régulation de l'Énergie*. The CRE has the status of an *Autorité Administrative Indépendante* (AAI). According to the definition of the *Conseil d'État*, AAIs are institutions that act 'on behalf of the state without being subordinate to the government and enjoy, for the proper conduct of their assignments, guarantees which enable them to act in a fully autonomous fashion, such that there action may not be directed or censured except by the courts' (Conseil d'État 2001). AAIs, which have existed since 1978, cover various policy areas and differ considerably with regard to their size and organizational structure. As pointed out by Jorion (1998, p. 42), AAIs are a 'completely remarkable rupture with the Napoleonic conception of a hierarchical system where the administration is subject to the orders of the executive' (quoted in Elgie 2006, p. 215).

The exceptional position of AAIs within the French administrative system is also reflected by the fact that the regulation of employment relationships and personnel policies differs considerably from the traditional career-based French civil service. In order to be more flexible, the AAIs are independent from the unilaterally regulated framework of the *droit de la fonction publique* and are not obliged to employ *fonctionnaires titulaires* (Süsskind 2010, pp. 169f.). Instead, they can hire so-called *fonctionnaires détachés* from other central government authorities on secondment or *agents contractuels* who are not *fonctionnaires* but non-permanent employees under public law contracts.[10] As to the CRE, Art. 30 of the Law on the Modernization and Development of the Public Electricity Service (*Loi n° 2000–108 du 10 février 2000 relative à la modernisation et au développement du service publique de l'électricité*) explicitly states that the agency may employ civil servants on a regular basis or on secondment, or may recruit public employees. While employed by an AAI, the *fonctionnaires détachés* are detached from their *corps* and subject to the employment conditions of the respective AAI. They cannot earn less than in their previous position, and once they have finished their secondment, *fonctionnaires détachés* continue their careers in the civil service. Furthermore, the secondment is revocable, and they can be sent back to their original authorities for disciplinary reasons (*Loi n° 84–16 du 11 janvier 1984* Art. 45). *Agents contractuels* are normally recruited when there are no *fonctionnaires* available with the competencies to fill a certain post. Their contracts are limited to three years and can be renewed for a maximum of three more years (*Loi n° 84–16 du 11 janvier 1984* Art. 4; *Décret n° 86–83 du 17 janvier 1986* Art. 6). Although these contracts specify the terms and conditions of employment,[11] 'the legal situation of contractual agents is not always very clear, as they obey public law principles without having the same protection as their statutory counterparts (they do not enjoy job security) and without benefitting from the judicial rules used for private sector wage-earners' (Rouban 2008, p. 244). For example, in contrast to private sector employees with fixed-term contracts, *agents contractuels* do not receive severance pay after the expiration of their contracts, as provided for in the French labour law (*Code du travail* Art. L122–3-4). As regards collective rights, there are no differences between *fonctionnaires* and *agents contractuels*. Both are free to form associations and have the right to strike; however, there is no legal provision for collective bargaining. At the agency level, the CRE has established a mandatory institutional body for social consultation, a so-called *comité technique paritaire* (CTP), which is made up of equal numbers of representatives for personnel and the agency as employer (*Décret n° 2002–691 du 30 avril 2002*). This body is consulted about issues that relate to organization and resources, the functioning of services or personnel status, as well as safety-related issues (Commission de Régulation de l'Énergie 2003, p. 85). However, CTPs generally have a merely consultative function and do not prevent unilateral action from authorities (Vincent 2008).

At the end of 2008, only 14 per cent of the CRE's 129 employees were *fonctionnaires*, while 86 per cent were *agents contractuels* (Commission de Régulation de l'Énergie 2008, p. 10), which is an exceptionally high share.[12] While in the following years the level of overall employment at CRE more or less stagnated, the share of fixed-term employees even increased, as the 2013 figures of 11 per cent *fonctionnaires* and 89 per cent *agents contractuels* show (Commission de Régulation de l'Énergie 2014, p. 21).

Sweden: Energimarknadsinspektionen (EI)

The Swedish *Energimarknadsinspektionen* (EI) was formed in 2005 as a functionally independent part of the Swedish Energy Agency (*Energimyndigheten*), which was established in 1998 with a broader scope of energy-related responsibilities. In 2008, *Energimarknadsinspektionen* became an autonomous agency responsible for the regulation of the electricity, natural gas, and district heating markets (Energimarknadsinspektionen 2009, p. 10).[13] Although the Ministry of Enterprise, Energy, and Communications is in charge of its activities, like all Swedish central government agencies, EI carries out its tasks and missions autonomously.

Energimarknadsinspektionen can be seen as an independent employer because in Sweden, employer responsibilities are almost completely delegated to central government agencies. Generally, the Swedish employment regime is characterized by a strongly decentralized system of collective bargaining both in the public and the private sector. As regards the central government level, job security and pensions are set in national collective agreements between the Swedish Agency for Government Employers (*Arbetsgivarverket*, SAGE)[14] and the unions, while working conditions and pay are negotiated at the agency level (for more details, see the description of the Swedish public employment regime in Chapter 5). EI is a comparatively small agency but with an increasing number of employees: its headcount rose from 68 employees on 1 January 2008 (Energimarknadsinspektionen 2009, p. 9) to 91 employees at the end of 2009 (Energimarknadsinspektionen 2010, p. 4) and reached 108 at the end of 2013 (Energimarknadsinspektionen 2014, p. 34).

Employment regulation

Entry requirements and recruitment

United Kingdom. Recruitment to the civil service in the Office of Gas and Electricity Markets (Ofgem) is based on guiding principles of the British Civil

Service, which have been subject to change since the 1980s (see Chapter 5). While the principle of selection on merit by fair and open competition is still fundamental today, since the beginning of the 1990s the system of recruitment to the civil service is strongly decentralized (Horton 1996, pp. 107ff.). Departments and agencies have the authority not only to determine the number of posts outside the Senior Civil Service but also to define their own entry requirements and qualifications and devise their own selection procedures (Civil Service Management Code 1.1.1 a, b).[15]

Thus, Ofgem has established a recruitment procedure which is tailor-made for its specific needs. The agency can choose between an internal appointment for vacant posts or it can advertise externally for an open competition (see subsection below on career advancement):

> [We] ... either test the market to make sure our internal candidates are the best or, if we haven't got the expertise, we go external. We use a variety of roots for that. We're obliged under the employment regulations of the civil service to advertise every job externally. When we go outside though, we would always advertise. And we... on the SCS-level, we use increasingly executive search companies as well as advertising. (Interview EUK)

The use of search companies for senior appointments is also encouraged by the Civil Service Commissioners because 'for many appointments it may be difficult to attract a strong field through advertising alone – at senior level it is often the case that people will only apply if they have been approached' (Civil Service Commission 2011, p. 9).

The formal recruitment process at Ofgem can be characterized as a three-stage 'sifting process'. In the first stage, Ofgem makes use of a private recruitment advertising agency, which assesses the applications against the required competencies of the grade of the vacant post. If the application passes this initial stage, it is sent to Ofgem, which in a second stage assesses the applicants against the key requirements of the vacant post. The third and final stage consists of an interview focused on competencies, which may include an assessment or a presentation for the more senior grades.

As to the employee's profile, the agency generally prefers employees which are early in their careers but have already gained some experience in the private sector, particularly in the finance sector, banks, consultancies, and the gas and electricity industry. This focus on the private sector is justified for three reasons. First, the agency values the expertise of these employees. Second, Ofgem considers the credibility of the employees as being higher when dealing with industry. Finally, Ofgem appreciates the specific attitude to work, because, 'by large and large, people coming from the private sector expect to work hard, put long hours and all the things that go with being in a private company' (Interview EUK). As a consequence of these preferences, between 60 and 70 per cent of its approximately 340 employees in 2010 have been recruited from the private sector:

> [W]e would not exclude the public sector by any means. If you take the other regulators I mentioned, the Office of Fair Trading, the Office for Rail Regulation, and there's a number of others. We would very easily take people from those regulators. There simply isn't enough to go around, and therefore we tend to go into the private sector, because the background we're looking for is in closest match. (Interview EUK)

Germany. Recruitment at the *Bundesnetzagentur* (BNetzA) in Germany follows a different course, since at the German central government level, an authority is only permitted to hire an employee if an appropriate post is vacant in its centrally defined budget. There are detailed staff numbers for each pay grade in the budget of the BNetzA, and the total number of employees in the staff appointment plan must not be exceeded at any time. The budget of the BNetzA, being a 'Higher Federal Authority' (*Höhere Bundesbehörde*), is part of the federal budget in the section of the overseeing Federal Ministry of Economics and Technology. However, recruitment and selection procedures are decentralized, and the BNetzA is responsible for the actual recruitment of its employees. While in the past – eased by the comparatively large size of the agency – internal recruitment for the filling of posts was the rule, external recruitment has gained importance more recently (Interview EDE).

With respect to external recruitment, however, the HR managers interviewed report that the agency is confronted with strong competition from the private sector, where excellent university graduates and experienced experts are often offered higher wages and more flexible career promotion. Addressing this challenge, personnel policies regarding recruitment and career advancement were redesigned. The HR managers state that recruitment procedures specifically address new labour market entrants such as university graduates, and are highly selective, including sophisticated assessments of the applicants' motivation for providing a public good. In addition, distinct features of the state as an employer, such as advanced work-life balance policies and equal opportunity, are highlighted.

New employees at the BNetzA normally start as public employees with two-year fixed-term contracts. These temporary contracts are intended to minimize risk in case the agency is not satisfied with its recruitment decision. However, the public employees are usually appointed to civil servant status after the termination of these contracts. Between 70 and 80 per cent of the fresh hires are university graduates, predominantly lawyers, economists, and engineers who usually possess key qualifications but have not yet acquired additional skills for specific positions. The high share of beginners can be traced back to the fact that the agency seeks to develop versatile generalists. This is typical for career-based systems with a focus on lifelong employment in the civil service. A minor share of the new employees is recruited from the private sector. In this context, the reform of the civil service law in 2009 aimed at improving the ability to attract career changers from the private sector, in that it is now possible to recruit employees at a higher level within a career category (*Bundesbeamtengesetz*, BBG § 20). The instrument is intended to increase the competitiveness of the public sector vis-à-vis the private sector (Schön 2009, pp. 16ff.) and in this regard is also appreciated by the HR managers of the BNetzA.

Although the BNetzA cannot compete with private sector wages and has only little control over the selectivity of the applicant pool, the interviewed HR managers are convinced that the strategies applied in recruitment are successful. They perceive their personnel as highly motivated, ambitious, and well trained. They also point out that turnover rates are low, that is, only a few of the BNetzA's employees have left the agency in recent years for a job in the private sector. The most important reason for this stability is, according to these managers, the high level of identification the employees seem to have with the agency and its public tasks. This enables the BNetzA both to recruit and retain the required personnel. As early as in the job interview, the agency attempts to sift out those applicants for whom mone-tary considerations seem to be the core career criteria and avoids hiring such applicants. Preferred applicants are those who, apart from possessing key qualifications, are able to demonstrate that they are attracted by the public tasks of the agency (Interview EDE).

France. In France, the government defines both the maximum limits for staff numbers and the personnel costs for AAIs (Süsskind 2010, pp. 167f.). AAIs are not entitled to create their own revenues, but are entirely financed by public funds. In consequence, the CRE does not charge fees from the regulated firms, and its resources are part of the annual state budget.

In contrast to the highly centralized and formalized entry requirements and recruitment procedures for the *fonction publique*, recruitment in the CRE is not based on a *concours*. Instead, the CRE's policy is geared towards finding candidates with abilities that are best suited for the agency's func-tions (Commission de Régulation de l'Énergie 2003, p. 83), which 'call for a high level of expertise in the field of energy but also those of financial auditing and law' (Commission de Régulation de l'Énergie 2009, p. 9). The focus is on the fit between the positions and the recruited employee's profiles (Interview EF). In general, employees are expected to have gained professional experience in at least one other job before joining the agency. Thus, at the end of 2009, only 18 out of 125 employees were in their first job at the CRE (Commission de Régulation de l'Énergie 2009, p. 9), and most of these new entrants had graduated from the *Grandes Écoles* of engineering or business or come from auditing firms. Job vacancies are generally advertised and open for applicants both from the *fonction publique* (as *fonctionnaires détachés*) and the private sector (as *agents contractuels*). As the number of *fonctionnaires* with suitable qualifications for the CRE to employ on secondment is not sufficient, a large share of personnel is recruited from outside the public sector as *agents contractuels*. Since its establishment, the number of *agents contractuels* at the CRE has grown steadily. While in mid-2001, 64 per cent of the 65 employees were *agents contractuels* (Commission de Régulation de l'Électricité 2001, p. 41), this percentage has increased to 86 per cent of the 129 employees in 2008 (Commission de Régulation de l'Énergie 2008, p. 10), and reached 89 per cent in 2013 (Commission de Régulation de l'Énergie 2014, p. 21). With regard to the employment background of the employees before joining CRE, at the end of 2007, only 30 per cent of the agency's staff had an employment history in public administration, 54 per cent had previously worked in private sector companies, 7 per cent had a university or other institutional background, and 9 per cent were graduates who had their first position at the CRE (Commission de Régulation de l'Énergie 2007, p. 139).[16]

Sweden. Swedish agencies such as the *Energimarknadsinspektionen* (EI) have a great deal of leeway in using their resources, including the determination of staff numbers. Also recruitment of employees is delegated to the agencies, including concrete recruitment procedures. The Swedish Constitution (*Regeringsform* Chapter 12 Art. 5) states that appointment to posts within the state administration has to be based only on objective factors such as merit and competence. Moreover, the 1994 Public Employment Act (*Lag (1994:260) om offentlig anställning* § 4) specifies that competence shall be the primary consideration for any recruitment to the public sector. When filling vacancies, agencies assess whether an applicant has sufficient competencies for the tasks he or she has to perform, and recruit the applicant who is considered to have the best qualifications for the post (Arbetsgivarverket 2009a, pp. 11f.; Swedish Ministry of Finance 1995, p. 37).

As the HR expert states, the recruitment policy of EI strongly reflects this focus on competence when filling vacancies and does not exhibit important particularities. Depending on the requirements of a position, the agency specifies the required competencies. As in the other energy regulatory agencies, most of the employees have a university degree in law, economics, or engineering. About 50 per cent of the agency's employees are recruited from the private sector (Interview ESE).

Pay

United Kingdom. The traditional pay and grading systems in the British Civil Service was centrally determined by HM Treasury in national negotiations with the concerned unions, and there was an annual seniority-related progression through pay bands (OECD 2005, p. 165; Burnham and Pyper 2008, p. 210; Bach 2009). With the introduction of the Civil Service

Management Code (CSMC) in April 1996, all departments and agencies were given full authority to determine pay, grading, and performance management arrangements (excluding pensions) of their employees, except for the Senior Civil Service (SCS), whose pay and grading structure is centrally managed by the Cabinet Office.[17] Since the late 1990s, central government departments and agencies have their own pay systems and conduct negotiations for their staff with local union representatives within the budgetary constraints of HM Treasury (Bach 2009; Kirkpatrick 2005, pp. 102ff.; Prowse and Prowse 2007, p. 54; Winchester and Bach 1999). This code ended the legacy of seniority-based pay increments and introduced individual objective-based PRP. A close link between pay and performance became one of the conditions for the delegation of pay policies to departments and agencies (CSMC § 7.1.2).

In 2010, Ofgem's grade structure consisted of five grades ranging from band A (typically administrative roles) to band E (defined as 'senior managers, technical experts or professionals who may lead a large number of employees through other managers or team leaders'). The five grades also defined pay ranges[18] (and grading structure and pay bands refer to so-called Core Competency Frameworks). Entrance to one of the grades is linked not to general educational qualifications but to job-related competencies. In general, as requirements for the entrance to a specific level of the civil service, educational qualifications and age limits 'were increasingly relaxed during the 1970s, in response to recruitment problems and to ensure equal opportunity' (Horton 1996, p. 108).

Upon recruitment of an employee, basic pay is set individually within the range of the respective pay band on the basis of skills and expertise, previous salary, and a comparison with the existing staff. Pay is reviewed annually on the basis of a performance appraisal system in which employees and their line managers agree on personal objectives. At the end of the process, performance logs and formal reviews, including a pay recommendation, are sent to Ofgem's HR department (Ofgem 2007). The performance assessments are the basis for the size of consolidated increases and non-consolidated payments in the form of bonuses.[19] At Ofgem, bonuses are considered to be an important HRM instrument and can add up to 10 per cent of the annual basic pay. The agency's focus on performance is also reflected in the handling of progression in the basic salary. In contrast to more traditional Civil Service departments and agencies providing automatic pay progression, progression within a pay band is dependent on performance at Ofgem. Thus, if not performing, an employee may receive no pay increase at all. The design of Ofgem's pay system and its tough handling of underperformance, which in the worst case even includes dismissal, illustrate that the 'working culture and environment here is very much like a private company' (Interview EUK). In this regard, Ofgem's strict link between pay and performance strongly resembles the overall aims of the Civil Service policy on tying performance management and pay since the late 1980s (Marsden 2004, p. 351).

Since October 2006, when the Cabinet Office issued the *Civil Service Reward Principles*, departments and agencies are explicitly supposed to adapt their pay arrangements to the principle that 'reward is one of the key tools that employers have to attract, retain and engage the optimal workforce to deliver high performance services to their customers' (Cabinet Office 2006). Although the reward package comprises more than just pay (for example, pensions and leave), the focus of the *Civil Service Reward Principles* is clearly on the pay aspect, and departments and agencies are encouraged to increase the proportion of pay that is contingent on performance, especially with regard to non-consolidated pay. Moreover, the *Civil Service Reward Principles* explicitly require departments and agencies to 'face the market'. That means that the cost of employees' skills on the labour market has to be taken into account when setting pay levels (Cabinet Office 2006).

The aspect of 'facing the market' dominates the design of Ofgem's pay structure. Competition for highly qualified employees with the private sector was considered as early as the establishment of Ofgem in 2000, and pay was regarded as the most suitable instrument for attracting the required personnel.

> [W]e had to design a pay-structure that could attract people from the private sector as well as the public sector, because if we had had just the constraints of the public sector, we would not have been able to attract the people we needed to do the job. (Interview EUK)

In order to enable Ofgem to recruit and retain staff from private companies, HM Treasury gives the agency some financial scope. Ofgem has used this flexibility to design a pay structure that is apparently comparatively competitive with private sector pay. In addition to pay, there might be other reasons to join Ofgem for employees who are at an early stage of their career:

> [T]he reason you want to come to Ofgem is, we are still competitive on pay, but not as much as the private sector. However, for your career and for your CV, having two or three years in Ofgem is definitely a very positive aspect, it is high-profile, highly responsible, and you are dealing with leading edge projects. (Interview EUK)

Despite its competitive pay structure, an interview partner indicated that 'there is a certain level, which is senior professional jobs, where we struggle to attract people, partly because they are very attractive to the outside, industry and the private sector' (Interview EUK). In order to deal with this challenge, Ofgem initiated a Graduate Development Programme in 2006 with the main purpose of filling those jobs for which Ofgem had difficulties in recruiting and retaining employees.

Germany. The remuneration of federal civil servants in Germany is governed by the Civil Servants' Remuneration Act (*Bundesbesoldungsgesetz, BBesG*) and is based on the 'alimentation principle'. The basic pay constitutes the core element of the remuneration of civil servants and also applies to the *Bundesnetzagentur (BNetzA)*.[20] Basic pay is independent of the function that a civil servant performs, but is determined by the office (*Amt*) that has been assigned and the corresponding pay scale grade (*Besoldungsgruppe*). The offices and their pay scales are governed by the federal remuneration schemes (*Bundesbesoldungsordnungen*), and each pay scale is composed of several pay levels (*Besoldungsstufen*).

The basic salary and pay increases were traditionally set according to pay scale and 'service age' (the so-called *Besoldungsdienstalter*) of a civil servant. This system was thoroughly reformed for the first time as part of the Civil Service Reform Law of 1997 (*Reformgesetz*). Since then, progression to the next pay level is not only determined by service age but is also dependent on the evaluated performance of the civil servant. If the civil servant does not meet the requirements, he or she remains at the current pay level until the requirements are met. However, the civil service reform law of 1997 left the principal system of progression according to service age untouched. This was changed as an element of the 2009 Law on the Modernization of the Civil Service (*Dienstrechtsneuordnungsgesetz*) which, among other things, abolished the system of progression according to service age. Since then, progression to the next pay level depends on the period of service (*Dienstzeit*) at a certain level and the performance of the civil servant (the so-called *Erfahrungszeiten*). If the performance does not correspond with the requirement of the office held by the civil servant, he or she remains in the current pay level (BBesG § 27 (5)) until a new performance appraisal indicates that the civil servant has fulfilled the required performance criteria (BBesG § 27 (6)). As indicated by Otto (2007), within the whole federal civil service there are no more than a dozen cases of a delay per year: 'It is thus safe to say that, apart from these few exceptions, all civil servants get a pay raise every two, three or four years' (Otto 2007, p. 8).

Since 1997, civil servants can be offered earlier progress to the next pay level in the case of consistently outstanding performances.[21] This so-called performance step (*Leistungsstufe*, BBesG § 27 (7); *Bundesleistungsbesoldungsverordnung*, BLBV § 3) is accompanied by two other instruments. First, the performance bonus (*Leistungsprämie*, BBesG § 42a; BLBV § 4) is a single payment (not-pensionable) for an outstanding particular performance that can be granted up to the amount of the first pay level of the civil servant's pay grade. Second, the performance allowance (*Leistungszulage*, BBesG § 42a; BLBV § 5) is paid monthly for a maximum of one year and shall not exceed 7 per cent of the initial basic pay of a civil servant. Among the different instruments, performance bonuses are used most often in the federal civil service. The instrument is considered to have 'the greatest impact as a reward for outstanding achievement, and it does not run the risk of being taken for granted' (Otto 2007, p. 8). According to BBesG § 41a (4), the budget for performance bonuses and performance allowances is 0.3 per cent of the personnel costs in the respective budget, and authorities are obliged to spend these funds fully.

In the BNetzA, the budget for PRP is equally distributed among directorate-generals, directorates, and divisions. Performance bonuses and performance allowances are granted by the line managers after consultation with their immediate superiors. In line with the general trend in the federal civil service, the BNetzA predominantly uses performance bonuses because performance allowances are regarded as too small for motivating employees over longer time spans. Although formally the bonus can be up to the amount of the first pay level of the pay grade, the BNetzA's HR managers reported that the performance bonus seldom exceeds EUR 1,500 before tax. Although the HR department would appreciate an increase of the tight budget for PRP, it is generally sceptical of the motivational effects on employees, as they regard other factors such as working culture, work-life balance policies, or chances for career advancement as more important. This finding is also supported by a study of the organizational culture in German agencies, which suggests that the employees are generally willing to go the 'extra mile' for the accomplishment of their tasks. The system of performance incentives is essentially based on this willingness and on non-monetary incentives such as the transfer of project responsibility (Bertelsmann Stiftung 2004, p. 27).

France. In line with its autonomous status as an AAI, the CRE has designed its own pay system, which is markedly different from the remuneration of *fonctionnaires* (see, for example, OECD 2005, pp. 114–19). There are no centrally defined regulations, and departments and agencies have a great deal of freedom in designing the remuneration for *agents contractuels*, whose terms and conditions are generally set out in contracts. For example, the salary could be based on the wage index of the *fonction publique* and thus relate to the remuneration of *fonctionnaires* with a similar function. However, remuneration could also be independent from the wage index and be based on fixed salaries or hourly wages.

Once working for the CRE, both *fonctionnaires détachés* and *agents contractuels* are treated equally with regard to pay and the evaluation of performance. *Fonctionnaires détachés* cannot be paid less than in their previous position, and the results of their performance appraisals are forwarded to their home authorities. The remuneration at the CRE, which consists of a basic pay and a one-off bonus at the end-of-the-year, 'is based on the recognition of professional abilities (level of training and experience acquired), taking into account the responsibilities exercised and the efforts made by each employee to achieve the objectives individually assigned' (Commission de Régulation de l'Énergie 2009, p. 10). Basic pay is individual and negoti-ated between the employee and the HR department when the employee is recruited. Neither unions nor staff councils are involved in the wage nego-tiations. Annual bonuses are based on a standardized performance appraisal system with objectified criteria. These bonuses can reach up to 30 per cent of the annual basic pay for the most senior positions (that is, directors) and up to 10 per cent for positions below directors. In the case of unsatisfactory results, no bonus will be allocated. Unsatisfactory results can also imply that the contract will not be renewed after three years. In the worst case, under-performance can even result in the termination of the contract.

> Yes, of course. Possible revaluations in the course of contract are obvious. There is the performance... Then somebody who in one year deals with a very heavy workload and which included a very difficult task and had many things to manage, and obviously, the salary... it is taken into account, and if we can make a revaluation, we do it. And obviously, the end-of-the-year bonus takes into account the performance and the work-load of the whole year and also the way in which the goals were achieved. Some are more productive than others, and all is connected. And what is interesting, is that it plays a stronger role in an authority than in a normal administration (AAI) where it is not possible to remunerate for the performance. (Interview EFR)

Although the CRE is independent in designing its pay system, budgetary restrictions limit its ability to compete with private sector wages. The agency has repeatedly complained about an insufficient operating and personnel budget in the face of its numerous and increasing tasks (Commission de Régulation de l'Énergie 2003, p. 84; Commission de Régulation de l'Énergie 2008, p. 12; Commission de Régulation de l'Énergie 2011, p. 9; Commission de Régulation de l'Énergie 2014, pp. 19f.). According to CRE, this results in a competitive disadvantage with regard to the private sector because it constrains the ability to recruit the required personnel (Interview EFR).

> Thus, in fact, one does not find civil servants in the French adminis-tration to carry out the expert report which must be drawn up by the Commission de Régulation de l'Énergie. Therefore, we are obliged to go and seek our staff in management consultancy and in the schools of engineers and others. Then indeed, traditionally, there is a true disparity between remunerations in the civil service and remunerations in the private sector. We are in the middle of both. In fact, it is a form of admin-istration and which works with the flexibility of a company. Despite everything, we do not have the means of remunerating the people as if they were in the large companies of the energy sector. Thus, in fact, much persuasion is necessary so that people agree to earn less money.

The wages are indeed not the same. Therefore, it is a true obstacle, it is a true handicap, you can say, this question of wages. (Interview EFR)

Sweden. In Sweden the *Energimarknadsinspektionen (EI)* has agreed with the local union representatives to use the individual pay-setting dialogue (for details see Chapter 5).[22] The individual dialogue between the line manager and the employee leads not to the payment of a single bonus but to an increase of the monthly pay for the following year. In case of unsatisfactory performance, the pay increase will be smaller compared to other employees.

As agreed in the central collective agreement (*Ramavtal löner inom staten,* RALS) and stated by the *Arbetsgivarverket* (Arbetsgivarverket 2009b, p. 19), the amount of individual pay is generally based on three criteria: 'a) level of responsibility and degree of difficulty of the work, b) performance and contribution to the operation's goals and c) the cost of equivalent labour on the labour market' (Arbetsgivarverket 2009d, p. 8). Education, age, and experience are explicitly excluded from the criteria for setting individual pay because they are considered to have an influence on an employee's performance and their contribution to the operation's goals (Arbetsgivarverket 2009b, p. 19). Agencies decide on how the criteria are to be interpreted and applied.

EI has concretized the criteria as follows. With regard to work tasks, EI recognizes changes in responsibility and difficulty. Wage criteria concerning individual competencies relate both to performance (accomplishment of planned tasks/assignments within planned time and with high quality; target-oriented handling of task modifications) and abilities such as service orientation, teamwork, being proactive and taking initiative, contributing to a good working atmosphere, and being able to represent the agency externally. These criteria are particularly relevant for the annual pay-setting dialogue. In the case that the employer is setting the salary for newly appointed staff, the cost of equivalent work on the private labour market is taken into account. Accordingly, if EI considers recruitment of a certain employee absolutely essential in order to fulfil its functions, the agency is flexible in minimizing existing wage differences with the private sector. As a consequence, competition for personnel is not considered to be a problem by HR managers.

Career advancement and further training

United Kingdom. Ofgem is rather independent in promotion policies given that promotion systems and promotion procedures are delegated to departments and agencies in the United Kingdom (CSMC § 6.4.1). A promotion generally means the move to a higher grade and thus leads to an increase in pay. The primary formal condition is that promotions are based on 'a considered decision as to the fitness of individuals, on merit, to undertake the duties concerned' (CSMC § 6.4.2a).

Departments and agencies can choose between either advertising vacant positions exclusively internally or both internally and externally. In the latter case, departments and agencies are required to follow the principle of openness as set out in the Civil Service Commission's *Recruitment Principles*. They must advertise the job opportunity publicly so that all prospective applicants have equal access to information about the job, its requirements, and the selection procedures (see subsection on recruitment).

When the required expertise is available within Ofgem, promotion opportunities are advertised exclusively internally (Ofgem 2009, p. 9). At Ofgem, a large share of vacant posts is advertised in this way, and thus only the current workforce has the possibility to apply. It is required that the line manager endorses the application, and applicants must attach their last two performance assessments.

A second possibility for promotion at Ofgem is labelled 'managed move'.

> So in terms of succession planning, when you're looking at people and you say: This individual is a high performer, they're showing a lot of capability, and we think they're ready for that next step, then a manager can make a business case to what we call personally promote that individual. (Interview EUK)

Due to equity and fairness considerations, according to the HR director, this procedure is used sparingly and reversibly at Ofgem.

Responsibility for further training is also delegated to departments and agencies, which generally aim at ensuring that employees 'have the knowledge, skills and competences to carry out their work and achieve the objectives of the organization' (Horton 1996, p. 136). In line with this general aim, Ofgem's further training policy is primarily linked to the fulfilment of its business needs in the sense that the focus is on individual courses and programmes that are relevant for the posts and roles of the employees.[23]

Besides offering courses on IT, personal skills (for example, on time management or presentation techniques), and on management, Ofgem emphasizes the development of professional qualifications. This includes, for example, the support for obtaining a chartered status or a master's degree. In these cases, the agency funds 80 per cent of the costs, while 20 per cent have to be paid by the employees. If the employees leave the agency within two years, Ofgem calls back the money that has been invested in the training (Interview EUK).

In 2006, Ofgem started a Graduate Development Programme on internal initial training, which has the main purpose of filling jobs in areas in which the agency faces difficulties in attracting staff, whereby upper-tier degrees in programmes with a strong emphasis on analytical methods are preferred (Interview EUK). During the 18-month programme, the graduates rotate through the major divisions and receive at least 25 days of training on different aspects. Afterwards they work for two more years on a middle professional level before they are ready to move to a senior professional level.

Germany. Promotion in the *BNetzA* follows the standard legal rules for civil servants, differentiating between the promotion (*Beförderung*, BBG § 22, BLV §§ 32ff.) and the advancement to the next service class (*Aufstieg*, BLV §§ 35ff.). A promotion is the conferment of a higher service grade (*Amt*) with a higher final basic pay level within one of the four service classes (that is, promotion from A9 to A10 or from A13 to A14). This is only possible when there is a vacant post with a higher service grade available in the budget of an authority. In contrast to new recruitments, which generally require an external advertisement (that is, on the internet, in an official journal, or in a newspaper; see BBG § 8, BLV § 4), the authority is not obliged to advertise higher positions externally. In the BNetzA, internal advertisement of higher posts is prevalent, and HR managers appreciate the large internal labour market for higher positions as a powerful means to retain highly qualified personnel experts. It is quite common at the BNetzA that senior managers directly approach employees that seem suitable for a vacant post and encourage them to apply. This is an example of what the Bertelsmann Foundation (2004, p. 30) has characterized as a 'positive competition' for employees between senior managers at the BNetzA.

The promotion opportunities at the BNetzA are institutionally restricted by the number of posts that appear in its budget; this refers especially to the relationship between the smaller number of higher service grades and the higher number of lower service grades (the so-called *Stellenkegel*). Thus, according to the HR managers interviewed, the internal competition for promotion opportunities is described as difficult. In this regard, following the legally established performance principle (for example, in BBG § 9), the results of performance appraisals (*dienstliche Beurteilungen*) are the only relevant criterion for promotion at the BNetzA (Interview EDE). Performance appraisals of civil servants are regulated by BBG § 21 and BLV §§ 48ff. The suitability (*Eignung*), capability (*Befähigung*), and professional performance (*fachliche Leistung*) of civil servants must be evaluated at least every three years. The relevant sections of the BLV contain only brief descriptions of these principles, which are further specified by service agreements (*Dienstvereinbarungen*) between ministries and employee representatives. The guidelines for the BNetzA's performance appraisal system are specified in the service agreement between the Federal Ministry of Economics and Technology and its main staff council, and apply to both civil servants and public employees. Except for a few employees – such as those who have spent less than six months in the authority – all employees are evaluated every two years. Since the evaluation is intended to provide a comparison, staff members are divided into reference groups according to their pay brackets and the similarity of their tasks. Performance criteria are: expert knowledge, work results, working method, general suitability, social skills, and leadership. Both the criteria and the overall results are based on a six-stage rating scheme ranging from X (employee surpasses requirements with constantly outstanding performance) as the best, A (employee surpasses requirements with predominantly outstanding performance) as the second best, until E (employee does not meet the requirements at all) as the worst possible rating.

The appraisals are conducted by the line manager (*Berichterstatter*, rapporteur) in cooperation with his or her immediate superior (*Beurteilender*, evaluator). In a first step, the *Berichterstatter* conducts interviews with the employees and prepares first drafts of the appraisal. This is followed by an evaluation meeting (*Beurteilungskonferenz*) led by the *Berichterstatter* and the *Beurteilende* in which the employees belonging to a reference group are ranked according to their performance. In addition, a quota system mandates the usage of the full scale. The best rating of X can be awarded to a maximum of 5 per cent of employees in a reference group, the rating of A to a maximum of 40 per cent, and the rating of B can also be awarded to 40 per cent. Below the rating of B no quota apply.[24]

Apart from a rating, the appraisals include a proposal for the further deployment of the employee (BLV § 49 (3)), although this proposal is not binding. The exact wording of the result of the performance appraisal has to be made known to the employee, and overall results of the reference groups have to be published in the form of a ranking (BLV § 50 (3), (4)). Employees are thus fully aware of their exact rank within their reference group. Although the BNetzA's HR department argues that the appraisal system is generally adequate for assessing the performance of its staff, because of this requirement, it considers the system to have inherent demotivating effects:

> It is sad to tell an employee who is above 50, who has done his work faithfully and to your absolute satisfaction, to give him in writing that he is somewhere in the lower third. ... As a practitioner I have an issue with instruments that leave my team more unmotivated after this a procedure than it has been before. (Interview EDE)

In contrast to a promotion (*Beförderung*), the advancement to the next service class (*Aufstieg*, BLV §§ 35ff.) requires the civil servant to obtain the educational qualifications for the respective service class as stipulated in BBG § 17. Once the civil servant has acquired the qualifications, he or she must wait for a vacant post in the higher service class available in the budget. Subsequently, he or she is conferred a service grade within the new service class (BLV § 40). This legally established link between career advancement and further education, typical of career-based systems, is clearly visible in the BNetzA, which actively supports individual career plans oriented towards the advancement to the next service class. For example, employees have the possibility to obtain a master's degree through distance learning while working full time. The agency pays the tuition fees and other expenses and supports the employees with special leave and working time flexibility. Once these employees have received their degree, they can apply for a vacant post in the higher service (Interview EDE).

Apart from further education measures that are connected with the advancement to the next service class, there are other more general forms of training for civil servants (*Dienstliche Qualifizierung*, BLV § 47). Civil servants are legally obliged to participate in these measures (BBG § 61 (2)), and a refusal can result in disciplinary consequences. As indicated by the HR department of the BNetzA, employees seem to be highly motivated to participate and often bring forward their own ideas for further training measures (Interview EDE).

France. Career advancement in the French *Commission de Régulation de l'Énergie (CRE)* differs considerably from the system of the French *fonction publique*. In fact, it is even arguable whether one can speak of a *system* of career advancement within the French energy regulatory agency. This is especially because of its comparatively small size, which restricts opportunities for promotion.

> There are not that many possibilities for promotion. On the other hand, as soon as we have the possibility to promote somebody, obviously, we do it. This is part of our competences. Which means, internally, we do everything possible, knowing that there are no significant opportunities. (Interview EFR)

Apart from lack of opportunities, the relevance of promotions is further limited by the relatively short retention time of most employees, whose contracts are limited to a maximum of six years. Thus, one could assume that employees who do not have future career prospects in the agency attach relatively little importance to promotion. This assumption is strengthened by the fact that the agency's further training policy is not geared towards supporting career prospects *within* the agency, but towards enhancing career perspectives in the private sector after the employees have finished working for the CRE.

> Well, as said before, I look after the staff members individually. I try to work with them after spending time at the CRE. Because I know that at the end of three years or six years, these people will leave. I work with them, I anticipate their needs for training to manage the 'afterwards'. ... Therefore, somebody who would like to obtain a master's degree in public administration or whatever he or she wishes to do, will be taken into account for one and a half to two years. I will provide financial

means, so that the time spent at the CRE constitutes a true value as regards training and the person then says: Good, not only have I worked at a regulatory authority, but moreover, I was trained to prepare for the time afterwards. (Interview EFR)

Individual training needs are identified in annual evaluation dialogues between employees and their line managers. Basically, the agency's further training policy aims at meeting three objectives: 'to develop specific skills required for regulation activities; improve personal efficiency (IT and foreign languages); support career plans, including acquisition of qualifications, linked to CRE's activities' (Commission de Régulation de l'Énergie 2006, p. 115). The last objective plays a key role for the ability to recruit the required personnel in the face of a competitive disadvantage with regard to pay (see subsection on pay). The training policy is explicitly geared towards compensating for the comparatively lower salaries by providing programmes which purposely make the employees even more attractive for private companies.[25]

We put special emphasis on the continuous training of our staff. We have two approaches as regards training: The first is that it is important that our staff members are trained for our projects. We invest a lot so that our staff can learn foreign languages or other things which they need in their day-to-day life. This is the first thing. The second, as I told you before, is that we have the problem of remuneration, which is less than in the private sector. But we do need staff members from the private sector. Since we cannot give them the level of remuneration which they have had in previous companies, we try to adapt to personal expectations by offering them training courses. (Interview EFR)

In 2010, more than half of the approximately 130 employees worked in private companies before joining the agency.

Sweden. Career advancement in Sweden in the *Energimarknadsinspektionen* (EI) is more in line with the general system. The traditional system of career advancement in the Swedish central government, relying on criteria such as the availability of a vacant post with a higher grade and seniority (Andersson and Schager 1999, p. 244), was abolished by the late 1970s as a result of the alignment of employment conditions in the public and private sectors. Since then, the system of career advancement is less-formalized and no longer predominantly based on promotion to a different position. Instead, promotion occurs through the development of the duties of a government employee within the same position. This is because the responsibilities of government employees 'are often broad and include considerable opportunity to improve both competence and pay levels' (Arbetsgivarverket 2009a, p. 12). Employees also have the possibility to apply for vacant posts. All vacancies are advertised, but agencies are not obliged to advertise externally (Bossaert et al. 2001, p. 363; Wilks 1996, p. 33).

Career advancement and further training of employees are inextricably linked. Evaluation dialogues (*Utvecklingssamtal*) 'between managers and individual staff members are generally used to review performance and potential future duties, results and training needs' (Arbetsgivarverket 2009a, p. 12). This general policy of career advancement and further training also holds for EI. Due to a flat organizational structure with few hierarchical levels and a small number of employees, there are only few promotion opportunities. The work of EI is mainly project-oriented, and a common method of career advancement is to become a project coordinator. This increases the level of responsibility and thus leads to an increase in pay (see subsection on pay).

One of the primary objectives of the agency is to match the skills and expertise of its employees with their tasks and responsibilities. Therefore, all employees are part of the agency's competence development strategy (Energimarknadsinspektionen 2015).

> We can talk of the competence process that is going on. ... In this you are going to identify what competences we have and what we still want. You have some differences between that and we are going to make some training programmes or competence activities. (Interview ESE)

> [W]e are looking several years ahead. What are the demands from the agency going to be? What can we see? What tasks can we see, old tasks, new tasks? What competence do we need to manage this? We are talking about both recruiting people, but also training for the already employed. (Interview ESE)

The central instrument for competence development is the *Utvecklingssamtal* between an employee and his or her line manager. The aims and procedures of such contracts are laid down in a collaboration agreement (*Samverkansavtal*) between *Energimarknadsinspektionen* as an employer and the local union representatives of Saco (*Sveriges akademikers centralorganisation*) and ST (*Fackförbundet ST*). The collaboration agreement forms the basis for the local cooperation between the EI as employer and the employee representatives at the agency. It is based on the 'cooperation for development agreement' (*Samverkan för utveckling*) for the central government sector, agreed upon in 1997, which builds on the concepts of participation, decentralization, and delegation and aims at enabling employees to influence their own work situation.

The evaluation dialogues fulfil a dual function in that they, firstly, aim at the development of employees and their careers in order to, secondly, supply the organization with the skills it needs for the fulfilment of its tasks. The evaluation dialogue takes place at least once a year. It has been characterized as a 360-degree-feedback system 'where performance appraisal is made not only by superiors, but also by peers, and/or subordinates' (OECD 2005, p. 55). This comprehensive feedback system includes the appraisal of staff members' views on the leadership of their superiors. At the end of the evaluation dialogue, training measures are set out in individual agreements which are evaluated in the next *Utvecklingssamtal*.

Job security and employment protection

United Kingdom. The general employment protection rules for public employees also apply to Ofgem. As set out in the Employment Rights Act 1996 (ERA), British civil servants are subject to the same rules of employment protection as are all other employees. The only difference is a separate Civil Service Compensation Scheme for civil servants in case of loss of office, including both involuntary and voluntary departures (Thurley 2010, p. 3).

Civil servants have no lifelong employment guarantee, and the Civil Service Management Code (CSMC) entails the procedures and conditions for dismissals. Civil servants can be dismissed for three reasons: on grounds of inefficiency, disciplinary misbehaviour, and compulsory redundancies. Decisions on dismissals are delegated to departments and agencies.

Germany. German *Beamte* have a lifelong employment guarantee and can only be dismissed as a consequence of a disciplinary procedure which is regulated by disciplinary law (*Bundesdisziplinargesetz*); this also applies to the civil servants at the BNetzA. Departments and agencies are not entitled to dismiss a civil servant on their own, but must bring action before the responsible administrative court, which decides over the dismissal. In case of dismissal, a civil servant loses all entitlements, can never regain the civil servant status, and cannot be appointed to another public employment relationship.

A dismissal is the hardest possible sanction following from a disciplinary procedure. Other sanctions are a letter of censure, a fine, a reduction of pay, or downgrading. The gravity of the sanction has to correspond to the severity of the misconduct. In 2008, disciplinary action was imposed on 0.17 per cent of all federal civil servants, and only 0.01 per cent of all federal civil servants have actually been dismissed.

France. As noted above, the French CRE employs *fonctionnaires détachés* from other central government authorities on secondment, and *agents contractuels* who are non-permanent employees under public law contracts. The secondment of *fonctionnaires détachés* is revocable; contracts of *agents contractuels* are limited to three years and can be renewed for a maximum of three more years (*Loi n° 84–16 du 11 janvier 1984* Art. 4; *Décret n° 86–83 du 17 janvier 1986* Art. 6,).[26] An *agent contractuel* leaves an authority after three years unless the contract is renewed. At the CRE, contracts are not renewed in case of unsatisfactory performance. The agency even makes use of dismissals of *agents contractuels* in cases of inefficiency:

We can even interrupt a contract in the course of a year. If the person is not performing. I mean, we do not have these restrictions, this slowness which you can have in the traditional administration where you cannot separate from a staff member who is not performing. We have contracts, which can be terminated in advance or not be renewed, therefore we have other possibilities. (Interview EFR)

Authorities furthermore have the possibility to dismiss an *agent contractuel* following a disciplinary procedure (*Loi n° 84–16 du 11 janvier 1984* Art 43, 44).

Sweden. In Sweden, the same general labour law applies to the public sector as to all other sectors of the labour market, and thus also holds for EI; that is, there is no lifelong employment guarantee for Swedish central government employees. Thus, the rules on job security set out in the 1982 Employment Protection Act (EPA) apply to almost all employees with permanent contracts in both the public and the private sector.

Employees can be dismissed either with notice (EPA § 7) or without notice in case of a summary dismissal (EPA § 18); EPA § 7 requires a dismissal to be based on objective grounds. Objective grounds are, on the one hand, redundancies as a consequence of economic, technical, or organizational needs. On the other hand, objective grounds can also imply circumstances that relate to an individual employee. There are no laws that regulate severance payments in case of dismissals with notice, but collective agreements provide payments in case of redundancies.

Generally speaking, 'up until the early 1980s those employed in the public sector had the security that the general growth of government made their jobs secure', and especially Swedish government employees 'have enjoyed considerable security of tenure and were usually dismissed only in cases of professional misconduct or criminal offence' (Wilks 1996, p. 33f.). The economic crisis in the early 1980s and the following reorganization of the Swedish public sector also had negative consequences for security of employment for central government employees.

Nevertheless, from a comparative perspective, the Swedish Employment Protection Act is rather beneficial for employees because although 'it is fairly easy for an employer to reduce the workforce due to business reasons, periods of notice are fairly generous and redundant staff are generally provided different kinds of help in finding a new job' (OECD 2008, p. 25). Furthermore, in 1990, a special Job Security Agreement (*Trygghetsavtalet*) between the Swedish Agency for Government Employees (*Arbetsgivarverket*) and the unions was established for government employees with the aim 'to prevent unemployment resulting from the considerable structural changes in the public sector' (Wilks 1996, p. 33). For central government employees, the agreement stipulates even more beneficial regulations in case of redundancies (OECD 2008, p. 25). For example, periods of notice for government employees are longer than demanded by law. The Job Security

Agreement also provides for 'benefits such as income supplements if a redundant employee receives a lower pay in their new employment than in government employment' (Arbetsgivarverket 2009d, p. 22). Finally, the Job Security Foundation (*Trygghetsstiftelsen*), which was established under the Job Security Agreement, individually supports redundant employees in finding a new job as quickly as possible.

Equal opportunity policies

With respect to equal opportunity policies, the energy regulation agencies in all four countries must respect the more or less codified national regulations for the civil service and public employment (see Chapter 5). The United Kingdom and Germany have both introduced a duty on public sector organizations to promote equal opportunities and to report on the outcomes. In 2008, France adopted a charter for gender equality in the public sector and introduced a general requirement for gender parity in recruitment committees. Sweden requires both public and private sector organizations to undertake gender audits and develop gender equality plans (Rubery 2013, p. 69). HR managers in the agencies report being well aware of the general, and in recent times, more mainstreamed principle of gender equality. According to estimates from HR managers in the interviews in 2010, men and younger employees seem to be overrepresented in the agencies.[27] The gender bias can be partly explained by the required type of qualifications, which generally exhibits a male dominance. The age bias, in turn, is presumably partly due to the young age of the agencies as organizations. Nevertheless, personnel tend to be mixed in terms of gender and age. In contrast, there are no indications that ethnic diversity or disability are specifically considered in the energy regulation agencies in any of the four countries.

Summary

As we have seen, regulations of employment conditions in the analysed agencies are primarily governed by the specific national regulations for employment at the central government level. They reflect the institutional frameworks regarding the civil service and public employment of the respective countries. However, the energy regulatory agencies in Germany, France, and Sweden, and in the UK as a reference case, have in common that they apply and interpret the respective institutional frameworks as flexibly as possible. Thus, nearly all dimensions of traditional civil service employment regulations are to some degree subject to change or circumvention.

While the legal civil servant status for employment in the agencies is maintained in all countries apart from Sweden (where that category of public employees was abolished well before the introduction of IRAs), personnel policies adopted are highly flexible (see Table 6.1).

Table 6.1 Dimensions of public employment regulation in energy regulatory agencies

Dimensions and characteristics	United Kingdom	Germany	France	Sweden
1. Regulation of employment conditions				
Legal status	Civil Servant	Civil servant/CS (~90%); public employee/PE (~10%) [data from 2010]	Civil servant/ *fonctionnaire détaché* (14%); public employee/ *agent contractuel* (86%) [data from 2008]	Employee
Collective regulations	Authoritative	CS: Authoritative/unilateral PE: Collective agreements	Authoritative/unilateral	Collective agreements
Regulation of labour conflicts	No active right to strike	CS: No right to strike PE: Right to strike	Right to strike	Right to strike
2. Personnel system				
Mode of advancement	Position-based	CS: Career-based PE: Position-based	Position-based	Position-based
Openness	High	Low	High	High
3. Personnel management				
Entry requirements	Non-formalized	CS: Formalized PE: Less-formalized	Non-formalized	Non-formalized
Recruitment	Agency's responsibility; recruitment both internal and external	Agency's responsibility; internal and external; new recruits usually start as public employees with two-year fixed contracts; afterwards appointment to civil servant status; general qualifications required	Agency's responsibility; recruitment both internal (as *fonctionnaires détachés*) and external (as *agents contractuels*); general qualifications required/ not based on examinations (*concours*)	Agency's responsibility; recruitment both internal and external (about 50% external); general qualifications required

Continued

Table 6.1 Continued

Dimensions and characteristics	United Kingdom	Germany	France	Sweden
Pay structure	Negotiation-based	CS: Determined by law (PE: Negotiation-based)	*Fonctionnaires détachés:* Negotiation-based *Agents contractuels:* Negotiation-based	Negotiation-based
Evaluation and assessment	Performance-based	CS: Attenuated seniority rules (years of tenure) and (to a small extent) performance-based (PE: Performance-based)	*Fonctionnaires détachés Agents contractuels:* Performance-based	Performance-based
Performance incentives	Yes	CS & PE: Yes, but small	Yes	Yes
Opportunities for promotion	Performance-based	CS: Seniority-based and performance-based; (PE: Performance-based)	Few; performance-based	Few; performance-based
Further education	Flexible	CS: Legally determined; (PE: Flexible)	Flexible	Flexible
4. Integration function of public employment regime				
Payment, social security		Medium (pay), high (social security)	Medium	Medium
Employment security	High	High	*Fonctionnaires détachés:* High *Agents contractuels:* Low due to fixed-term contracts	Medium
Equal opportunity and treatment at the workplace	High	High	High	High
5. Specificity of public employment regime				
Difference as compared to private sector employment regime	Low	High	Lowered	Low

This is most obvious at Ofgem in the UK, where the agency (like all IRAs in the country) has broad discretion in all matters of HR management, which allows for the adapting of recruitment policies, pay, and advancement regulations to 'business needs'. Thus, recruitment of young employees with private sector experience, PRP (including a tough handling of underperformance) as well as position-based promotion and individual (as opposed to unilateral or collective) agreements have become core features of employment regulation.

At the Swedish EI, too, we find a mixture of internal and external recruitment, position-based advancement, and a performance- and negotiation-based pay structure. However, a common HRM policy across all agencies in Sweden and collective agreements provide a more employee-friendly framework for interest representation than in the United Kingdom.

High flexibility in personnel policies in the case of the CRE in France can be traced back to the special administrative status of the agency, which is not subject to the still career-based institutional framework of the *fonction publique*. With the option of recruitment of young graduates from the *Grandes Écoles* instead of making use of *fonctionnaires détachés*, fixed-term contracts, and a high emphasis on PRP, alignment with the private sector is quite high. Since restrictions in pay levels are perceived of as a competitive disadvantage, compensation is sought through a specific continual training policy, thus also counterbalancing the low employment security for the majority of contract employees.

Only in the German BNetzA do the central government civil servant regulations fully apply. Nevertheless, pockets of flexibility identified in HRM unfold within the restricted framework of the civil servant career system, which does not allow for competitive pay structures, substantial performance incentives, or position-based advancement. Instead, personnel policies geared towards gaining and retaining highly qualified staff focus on offering family-friendly working conditions, job rotation, and enhanced chances for career advancement within a large internal labour market. These policies earned the agency the reputation of having an innovative organizational culture as part of the public administration (Bertelsmann Stiftung 2004) and, at the same time, resemble management strategies in business.

Thus, employment regulation in the energy regulatory agencies analysed in this chapter departs from the standards of the traditional ideal type of the civil servant, although the civil servant status may be maintained. While the extent of change varies, with Ofgem and EI being most advanced, common features of alignment with private sector employment are external recruitment and a strong emphasis on performance regarding assessment, pay, and promotion. Findings presented here establish that these commonalities by sector across countries reflect the shared competitive challenge that regulatory agencies need substantial numbers of highly qualified experts for effective market control, who usually find better pay and more flexible career prospects in private firms. Both the relative independence of the agencies from government and central administration as well as a substantial autonomy in personnel policies support the agencies' strategies to meet the challenges of competition on the labour market. At the same time, the agencies developed HRM strategies that are similar in focus and design, irrespective of the different national public employment systems.

Nevertheless, the distinct national systems strongly predetermine employment regulations in the energy regulatory agencies, and differences between the agencies under study reflect differences in the national regulations. The flexibility of HRM in the British Ofgem and the Swedish EI conform to a high degree to the respective conception of national public employment regulation. On the other end of the spectrum, the same holds true for the bureaucratic structure of the BNetzA, whose employment regulation closely follows the German civil service career-based system, whereas personnel policies in the CRE in France have developed in stark contrast to the national bureaucratic public employment regime.

7
Waste Collection

Introduction

Waste collection is one of the long-established core public services provided at the local level. In many urban areas, public waste collection was established in the mid-19th century with the main aim of securing public health in an era of rapid urbanization and industrialization (Hafkamp 2002; Hemmer et al. 2003). Until the 1970s, municipal responsibility and service provision by a public workforce were major characteristics of the organization of waste collection throughout Europe (Hafkamp 2002, p. 13). Despite technical innovations that led to improvements of working conditions, waste collection is still very demanding in terms of human resources and remains largely heavy labour for employees (European Commission 2001, p. 19). Except for a few technical or coordinative professions, tasks are performed by drivers, collectors, and other manual occupations (European Commission 2001, p. 24). Workers often have little formal qualifications and belong to a group that is often affected by relatively low pay and high unemployment rates in the private sector (Sengenberger 1987; Keller 2008). By contrast, in the 'Golden Age' of TRUDI, the public sector constituted a large, protected, internal labour market with a high degree of job security and – for the lower pay grades, such as in the field of waste collection – pay premiums in comparison to the private sector (Sengenberger 1987; Tepe and Kroos 2010). Furthermore, employment regulations in the public sector often served as a reference point for those areas of the private sector where the service was publicly funded but provided by a private company, as in the case of private waste collection (Ambrosius 2008).

Since the late 1980s, rising amounts of waste, increasing hazardousness of substances, but also increasing value of discarded material, and increasing environmental awareness by the public led to profound changes in waste management. While public health is still a main aim, environmental hygiene, management of resources, and producer responsibility became relevant as well. Today, municipalities are still legally obliged to guarantee the service of waste collection,[1] but they can choose between provision by a public institution (for example, a public sector department or a public company) or contracting out the service to a private company. Further options include public-private partnerships, contracting out the service to other municipal companies, or joint waste management authorities with other municipalities. Thus, waste collection represents a field where the political and decision-making responsibilities remain with the state, whereas the provision can be either public or private. Due to scale effects, the collection of household waste is generally organized as a local monopoly (European Commission 2009). Thus, in the case of outsourcing, competition occurs through periodic tendering processes, in which companies bid for time-limited monopolies over service provision. Liberalization and privatization policies on the European level set in motion reform processes which generated a constellation in which public providers are still relevant, but the share of private service provision has increased. The relative shares of public and private service provision of waste collection differ across countries (Dijkgraaf and Gradus 2008; European Commission 2001; Dijkgraaf et al. 2009; Hall 2010). However, in most Western European countries, public service providers are still important actors with shares of about 50 per cent of the total volume. Furthermore, as a result of a process of market concentration in the private sector, the counterparts of public service providers are often large international companies with several thousand employees (Hall 2010, p. 3; Davies 2003, p. 19). Given that the sector is labour-intensive, labour costs are a major factor in competition.[2]

In the present chapter, we study the evolution of public employment regimes in waste collection in Germany, France, Sweden, and the United Kingdom. In contrast to energy market regulation and the police, differences in the legal conceptions of public services and different systems of municipal self-administration in the four countries are important background factors that need to be taken into account to understand public employment regimes in the waste collection sector. In addition, we must distinguish between two forms of competition. First, in *direct competition*, contracts are awarded after competitive bidding. This is mainly the case in the UK, as well as for packaging waste in Germany. Second, *indirect competition* takes place if service provision is confided to a public organization by political decision. In this case, the political decision for public service delivery has to be justified by benchmarking and cost comparisons within the public sector or between public and private companies (Nullmeier 2005, p. 111). The importance of indirect competition for service provision has increased since the 1990s in the process of liberalization and privatization of public services, but it has also been a measure of austerity politics at the municipal level (Hemmer et al. 2003, pp. 6ff; Davies 2003).

Employment conditions in the public provision of waste collection

Irrespective of market liberalization and fiscal pressures on municipal public budgets, the public provision of waste collection still constitutes one of the basic infrastructures provided by the state on the local level. The organization of waste collection varies across countries, not only with respect to the extent of privatization and competition but also regarding the different types of waste in some countries. For example, in Germany, the collection of packaging waste is generally put out for tender, whereas the decision about the organization of household waste collection is made by the municipalities. In addition, the state structure and autonomy of the local level influence the organization of this service and generate not only variation *across* countries but also *within* countries. The organization of waste collection ranges from very close administrative control by the municipality, to more independent organizations based on public-law, to privately owned companies. Furthermore, the competitive context differs. The following account is based on interviews with HR managers in public waste collection.[3] In addition, empirical research on the terms and conditions of sector-specific developments and employment regulation was taken into account, supplemented by a comprehensive document analysis covering the evaluation of laws, administrative regulations, collective agreements, and sector-specific national stakeholder documents.

United Kingdom. Waste collection was generally considered a public service in the United Kingdom until the end of the 1970s. Like many other public services, waste collection was exclusively provided by the state and the public workforce. The Thatcher government, however, radically reformed the organization of the waste collection sector. With the Local Government Act 1988, compulsory competitive tendering (CCT) was introduced for municipal services, including public waste collection. Municipalities were obliged by legislation to prove their cost competitiveness in comparison to private sector providers (Domberger and Jensen 1997). Thus, public service provision was set in direct competition with the private sector. Nevertheless, many municipal providers successfully competed with the private sector. In 1996, 71 per cent of waste collection was still provided by public organizations (Szymanski 1996, pp. 7f.), and in 2006, a study still reported a rate of 50 per cent for public provision (Hall 2006). Within the British administrative system, which is divided into central and local government employment (see Chapter 5), employment in public waste collection belongs to the local level. The regulation of public employment in the United Kingdom is generally based on private labour law, and collective bargaining was traditionally organized at the national level.

Until the Thatcherite reforms, public employment was distinct from the private sector due to its highly centralized personnel system, standardized employment practices, paternalistic styles of management, and collectivist patterns of industrial relations. Public organizations operated at higher standards than the national minimum legislation. The explicit aim was to act as a 'good employer' in order to attract and retain staff and to achieve good labour relations (Horton 2000, p. 211).

The transformation described above with regard to the organization of public services was accompanied by a restructuring of employment regulations, both developments being part of the overall framework of reforms based on the New Public Management (NPM) paradigm (Hood 1991; Christensen and Laegreid 2003; OECD 2004) under the Thatcher government. Former practices of collective bargaining were disregarded (Crouch 2003), and the Conservative governments from 1979 until 1997 passed a series of laws that established elements of private sector management in the public sector (OECD 2004).[4] Thus, the traditional politically and functionally strong self-governance of the local administration was replaced by a centralization of control and financial restrictions on the one hand, and a decentralization of organizational responsibility by the introduction of market competition, a split between purchaser and provider roles, and the introduction of market testing on the other (Ferner 1994, p. 55).

Furthermore, waste collection was also affected by the fact that the unions' strike capacity, which in the UK is not based on a positive right to strike anyway,[5] became even more restricted. Regarding the legal framework, the relevant individual labour laws are the Employment Rights Act 1996, the Minimum Wage Act 1998, and the Equality Act 2010. Collective labour law is regulated in the Trade Union and Labour Relations (Consolidation) Act 1992 (TULCRA) and the Employment Relations Act 2004. The framework for pay and work conditions for over 1.4 million workers in local government services is determined by the National Joint Council (NJC) for Local Government Services (Local Government Association, LGA).[6] The Single Status Agreement, reached in 1997, harmonized formerly separate agreements for manual, administrative, professional, and clerical staff at the local level. It comprised regulations on pay and grading, working time arrangements, tendering, and bonus systems. However, like collective agreements in the United Kingdom in general, it is not binding.

Reviewing studies on the coverage of collective agreements, Morgan and Allington (2003) found that, at least until the end of the 1990s, the share of manual workers covered by a collective agreement declined. According to the Workplace and Industrial Relations Survey of 1992 (WIRS92), the coverage of public sector manual workers declined from 91 per cent in 1984 to 78 per cent in 1990. For all major public sector occupational groups, the WIRS98 reports an average decline in collective bargaining coverage to 63 per cent in 1998, which is attributed to CCT and new arrangements for pay review bodies (Morgan and Allington 2003, p. 37). In addition, the decentralization of collective bargaining has had an adverse effect on the working conditions of public employees because local agreements are generally less favourable than those negotiated at the national level (Morgan and Allington 2003, p. 37).

Thus, the state as the main producer, provider, and distributor of services was questioned and, at the same time, the traditional practices of public employment were challenged (Page and Wright 2007). As a result, employment at the local government level declined sharply. Three years after the introduction of CCT in 1988, waste collection had lost about 16 per cent of all jobs, which, next to building cleaning, is the largest decline on the local level (Kerr and Radford 1994). Furthermore, municipal employers began to make extensive use of flexible work arrangements (Horton and Farnham 2000; Bach and Winchester 2003). By the early 2000s, a large share of the workforce at the municipal level was employed on part-time contracts or on a temporary basis (Bach and Winchester 2003). Nevertheless, there is a large discrepancy between collective bargaining coverage in the public and private sectors, with collective bargaining still covering about two-thirds of public sector employees in 2012, compared to 16.9 per cent in the private sector (Fulton 2013).

With regard to job security, terms of employment, and union recognition, the law on Transfer of Undertakings Protection of Employment (TUPE), enacted in 1981 for the private sector, was extended to public sector employees in 1993 (Winchester and Bach 1999, p. 29). Even though TUPE regulations require that workers transferred to a new employer retain their terms and conditions of employment, trade unions criticize that these regulations merely provide a temporary protection of terms and conditions (Unison 2003). In addition to TUPE, the government introduced the so-called two-tier code ('Code of Practice on Workforce Matters in Local Authority Service Contracts'), which demanded that providers of outsourced public services do not apply different regulations to their staff. This code was established in 2005, but abandoned in 2010 in order to remove 'a significant barrier' to smaller organizations delivering public service contracts (Cabinet Office 2010).

Germany. The German system of waste collection is characterized by a division of responsibility for household waste and packaging waste. Different regulations for competition apply. Municipalities are responsible for household waste collection, and tendering is not relevant if a municipality chooses to provide the service itself. In the field of packaging waste, in contrast, the implementation of a new regulation in 1991 shifted the responsibility for packaging waste to the private sector.[7] Consequently, contracts in the packaging waste sector are put out for tender. While about 50 per cent of household waste collection is provided by public utilities, the public share in the collection of packaging waste has been reduced to about 10 per cent, most of which, however, are actually subsidiary firms of municipal companies that collect household waste (DGB 2007, p. 6).

The major differences between personnel policies in the fields of household waste and packaging waste can be traced back to the form of competition. As almost all municipalities belong to the employers' associations of the municipalities on the *Länder* level (*Kommunale Arbeitgeberverbände*, KAV), with an umbrella organization at the national level (*Verband der kommunalen Arbeitgeberverbände*, VKA), employment in all municipal companies in household waste collection is based on the regulations laid down in the collective agreement for the public sector (*Tarifvertrag für den öffentlichen Dienst*, TVöD) agreed upon in 2005. This collective agreement contains a special supplement for the waste sector (TVöD-E/*Entsorgung*).

In contrast to collective agreements in the private sector, the TVöD is characterized by comparatively high employment security and pay. Employment in packaging waste collection is less favourable. Since contracts for the collection of packaging waste are awarded for a limited time frame, employment is only secured for the contracted period. In order to reduce costs and to keep up with their competitors, public companies ensure numerical flexibility by using fixed-term contracts or employing temporary agency workers. However, terms and conditions of employment differ not only between household waste and packaging waste collection but also between the workforce with long-term pay scale agreements and workforce employed after the introduction of the TVöD. While workers who have been employed before 2005 often enjoy tenure and pay supplements that were abolished with the introduction of the TVöD, pay and work security is often less favourable for new employees.[8] Further differences exist between municipalities because these can choose to organize their waste collection enterprises according to either public or private law (*Deutsche Gemeindeordnung*, § 5). In municipal organizations based on public law (administrative units or so-called *Eigenbetriebe* or *Regiebetriebe*), which are the traditional form of public service provision under administrative supervision of the municipality, employees are contracted directly by municipalities and are generally employed on the basis of the public sector collective agreement (TVöD). In contrast, public companies based on private law are independent employers which are not necessarily bound by the public sector's collective agreements (Bremeier et al. 2006).

Studies on the transformations in public governance at the municipal level show that independent employment regulation is an important argument for formal privatization (Edeling et al. 2004; Bremeier et al. 2006). The pay reform in the public service collective agreement introduced with the TVöD 2005 aimed at increasing individual effort and responsibility in order to improve the competitiveness of municipal utilities. It was a response to the 'escape from the BAT' (*Bundesangestelltentarifvertrag*, the former collective agreement), which had itself become a driving force behind the outsourcing of public services before 2005 (Bremeier et al. 2006, p. 18).

As reported by a trade union representative, public waste collection is, however, fully covered by collective agreements, mostly the TVöD, but in some cases also by the collective agreement of the private sector (Mendroch 2008, p. 133). By contrast, the collective agreement for the private sector only covers a minor share of employees, about 20,000 of the estimated 70,000 workers (Mendroch 2008).

Major pay gaps between the collective agreements and the company agreements motivated the trade union and public employer associations to deliver a petition for a minimum wage based on the *Arbeitnehmer-Entsendegesetz* (Employee Secondment Act) to the Federal Ministry of Labour and Social Affairs. It was successful and the minimum wage regulation was declared generally binding in 2009 (BMAS 2015).

According to our expert interviews, employment regulation differs in public waste collection between in-house provision and competitive provision. In public household waste collection with in-house provision and an absence of direct competition with the private sector, the workforce is generally employed within the TVöD framework. Apart from fixed-term contracts used to cover temporary shortages, job security is high. In packaging waste collection, confronted with direct competition from the private sector, all three interviewed companies make use of their independence with regard to the application of collective agreements. As a result, the collective agreement of the private sector or even less favourable company agreements apply. Furthermore, job security in packaging waste collection is much lower because of the limited terms of a service contract.

France. In France, neither compulsory tendering as in the United Kingdom nor a dual structure as in Germany exists in the field of waste collection. Municipalities can autonomously decide whether they provide the service in-house or whether they outsource it to the private sector. Since the early 1990s, an increasing number of municipalities have outsourced waste collection. While the share of public provision was 70 per cent in 1995, only about half of the waste volume was collected by public organizations in 2010 (ADEME 2009, p. 8). Some larger cities divide the task and allocate part of the city to public utilities and other parts to private firms. 'We decided to share the city between private and public for a lot of reasons. First thing is that we can make comparisons' (Interview WFR1).

Until the 1980s, the municipal workforce was employed under a variety of employment conditions (Mossé and Tchobanian 1999, p. 133). Since the enactment of the threefold system of the French public sector in 1982, waste workers belong to the *fonction publique territoriale* and are thus civil servants.[9] Even though the Local Government Act 1982 entitled municipal employers to employ a workforce on a temporary basis, the studied municipalities did not make use of this opportunity for flexibility on a regular basis; however, temporary workers are relevant for replacements in case of sickness. In practice, employees with fixed-term contracts are typically offered a permanent position after the termination of their contract. In the private sector, a national collective agreement, which has been extended by law to the whole waste collection sector, comprises exact regulations on wage-setting, holidays, and sick pay.[10]

Sweden. The Swedish waste collection sector was dominated by public provision of services until the end of the 1980s (Bryntse and Greve 2002). Since the early 1990s, following the adoption of the Local Government Act of 1991 that aimed at giving municipalities a free hand in organizing their committees, administrative structures and staff municipalities have been dramatically transformed (Montin 1993; Bäck and Larsson 2008). A considerable number of municipalities began outsourcing the delivery of services (Wollmann 2008, p. 304). As a result, in the mid-2000s, only 25 per cent of all municipalities maintained the in-house approach (Avfall Sverige 2007), which is the lowest share in all four countries under comparison. Employment contracts in the waste collection sector, as public employment in Sweden in general, are based on private labour law and collective agreements. Their legal fundament is the 1982 Employment Protection Act (*Lag (1982:80) om anställningsskydd*). In addition, rights and responsibilities of the social partners are based on the 1976 Co-Determination Act (*Lag (1976:580) om medbestämmande i arbetslivet*). Moreover, some regulations of the 1994 Public Employment Act (*Lag (1994:260) om offentlig anställning*) also apply to municipal employees, such as regulations about secondary employment (§ 7) or work-conflicts (§§ 23–29). In the context of broad municipal autonomy that 'is rooted in Sweden's history more deeply and endurably than in any other European country' (Wollmann 2006, p. 259), Swedish municipalities are autonomous employers (Wollmann 2004, p. 647). In addition, similar to Germany, municipal companies can contract their own workforce.

Despite this administrative and organizational fragmentation, collective bargaining is highly coordinated because all municipalities are members of the Association of Local Authorities (*Sveriges Kommuner och Landsting*, SKL), the employers' association entrusted with collective bargaining. In addition, the employers' organization representing public companies based on private law, PACTA (*Arbetsgivarförbundet för kommunalförbund og företag*), is well-integrated in collective bargaining with SKL. Most of the other public companies in the waste collection sector are represented by the employers' organization for companies in the municipal and county council sectors (*Kommala Företagens Samorganisations*, KFS).

Negotiations take place separately for co-determination, dispute regulation, and collective agreements (Eriksson 2010), the latter being most relevant for personnel policies. Negotiations typically start with a preliminary nationwide collective agreement for the whole municipal sector, comprising a framework for pay and general employment conditions (*Huvudöverenskommelse om lön och allmänna anställninsvillkor*, HÖK), but also leaving room for further specifications in certain areas such as pay by municipal, company, or individual bargaining.

In a second step, the agreement is specified on the municipal or company level. An amendment to the agreement regulates specific entitlements, which employees can claim in cases of privatization or any other decision by the employer that causes changes in the employment conditions of the individual employee.[11] The aim of this regulation is to support and assist workers in the transition to a new job and to provide workers in the transformation process with financial security (*Omställningsavtal* KOM-KL supplement 1 § 1). When applied, employees can claim pay during leave from work (§ 10), which is a special or additional transition fee (§§ 11 and 12). In contrast to the regulations in the United Kingdom, the Swedish approach was already established in the 1970s for the central administration and was approved by the social partners. It has become accepted for three reasons: it is based on a consensus among the social partners; it is funded by the employers; and it provides more flexibility for both parties. In a third step, individual bargaining for wages can take place; this possibility has recently been extended to the whole workforce (SKL 2013).

In the private sector, no national minimum wage exists because practically the whole labour market is covered by collective agreements. Minimum wages are negotiated as part of the collective agreements at the sectoral level between the social partners (Kullander 2009, p. 8).

Employment regulation

Entry requirements and recruitment

The main job types in the waste collection sector are collectors and drivers. These jobs require little formal qualifications, and recruitment does not pose any specific challenges for public employers. Rather, public employers enjoy a comparative advantage over the private sector since they offer jobs with higher job security and better pay for individuals with fewer or lower qualifications. However, as waste collection is still demanding in terms of human resources, labour costs are major factors in competition (European Commission 2001).

United Kingdom. In the United Kingdom, recruitment for public employment at the local level is decentralized, and municipalities or municipal units recruit their own workforce (Wollmann 2006, p. 78). As in the British public sector in general, no statutory entry qualifications exist, but requirements are related to the specific tasks (Bossaert et al. 2001, pp. 368f.).[12] Drivers are required to possess a driving license for large vehicles, as well as sufficient physical fitness and stamina. External recruitment takes place for both the positions of collector and driver. According to job advertisement displays, recruitment procedures are neither formalized nor generalized, and the selection of employees is based on previous employment records and successful job interviews. Applicants for driver positions may be examined for their driving skills, and some municipalities require job references. Nevertheless, according to a report of the Incomes Data Service about recruitment and retention in local government conducted in 2003, over 90 per cent of the municipalities reported difficulties in attracting and retaining staff (IDS 2003, p. 5). Among the identified factors were general shortage of key staff, relatively poor pay and working conditions, competition from the private sector and from other local authorities, the high cost of living in some areas, tight labour markets, and a perceived lack of career progression in local government (IDS 2003, p. 22). However, the problem appears to be less severe in waste collection because only 1 of the 75 cases reporting recruitment problems referred to this sector (IDS 2003, p. 18).

Germany. Since the principle of subsidiarity (*Subsidiaritätsprinzip*)[13] grants German municipalities and municipal organizations comprehensive rights of self-regulation, they are independent employers (GG Art. 28 Para. 2; see section on employment conditions) and hence, recruitment is also decentralized. In contrast to the civil service, where statutory career-specific formal entry qualifications are relevant (Bundesministerium des Innern 2006, p. 34), workers in public waste collection are usually public employees who are recruited for specific tasks and are thus hired according to specific qualifications necessary for their jobs.

Our interview partners reported that, besides the large-vehicle driving license for drivers, physical capacity and social competences, no specific requirements are necessary for jobs in public waste collection. The interview partners also reported that the recruitment of the workforce in the waste collection sector is unproblematic. One HR manager stated that up to 100 persons applied for one open position (Interview WDE1), and applicants' qualifications have substantially increased during recent decades, a development repeatedly mentioned in the interviews (Interviews WDE1, WDE3).

In general, recruitment is not conducted internally but rather through the labour market. However, in cases where different regulations exist in parent companies and subsidiary enterprises, internal recruitment is also relevant. This is mostly the case in municipalities where both household waste collection and packaging waste collection are provided by public organizations. In these cases, recruitment for household waste collection is restricted to applicants from the subsidiary companies (Interview WDE3). Since pay and job security are much higher in household waste collection than in packaging waste collection, there is interest from the employees' side to change positions. From the employers' perspective, internal recruitment is seen as an extended probation time and as a means to comply with the employers' responsibility towards the workforce (see subsection on the integration function of the public sector).

France. In contrast to the other countries, entry requirements and recruitment in France are centralized and highly standardized for the whole civil service (Auer et al. 1997, p. 40). Even though municipalities contract their own workforce, a national organization for the civil service of the local government, the *Centre National de la Fonction Publique Territoriale* (CNFPT), defines recruitment criteria and recruitment procedures for specific tasks. As in the civil service in general, the recruitment competition – the *concours* – is the normal entry procedure for local government (CNFPT 2010a, p. 17). However, in waste collection as in other fields of the lowest employment category (*Catégorie* C), exceptions and direct employment by the municipalities or municipal organizations are possible for the lowest entrance positions (CNFPT 2010a, p. 19). Furthermore, at the national level, standardized job descriptions exist which locate the jobs in the classification of the French system of public employment. These descriptions comprise principal activities, relevant competences for the job, as well as the conditions for access (CNFPT 2010b, Fiche no. 05/C/20). Besides a driving license for large vehicles for drivers, only general skills are required.

The interviewed HR managers reported that, in practice, the *concours* is not used as a selection process, but recruitment takes place after successful job interviews. New entrants into the French public workforce start at the lowest level, and the subsequent career development follows a stable pathway, which is linked to seniority, at least to some degree. This also holds for the waste collection sector. Even though the position of driver is a first career step, access from the external labour market is possible (CNFPT 2010a, pp. 17, 143). Like their German counterparts, the interviewed HR managers in France stated that they observed a general trend towards higher educational backgrounds of applicants. This trend is explained by the high unemployment rate:

> And with the economic crisis we have a new kinds of candidates who are people who were butchers, bakers, lorry drivers [...] And this is good for us because those people are more trained, more accustomed to work in teams. (Interview WFR1)

Sweden. There is no unified recruitment procedure in the Swedish public sector since the various authorities are responsible for their own recruitment systems. This implies that the selection process for public employees is similar to the private sector (Auer et al. 1997, p. 44; Bossaert et al. 2001, pp. 98f., 270). As in the other analysed countries, apart from the driving licence for large vehicles for the drivers, no specific qualifications are required. Nevertheless, most applicants have a background of at least 12 years of school education, and this condition has now developed into an informal but 'common' demand (Interview WSE2). While in the other countries this development is mainly attributed to the economic situation, in Sweden, the increased standard of education is mentioned as a cause.

To summarize, recruitment procedures in public waste collection reveal a low degree of formalization. Corresponding to the tasks that – besides the driving licence for large vehicles for the job of a driver – demand no specific qualifications, no specific recruitment criteria are mentioned. Comparing the four countries, the most formalized system for recruitment is established in France, where a nationwide unified job description and general recruitment criteria exist, and a formal recruitment procedure is specified. However, even within the French civil service system, the recruitment procedure is exceptional since the entrance exam, which is generally required for a position in the civil service, is not obligatory. Thus, recruitment procedures and entry requirements in all four countries can be characterized as position-based, and even though recruitment is decentralized and entry requirements as well as recruitment procedures are not standardized, no major divergences between the countries can be observed. In practice, although the regulative parameters have not changed since the 1990s, recruitment criteria have been implicitly upgraded because of a broader supply of workers and increased availability of applicants with higher educational levels.

Pay

Pay in the public sector was traditionally based on centrally determined grading systems with fixed pay scales. Progression is predominantly based on seniority, with equity and consistency being core values. This resulted in public sector pay premiums on the lower end of the pay scales in comparison to the private sector. Since the late 1980s, this has changed considerably, and in many countries pay determination contains elements of NPM, such as performance-based pay. Moreover, when fields that are very demanding in terms of human resources are exposed to competition with the private sector, as in public waste collection, the processes of market building and privatization have exerted a downward pressure on wages (Bach 1999, p. 19).

United Kingdom. Municipalities in the United Kingdom are independent employers, and the central government has little direct control on pay and employment conditions. However, it can exert influence through the allocation of funds or through legislation. Until the end of the 1970s, a model of benevolent paternalism and absenteeism of central governmental influence was prevalent. Methods of pay settlement were traditionally characterized by a joint regulation through nationally coordinated collective bargaining, which was organized along both sectoral and occupational lines (White 1999, p. 73; Kirkpatrick and Hoque 2005). At the local government level, 15 negotiating groups existed. Waste collectors belonged to one of the largest groups, the manual workers. While differences existed between civil servants, white-collar employees, and blue-collar workers, as well as between different occupations, there were no geographical differences in basic pay-setting arrangements (White 1999, p. 74). Pay progression was traditionally based on length of service (Local Government Employers, LGE 2004, p. 4). Although basic pay was set in national agreements and there was little scope for negotiations at the local level, individual local authorities, being independent employers, had some leeway in exceeding national guidelines and setting up incentive pay schemes (White and Hutchinson 1996, p. 186). Central governmental influence was limited.

The Conservative governments from 1979 to 1997 radically changed this system by restricting the financial scope of local governments, imposing pay limits on public services, and introducing CCT. Furthermore, the collective power of employees was curtailed, and centralized pay bargaining was hindered.[14] Controlling the financial resources, the government was able to penalize authorities for exceeding pay guidelines by refusing to provide the necessary budgets (White and Hutchinson 1996, p. 189). As a result, 'the formal situation in which local authorities are independent employers, who voluntarily cede certain rights to national and regional representative institutions, no longer matches reality' (Walsh 1981, cited in White and Hutchinson 1996, p. 209). While in the beginning of the 1980s, financial constraints resulted in pressure to centralize collective bargaining, by the early 1990s, CCT became a 'major catalyst' of bargaining decentralization for manual workers' wages, as it allowed for more flexibility in order to compete with private sector service providers (White and Hutchinson 1996, p. 209). 'If they are to compete then local authorities must be able to reduce their costs below those of private contractors. [T]he private sector will generally offer lower levels of pay, and have poorer conditions such as holidays, sickness pay and benefits' (Department of the Environment 1991, cited in Kerr and Radford 1994, p. 38).

However, by 1997, national collective agreements were still relevant for a large majority of municipalities following nationally agreed rates, and only about 40 councils had developed their own pay structures (White 1999, p. 91; OECD 1994, p. 75). According to a study commissioned by the Department of the Environment on the effects of CCT, 'the impact on take-home pay of other changes to conditions, particularly with regard to bonus schemes, was considerable. Overall, 32 per cent of bonus schemes were changed and 15 per cent were abolished altogether' (Department of the Environment 1991, cited in Kerr and Radford 1994, p. 38).

In 1997, the National Joint Council introduced the Single Status Agreement, which was a radical reform of local government payment aiming at abandoning the status division between manual and non-manual employees by establishing one single pay spine (National Agreement on Pay and Conditions of Service). Besides the harmonization between the two status groups, the agreement aimed at the equalization of pay and work conditions by introducing a scheme for the comparative evaluation of skills and knowledge demanded for specific jobs.[15] However, municipalities were not required to use a particular scheme, and the agreement allowed for local variation in grading structures and their relation to the pay spine (Perkins and White 2010, p. 249). The National Joint Council agreed local pay reviews should be completed and implemented by 2007. However, the process of implementing the Single Status Agreement was very slow, with only about one-third of the municipalities having completed the pay and grading review by 2004 (Perkins and White 2010, pp. 247, 250; LGE 2004). Two studies by the employers' associations on the local government level reveal that pay structures, methods of allocating jobs to pay bands, as well as the systems of pay progression differ between municipalities (LGE 2004; 2006). Although some municipalities use the arrangements available according to the agreement – such as broad pay bands, systems of career grades, and spot salaries – most municipalities make use of narrow pay bands. The allocation of jobs to pay bands is mostly accomplished by job evaluation. Sometimes pay bands are linked to market rates or job families. With regard to pay progression, municipalities reported to adhering to the traditional model of progression solely by length of service. Some municipalities combine the system of progression by length of service with other measures, whereas other municipalities abolished this system altogether (LGE 2004, p. 4). Given that only 30 of the 500 municipalities had concluded separate bargaining arrangements by the late 2000s, the Single Status Agreement is of major importance for the local public sector (Perkins and White 2010, p. 247f.).

Given the broad pay bands within the Single Status Agreement and the existence of separate regulations, pay policies in public waste collection in the United Kingdom varied considerably in the late 2000s. On the one hand, median hourly wages range from GBP 5.32 to GBP 7.41 between municipalities. On the other hand, bonus systems vary considerably, being in some cases worth up to 50 per cent of basic pay (IDS 2003, p. 58). The Local Governments Earnings Survey 2010/2011 underscores these findings by reporting regional differences between basic pay, as well as differences between basic pay and gross pay within municipalities (LGA 2013). Pay of public sector workers employed in the services subject to CCT is significantly more favourable than of those working for private contractors (Kerr and Radford 1994, p. 38). A minimum regulation is provided by the Minimum Wage Act 1998, with a minimum hourly wage of GBP 6.50 for workers aged 21 years and older in 2015.

In sum, until the 1980s, pay in the British public waste collection sector was characterized by centralized national bargaining for basic pay and pay progression by length of service. Even though collective bargaining at the national level is still influential, different pay and progression systems – as well as a broad variation in actual pay in the sector – reveal a development of decentralization and fragmentation within the sector. However, pay and working conditions in local government are still better in the public sector than in the private sector. The existence of a minimum wage ensures a minimum standard in the private sector, and at the same time limits the public-private wage gap and thus limits the competitive pressure.

Germany. Until 2005, the remuneration of German public employees was based on the career-based model with seniority-based pay progression and family allowances (Czerwick 2007, p. 171). The collective agreement of 2005 (TVöD) introduced a single pay scheme for public workers and employees; also, non-work-related wage supplements were abolished, and elements of performance-related pay (PRP) were added.[16] In contrast to the former connection between pay progression and age, the new contract focuses on length of service. Conditional on at least average performance, advancement to the next higher level is scheduled after 1, 3, 6, 10, and 15 years (TVöD §16 (3)). In case of extraordinary performance, these intervals can be shortened, whereas advancement can also be delayed in case of bad performance (TVöD §17 (2)). In practice, waste collectors are in the lowest wage groups (E3 and E4), whereas drivers belong to the second wage group (normally E5, but E6 in the case of a three-year professional driver training). Local regulations as well as opinions about PRP vary. Some interviewed HR managers state that individual performance in the field of waste collection is not measurable, and thus pay differentiation would not result in increased motivation, but rather dissatisfaction among the workforce; thus, they did not actively pursue PRP strategies (Interviews WDE4 and WDE2). In one case, an elaborate system of performance measurement was established. As a result, 98 per cent of the workforce reached the norm and thus obtained the 1 per cent pay increase; the system was abandoned in the following period (Interview WDE5). In another case, the 1 per cent of the aggregated payroll available for PRP was divided, with one part distributed equally to all employees and another part used for awards for extraordinary performance (Interview WDE3). Only in one case was satisfaction from employers as well as employees reported (Interview WDE3).

In the area of packaging waste collection, where public companies compete directly with the private sector, pay is generally lower than in household waste collection. The overall coverage of collective agreements is less than 30 per cent, and given that public providers make up only 10 per cent of providers in this field, the public sector agreement too is of minor importance with a coverage of only 6.75 per cent (ver:di 2012, p.10). Especially, in the private sector firms, many companies only pay the minimum wage. The interviewed HR managers view the private companies as the main drivers toward low standards and pressure on wage levels. Moreover, they report differences with regard to pay between core staff and temporary agency workers (Interview WDE4).

> The pay structure is different. It's not the TVöD [collective agreement for the public employees of the federal state and the municipalities; the authors] that is applied but the BDE [collective agreement of the private

sector in the field of waste management; the authors]. The company is based on low-wages – sometimes I am shocked when I see with how little wage the colleagues have to get along with. But that seems to be normal in this industry – there are companies that pay even less. (Interview WDE4)

In sum, until the early 1990s, pay in public waste collection was character-ized by the career-based system with non-work-related allowances and pay levels and increases referring to seniority and the age of the employees. Due to centralized bargaining, pay was rather uniform throughout Germany. Since the reforms, pay progression is based on the length of service, and due to the abolishment of non-work-related supplements such as family allowances and the introduction of PRP in the collective agreement of 2005, pay systems are generally more aligned to private sector standards. So far, compared to the overall payroll, the share of PRP is almost negligible, and variations with regard to the amount as well as the procedure exist. Overall, the relevance of PRP is rather symbolic, and there seems to be no fervent support for this element of NPM on the side of HR managers and the employees' representatives.

France. For employees in waste collection in France, the general pay regu-lations for civil servants apply. Pay is regulated by law in a uniform frame-work for the three levels of public employment. Even though the state has the power to regulate pay unilaterally, in 1983 trade unions obtained the formal right to negotiate issues of remuneration with the government (*Loi n° 83–634 du 13 juillet 1983* Articles 20ff.). Collective agreements have no legal status, and they do not suspend the government's unilateral power of decision-making. The government also decides on the timing of pay nego-tiations and defines strict parameters of negotiation. However, as the agree-ment is the outcome of a political compromise, all players, including the government, adhere to it. Given that bargaining takes place at the central level and encompasses the whole public sector, the local actors are not involved in the negotiations (Burnham 2000, p. 109). As a result, the French public sector is referred to as 'the most centralized wage-setting system of all 27 EU Member States' (EUROFOUND 2007, p. 29). Remuneration comprises a base wage amended by job-related supplements as well as non-work related supplements such as housing and family allowances. Premiums exist for certain functions.

The actual wage is calculated from a system of index points, which cover all grades and employment levels, and the work-related supplements. Depending on the level of technical expertise or responsibility attached to certain jobs or functions, further index points are added, which are based on the NBI (*novelle bonification indiciaire*). The value of one hundred index points is determined in annual pay negotiations (Burnham 2000, p. 110). In 2010, one hundred index points were equivalent to an annual pay of EUR

5556.35 (*Décret n° 2010–761 du 7 juillet 2010*), with the minimum wage set at 280 index points.

After entry in the public service, civil servants start at the lowest possible number of index points for their grade and, if their performance is not explicitly unsatisfactory, they then progress through the scales. Supplements, such as residential allowances and family allowances, are fixed amounts. Municipal workers in public waste collection are technical assistants (*adjoints techniques territoriaux*) belonging to the technical *corps* in the *category* C. Four hierarchical levels are differentiated,[17] entailing different salary scales. Progression within these levels depends on length of service. As a result, pay is uniform for the same occupations throughout the whole public sector in France. The lowest level (*adjoint technique de 2eme classe*) has 297 index points and, thus, minimum annual pay in public sector waste collection is EUR 16,502. Although PRP was introduced in the French public sector the 1990s as a new management approach, so far it has not been implemented for manual work such as waste collection. From the perspective of HR managers, PRP is referred to as 'a dream':

> The trade unions want a kind of equality: the same wages for the same jobs. We have a lot of problems trying to promote the best instead of the older. [...] We have permanent discussions with the trade unions explaining that we need to promote the better instead of the older. (Interview WFR1)

In the private sector, pay is also highly regulated. Like in the public sector, the number of index points depends on the knowledge and skills required for the respective job. In addition, a sector-specific minimum pay level is defined (132 index points CCNAD III-2 Art 3.5). Job-related supplements such as dirty or heavy work premiums are expressed by index points and added to the basic pay (CCNAD III-2). Each index point is worth EUR 14.81 in 2015. Collectors and drivers are located in the range of 100 to 107 and 110 to 118 index points, respectively. Both are below the 132 index points of the minimum wage.[18] Furthermore, according to pay progression based on work experience, the wage increases by 2 per cent every two years (CCNAD III-2 Art 3.15.). In contrast to the public sector, residential allowances and family-based allowances do not exist in the private sector.

In conclusion, given that employees in public waste collection are part of the *fonction publique territoriale*, salaries are unilaterally set by the government after negotiations with the trade unions. Traditional pay components such as residential supplements and family allowances exist. Given that wages are set at the central level and PRP is not applied for this group of public employees, local governments have no leeway for differentiating wages. In contrast to Germany, the difference in pay between public and private sector employment is comparatively small, since nationally binding collective agreements exist for the private sector that resemble the public sector to a large degree.

Sweden. Collective wage bargaining for Swedish public sector employees was introduced in 1966, and the first elements of local flexibility amounting to up to 1 per cent of salary were added in 1978. In 1985, the Swedish Parliament passed the government's Personnel Policy Bill, which committed the public sector to give priority to results and efficiency over other considerations. While central wage agreements had determined wage levels and defined the scope for wage increases until the late 1980s, from then on bargaining has been decentralized in order to give local employers more influence over the size and distribution of pay increases (SKL 2006, p. 9).

According to the new system, a central collective agreement sets minimum wage levels and wage increases for all municipal employees and entails recommendations for local collective agreements.[19] This national agreement also includes major public companies.

A second important collective agreement for employees of municipal companies in the waste sector is the *Återvinning* (until 2012: *Renhallningsavtalet*), which is also set at the central level and includes minimum wages and ranges for wage increases. For municipal workers, the monthly minimum wage in 2015 is SEK 20,120 (EUR 2,193.63). Furthermore, municipal employers have some leeway for individual negotiations (SEK 600 per employee, Löneavtal § 2). In contrast to the past when a minimum increase was guaranteed for each employee, the whole amount is now subject to individual negotiations (SKL 2010; SKL 2013).

> The aim is to create a process where the worker's results and wages are linked together so that the positive relationship between wages, motivation, and results is achieved. It is, therefore, of great importance that a dialogue exists between manager and employee about goals, expectations, requirements, performance, and salary. (SKL 2010, Löneavtal § 1, translation by authors)

In this vein, the collective agreement has been amended by a section in which the social partners list requirements for individual wage settlements. Besides transparency and the setting of concrete and measurable targets, it also defines criteria for performance-related individual pay. While no provisions for general pay supplements are made, in the agreement the social partners emphasized that the experience of older workers should be taken into account in individual evaluations, and thus recommended at least some progression by length of service (SKL 2013 Bilaga 5). Regarding individual wage settlements, the three interviewed municipalities follow different approaches. While in one municipality, individual pay negotiations for workers in public waste collection have already been established, a second municipality reported that plans exist to introduce it in the near future, and the third municipality did not refer to any range for individual bargaining. Individual wage settlements are reported to be the result of annual dialogues between the employer and the individual employees. In the three municipalities, the pay level is above the minimum defined in the collective agreements. With regard to PRP, wage settlements formerly entailed individual components in the form of an accord system with about 30 per cent of the payroll depending on the number of bins emptied. This system was abolished for two reasons. First, the system induced workers to disregard safety rules, resulting in increased accident rates. Second, it was argued that individual performance was not comparable because of differences between collection areas. In contrast to the former accord system that defined performance quantitatively by the length of time needed for a specific number of bins emptied, the new system was geared toward qualitative aims by measuring performance as service orientation: 'it's to be polite with the citizens to make a nice work. Go nice and slow in the traffic, don't rush, follow the traffic rules' (Interview WSE3).

In sum, pay in public waste collection in Sweden was already close to the position-based model in the 1980s, and developments since then strengthened the flexibility of pay settlements. Even though the general framework is set at the national level, these regulations merely define minimum standards such as minimum pay and guaranteed wage increases for individual employees. Municipalities have some scope to adapt their own pay policies. In practice, not all employers make use of their independence to individualize pay.

Career advancement and further training

In general, the field of waste collection offers few career prospects, and opportunities for further training are very limited in all countries under study.

United Kingdom. Career advancement in the public sector of the United Kingdom is position-based: 'Movement to a higher grade should be linked to the employee taking on the new demands, rather than just to time in post or qualifications received' (NJC 2005, p. 183). Against this background, further training and career prospects are part of the 'key national provisions' of the collective agreement for the local government employees (NJC 2005: 2.1). 'Training and development should be designed to meet the corporate and service needs of authorities both current and in the future, taking into account the individual needs of employees. Local schemes on training and development should enable authorities to attain their strategic objectives through development of their employees' (NJC 2005). The agreement demands authorities to pay for all further training expenses, including payment of normal earnings. In order to encourage and support further training programmes, partnerships with trade unions and coordination with statutory programmes are suggested. Local governments are expected to set their own guidelines and to conduct reviews (NJC 2005). However, in line with the general pattern that collective agreements are not binding in the United Kingdom, these provisions do not entitle employees to a legal claim to further training. Moreover, in public waste collection, the only possible advancement is from collector to driver.

Germany. In Germany, traditionally two forms of career advancement for public employees existed. In case public employees met a set of required qualifications, they could apply for open positions in a higher wage group. In addition, a specific form of automatic career progression was in place. After a certain time span – usually five years for blue-collar workers – employees were eligible for a promotion to a higher wage group even without having the respective qualifications normally required by this wage group (Brandes and Buttler 1990, p. 98). This so-called *Bewährungsaufstieg* (BAT §23) was discontinued after the TVöD became effective in 2005. Since then, career advancement is based on a successful application for a vacant post or on the assignment of tasks that are related to a higher wage group (TVöD § 14). Further training is regulated by the general labour law of the *Länder*. Twelve of the 16 *Länder* adopted rules for continual training, offering employees up to five days of paid leave per year for further training (see, for example, *Bremisches Bildungsurlaubsgesetz*).[20] With the TVöD, further training has for the first time become a subject of collective regulation (TVöD § 5). Continual training is highly valued, and lifelong learning as well as a high level of qualification is considered important for both employees and employers. Continual training is regarded as a means to increase the effectiveness and efficiency of the public service (TVöD § 5). Even though employees are not legally entitled to further training, Dörring and Kutzki (2007, p. 2) interpret the new regulation on further training in the TVöD as a new guiding principle.

Career advancement in the public waste collection is connected to a new position in a higher wage group. In practice, due to the lack of legal regulations and municipal self-government, career advancement and further training differ considerably between municipalities. A common form of career advancement reported in all municipalities is advancement from collector to driver. However, while in some cases the employer bore the costs, in other cases employers obtained public funding earmarked for training of low-skilled workers. External factors such as new regulations, technical demands, or specific programmes of individual *Länder*, but also labour shortages, often result in offers for internal further training. For example, a regulation was enacted in 2006 that demanded additional qualifications and continual training for all professional drivers of large vehicles (*Berufskraftfahrer-Qualifikations-Gesetz*). This led to comprehensive internal training programmes, and municipalities report that they provided the necessary training. In some cases, these programmes resulted in additional offers of further training for all employees. One municipality reported that it established an internal driving school and introduced a company agreement guaranteeing all employees the right to obtain a driving license for large vehicles (Interview WDE5). Furthermore, in cooperation with a *Länder* programme supporting further training of low-qualified employees (WeGebAU, *Weiterbildung Geringqualifizierter und beschäftigter Älterer in Unternehmen)*, training programmes for obtaining a driving license for large vehicles was offered in two municipalities (Interviews WDE3 and WDE4). In addition, one municipality offered further training to qualify its employees for other fields of employment in the company, for example in administration (Interview WDE5). Two municipalities, however, did not report specific programmes for further education. Career advancement in companies in the competitive field of packaging waste collection is scarce. Rather, the change from fixed-term employment or temporary agency work to a permanent contract, or from the subsidiary company to the mother company, is reported as a kind of career advancement.

France. In France, career advancement in the public sector is regulated by law, centralized, and highly formalized. The system rests on the general statute of the civil service that applies to all civil servants (*Loi n°83–634 du 13 juillet 1983*). Furthermore, particular statutes have been enacted for each *corps*, which outline career pathways of civil servants within a *corps*. In general, advancement in the French civil service is career-based. Civil servants start their career as trainees, typically for a period of one year. If they properly fulfil their duties, they are granted a tenured civil service position (*titularisation*). Uniformly throughout the civil service, employees are guaranteed to climb the steps within a grade by length of service. In most *corps*, the time span spent in a certain pay bracket can either be shortened as a reward for good performance or extended as a sanction for bad performance. Finally, an internal competitive exam can be necessary to access the highest class of a *corps* (UN 2006, p. 13). Career advancement for employment on the local level is administrated centrally by the so-called management centres of the local government service (*Les centres de gestion de la fonction publique territoriale*, CDG). Career advancement for workers in the public waste collection, as for those in the technical services of the municipalities (*adjoints techniques territoriaux*) in general, encompasses three steps.[21] In case of entry to the civil service at the second entry level (that is, as drivers), two further levels can be reached (CDG 61 2011).

The HR managers interviewed referred to these possibilities of advancement as 'a linear career', which is 'a progression that is very slow, but secure. If one does the work properly, he will arrive there' (Interview WFR2).

In addition, French civil servants have comprehensive rights for continual training. Traditionally, in-service training was the prerogative of technical *corps*, mainly aiming at developing and improving skills. Beyond that, further training is also relevant for career advancement, as it prepares employees for competitive exams (UN 2006, pp. 14f.). Depending on the size of the municipality and the respective sector, continual training on the local level is provided either by the municipality or the CDGs. As explained above, career progression in public waste collection is based on two criteria: the length of service and the achievement of a specific pay level. Jointly, the two principles constitute a seniority-based model with automatic progression to the next pay level, conditional on the absence of negative performance evaluations. Bad performance evaluations delay progression of pay levels and career advancement but are not a general hindrance. With regard to the first career step to the *adjoint technique de 1ère classe*, where external recruitment is also relevant, two possibilities for career advancement exist. Having obtained at least three years of experience as an *adjoint technique de 2ème classe* and having reached the fourth pay level qualifies workers to take an exam for career progression. Otherwise, they step up after at least ten years of work experience and having reached the seventh pay level. As advancement is rather career-based than position-based, a career step does not automatically imply changing work content. 'They can be chief technical officer, second class or first class, but still be refuse collectors' (Interview WFR3). Beyond that, further career progression is possible after passing a *concours*.

In practice, further training was reported to be relevant and employees in the waste collection sector make use of their possibilities for continual training, in particular with courses preparing for career advancement. In addition, literacy and language courses are also booked. Besides professional training, civil servants have the legal right for paid continual training in their own fields of interest, capped at 20 hours per year. While the rights and opportunities for further training are present in the other countries too, only in France is it considered relevant in the waste collection sector (Interview WFR2).

In the private waste collection sector, possibilities for career advancement must be reviewed on a regular basis based on the needs of the company and the employees' qualifications.[22] Trade unions must be informed about the evaluation and the number of employees promoted. The individual right to training was established in labour law by *Loi n° 2004–391 du 4 Mai 2004*, and is now the subject of the *Code du travail* Art. L 6323–1. It complements other methods of training for employees throughout their working lives, including individual training leave (*Droit individuel à la formation – DIF*, CCNAD Art. 4–2) and the training plan.

Sweden. Career advancement in Sweden is not formalized, and automatic career advancement does not exist. As in position-based systems in general, employees are contracted with regard to their qualifications meeting the demands of a specific job. Depending on their qualifications, employees might change their position within the company by applying to open positions, but no specific programmes exist. Furthermore, no specific regulation and no coordinated national system exist with regard to further training. In the collective agreement for local employees, the importance of competency development is stressed (SKL 2010, pp. 29, 139), and staff motivation, efficiency, and better work environment are mentioned as important effects. 'Although social partners in some sectors regulate CVT [continual vocational training; insertion by the authors] by collective bargaining at the sector level, this issue is traditionally not a top priority of the collective bargaining agenda' (Brunk and Wahmann 2009). The collective agreements do not set up any specific measures, and employees cannot legally claim further training. They are, however, eligible for (non-paid) educational leave on grounds of general law. In the context of strong local self-government and missing formal regulations, career advancement and further training differ between municipalities. Several interview partners reported that advancement from collector to driver is common, but there are no structured programmes in place. In order to reach high ecological standards, courses in eco-driving are mandatory. In practice, career advancement and further training largely depends on the financial situation of the municipality (Interviews WSE1, WSE2, and WSE3).

Job security

As described above, for most occupations in the waste collection sector, formal qualification is not important and a large share of the workforce is low-qualified (European Commission 2001, p. 2). For these workers, high employment security is particularly important because they are more likely to face disadvantages on the labour market and have a higher risk of unemployment than qualified staff. This argument is even stronger for the workforce in public waste collection, which shows other characteristics that are connected with disadvantages on the labour market, such as a foreign nationality or relatively high age; a combination of these factors might even worsen the situation of employees on the labour market (Keller 2008, p. 208). Furthermore, waste collection work is physically demanding and entails a number of high-risk activities, such as jumping on and off trucks, carrying waste bins, working in close proximity to large refuse collection vehicles, and walking on busy roads collecting waste from both sides of the pavement. Therefore, the risk of accidents in this field of employment is extraordinarily high. For example, in the United Kingdom, the share of accidents in the waste collection industry is around four times the national rate, and the fatal injury accident rate is ten times the national rate (Health and Safety Executive 2004, p. 68). Thus, besides regulation for job security, a high standard of work security, as well as means enabling employees to work until their pension age, are also crucial to secure work income for employees until they receive their pension. Here the inclusion of a workforce with restricted or reduced capabilities (such as older employees), or staff that suffers from work accidents, can be critical. However, as we will see, in the course of transformations based on NPM measures, the traditional role of the state as a 'good employer' granting high job security and integrating disadvantaged labour market groups is questioned.

United Kingdom. Employment protection for the public workforce in the United Kingdom is based on the general labour regulation laid down in the Employment Rights Act 1996 (ERA). Even though public employees can generally be dismissed, in view of stable industrial relations, the orientation towards service quality and the self-perception of the state as a 'good employer' and a role model for the private sector, job security in the public sector was traditionally very high (Winchester and Bach 1999, p. 26). However, the public sector management reforms in the 1980s, especially the organizational restructuring of local government services, affected job security at the local government level. Mandatory legislation required municipalities to expose activities traditionally supplied in-house to periodic competitive tendering. Contracting out fundamentally changed the provision of many public services, regardless of who provided the services. The required tendering created potentially market-inclined pressures within public organizations. In-house providers were instructed to operate as if they were independent contractors: maintaining their own accounts, generating returns on their assets, and providing or purchasing their own support services (such as finance, payroll, or personnel) (Sachdev 2001, p. 11). At the same time, over the course of the decentralization of collective bargaining, the trade unions' capacity to defend the formerly high standards of work security declined along with the influence of trade unions. Obligatory tendering emphasized economic efficiency, and measures of cost reduction were enforced irrespective of public or private ownership. More generally, research on services under CCT (referring, among others, to building cleaning) shows that efficiency gains were reached by increasing workloads and at the expense of good pay and working conditions.[23] Job security in local government services further declined with the increase of the share of non-standard employment, such as part-time work, fixed-term contracts, or temporary agency work. In a case study of two local authorities, Colling (1999) reported that, along with the overall decline in job security, fixed-term employment and temporary agency work expanded in the public waste collection sector.

Germany. In contrast to German civil servants, public employees such as those in waste collection have no tenure. Nevertheless, job security for employees is high, and after 15 years of service and reaching the age of 40 years, employees were guaranteed a position for the rest of their working life (MTArb § 58; TVöD/TV-L §34 (2)). This regulation has not been adopted for employees of the *Länder* that had formerly been part of the German Democratic Republic (TVöD/TV-L § 34). Thus, after reunification, different regulations exist in the 'old' and the 'new' *Länder*. Irrespective of the relatively high job security, public employees can still be dismissed for a 'just cause' (TVöD/TV-L § 34 (2)), such as a serious violation of the employment contract, but also for individual reasons like the incapacity to fulfil the employment contract (Linde and Jansen 2009, p. 197). Furthermore, a special supplement for the field of waste management exists (TVöD-E/*Entsorgung*) which entails regulations allowing for temporary employment up to four years longer than the TVöD.

In practice, job security in the public waste collection sector highly depends on the competitive situation faced by the organization collecting waste. The household waste collection sector with contracts based on the TVöD is generally characterized by high job security, while in the packaging waste collection sector, jobs are only secure for the contracted period. Furthermore, temporary agency work with lower standards of job security is common in the packaging waste collection sector.

Nevertheless, competition also impacts job security in the household sector because employees are continuously threatened by the possibility of privatization. Workers' representatives and trade unions have been able to negotiate job security provisions in some instances. Two of the municipalities analysed in this study have concluded work agreements prohibiting dismissal for redundancy for a few years into the future, implying that employment security in these cases even exceeds the general regulation of the TVöD. The HR managers in these municipalities justify these agreements as an element of social responsibility as a public employer, and also point to the high transaction costs involved.

> What do we do with 250 waste collectors when we no longer provide the service? And simply to sell them [with the company] in a situation of ever decreasing wages that has developed in this field in recent years would be a financial disaster for the workers. We would not just do that. This would mean: The city retains workers and has to pay them in addition to the contracted service. Only if this would still be cheaper, it would be a useful business. (Interview WDE1)

In another municipality, plans to privatize waste collection have been averted by reducing labour costs: staff reductions are conducted by not replacing all retired employees. However, in light of the unclear future of public waste collection, new employees tend to only be hired on fixed-term contracts (Interview WDE2). Thus, at least some municipalities have started to evade the strict and employee-friendly regulations of the public employment regime by an increased use of 'atypical' employment modes avoiding guaranteed lifetime employment.

Notwithstanding the general high job security in the TVöD, especially for employees in the 'old', formerly Western German *Länder* described above, workers in the public waste collection sector are still facing the risk of unemployment in case of health problems. One of the interviewed HR managers stated that almost no workers remain in the sector until retirement age (Interview WDE3). In order to prevent the unemployment of their workforce, some municipalities attempt to maintain staff that 'left their health in the company', for example by guaranteeing alternative, less physically demanding employment in street cleaning or gatekeeping (Interview WDE3). In the studied municipality, employees who have reached their fiftieth birthday and who have worked for the company for more than 20 years are entitled to another position under retention of their former payments. Workers who do not fulfil these criteria can change to another position conditional on a 10 per cent reduction of their wages (Interview WDE3).

All municipalities reported that they attempt to include workforce with reduced capabilities, although they emphasize that capacities are limited. At the same time, the HR managers stated that the disentangling of services reduces the scope of functions, and thus their means to integrate workforce with disabilities. Furthermore, increasing work intensification and PRP challenges the ability of public companies to integrate employees with reduced work capacities.

> These are contradictions within itself and at the moment this also tears apart the trade unions: On the one hand, they recognize that the public service must develop into a service company, and this of course entails performance incentives – those who work more, earn more. On the other hand, the young ones do not get the opportunity to get the pay premiums because they have to work together with the old workers. If you do this a few times, you will have social unrest after a while. Then it's said 'we do not work with the old people because with them we do not make enough money'. There are these contradictions. (Interview WDE1)

Thus, the increased performance expectations lead to a paradoxical incentive structure for HR managers in the public sector, as there is a contradiction between the state as an employer with social responsibilities on the one hand and the state as a service provider which, in the interest of its citizen-customers, is obliged to provide cost-efficient services on the other.

France. Job security in the French civil service is very high. The lifelong employment guarantee for *fonctionnaires* means that the large majority of the workforce cannot be dismissed. On the municipal level, employers can make use of fixed-term contracts, but employers make very little use of this type of employment in practice. Thus, in the public waste collection sector – as in the public sector in general – job security is very high: 'We are bound to them until they die', as a HR manager put it (Interview WFR1). Furthermore, pension age in the French public waste collection is 55 years, which is five years below the general French standard and about ten years below the pension age in other countries. As a result, the workforce is much younger. The average age in the interviewed municipalities is between 39 and 41 years, so that an ageing workforce and physically exhausting work is less of a problem for public employers in this sector.

Sweden. The Swedish public workforce is subject to private labour law. As stated in the 1982 Employment Protection Act (*Lag (1982:80) om anställningsskydd*), employees can generally be dismissed for 'objective reasons', such as redundancies. Job security regulations based on collective agreements (*Trygghetavtal*) are relevant for employees of municipal private companies that belong to the employers' association of municipal companies (*Kommunala Företagens Samorganisation*, KFS). These employers are obliged to longer periods of notice before dismissal, leave for vocational training, supplementary pay, and the support of the Job Security Foundation (*Trygghetsstiftelsen*), which individually supports redundant employees in finding a new job. Thus, the risk of redundancy is counterbalanced by more generous unemployment benefits and an active and individually tailored labour market policy.

Even though employees can be dismissed in case of redundancy, in one of the cases under study, comprehensive restructuring did not result in unemployment. After the contract with a private service provider ended, the shares of public and private division were restructured and new contracts were awarded. In the course of this operation, the municipality took over all workers employed in the waste collection sector.

> Some of the people go over to the new company, the private one. Some will be retired and a couple of them will get a new job. I think more or less everyone is taken care of. I think [we are] sending home two persons one year ahead of retirement. I think they are about 64 [years old]. (Interview WSE1)

Equal opportunity policies

Equal opportunity policies are relevant in the public waste collection with respect to two aspects. In view of an almost entirely male workforce, which is mainly due to the demanding physical requirements of the jobs, equal opportunity policies for women constitute a challenge. In addition, the high share of migrant workers in the workforce, which is partly a consequence of the rather unattractive job profiles, exposes the sector with respect to anti-discrimination policies. While in all four countries the general equal opportunity regulations apply, HR managers' perceptions of the relevance of these regulations for this sector's workforce vary.

A common view among German as well as French HR managers is that employment in waste collection is not attractive for women due to the physical strength required. The French HR managers interviewed for this study also emphasized the difficulties of reconciling working times comprised of early morning and night shifts with family life, which, they claimed, particularly affect women. Against this background, the gender imbalance in the workforce is not seen as a real problem. However, interestingly in one case in Germany, an HR manager was very much in favour of hiring more women. He argued that women, due to being physically weaker than men, would have to make use of more efficient and thus healthier work strategies, for example when lifting garbage bins, and that this could contribute to better working conditions for men too (Interview WDE5). Thus, he turned around the traditional view that physical strength is a precondition for a job in the waste collection sector, but rather presented women as role models for male workers.

In Sweden too, HR managers perceive the male dominance of the workforce as a result of the fact that women do not apply for jobs in waste collection. However, unlike their German and French counterparts, they unanimously report a strong interest in increasing the share of women because of pressures on the male-dominated waste sector generated by the overall equal pay policy in the Swedish public sector. Swedish public employers have to survey and analyse pay differentials and 'to determine whether these are objectively based and have no connection with gender' (Diskrimineringsombudsmannen 2009). The legislation on pay surveys has influenced the country's collective agreements, and public employment is covered by agreements prescribing that regulations on pay have to incorporate principles concerning equal treatment and equal pay. These regulations also include prohibitions of discrimination. The aim of these rules is to achieve equal pay between women and men, not only within but also across sectors and occupations. The problem Swedish HR managers in waste collection refer to concerns the pay level in the waste collection sector, which is reported to be higher than in female-dominated jobs with similar qualification requirements. In this regard, efforts to increase the share of women are interpreted as a way to counteract pay differentials: 'So this is a typical men's work. [...] And it's a problem because our salaries are higher than if you work with room cleaning. So we are in the centre of the equalization' (Interview WSE3).

Finally, with regard to the share of the workforce with a migration background, all countries report a diverse workforce. In contrast to other fields of public employment such as the police, no special emphasis on diversity policies to attract or retain such workers seem to exist. Moreover, HR managers did not refer to potential discrimination as a problem within this sector, although the fact that workers with a migration background are overrepresented in the sector may be considered an element of societal discrimination. In France, where strict regulations for public authorities not to record ethnic background are in place, it has been stressed that 'there is no discrimination whether positive nor negative' (Interview HRM WFR3).

Summary

In all four countries, waste collection is characterized by a substantial decrease in the share of public service provision, and competition with the private sector has become more important. As waste collection is a labour-intensive sector, enhanced competition mainly induces cost containment in personnel expenditure. This sector-specific trend, observable in all four countries, affects a low-qualified workforce, which in the past notably profited from the state's role as a 'good employer' providing higher pay levels, better chances for pay progression, and higher employment security than in the private sector. Therefore, it does not come as a surprise that changes in employment regulation mainly target pay levels and employment security and often imply downgrading, whereas promoting policies and incentives by performance, which had been of minor relevance for this workforce from the outset, remain less important.

However, depending on the country's institutional and public sector reform background, the scope of privatization and the type of competition with the private sector varies, as does their impact on personnel policies. Two forms of competition are relevant. In the United Kingdom and in the field of packaging waste collection in Germany, we find direct competition for service contracts between public and private providers. In contrast, in Sweden, France, and in the case of household waste collection in Germany, direct competition between public and private providers is not relevant. However, as policy decisions for public provision in all countries have to be justified in terms of efficiency, increasing shares of private service provision can be seen as a form of indirect competition. In this context, the preservation of distinct public employment regulations on the one hand, and the alignment to private sector employment and working conditions on the other hand, unfold in different ways.

In the United Kingdom, where direct competition with the private sector is of major importance and the specific regulations for public service personnel policies were abolished, an alignment of public employment to the private sector has taken place, negatively affecting pay levels and employment security (see Table 7.1). However, the general minimum pay sets a standard for both sectors. In packaging waste collection in Germany, equally exposed to direct competition, we also find a trend towards downward adjustment to private sector employment conditions, as coverage by collective agreements is low, resulting in relative low-wages (though limited by a minimum wage threshold). Moreover, a growing temporary workforce suffers from reduced employment security.

Employment conditions and personnel policies in the waste sector in the United Kingdom follow the country-specific trend of an early efficiency- and market-oriented public sector reform promoting privatization and flexibility of employment regulation in the public sector (see Chapter 5).

Table 7.1   Dimensions of change in public employment regulation: Waste, UK

Dimensions and characteristics	Pre-1990s	Early 2010s
1. Regulation of employment conditions		
Legal status	Employee	Employee
Collective regulations	Collective agreement	Collective agreement, minor relevance
Regulation of labour conflicts	No active right to strike	No active right to strike
2. Personnel system		
Mode of advancement	Limited opportunities for advancement: Position-based	Very limited opportunities for advancement: Position-based
Openness	High	High
3. Personnel management		
Entry requirements	Non-formalized, low	Non-formalized, low
Recruitment	General qualification	General qualification
Pay structure	Negotiation-based, highly coordinated	Negotiation-based
Evaluation and assessment	*No information available*	*No information available*
Performance incentives	No	
Opportunities for promotion	*No information available*	Very limited: Performance-based
Further education	*No information available*	*No information available*
4. Integration function of public employment regime		
Payment, social security	High	Low
Employment security	High	Low
Equal opportunity and treatment at the workplace	*No information available*	*No information available*
5. Specificity of public employment regime		
Difference as compared to private sector employment regime	Private sector close to the public sector (the state as 'good' and 'model employer')	Public sector close to the private sector

The picture of waste collection in Germany is more diverse, as exposure to competition varies between packaging waste and household waste, with the latter not being subject to direct competition (see Table 7.2). At least for the core workforce, employment regulation still provides for better conditions with respect to wages and employment security compared to the private sector. Nevertheless, the abolishment since the personnel reform in 2005 of non-work-related allowances and seniority rules in pay applying to all employees in the public service, indicate that the distinctiveness of public employment has declined with respect to regulations particularly relevant for a low-qualified workforce.

Table 7.2 Dimensions of change in public employment regulation: Waste, Germany

Dimensions and characteristics	Pre-1990s	Early 2010s
1. Regulation of employment conditions		
Legal status	Employee	Employee
Collective regulations	Collective agreement	Collective agreement
Regulation of labour conflicts	Right to strike	Right to strike
2. Personnel system		
Mode of advancement	Limited opportunities for advancement: Position-based	Very limited opportunities for advancement: Position-based
Openness	High	High
3. Personnel management		
Entry requirements	Non-formalized, low	Non-formalized, higher
Recruitment	General qualification	General qualification
Pay structure	Negotiation-based, highly coordinated	Negotiation-based
Evaluation and assessment	Seniority rules	Seniority rules abolished
Performance incentives	No	Very limited
Opportunities for promotion	Very limited: Seniority-based	Very limited: Performance-based
Further education	Very limited	Very limited
4. Integration function of public employment regime		
Payment, social security	High (but private sector close to public sector pay regulation)	Core workforce, household waste: Comparatively high; Others, packaging waste: Very low
Employment security	High	Core workforce, household waste: Comparatively high; Others, packaging waste: Very low
Equal opportunity and treatment at the workplace	Not of major relevance	Not of major relevance
5. Specificity of public employment regime		
Difference as compared to private sector employment regime	Private sector close to the public sector	Public sector close to the private sector (especially in packaging waste collection) For core workforce, household waste: Some public sector employment aspects still in place

Table 7.3   Dimensions of change in public employment regulation: Waste, France

Dimensions and characteristics	Pre-1990s	Early 2010s
1. Regulation of employment conditions		
Legal status	*Fonctionnaire* (*fonction publique territoriale*)	*Fonctionnaire* (*fonction publique territoriale*)
Collective regulations	Authoritative/ Unilateral	Authoritative/Unilateral
Regulation of labour conflicts	Right to strike	Right to strike
2. Personnel system		
Mode of advancement	Career-based	Career-based
Openness	Low	Low
3. Personnel management		
Entry requirements	Low	Low
Recruitment	General qualification	General qualification
Pay structure	Determined by law	Determined by law
Evaluation and assessment	Seniority rules	Seniority rules
Performance incentives	No	No
Opportunities for promotion	Seniority-based, internal exam	Seniority-based, internal exam
Further education	Legally determined, standardized	Legally determined, standardized
4. Integration function of public employment regime		
Payment, social security	Similar to or lower than in the private sector	Higher than in the private sector due to wage decreases in the private sector
Employment security	High	High
Equal opportunity and treatment at the workplace	*No information available*	Low
5. Specificity of public employment regime		
Difference as compared to private sector employment regime	High	Medium (elements of civil service employment also in the collective agreements in the private sector)

As Table 7.3 shows, this is far less the case in public waste collection in France, where personnel policies have barely been subject to change. Based on long-standing legal regulations, employment conditions include lifetime employment and a pay system providing for automatic progression and additional non-employment-related components. In contrast to the other

Table 7.4   Dimensions of change in public employment regulation: Waste, Sweden

Dimensions and characteristics	Pre-1990s	Early 2010s
1. Regulation of employment conditions		
Legal status	Employee	Employee
Collective regulations	Collective agreement	Collective agreement
Regulation of labour conflicts	Right to strike	Right to strike
2. Personnel system		
Mode of advancement	Limited opportunities for advancement: Position-based	Very limited opportunities for advancement: Position-based
Openness	High	High
3. Personnel management		
Entry requirements	Non-formalized, low	Non-formalized, higher
Recruitment	General qualification	General qualification
Pay structure	Negotiation-based, highly coordinated within the public and between the public and the private sectors	Negotiation-based, highly coordinated within the public and between the public and the private sectors
Evaluation and assessment	*No information available*	*No information available*
Performance incentives	No	Very limited
Opportunities for promotion	Very limited	Very limited: Performance-based
Further education	Very limited	Very limited
4. Integration function of public employment regime		
Payment, social security	High (but private sector close to public sector pay regulation)	Lower (but private sector close to public sector pay regulation)
Employment security	High	Lower, but against the background of comprehensive general security regulations in the Swedish welfare state
Equal opportunity and treatment at the workplace	Not of major relevance	Not regarded to be of specific relevance
5. Specificity of public employment regime		
Difference as compared to private sector employment regime	Private sector close to the public sector	Public sector close to the private sector

countries, even in the field of waste collection, a legally regulated career pathway and entitlements for further education exist, underlining that employment regulation in this sector highly corresponds to the overall civil service system in France. However, it must be noted that many of the civil servant elements in waste collection are present in the respective national collective agreement for the private sector too, indicating a persisting role model function of the public sector.

In Sweden too, the personnel policies in public waste collection correspond to the private sector (see Table 7.4), but unlike in France and in line with the early public sector reform in Sweden, employment in the public sector is based on private law and personnel policies are relative flexible. Encompassing PRP and some scope for dismissal, counterbalanced by generous unemployment benefits and active labour market policy, complete the picture of an early adopter of change under favourable economic conditions. Relatively high levels of pay and social security and a highly coordinated pay regulation between the public and the private sector are also contrasted by the equally flexible employment regulation in the waste collection sector of the United Kingdom.

Thus, overall we observe a trend toward declining differences between the employment conditions in the public and private areas of the waste collection sector. On the one hand, this general trend can be attributed to the financial and ideological pressures towards privatization, as well as the pressures exerted by competition omnipresent in waste collection across all countries. On the other hand, differences in the extent of alignment to less favourable private sector employment conditions reflect variations in the structure and reform of the respective national public employment systems. Moreover, comparing regulations in waste collection in the United Kingdom and Sweden, both forerunners in re-regulation of the public sector, reveals contrasting pathways of employment flexibility.

8
The Police

Introduction

The societal role of the police is to prevent and fight crime, to maintain order, and to deliver a variety of related services to communities. Notwithstanding social and cultural differences (Hills 2009), the state's monopoly on the legitimate use of force and its connection with what is called 'policing a social order' are societally accepted elements of the self-understanding of police forces in Western democracies (Lange and Schenck 2004; Monjardet 1996). Inasmuch as policing is understood as a core state function, it is argued that police services cannot be privatized – at least not without careful considerations. The police incorporate the social contract between the state and its citizens, in which the latter have to obey to the law in order to be protected by the state. The distinctive feature is that the public police exercise authority in the name of law and order (the state) over the respective population (the nation). As the maintenance of (social and public) security is defined as the direct task of the state, the police are said to render a key service to the interior stabilization of a nation-state. Thus, the distinctiveness of the police lies not only in their production of a public good but also in being the 'specialist repositories for the state's monopolization of legitimate force in its territory' (Reiner 2000, p. 1; see also Brodeur 2010).

However, since the end of the 'Golden Age' of TRUDI, the strong tie between the state and the police has loosened. Security provision is abandoned by the central state in different dimensions: outwards to commercial security markets, downwards to municipalities and private organizations, and upwards to transnational institutions (Loader and Walker 2001, p. 10). Referring to these trends, the UK Government speaks of extending the 'police family' (Home Office 2001), and governments aim for a broadened 'security architecture' (the German conceptual equivalent to the term 'family') on the local, national, and global scale. Obviously, the thrust towards privatization of state functions has not halted before the police, and the emergence of commercial and non-profit security markets is a reality (Eick

2011; Wakefield 2003),[1] often summarized as the 'pluralization' of policing (Jones and Newburn 1998; Loader 2000). Nevertheless, the 'regulatory state' (Grande 1997) is still the sole provider of public police, understood as the 'monopoly of legitimate coercion, the delivery of civic governance, the guarantee of collective provision and the symbolism of state and nation' (Loader and Walker 2001, p. 9).

With regard to recruitment and qualification, policing represented an occupational culture with a strong focus on police experience and daily work. Typically, policing was considered a job for the average citizen, with physical attributes and moral persuasions more important for recruitment than actual specific skills or qualifications.[2] This conception began to change after the Second World War. From the 1970s onwards, higher demands on the delivery of security and public order and new technologies required more specific skills and competencies. Since then, police work has successively professionalized, emphasizing systematic and theoretical training in specific training institutions (Fyfe 2013; Haselow and Kisman 2003; Karp and Stenmark 2011; Roché 2005, pp. 322–4; White and Escobar 2008). Recruitment strategies reflected not least quests and needs for gender and ethnic diversity. While high public reputation, specific employment conditions, and a unique work ethos make the police an attractive employer (Kroos et al. 2011), hiring personnel for specific tasks, such as management positions and IT, and representing the growing diversity of the society still constitute major challenges. Although entry requirements are relatively low in the countries under study, most police forces struggle to recruit women into a profession biased in favour of men, and to increase diversity within an ethnically homogenous 'white' institution.[3]

The legal, organizational, and executive responsibility for the provision of public policing continues to be located in the state. As we show in this chapter, this continuity is reflected in the stability of the police's employment system, based on special employment conditions (Kroos et al. 2011). Nevertheless, all four countries implemented NPM features at the organizational level (Briken 2014). The purpose of the following section is to conceptually locate the police sector in the public service of Germany, France, and Sweden using the United Kingdom as reference case.[4] We then illustrate the core employment conditions of the police forces across the four countries. The chapter ends with a summary highlighting common features and differences of employment regulation across countries, and identifying sector specific differences within national employment regimes.

Apart from a document analysis, information on sector-specific employment regulation is based on an exploratory survey and expert interviews in Germany, France, and Sweden with different actors within the police. Since HRM in the police in these countries is, at least to some degree, part of the negotiations between the employer and the unions, the expert interviews include HR managers and union representatives. With the exception of Germany, all interviews were conducted at the central state level. For the German case, three distinct *Länder* were chosen to reflect the heterogeneous structure of the German police. From December 2009 to March 2010, 22 interviews were conducted across the three countries. In Sweden, the interviews took place in Stockholm and covered both HR managers (n=3) and union representatives (n=2). In France, two members of the *Direction de la Formation de la Police* and one member of the *Direction de l'Administration de la Police* (n=3), as well as three union representatives (n=3) from the three main police *corps*[5], were interviewed in Paris. In Germany, the interviews represented HR management (n=6) and union representatives (n=5) from the three *Länder* of Bremen, Baden-Württemberg, and Brandenburg. This sample reflects the basic structure of the German federal state, including a so-called city-state (Bremen), a prosperous regional state (Baden-Württemberg), and a regional state from the former German Democratic Republic (Brandenburg). Over all countries and positions, the questionnaire focused on the interviewees' perception of the most recent changes in core work and employment structures.[6]

Overview: basic features of the police

In this section, we focus on the police as a modern democratic institution whose organization varies in the way the central state exerts control. The administrative systems range from an until recently locally appointed and locally accountable police (Sweden),[7] to that of a local police accountable to a central government (UK), to that of an accountability system on a *Länder* level with an overlapping Federal Police (Germany), to that of a strictly centralized system (France).

United Kingdom. The origins of the British police can be traced back to the 19th century.[8] In 1829, the Metropolitan Police Service (Metropolitan Police Act 1829, c. 44) was established by the Conservative politician Robert Peel in London. The responsibilities for the police were added to the Home Office. With the Municipal Corporation Act 1835, this 'Peel model' was exported to the rural areas and ended the rather uncontrolled and heterogeneous interplay of the 'police' forces in the parishes and privately paid watchmen. In contrast to the bureaucratization and the rise of strict central administrative structures characteristic of the French nation-state and Prussia (see Chapter 5), the Home Office would not intervene directly on the local (communal) level (Knöbl 1998, p. 194). Additionally, the Peel model introduced a strict distinction between the military forces and the police. Even today, the British police remain unarmed.[9]

The relatively autonomous structure changed fundamentally with the introduction of the Police Act 1964. Command-and-control structures were centralized within the Home Office. Police power was divided into a tripartite system between the chief constables, local authorities, and the

Home Office. Over time, the power of the Home Office within this system increased. The Home Office became responsible for police administration, decisions on the general budget lines (Johnston 1992, p. 7), and the setting of the general missions for the police. England and Wales are policed by 43 territorial forces staffed with around 220,000 police officers. In addition, Special Forces (such as the British Transport Police, Civil Nuclear Constabulary, Ministry of Defence Police) provide policing focusing on particular tasks, such as transport or energy.

The territorial forces differ in manpower and resources according to the size of the respective territory. The Metropolitan Police of London is a 'giant', staffed with 33,367 officers, overseen by a commissioner (the London equivalent of the chief constable). The second- and third-largest police forces with about 8,000 officers each are the West Midlands Police and the Greater Manchester Police. In stark contrast, more than half of the remaining 41 provincial police administrations rely on a police force of only about 1,000 to 2,000 officers.

The British police have institutionalized the single career principle. Every sworn police officer in England and Wales is a 'constable' regardless of rank. By a sworn oath and warrant, the Office of Constable provides the constable with additional legal powers to arrest and to control the public. Those powers are not 'delegated' powers because police officers are not employees, but rather office holders. The system is based on a standardized set of ranks every police officer has to go through during his or her career.[10] The commissioner of the Metropolitan Police is often considered to be the highest-ranking UK police officer. In general, every chief constable and two additional commissioners are supreme over their respective forces and are not answerable to any other officer. Police officers do not belong to the very small group of British civil servants, but are sworn officers. This means they have a similar status as civil servants, based on statutory regulations instead of regular labour law (Gash 2008, p. 27), entailing prerogatives such as higher employment security and more extensive social benefits. Nevertheless, roughly 40 per cent of the police staff are non-uniformed civilians fulfilling tasks defined to be 'sovereign duties' without sovereign powers. Furthermore, the police officers are supported on the street by uniformed non-sworn staff. The two groups are part of what the Home Office named the 'extended police family' in 2001 (Home Office 2001) and consist of uniformed non-sworn Police Community Support Officers (PCSOs), civilian staff integral to the Neighbourhood Policing Teams (implemented by the Police Reform Act 2002), and uniformed Special Constables, a volunteering force spending a minimum of four hours per week policing their neighbourhood streets. The Police Reform Act 2002 allowed the delegation of limited legal powers to a semi-civilian police category and even to the volunteer constabulary, with the effect of increasing visible police presence without increasing costs.

Over the last three decades, police resources have been extended and the police force peaked in 2010, when its numbers were nearly twice as high as in 1980 (see Table 8.1). However, beginning in 1988, the police were scrutinized by the Audit Commission (AC), an independent body established by the Local Government Finance Act 1982 to monitor and promote economy, efficiency, and effectiveness in the management of local government. While the first reports focused on the financing of police funding and budget allocation, later reports focused on operational matters, including crime management and patrol work (Audit Commission 1996). Though the commission's recommendations were not prescriptive, they have been commonly implemented (Mawby and Wright 2005, p. 7). Under the then Labour government, 'Best Value' indicators were implemented, and within the Police Performance Assessment Framework of 2004 (PPFA), police authorities were put under a national benchmarking scheme, the results of which are made publicly available. From 2010 onwards, this performance culture was combined with a stronger focus on the reduction of spending and crime rates. Crime statistics were refined and a new control body, the Police and Crime Commissioners, was set up in order to control the budget on the local level instead of on the level of the police authorities (HMIC 2014). Furthermore, the government ordered a 20 per cent cut of all territorial police force budgets within four years.[11] To reach these tight goals, most police authorities initiated reductions in personnel by reducing their civilian police staff, convincing sworn officers to retire once they reached their 30 years of service and cutting some of the higher-ranked senior positions (see Table 8.1). Some forces also engaged in extensive outsourcing of back office services and contracted with private security.[12] These reforms from 2010 onwards led to a decline in police employment, affecting mainly the share of civilian employment. Irrespective of the quantitative employment dynamics, the share of women in the police forces has increased, reaching 27.8 per cent in 2014 (see Table 8.1).

As to interest representation, under UK labour law the police are legally prohibited to join trade unions to defend pay and working conditions, but they are allowed to associate. In 1919, the Police Federation was established by the Police Act as an alternative system to resolve disputes through arbitration. As of January 2014, the Police Federation of England and Wales is the statutory staff association for police constables, sergeants, inspectors, and chief inspectors in the 43 territorial police forces, with approximately 127,000 members. The higher ranks are represented by the Police Superintendents' Association of England and Wales (PSA). The civilian police staff is organized in the service union UNISON and possesses all rights for industrial action.

Germany. In 1848, Prussia established a strong and tightly organized police force, coordinated by a civil administrative body but following the military model (Funk 1986, p. 61). After the unification of Prussia with the other

German states in 1870, the Prussian model became the benchmark model of police organization. Recruitment was largely from the military: serving in the army for a minimum of nine years was a pre-condition to becoming a police officer in Prussia until 1893 (Funk 1986, p. 290). The further sophistication of police organization in the Weimar Republic was interrupted by National Socialism, which transformed the police into an instrument of Nazi dictatorship.

The development of a modern and democratic German police force started after 1945. For a short period, the German police were under the supervision of the Allied governments, who also started setting up police schools for training. In 1950, the 11 West German *Länder* obtained the power to establish their own police forces, and the police are part of the executive force according to the German Constitution (GG Art. 20 Para. 3). Until the mid-1970s, a *Polizeigesetz* (Police Law) was established in all *Länder*, defining the core functions of the police. After reunification in 1990, the police forces in the five East German *Länder* followed the structure of their Western counterparts. The German Constitution refers the regulation, planning, design, and supervision of the police to the parliaments of the *Länder*, which are the main arenas of political decision making in relation to issues of internal security, while the ministries of the interior are in charge of the implementation. Even though the police are subordinated to the Ministry of the Interior, the administration of the police is governed in two different ways. In some *Länder*, the police are integrated into the central administration (*Einheitsverwaltung*), and a ministerial department is the responsible authority. In others, the police have their own administration (*Sonderverwaltung*), with a police president as head of the police, appointed by the president of the *Land*. An assessment of the hierarchical and organizational structure of the police forces shows that every state has its own structure and wording for different units and departments, making it difficult even for police experts in Germany to compare the police forces (Groß 2008). In 2010, more than 260,000 individuals were employed in the 16 *Länderpolizeien*, the largest one being North Rhine-Westphalia (up to 40,000), and the smallest being Saarland (approximately 2,800). In terms of police density, Berlin has about 162 inhabitants per police officer, whereas North Rhine-Westphalia counts 404 inhabitants per police officer (Groß 2008, p. 21).

In all *Länder*, the police are integrated into the overall civil servant employment and career scheme (see Chapter 5). Each police trainee has to pass the same basic training, based on framework guidelines by the German Ministry of the Interior since 1967, in specific police schools or in a university of applied sciences before entering the police force. The majority of German police officers are civil servants, whereas about 17 per cent are public employees. In Hamburg, Hesse, Berlin, and Saxony, the latter are called *Angestelltenpolizei* (public employee police). Their number remains relative stable over time, and the police public employees fulfil tasks like traffic control, handling of administrative offences, or object protection. As in the United Kingdom, from the mid-1990s onwards, civilians have been recruited to strengthen the link between the police and the population in some states (*Freiwilliger Polizeidienst* in Hesse; *Sicherheitswacht* in Bavaria and Saxony; *Sicherheitspartner* in Brandenburg; since 2006, *Freiwilliger Ordnungs- und Streifendienst* in Lower Saxony). The uniformed volunteers work closely together with the police, and in Baden-Württemberg they even carry weapons (Groß 2008, p. 48). In sum, around 4,500 to 5,000 individuals are involved in this supplementary police service (Pütter and Kant 2000, own account). At the same time, the number of security partnerships between the police and commercial security increased. According to the German Ministry of the Interior, 32 partnerships in 10 of the *Länder* were counted in 2011. While no direct police tasks are outsourced, information and communication are shared, and commercial and public security forces cooperate in case of specific incidents such as burglary (IMK 2011).

The introduction of NPM ideas started in most of the German *Länder* with the decentralization of budget responsibilities from the Ministry of the Interior or the central police governor to the sub-units. The first mover, Baden-Württemberg, started in 1993, the others followed in the years between 1997 and 2001 (Lange and Schenck 2004, pp. 151–90). By 2011, controlling and target agreements have been introduced in all German police forces, while the so-called impact-oriented police work (*wirkungsorientierte Polizeiarbeit*) and the use of balanced scorecard models frame the working conditions for the officers (Lange and Schenck 2004, pp. 151–90; Ritsert 2011).[13]

The German police forces are unionized, but due to their civil servant status, they have no right to strike. Two major unions aim to represent the overall police forces, namely the *Gewerkschaft der Polizei* (GdP) and the *Deutsche Polizeigewerkschaft* (DPolG). The much smaller *Bund deutscher Kriminalbeamter* (BdK) organizes the detective constables. DPolG and BdK are both part of the German Association of Civil Servants (*Beamtenbund und Tarifunion*, DBB), whereas the GdP is one of the eight unions under the umbrella of the German Federation of Trade Unions (*Deutscher Gewerkschaftsbund*, DGB).

France. The French police appeared as a specialized and public organization in 1667 (*édit royal de mars* 1667). Until 1699, the post of a *lieutenant general de police* (general lieutenant of the police) was created in every French city to serve the demands of the feudal elites for security, thereby forming the first network constituting a national police system. During the French Revolution in 1789, these first forms of police organization were abolished. The new government transformed the forces into the *police municipale* with the respective mayor holding the responsibility for the force. A first uniformed, preventive patrolling force was established in 1829. Unlike the

English 'bobbies', the French *sergents de ville* were armed with a cane by day and a sabre by night. A high proportion of *sergents* were former soldiers, and an emphasis on military discipline characterized the Parisian police. In the Third Republic, the first police training school was opened in Paris in 1883, offering a three-month training to the recruits. During the phase of rapid industrialization and urbanization, urban unrest and strikes led the elites to establish a state police (*étatisation*), but still the mayor fulfilled the main oversight functions. In the provinces, training was poor, and policing varied across the country in both quality and strength. The Vichy regime central-ized control over the different police forces in 1941. The *Police Nationale* was founded (*Loi du 23 avril 1941*) and became responsible for policing all towns with a population of 10,000 or more. Despite this centralization, France has three different types of police forces. At the national level, the centrally controlled civilian force is subordinated to the French Ministry of the Interior (the National Police) and a centrally controlled, militarized force (the *gendarmerie*, circa 98,500 soldiers) was subject to the Ministry of Defence[14] and responsible for policing the rural areas. At the local level, a multitude of municipal forces are paid by and answerable to the mayors (*police municipal,* circa 18,000 in 3,500 municipalities).

In 2010, about 141,000 individuals worked for the French National Police. The majority of police officers are employed under civil servant status (*fonctionnaire*). The National Police comprises four *corps,* each with its own tradition, its own territorial competencies, its own career ladder and rules for recruitment, training, promotion, and remuneration, as well as its own trade unions. This structure mirrors the hierarchical and segmented struc-ture generally characteristic for professions in France (OECD 2012, pp. 189f.; Horton 1996, pp. 53ff.). Three hierarchical levels are differentiated: the *corps d'encadrement et d'application* (surveillance and enforcement), represented by the *gardiens de la paix* and *brigadiers*; the *corps de commandement* (command), consisting of the *officiers*; and the *corps de conception et de direction* (strategy and management), composed of *commissaires.*

Since 1997, auxiliary police workers on fixed-term contracts, concluded after a three-year period and eligible for one renewal for another three-year period, are integrated as so-called *contractuel* or *adjoints de sécurité*.[15] In addition, in 1987, young men doing their national service were admitted as 'short-term police officers', and their number increased to 10 per cent of the total workforce in the mid-1990s (Horton 1995, p. 125). Moreover, the *poli-ciers municipals* form an increasingly formalized part of the French policing system. In 1994, their status was strengthened by integrating them officially into the *fonction publique territoriale* (FPT, see Chapter 5).[16] Since that time, their role has been professionalized both in terms of function and career (Cayrel and Diederichs 2010, pp. 10ff.).

Each of the status groups has its own trade union. French police trade unions have a long and complex history of mergers, separations, and emergence of new trade unions. Today, there are five main trade unions according to the results of the *élections professionnelles* (Loubet del Bayle 2010, p. 65). The UNSA-Police and *Alliance Police Nationale* represent the *gardiens de la paix*. SNOP-UNSA and *Synergie Officiers* both represent the *officiers*. The smallest group of the police workforce, the *commissaires*, is represented by a single trade union, the SCPN. UNSA-Police and SNOP-UNSA traditionally support left-wing policies, whereas *Alliance Police Nationale* and *Synergie Officiers* are closer to right-wing parties (Loubet del Bayle 2010, p. 166). In total, and in stark contrast to other sectors, 70 per cent of the police are trade union members (Loubet del Bayle 2010, p. 60).

NPM reforms reached the French police by the end of the 1990s. Under the Socialist government of Lionel Jospin, the French police followed the trend of adopting its own concept of community policing (*police de proximité*) in order to increase the presence of the police in the public sphere (Mouhanna 2009).[17] However, it was only under the Conservative government of Nicolas Sarkozy (2007–12) that the implementation of more NPM-focused reforms took place. First, Sarkozy abolished the *police de proximité*, increased personnel and technical equipment, and focused on the repression of delinquency and crime.[18] He also established a culture of results, the so-called *politique du chiffre,* including performance indicators. Moreover, Sarkozy announced the reward of good performance with bonuses (*prime aux résultats exceptionnel*) and the creation of more career opportunities for the higher ranks (Matelly and Mouhanna 2007). The individual performance-related pay system was introduced in 2008, but applied within the police forces only to the (few) top positions since the police officers successfully defended the principle that police work is teamwork (Mouhanna 2009).[19] In 2013, the performance-oriented *prime* system was abolished for the public service in general (see Chapter 5).

Sweden. By 1848, the development of a modern Swedish police force in the sense of an organized and trained force gained momentum and was based on the benchmark model of the time, the London Metropolitan Police (Furuhagen 2004, 2009; Nyzell 2014). In line with the administrative structure of the Swedish state (see Chapter 5), responsibility for the police remained with the municipal advisory citizens' boards until the 1920s. In 1925, the national government began to coordinate police operations nationwide. Furthermore, in response to the worldwide economic depression of the 1930s and increasing crime rates in the urban areas, the central government established state police forces to reinforce local police (Becker and Hjellemo 1976; Lord 1998).

The Swedish Police Service was nationalized in 1965. A local government reform consolidated the 554 separate police districts into 118, each headed by a county police commissioner appointed by the government. While local police chiefs were independent in operational decisions, the budget was centrally allocated out of national resources (Becker and Hjellemo

1976; Gurr et al. 1977). Local authorities are controlled by police boards, whose task it is to control adherence to the governmental guidelines and the efficient use of resources. The local police board also decides on the operational plan, budget, internal organization, and rules of procedure for the authority, while the chief commissioner has responsibility for the day-to-day operations and finances. Between 1965 and 1991, the prospering economy allowed the National Police Board to provide the districts with the majority of requested resources, such as equipment or training for officers (Weiland 1995). During the 1990s, the autonomy of local police chiefs was even extended by a new system of central government grants, entailing less detailed regulations from the centre as well as increasing autonomy related to budgets.

With the reform of 1965, however, long-term planning responsibilities shifted from the local to the central administration, where the *Rikspolisstyrelsen* (National Police Board, NPB) was created (Rikspolisstyrelsen 1973; Ivarsson Westerberg 2004, pp. 78f.). The NPB is the central administrative and supervisory authority of the police.

At least from the late 1990s onwards, the number of police in Sweden constantly rose. In response to an increased feeling of public insecurity at the end of the 1990s, the visibility of police in the streets and in the rural areas was raised (Lindstrom 2015).[20] Between 2000 and 2010, the resources allocated to the police forces grew by more than 40 per cent, and the number of police employees increased by 26 per cent to 28,000, of whom 20,300 were police officers. The number of employees varies between the different police authorities. The largest police authority is the Stockholm County Police with about 6,500 employees, of which 5,000 are police officers (SCP 2009, p. 12). The smallest police authority is the Gotland County Police with 140 employees, of which about 100 are police officers.

The Swedish police are organized according to the single career principle with a strong emphasis on systematic training.[21] After the training phase, each Swedish police officer enters the police force as *Polisassistent* (police constable) with the possibility, in principle, to advance through the full scale of ranks. The Swedish police have a long tradition of civilian police staff, and the share of civilians has remained relatively stable at about one-third of the workforce (Swedish National Police Board 2012, p. 63). The abolition of the civil servant status in most of the public services (see Chapter 5), combined with the rise of administrative tasks during the 1970s due to computerization and the introduction of new accounting principles, led to the early integration of non-police officers, and the term 'civil employee' was first used in 1973. Since then, the share of civil police employees has been rising on all levels (administrative, technical, as well as scientific support) (Ivarsson Westerberg 2004, pp. 87f.). Nevertheless, no extension or further differentiation of street patrol or uniformed forces, like in the United Kingdom, has taken place. Although the Swedish Police

Service integrated the British community policing model into their organizational concept, they did not outsource duties to the extent that Britain did. Instead, the Swedish Police Service tightened its ties to 'supplementary' public order providers and forged security partnerships with commercial security companies, public transport guards, and voluntary neighbourhood watch schemes (Rolandsson 2015, p. 32).

In Sweden, NPM policies were carried forward both by left- and right-wing governments. Three major waves can be distinguished (Auffenberg and Kittel, 2015). During the 1990s, police tasks were devolved and more autonomy in organizational issues was transferred to local police authorities. Each local unit overlooked a global budget with full responsibilities regarding spending. In this way, the NPB's influence declined and its role changed from a directing to a more service-oriented agency (Ivarsson Westerberg 2004, p. 101, pp. 123ff.) Moreover, the Swedish version of community policing (*närpolisreform*) with a strong focus on citizens' well-being was introduced. In order to implement the reform, the number of so-called contact officers on the municipal level was increased at the expense of cuts in other fields of the police (Auffenberg and Kittel 2015). In the second wave, output orientation and performance measurement were put on the agenda. Clearance rates, delinquency rate, and citizens' trust in the police served as main statistical indicators to measure the efficiency of police work. The third wave was initiated in 2005. While the police staff increased, a bundle of new management methods like the balanced scorecard model and total quality management (TQM) were tested and implemented.

In 2010, the Police Service became the largest state-controlled activity in Sweden, but neither the rise in the staff level nor the new police government methods led to a fall in crime rates. For this reason, the Swedish Government initiated a further major police reform by restructuring the police 'multi-agencies' and the autonomous local and regional agencies, and by unifying them in one central agency (Statskontoret 2010).[22] The goal was to form an integrated 'mono-agency'. As of 1 January 2015, the Swedish Police Service was fully centralized and the county police lost their autonomy to pursue their own strategies and to control the budgets. Now the NPB is responsible for setting the budgets as well as stipulating the recruitment strategies on the local level. It also has the supervisory authority over the National Laboratory of Forensic Science and is responsible for the development of new work methods and technological support. All law enforcement services in Sweden are provided by one single police organization. Through the National Police Academy, NPB is responsible for the training of police officers. NPB is the central administrative and supervisory authority of all police services and reports to the Swedish Ministry of Justice in charge of developing overall police strategies. In addition, each of the county police authorities, which have been reduced to 21, is responsible for maintaining public order and security and preventing crime in its own county, headed

Table 8.1   Development of police forces in the UK, Germany, France, and Sweden, 1980–2014

	Development of police force numbers	Share of civilian employment	Share of female employment	
			Among total police force	Among civilian employees
UK (England and Wales)	1980: 112,958[p]	1980: 0%	1980: 8.5%[p]	1980: n/a
	1985: 118,620[p]	1985: 0%	1985: 9.3%[p]	1985: n/a
	1995: 186,622 FTE[q]	1995: 31.8%[q]	1995: 14.0%[p]	1995: n/a
	2005: 223,426 FTE[q]	2005: 36.1%[q]	2005: 21.1%[q]	2005: 66.5%[q]
	2010: 244,497 FTE[r]	2010: 41.2%[r]	2010: 25.7%[r]	2010: 63.7%[r]
	2014: 207,843 FTE[s]	2014: 38.2%[s]	2014: 27.9%	2014: n/a
Germany (only *Länder*; before 1990 only West-Germany)	1980: 199,801[g]	1980: 17.1%[g]	1980: 11.2%[g]	1980: n/a
	1985: 207,637[h]	1985: 17.0%[h]	1985: n/a	1985: n/a
	1995: 280,103[i]	1995: 17.7%[i]	1995: 18.4%[i]	1995: 57.3%[i]
	2005: 269,096[j]	2005: 15.7%[j]	2005: 22.9%[j]	2005: 59.6%[j]
	2010: 263,316[k]	2010: 14.7%[k]	2010: 24.9%[k]	2010: 59.9%[k]
	(FTE: 252,369)[k]	2013: 37.6%[x]	2013: 69.9%[x]	2013: 22.5%[x]
	2013: 266,291			
	(FTE: 255,921)[x]			
France	1980: 112,677[a]	1980: n/a	1980: n/a	n/a
	1986: 123,325[a]	1985: n/a	1985: n/a	
	1996: 129,235[a]	1995: n/a	1995: n/a	
	2005: 147,772[b]	2005: 1.9%[d]	2005: 22.0%[d]	
	2010: 141,126[c]	2006: 8.2%[e]	2009: 27.3%[f]	
	(FTE: 139,061)[c]	2010: 7.3%[c]	2012: 25.6% [y]	
	2012: 138,959	2012: 10.9 [y]		
	(FTE: 136,758)[y]			
Sweden	1980:	1980:	1980:	1980:
	1985:	1985:	1985:	1985:
	1997: 22,755[l]	1997: 26.2%[l]	1995:	1995:
	2005: 23,940[m]	2005: 28.7%[m]	2005: 35.7%[n]	2005: 71%[n]
	2010: 28,017[m]	2010: 27.6%[m]	2010: 39%[o]	2010: 69%[o]
	2014: 28,689	2014: 30.1%	2014: 42%	2014: 68%

FTE: Full-time equivalents; n/a: no data available.

Note: Due to country specific-statistics, the latest figures available vary from 2012–14.

Sources: a: Ministère de la fonction publique et de la réforme de l'état 2004, pp. 86f; b: Ministère du budget, des comptes publics, de la fonction publique et de la réforme de l'état 2009, pp. 386f; c: Ministère de la réforme de l'état, de la décentralisation et de la fonction publique 2012, p. 294; d: Ministère du budget, des comptes publics et de la fonction publique 2007, p. 248; e: Ministère du budget, des comptes publics et de la fonction publique 2008, pp. 296f; f: Ministère de la fonction publique 2011, p. 314; g: Statistisches Bundesamt 1982, pp. 47, 57, 59, 60, 62, 63, 64, 68, 74, 75; h: Statistisches Bundesamt 1987, pp. 40, 42, 44, 46, 94; i: Statistisches Bundesamt 1997, pp. 72, 78; j: Statistisches Bundesamt 2007, p. 82; k: Statistisches Bundesamt 2011, pp. 63f., 69. l: Rikspolisstyrelsen 2010; m: Rikspolisstyrelsen 2013; n: Körlin et al. 2006, p. 5; o: Rikspolisstyrelsen 2011, p. 46; p: Grahame 2001, pp. 13ff., 20, 25, 35; q: Nasreen et al. 2004, pp. 3, 5, 13f., 19f; r: Sigurdsson and Dhani 2010, pp. 3, 14, 21f; s: see Home Office 2015; x: Statistisches Bundesamt 2014, pp 46, 47, 49; y: Ministère de la fonction publique 2012, pp. 275, 288.

by a county police commissioner. The County Police Board, comprising local politicians and the commissioner, the latter appointed by the government of Sweden, reports to the NPB.

Collective bargaining in the Swedish police sector is framed by the central collective agreement (*Ramavtal löner inom staten*, RALS) and concluded at the central level by the Swedish Agency for Government Employers (*Arbetsgivarverket*) (see Chapter 5). In the police sector, the *Rikspolisstyrelsen* and the *Polisförbundet* conclude the local agreement, which is then further specified by the local police departments (Polisförbundet 2013). The Swedish Police Union *Polisförbundet* organizes more than 96 per cent of all police officers in Sweden (Polisförbundet 2013). In 1977, the right to take action, such as going on strike, was restricted both by the Public Employment Act and by collective agreements in order to avoid conflicts that could endanger public safety, especially in sectors such as healthcare, firefighting, and police work. Yet, the 'doctrine of freedom of the labour market' (see Chapter 5) is a very strong, fundamental principle in Swedish industrial relations, and forcible intervention by the state is very rare. Consequently, the overall 'ban' on strikes is self-imposed and confirmed in every collective agreement but is not registered in labour law (Stokke and Thörnqvist 2001, pp. 246ff.).

Work and employment regulation in the police

In this section, we focus on work and employment relations, namely the entry requirements and recruitment, pay system, career advancement and further training, and equality politics in the countries under study.

Entry requirements and recruitment

United Kingdom. In England and Wales, there are few formal educational or physical requirements to enter the police service. The profession is open to persons of all ages with a minimum age of 18 and a structural limit set by the retirement age, and all (or even no) schooling backgrounds, that is, graduates, individuals in possession of a Higher National Diploma qualification, and non-graduates alike. Recruitment and selection procedures are managed by the local police forces, applying a nationwide competency-based framework. Entry is open to British and Commonwealth citizens, European Community and European Economic Area (EEA) citizens, and foreign nationals who have no restrictions on their leave to remain in the UK. However, since 2012, a Certificate in Knowledge of Policing (CKP) exists, initially intended to be compulsory for the Metropolitan Police Service only but later adopted by several other local police forces as a prerequisite for joining. The course includes law, national policy, and the like required to be a police officer and costs about GBP 500–850. Furthermore, since 2014, for the very first time in its history, the British police opened its organization for direct entrants at a higher hierarchical level, namely the superintendents for the Metropolitan Police. According to the lead programme superintendent, Nicola Dale, the direct entry intends to attract senior leaders from outside the police force to fill positions at superintendent rank (about 800 positions in the 43 police forces) in order to integrate financial and business leadership expertise (Guardian 2014).[23] The direct entry programme was initiated in November 2014 with nine successful applicants. All probationary police constables in England and Wales go through a professional training programme (Initial Police Learning and Development Programme IPLDP), preparing for the Level 3 Diploma in Policing (QCF) during their first two years of service. Training takes place at different venues and throughout a number of workplace assessments.

Since 1997, specific legal qualifications are no longer a requirement for all posts for the civilian police staff, with the exception of specific qualifications attached to the role (that is, specific qualifications and expertise in forensics). Most back office work is done by civilian employees on all hierarchical levels from accounting to administration, finance to forensics, HR to IT, and occupational health to operational support.

Germany. Entry requirements and recruitment for the German police are defined according to the different *Länder*. In general, applicants must be either German or EU citizens, and in some cases even Non-EU citizens are allowed to become police officer. Application is possible for two different career brackets, one based on occupational training geared towards medium-level careers (*mittlerer Polizeivollzugsdienst*), the other based on university studies geared towards management and specialist positions in the higher career class (*gehobener Polizeivollzugsdienst*). For the occupational training pathway, police recruits are required to have completed at least intermediate education and be aged 24 at maximum. This training consists of two-and-a-half to three years of courses in special training institutions with a broad set of subjects taught.[24] Police training at universities of applied sciences, established in the 1970s, requires a higher secondary school certificate and takes three years with a maximum entry age of 36 years. It represents a more professionalized path combining scientific and practically oriented knowledge for police work. Moreover, with this kind of training, the students acquire the same kind of education as other employees in the state administration (Pagon et al. 1996). The entry exams vary but focus on physical capabilities, general knowledge, and social skills.

France. Entry requirements and recruitment for the French *Police Nationale* are centralized and highly standardized, following regulations for the whole civil service (see Chapter 5). Entry is through competitive exam (*concours*) for all hierarchical levels, and all applicants must be of French nationality, under 35 years of age (under 30 for the *adjoint de securite*), and have proof of specific physical qualities. The *adjoint de sécurité* do not need a diploma but can directly participate in the *concours*. For the *gardien de la paix*, the grade *baccalauréat* (or similar) is required, while for *officiers* a *licence* (or

BAC+3) is needed, and for the *commissaire* the Master 2 (or BAC+5). The different *concours* are also open for internal applications. The officer's rank often depends upon his or her educational level, whether secondary or post-secondary. Once selected, police recruits for the highest *corps* attend the Saint-Cyr School at Mont d'Or for ten months, while the *officiers* attend the Canet-Cluse School for six months, and *gardien de la paix* attend the Superior School for six months.

Sweden. Unlike in other parts of the Swedish public sector (see Chapter 5), there is a single recruitment procedure for the Swedish police. Application to the police is open to all persons with a high school degree or the equivalent. The Swedish police are a very popular employer, and only 5 to 10 per cent of all applicants can be offered a position.[25] To enter the Swedish police, the potential police officers must apply for a studentship at the Swedish National Police Academy. The Academy has two recruitment dates each year, one in March and the other in September. After an admission test, recruits undergo basic training at the academy. Since 2000, police education and training was established at the Universities of Umeå and Växjö. In 2002, distance learning courses, comprising the same subjects, content, and duration as the on-campus courses, began to be provided for prospective police officers. The Swedish recruits' training consists of four terms of full-time study. The goal is to offer both theoretical and practical foundations. At the end, the recruits are placed in police departments where they are assigned to senior officers who evaluate their ability to perform specific skills.[26] Whereas recruits were paid during training prior to 1994, now students must pay their own fees and are only paid for the six months of practical work after training.

The civilian staff is in charge of duties such as corporate issues, staff development, legal and financial matters, IT, and crime investigations and is recruited according to the special skills needed. The turn to NPM-inspired practices is reflected in the hiring of economic specialists instead of legal specialists for administration, and placing new emphasis on the development of leadership skills (Anderson and Tengblad 2009; Elefalk 2001). Recruitment strategies in this area depend on the specific needs of each and every unit.

Pay

United Kingdom. Irrespective of the decentralized organization of the British police forces, pay and conditions have been set centrally since the Desborough Committee Report of 1919. Since 1978, pay and terms of employment of all UK police officers are negotiated through the Police Negotiating Board (PNB), set up after an inquiry by Lord Edmund-Davies on conditions of police service and pay (Police Act 1996 § 61).[27,28] Wages are fixed by the Home Secretary on advice from the PNB. Until 1994, sworn police officers benefited from rent and housing allowances.

Within the PNB, the local government employers represent the employers, while the police officers are represented by the Police Federation, the Association of Superintendents, and the Staff Association of the Chief Police Officers. Among the issues negotiated through the PNB are hours of duty, leave, pay, additional allowances, and pensions. The PNB negotiates agreements between the employers and employees, which are then recommended to the Home Secretary. If accepted by the Home Secretary, they are placed within a draft statutory instrument, called Police Regulations, and submitted to Parliament for approval. Once placed in the regulations, PNB agreements are legally binding. For the civilian staff, the Police Staff Council's (PSC) national agreements are only binding if police authorities and chief constables agree to incorporate them in the employment contracts of their employees. The Metropolitan Police Service, City of London, Kent, and Surrey police forces, for example, do not take PSC agreements into account.

In general, the pay system can be described as a career-based remuneration system. Salaries are determined by working hours and length of service within a specific rank. In 2002, special priority payments were agreed upon as part of a new pay and conditions settlement. These include up to GBP 400 on top of the basic salary for all the federated ranks and bonus payments for occasional work of an outstanding, demanding, unpleasant, or important nature, as well as competency-related payments.[29] In addition, a competence-related 'threshold payment' can be awarded to constables at the top of their pay scale who could only earn more by being promoted. Although this award was originally only meant to reward highly competent performance, it had become an automatic annual payment for most of the eligible officers. However, it was abolished for new entrants in 2012. A general overtime pay agreement exists. Contrary to the public sector in general, police officers are allowed to retire after 35 years of service, regardless of their age.

For the civilian police staff, pay is also based on hours of work and length of service, but there is no standardized system of promotions, and pay increases are less substantial than for police officers. In general, their pay is lower than police officers' pay, and neither police-specific pension schemes nor special retirement agreements exist. Since civilian police staff have the right to unionize, pay is negotiated by the public service sector union UNISON.

Germany. The pay system for German police officers is similar to the public service system in general (see Chapter 5), and thus standardized and directly linked to ranks. Pay supplements are awarded for so-called heavy working conditions and for shift work. On top of this, there exists a specific supplement for the police (*Polizeizulage*), mainly meant to compensate for the dangerous aspects of police work. Police officers normally retire at the age of 62 instead of 65. As functions are not directly linked to ranks, a large share of police officers are not paid in accordance with the functions they fulfil, due to budget restrictions. Performance-based bonuses, though allowed by civil service law, so far have not been implemented, both for budgetary reasons and because of the common understanding that police work is teamwork (Behr 2000; Lange and Schenck 2004).

France. In the French police system, as in the general French civil service, pay is career-based and depends on hierarchical status and length of service. Pay increases, thus, are similar to the general pay scheme for the public sector (see Chapter 5). Like in other sectors, employees benefit from police-specific pay supplements for shift work and dangerous jobs. In addition, the French police have a long-standing tradition of informal performance-related bonuses, paid in cash and on a small scale. Heavily criticized by the *Cour des Comptes* in 1998, the system was transformed into an additional allowance for all police officers that can be topped up if necessary. Twenty-five per cent of the *commissaires* (highest hierarchical level) and 25 per cent of the *officiers* (mid-level) are paid special police allowances that can be topped up to between EUR 100 and 200 per month. Since 2004, individual bonus payments for exceptional performance by higher-ranked officers or collective bonus payments for very successful units can be distributed. Even though it seems to closely follow quantitative results, the system lacks a clear definition for the distribution of funds between the forces and rather reflects the power relations inside the institution instead of performance (Matelly and Mouhanna 2007).

Sweden. The Swedish police salary structure is established by framework agreements on salaries for employees in the public service, RALS (*Ramavtal löner inom staten),* and is negotiated in collective agreements between the parties in each agreement area. Central agreements regulate matters such as pensions, holidays, work hours, and other general employment conditions (see Chapter 5). After conclusion of the central agreements, local negotiations are conducted within the police between the Swedish National Police Board and the four local unions (the Swedish Police Union, ST-The Union of Civil Servants, Saco-S, and Seko). The local agreements contain principles for setting salaries within the police, where there are a number of collective agreements which have adopted the rules and regulations to the exigencies of police activities. For example, the police have their own agreements on work hours, holidays, reimbursement of expenses, parental allowances, extra pension allocations, reimbursement for loss of income in case of work-related injury for police officers, and collaboration. Salaries of individual employees are regulated by the police authorities, and pay is individually negotiated, at least within a fixed frame for mid- and high level positions in the police. Special police allowances were reduced in a collective agreement in 2008 (Polisförbundet 2008), which means that the pay-setting system has become even more comparable to the rest of public employment. Nevertheless, from the HRM point of view, this is compensated by the pension scheme now allowing police officers to retire much earlier than by the age of 65.

But they gained so many other things. There is a pension agreement, they have. It is unique in the whole public service! I do not think you can find it in any other sector or even in the industry. (Interview PSE3)

Swedish police officers benefit from extra pay for heavy work and shorter working hours compared to general working hours in the public sector (34 hours instead of 40). This changed somewhat with the implementation of a new shift system in 2008, according to which police officers work up to 36 hours a week. While the police unions officially complained about the worsened working conditions, they successfully negotiated a special pension system. A small portion of police officers' pay is used to finance early retirement schemes. Unlike other public sector employees, the police have the opportunity to retire at the age of 60 (Polisförbundet 2008, 2010) As regards the civilian employees, pay and social benefits are less generous than for comparable police officers. However, in professions where the police compete with the private sector to recruit individuals with 'high potentials' for specialized fields (such as cybercrime), the police must adjust remuneration upwards to market salaries. For this reason, in 2006 the National Police Board provided funding to hire 300 such specialized experts (Anderson and Tengblad 2009).

Career advancement and further training

In general, career advancement in all four countries is 'through the ranks' and has a long tradition. Further training, too, is an integral part of the overall training schemes and has become an important issue for police departments from the 1970s onwards in reaction to technological innovations, changes in society, and a more theoretical approach to policing strategies.

United Kingdom. Career advancement in the British police forces follows a strict pathway, and all senior officers once started at the bottom. Even though the procedures for promotion differ between the regional police authorities, in general, promotion to the ranks of sergeant and inspector must be based on qualifying examinations. Since the 1990s, the Home Office set in motion programmes to standardize the promotion exams, ascertaining that all officers are trained to a minimal standard defined internally by the police. Within the context of development centres, exercises and competency-based interviews are validated and assessed against the police's National Competency Framework (NCF) by comparing skills and abilities to the defined standards. In March 2013, a new method for promoting police officers through work-based assessments was announced. With the proposed system, officers who are deemed eligible for promotion and who have passed their legal examinations would enter a selection process at the local level to assess their ability to perform at the next rank. The successful applicants would then be given a temporary promotion for

12 months and, if they passed that work-based assessment programme, would be substantively promoted. Alex Marshall, Chief Executive of the College of Policing, underlined that the introduction of the scheme would represent 'the first significant change to the promotion process for many years' (see SFJUK 2013).

As for further training, the National Police College has provided junior, intermediate, and senior command courses since 1948 for inspectors and chief inspectors, superintendents, and chief superintendents, respectively. Special courses for sergeants were also offered. Further training was put on the agenda again in 1999 within the framework of the report 'Managing learning: A study of police training' (HMIC 1999). In essence, further training was implemented as a standardized tool by linking training and career progression to training needs analysis in order to better meet the given performance plans. With the Criminal Justice and Police Act 2001, the Central Police Training and Development Authority (Centrex) was established. Renamed and reorganized twice since then (National Policing Improvement Agency [NPIA] in 2007, College of Policing since 2013), it constitutes the first step to standardizing training measurements and assuring a nationwide comparable level.

Germany. Career advancement in the German police is highly formalized and was originally channelled into four different service classes. Over the course of the 1990s and 2000s, the lowest service (*Einfacher Dienst*) has lost ground in all *Länder* due to job cuts and higher qualification requirements. In some *Länder*, starting in 2000 in Bremen, a more condensed two-tiered service class system (*zweigliedrige Laufbahn*) has been introduced.[30] Even though police unions and HRM stress the positive motivational aspect for police officers, the costs are still deemed high, and due to the restricted number of posts in the higher ranks, not every police officer can advance upwards on the career ladder as expected (see below).

In general, career advancement is through the ranks and follows either a promotion (*Beförderung*, BBG §22, BLV §§ 35ff.), meaning the conferment of a higher service grade within the same service class, or advancement to a higher service class (*Aufstieg*, BBG §17; BLV § 35), with the latter based on meeting pre-described qualification requirements. Since all new appointed officers start in the lowest position within the career bracket corresponding to their entry qualification, promotion is the normal mode of advancement. Procedures for promotion take into account performance, but also time served in terms of experience; thus advancement is still linked to seniority. Performance appraisals entail the evaluation of suitability (*Eignung*), capability (*Befähigung*), and professional performance (*fachliche Leistung*), with the latter gaining more and more ground, as one HR expert underlined:

I mean, I am an advocate of the idea, I mean, 'Suitability, Performance, Qualification', even if it sounds a bit flawed, but it takes more and more space. Sure, seniority, that still exists. Within the last reform (*Dienstrechtsreform*),[31] the age groups have been adapted and extended. ... Now we have some funds to promote a colleague slightly earlier in case he did a good job. But it must all fit in ... all boxes ticked. (Interview PDE10)

At the same time, several interviewees (PDE2, PDE3, PDE5) referred to the concept of 'social promotion', meaning that if an older police officer did a decent job for a long time, but is not performing as well as a younger officer, the older officer is nonetheless perceived of as deserving a promotion.

And if we would follow the performance principle, and we would have a look at one specific year only, the staff that had shown a good but not outstanding performance over several years would never be promoted, because the year's outstanding staff would get all the promotions. This is something we would say, it's about – how can I put it – to a certain degree, social aspects play a role. (Interview PDE2)

Tensions between performance and seniority have become aggravated since both the advancement to higher service grades within a given service class, and the advancement to a higher service class (*Laufbahngruppe*), are institutionally restricted by the number of posts defined in the respective budgets. On the one hand, according to evaluation-based promotion, only those officers who receive the best grade in the performance assessment can be promoted. On the other hand, grades are apportioned. For example, only a given share of applicants can achieve an 'A' on the assessment. Therefore, in order to be able to promote older officers for social reasons, young officers often only receive mediocre grades even if they are high performers. This bottleneck in promotion (addressed as *Beförderungsstau*), while characteristic for German public administration in general, is perceived of in the police as particularly demotivating and counterproductive, especially given the rising public demands for high-quality police work (Interviews PDE2, PDE7, PDE10). Mobility restrictions also occur in the rare cases of advancement to higher service classes by way of examination, since here too, the number of available posts at each level in the hierarchy is fixed annually with the police budget and usually does not match the organizational requirements of the police. Therefore, many police officers occupy posts that are usually linked to a higher rank, and even if the respective officer is eligible for promotion, this might not be possible for budgetary reasons. In practice, therefore, many police officers do not receive the pay they would deserve for their performance (Interviews PDE2, PDE 3, PDE 8). In some German police forces (for example, in Bremen), this challenge is met by attempts to establish the idea of 'expert careers' within the police by becoming a specialist without a management function.

France. Even more pronounced than in Germany, advancement in the French civil service is generally pre-determined by the established, strict career group system (*corps*) (see Chapter 5). Reforms of this system in the police, starting in the 1970s with the merger of the formerly separated uniformed and non-uniformed *corps*, impacted the career chances of the respective groups, though with different group effects, as the more recent reforms show. In 1995, the 'reform of *corps* and career' (*réforme des corps et des carrières* I) led to a fusion of *corps* into three new *corps*. In 2004–05, a follow-up reform (*réforme des corps et des carrières II*) aimed at widening the lowest *corps* and integrating the majority of *gardiens* (46 per cent of police staff) into one *corps*.[32] This was combined with a reduction in size of the higher *corps*, which decreases chances for promotion in the longer run. On the other hand, the lower levels profited from better chances for internal mobility, as one HR manager stressed:

> In terms of individual careers, we facilitated the passages. A *gardien*, for example, he didn't have much of a choice, he could choose between two different careers, the public security or the riot police. Today, with the same educational level, he has a whole range of different career paths to choose from. In the past, we also had a very localized approach. You started in one department and made your career there. Today, we have a lot more freedom of movement, and you can do your career by passing through investigation in this department, and doing public security in another department and so on. We really facilitated the changes. Changes that are, from our perspective, extremely enriching. (Interview PFR3)

Modes of career advancement encompass seniority and performance. While promotions within a *corps* are mainly seniority-based, promotions into higher *corps* are based on entrance examinations or performance-based selection processes. However, the share of internal promotions has increased at the expense of external staffing. Furthermore, similar to Germany, the notion of 'social promotion' of older police officers exists. Or, as one HR manager put it,

> And without being the exception, the last resort that remains is the criterion of seniority. You are comparing staff, you compare the marks, you compare the jobs they do. The more important a job is, the higher the chances to get to the superior level. If we have competing candidates that have the same important job, the same responsibilities, the same performance, we still have seniority, and we will take the most senior in that case. That's it. (Interview PFR3)

Despite the fact that career pathways through the *corps* are outlined and flexibility has increased, employees are increasingly faced with restricted entry and advancement chances due to limited availability of posts. Even though about 73 per cent of the *adjoints de sécurité* find a job after termination of their contract, it is difficult for them to continue their career within the police. Internal vacancies have been restricted by the General Review of Public Policies (Révision générale des politiques publiques, RGPP), and the number of *concours* has been reduced. For example, between 2006 and 2011, only three of these contests for internal vacancies took place. This is also the case for the three bodies of the national police, where access to senior positions has tightened since the RGPP.[33]

In response to two government reports in the 1980s indicating poor qualifications and competencies of police officers, training and advanced training have been professionalized. The Socialist government initiated a programme aiming at the modernization of equipment and eliminating the nepotistic structures of the old regime (Roché 2005). This programme entailed a so-called real training policy, which had notable effects on the level of recruitment and initial training. Whereas up to the early 1980s, the sole selection criteria were traditional computing and orthography skills, the 1982 Police Training Charta defined management tasks and leadership concepts for the first time. New training schools were opened and curricula for in-house training were developed. Since 1990, 40 hours of in-house training are mandatory, and since 1992, *commissaires* and higher ranks must participate in police management workshops (10–15 days within a two-year period). Since then, continual training is not only linked to the general improvement of competencies, but half of it is also dedicated to the preparation for exams necessary for internal promotions or for exams which follow promotions. In other words, French police officers have the duty to participate in job-specific further training and the right to participate in promotion-oriented training.

Sweden. In Sweden, both career advancement and further training have been modernized. Although a career-based system persists, the so-called glass ceiling reform of 1997 eased career advancement and partly overturned standardized promotion paths. For example, career trajectories allow for leaving out one or two steps on the career ladder in order to advance directly to higher positions. According to one HR manager,

> It has opened up, yes. Today, you also have this that you can, as a civilian, join our programme and be within the leader organization of policemen. Of course, you have to practice some theory within that. You are not allowed to go out and work on the street, still you are in a leading organization of the police. (Interview PSE3)

Although a rank system based on seniority still exists, especially in rural areas, it is perceived by the interviewees as a 'nostalgic' element. Apart from some general requirements for promotion to senior positions, promotion procedures still differ between police authorities. The 1997 reform also abolished the requirement of a law degree for becoming a regional police chief in favour of other university degrees, such as business or engineering. Promotions based on seniority were perceived as unjust by all interviewees:

> But we are quite clear in our policies what it is about: competencies are first and seniority is second. We are coming more and more to very clear recruitment processes where the profiler...[A competence profiler?] Yes. In the recruitment process where you have to start with the analysis about what do we need today and in the future? So you just do not recruit the same person as the one who had left. You have to make a very clear and neutral profile and an open transparent process. We just launched the recruitment process and it is very...people have been...the authorities have been longing for it. It is a big impress and it has got a lot of approvers, people really like it. I think it is needed, because you had to see the whole process. We are definitely more about competences, not persons or seniorities...(Interview PSE2)

In line with these changes, assessment centres are increasingly relied upon in decisions regarding the internal staffing of vacant posts, and annual individual assessments have been introduced. Even though they so far have not impacted individual pay levels, the HR managers interviewed considered this linkage as a logical further step.

Like training, advanced training has a long tradition in the Swedish police, with courses offered in the national police training centres for senior constables, inspectors, and commissioners from the 1950s onwards (Lord 1998). Career development initiatives in the Swedish Police Service are focused on leadership training and on broadening the base from which managers are recruited. Career development takes various forms, from counselling or tailor-made programmes for a specific member of staff to courses arranged for a group of employees at the request of a police authority. Leadership issues are coordinated by the National Police Board. In order to keep up to date in this field, the NPB has set up a Leadership Training Centre (LTC) at the National Police Academy. The LTC is a knowledge management centre which tracks developments in the Police Service and other organizations, monitors the publication of books, articles, and research papers in the field, provides advice on leadership strategies, and supports pilot schemes at the police authorities. In addition to providing leadership training, the Police Service arranges competence development courses for both police and civilian staff, for example in the use of IT or crime investigation duties. The police authorities usually prioritize training courses focused on operational duties, such as tactical police work and various practical skills (NPB 2005; 2010).

Job security

Job security in all four countries is high and combined with an unlimited employment status. Police officers usually cannot be dismissed unless they violate specific rules of conduct. The majority of complaints stem from citizens accusing police officers of inappropriate behaviour, such as racism or excessive violence. However, most of the proceedings are rejected and the number of dismissals within the police is minimal.[34]

United Kingdom. Police officers, in general, cannot be made redundant, but they can be obliged to take compulsory retirement after 30 years of service. Only a very small proportion of sworn police officers are dismissed, but no overall statistics are available. The Metropolitan Police reported 124 dismissals due to misconduct between 2006 and 2011.[35] In contrast to the high job security of the sworn officers, according to the general regulation, all non-sworn and civilian staff can be made redundant, as is the case with employees in private sector. Thus, since the announced cost cuts in 2010, the proportion of civilian staff having left the police is higher than the number of sworn police officers.[36]

Germany. German police are civil servants and thus have a lifelong employment guarantee. Dismissal is only possible after a disciplinary procedure, which is regulated by disciplinary law (*Bundesdisziplinargesetz*). In order to dismiss a civil servant, departments and agencies must bring action before the administrative court that decides on the dismissal. In case of dismissal, a civil servant loses all entitlements and can neither regain the civil servant status nor be appointed to another public employment position. A dismissal is the hardest possible sanction stemming from a disciplinary procedure. Other sanctions include a letter of censure, a fine, a reduction of pay, or downgrading. The gravity of the sanction must correspond to the severity of the misconduct. The number of police officers dismissed usually is neither published nor made available to the public, but must be requested by the political parties that are members of the *Länder* parliaments via 'minor interpellations' (*Kleine Anfragen*).

France. In France, the majority of the police are still employed as *fonctionnaire* and benefit from high job security (see Chapter 5). However, with a new regulation implemented in 2010, police officers can be dismissed if they refuse replacement three times.[37] The *adjoints de sécurité* or *contractuels*, employed on a fixed-term contract, enjoy less employment security. Prior to 2012, the contracts, which are usually issued for a three-year period, could only be extended for another three years, thus making conversion into the police force impossible. Since 2012, however, a new regulation for contracted staff allows the employer to issue permanent contracts.[38]

Sweden. The Swedish police staff benefit from the job security set in national collective agreements between *Arbetsgivarverket* and the unions. Police employment in Sweden is barely distinguishable from private sector employment, and due to the harmonized employment relations (see Chapter 5), job security for the police forces is rather high.

Equal opportunity policies

In all of the countries under study, equal opportunity policies regarding gender and ethnic diversity have become relevant in the police as a consequence of both the admission of women to the police forces and the increasing ethnic diversity of the population. Given the tradition of a predominantly male workforce and a male occupational culture, one challenge has been the inclusion of women in both the civilian and the police staff. Additionally, the colonial past of some of the countries and the rise in migration flows towards Western Europe have increased social diversity, thus challenging the traditional ethnic homogeneity of the police forces.[39] While women's quest for access to the police goes back to the beginning of the 20th century, the demand for more ethnic diversity is more recent. From the 1970s onwards, not least stipulated by EU anti-discrimination policies, most police forces in the Western European sphere have emphasized equal opportunity policies, with the aim of recruiting more women and people of diverse ethnic backgrounds.[40]

United Kingdom. In the United Kingdom, female police officers were fully attested in 1923 but had limited powers to arrest and worked in separate units. It was not until 1973 that female police were integrated into the main force. The Sex Discrimination Act 1975 required the police to abolish separate departments and career structures for women and to integrate women fully into the service. From then on, male and female officers competed on equal terms for entry, promotion, and transfers, and subsequently, the number of female officers increased. The British Association for Women in Policing was founded in 1987 in order to support women at all levels and to lobby for equal rights. While in 1998, women made up only 16 per cent of the total sworn police constable population (Westmarland 2001), this share grew to 27.3 per cent in 2013 (Home Office 2013). However, women are still underrepresented in higher ranks. In 2013, women in senior ranks across England and Wales only accounted for 18 per cent of the total police workforce as compared to women at the constable level representing 29.7 per cent of the total workforce (Home Office 2013). In order to tackle this issue, a wide range of mentoring and development programmes for female police officers and female police staff have been initiated, both on the level of the regional police forces and on the level of the training institutions (Carson 2009).

In 2013, the share of ethnic minority police officers within the police forces in England and Wales reached 5 per cent (Home Office 2013). Until the late 1990s, verbal racism was reported to be endemic to the police in England and Wales (Smith and Gray 1985, pp. 388–89; Holdaway 1996). This is in line with the Scarman Report (Scarman 1981) and the Macpherson Report (Macpherson of Cluny 1999), which uncovered structural racism within the police forces. In consequence, sensitization programmes were set up and the recruitment of ethnic minorities was encouraged (Silvestri et al. 2013).

Germany. Women were fully integrated into the main police forces of the German *Länder* by the end of the 1980s (Wilz 2005, p. 159). While quotas or positive action for female police officers do not exist, the general gender equality regulations for the civil service and public employees apply.[41] In line with the general German policy orientation emphasizing reconciliation of work and life rather than equal rights, concepts to manage work and life are fostered in all police forces, be it through part-time work offers, programmes to reintegrate female police officers after parental care leave, or provision of childcare services. With a share of less than 20 per cent, women are still underrepresented in the higher-level career groups.[42] While interviewees stressed the fact that the police follow the rules set up for the public service in general, at the same time there are reservations with respect to the 'fit' of equality norms for the police, as the following interview sequence illustrates:

On the beat, we have around 30 per cent female police officers. Physical characteristics could be extremely different – even though we have standards while recruiting. Some women won't go on the beat with another woman. According to them, they feel uncomfortable in a conflict situation without a male partner. If the share of female police officers gets too high, in some areas, this is seen as discriminating – by men also. We try to handle this. But that's why I am against quota. You need to specify the area. In which areas does gender play a role? It isn't about gender, it's about the tasks the people can fulfil. (Interview PDE9)

The same holds true for ethnic minorities. Ethnic minorities are still underrepresented, and figures in the German police forces vary from 0.4 per cent in Mecklenburg-Western Pomerania to 17.6 per cent in North Rhine-Westphalia, which approximates the roughly 20 per cent in the overall population (Die Zeit 2014). Following the general rules applied to the public service, no positive discrimination can take place.

There isn't a quota for colleagues with ethnic background. We wouldn't agree with that, because this just wouldn't work. We expect people to do the training, and we don't want to decrease the standards.... We want the same standards and from that point on everybody is welcome. And we already have colleagues with ethnic background, quite a few. (Interview PDE11)

However, police recruitment strategies have recently had a stronger focus on ethnic minorities, and both police and academic research have investigated the barriers for ethnic minorities to enter the police (Hunold et al.

2010; Regge 2013). According to our interviewees, more targeted recruitment is successful; the number of applicants is already increasing, and some change in the composition of the workforce is expected within the next years. (Interview PDE10)

France. In France, women have been able to become police officers in the highest *corps* since 1974, in the middle *corps* since 1976–77, and in the lowest *corps* since 1979. Until 1992, negative quotas officially restricted the share of women in the police. Since then, the share of female employees has increased to values ranging from 17 per cent for *gardien de la paix* to 22 per cent for *commissaires* and *officiers*. In this context, the higher representation in the higher *corps* (*officiers* and *commissaires*) can presumably be attributed to the system of multiple entry points and exam-based recruitment and promotion procedures. At the same time, neither positive discrimination nor positive action exists, and interview partners disapproved of positive action, as careers in the *fonction publique* are supposed to be based on merit and *égalité des chances*. However, all interview partners agreed that policing is a predominantly male job, and assumed that women are more prone to prioritize family or care work.

> But we have the problem with the female condition. The police occupation is an extremely hard job, with flexible working times, and I think, there's a moment in which the women will have difficulties in combining work and family life, especially if she wants children. She will be absent, she will get on parental leave, she will take, one, two, three years, because that's the right you have in the public service. And once she's back, she will take part-time. (Interview PFR5)

Due to the French republican approach to citizenship, no statistical account exists for ethnic minorities. According to our interview partners, there is still a distinct underrepresentation of these groups in the French police. To them, this can be explained by the problems in policing groups from the same racial or ethnic background.

> So, in France, it's forbidden. But,...but admittedly, we do it anyway. The time we created the *adjoints de securité* [in 1997], it was Jean-Pierre Chevenènement, the then minister. He said: We need to recruit the police that look like the population in the *quartiers*. Off the record, this meant to recruit black and Arab people. So that's what we did. It didn't work neither better nor worse. Because in any way, the moment the police officers arrests someone, it doesn't matter whether he's black or Arab,...So it didn't change a lot. (Interview PFR6)

Sweden. In Sweden, the first women entered the police as early as 1908, although they were not yet accepted as part of the official police (Dahlgren

2007, p. 37). From 1958 onwards, women were allowed to go on the beat, and equal access to all functions was established in 1971 (Dahlgren 2007, p. 52). In 2008, women made up about 25 per cent of all police officers, and in 2006, the share of women in managing positions stood at about 19 per cent. Until 2014, the respective shares rose to 31 and 20 per cent (Polismyndigheten 2015, p. 61). Female careers have been facilitated by way of recruitment efforts, as well as mentoring programmes and leadership training programmes designed for women, but quotas have not been implemented.

> No, we have very explicitly chosen not to do that. We think the way, and I think we had some really good reasons for thinking so, is that transparent processes where you do not pick a person, where you say we need this and this and you have an open search..., good competence development, clear career path etc. is promoting women. Because nothing is more about taking away obstacles rather than telling women, go to this programme then you would be a better leader. I mean, the problem is not with the women, the problem is in the organization. (Interview PSE1)

Women obviously benefit from the increased use of assessment centres in promotion procedures, as they allow for objective decision making (see interviews PSE2, PSE3). However, from the point of view of our interviewees, women still have to perform better than men to achieve the same hierarchical level.

> She has to work, I think, two or three or four times as hard as anyone else to get the mandate from her own organization to succeed, I guess. She needs a lot of support. (Interview PSE2)

The integration of ethnic minorities follows generally applicable equal opportunity rules, and no further programme or specific support exists. However, the integration of ethnic minorities in the Swedish police forces remains critical. Recent research underlines the fact that already during the recruitment process, applicants with an ethnic minority background have to demonstrate a greater share of loyalty, and this is seen as a barrier to successful recruitment and integration (Peterson and Uhnoo 2012; Uhnoo 2015).

To sum up, while the inclusion of women in the police has progressed, with the Swedish Police Service being a forerunner, evidence on better integration of ethnic minorities is poor, presumably not only due to a lack of statistical documentation. All police forces claim to improve and change the male-biased, 'white' police cultures, but advancement still seems to be slow (Rabe-Hemp 2007; Silvestri et al. 2013; Fassin 2011; Loftus 2008).

Summary

In all countries except for Germany, the size of the police forces has grown considerably since the 1980s, unlike most other areas of public employment. At the same time, police forces in the UK and, to a lesser degree, Sweden diversified their workforce and increased the number of civilian staff. This change in the workforce structure is a major factor accounting for the increase in the share of women, contributing to an overall share of women in the police force of more than one-quarter in the United Kingdom, Germany, and France. In Sweden, where the police have a strong tradition of service in the sense of care for the community and where women are highly integrated into the labour market, the female share even rose to more than 40 per cent in 2014 (see Table 8.1), thus strongly attenuating the male culture generally attributed to the police. With regard to career advancement, women are less underrepresented on higher hierarchical levels in France and Sweden than in Germany and the United Kingdom. This suggests that formalized, non-bureaucratic promotion procedures, such as assessment centres or exam-based recruitment, ease female career development within the police. In contrast to the inclusion of women, reaching ethnic diversity

Table 8.2 Dimensions of change in public employment regulation: Police, England, and Wales

Dimensions and characteristics	Pre-1990s	Early 2010s
1. Regulation of employment conditions		
Legal status	Sworn officers	Sworn officers (SO) Civilian staff (CS)
Collective regulations	Unilateral	SO: Unilateral, external negotiation agency CS: Collective agreements
Regulation of labour conflicts	No right to unionize; No active right to strike due to executive powers	SO: No right to unionize; No active right to strike due to executive powers CS: Right to strike
2. Personnel system		
Mode of advancement	Career-based	SO: Front-line police: Career-based; Back office: Position-based for specific tasks (IT, Forensics, Management) CS: No specific pathway
Openness	Low	SO: Front-line police: Low; Back office: High for some special tasks CS: High

Continued

Table 8.2   Continued

Dimensions and characteristics	Pre-1990s	Early 2010s
3. Personnel management		
Entry requirements	Formalized, low	Formalized, low
Recruitment	Special police training pathways through the ranks	SO: Special police training pathways through the ranks; Open for other disciplinary backgrounds in some specialized areas CS: Minor special training
Pay structure	Negotiation-based, centralized	Negotiation-based, centralized
Evaluation and assessment	Yes (police unit level)	Yes, increasingly individualized
Performance incentives	No	SO: Few, higher ranks, collective rewards on unit level CS: None
Opportunities for promotion	Seniority-based	SO & CS: Partly individualized, performance-based
Further education	No	SO & CS: Flexible, customized
4. Integration function of public employment regime		
Payment, social security	High	SO: High CS: Low
Employment security	High	SO: High CS: Low
Equal opportunity and treatment at the workplace	High	SO: Average public sector CS: Average public sector
5. Specificity of public employment regime		
Difference as compared to private sector employment regime	Average	SO: Lowered CS: None

Note: SO: Sworn Officers; CS: Civilian staff.

in the police workforce still poses a challenge, although equal opportunity and anti-discrimination norms apply in all countries studied.

Although police forces in all countries under study have been subject to efficiency-oriented organizational reforms and to some extent also to re-regulation of employment, employment conditions in the police still *correspond to the ideal type civil servant* in many dimensions. This is most obvious with regard to employment security. Not only in Germany (see Table 8.3) and

Table 8.3 Dimensions of change in public employment regulation: Police, Germany

Dimensions and characteristics	Pre-1990s	Early 2010s
1. Regulation of employment conditions		
Legal status	Civil servant (*Beamter*)	Civil servant (*Beamter*)
Collective regulations	Authoritative/ unilateral	Authoritative/unilateral
Regulation of labour conflicts	No right to strike	No right to strike
2. Personnel system		
Mode of advancement	Career-based	Career-based
Openness	None	Low for core policing tasks; High in specialized areas such as IT, forensics, strategic planning
3. Personnel management		
Entry requirements	Formalized, low	Formalized, high (*Abitur*)
Recruitment	Special police training pathway	Special police training pathway
Pay structure	Determined by law	Determined by law
Evaluation and assessment	Seniority rules	Performance-based but on collective level (units, not single staff)
Performance incentives	None	None
Opportunities for promotion	Seniority-based	Seniority-based but focusing more on performance in case of competing candidates
Further education	Legally determined, standardized	Legally determined, customized
4. Integration function of public employment regime		
Payment, social security	High	High
Employment security	High	High
Equal opportunity and treatment at the workplace	Low	High, but mismatch between equal opportunity programmes (talk) and diversity within the forces (action)
5. Specificity of public employment regime		
Difference as compared to private sector employment regime	High	High

France (see Table 8.4), where a legally based and unaltered civil servant status is dominant, but also in the United Kingdom (see Table 8.2), where a special status of sworn officer applies, and in Sweden (see Table 8.5), where the civil servant status had been abolished in the 1970s, the police workforce enjoy either tenure or unlimited contracts, and dismissal is strongly regulated and restricted. Moreover, in all countries some form of collective interest representation is in place, counterbalancing the unilateral power of the state as employer and allowing for some negotiation with regard to pay and working conditions.

Reluctance in the alignment to the ideal-type service provider is also observed in the pay structure, where no major changes occurred. Only in Sweden does the introduction of individual performance-related pay systems as a significant characteristic for the service provider model go beyond mere rhetoric. In the other countries, performance-related incentives are small and only apply to the higher ranks, whereas on the level of the police units, if at all, small collective rewards dominate. This reflects the understanding of police work as teamwork, as well as caveats with regard to performance measurement, especially when it is linked to crime rates and crime solving. Nevertheless, in all four countries, the focus on collective performance has strengthened, and either New Police Management as in the United Kingdom (Metcalfe 2004), the balanced scorecard or comparable models, or value-for-money concepts were introduced to improve the police units' performances and to identify 'objective' results for legitimizing the distribution of resources.

Further *commonalities* in the development of employment in this sector refer to recruitment and training. In all countries except the United Kingdom (where everyone can apply if he or she fulfils the general physical requirements and only a few authorities have started introducing compulsory certificates), entry requirements have increased, and in all countries training has become more professionalized. Likewise, further training has been enhanced, strengthening the role of both compulsory and voluntary continuing education.

Irrespective of these commonalities, important *differences* in the employment regulation and personnel policies can also be observed. To some extent, they are in line with the specificities of the national trajectories in public employment. Thus, the police in Germany and France, in accordance with the persistent bureaucratic features of their civil service in general, still adhere to a career-based system and tend to privilege years served over performance, although the restructuring and condensing of career classes and the growing emphasis on performance contribute to more flexible and competitive advancement. The police in Sweden and the United Kingdom, in contrast, show a stronger performance orientation and more leeway for position-based advancement, be it by fast track programmes or staffing by external recruitment, corresponding to the more far-reaching change of the national public employment towards a service provider model.

Table 8.4   Dimensions of change in public employment regulation: Police, France

Dimensions and characteristics	Pre-1990s	Early 2010s
1. Regulation of employment conditions		
Legal status	Civil servant (*Fonctionnaire*; *Fonction publique d'Etat*)	Civil servant (*Fonctionnaire*): *Police Nationale* (PN): *Fonction publique d'Etat*; *Police Municipale* (PM): *Fonction publique territoriale* Public employee (*Non-fonctionnaire*): *Adjoint de sécurité* (ADS)
Collective regulations	Authoritative/ unilateral	Authoritative/unilateral
Regulation of labour conflicts	No right to strike	PN: No right to strike PM: Right to strike ADS: Right to strike
2. Personnel system		
Mode of advancement	*Corps* model	*Corps* model
Openness	None, internal examinations	PN: None, internal exam PM: High ADS: High
3. Personnel management		
Entry requirements	Depending on *corps*	Depending on *corps*
Recruitment	Special police training pathways	PN, PM, ADS: Special police training pathways
Pay structure	Determined by law	Determined by law
Evaluation and assessment	Seniority rules	PN: Mix of seniority rules and performance-based (for higher ranks) PM: Seniority rules ADS: –
Performance incentives	No	PN: Few for higher ranks, collective rewards on unit level PM: No ADS: No
Opportunities for promotion	Seniority-based, internal exam	PN: Seniority-based, internal exam PM: Internal exam ADS: Internal exam to get into PN
Further education	Legally determined, standardized	Legally determined, standardized

Continued

Table 8.4   Continued

Dimensions and characteristics	Pre-1990s	Early 2010s
4. Integration function of public employment regime		
Payment, social security	High	PN: High PM: Average, high ADS: Low, low
Employment security	High	PN: High PM: High ADS: Low
Equal opportunity and treatment at the workplace	Low	Low
5. Specificity of public employment regime		
Difference as compared to private sector employment regime	High	PN: High PM: Average ADS: Low

Note: PN: *Police National* ; PM: *Police Municipale* ; ADS: *Adjoint de Sécurité*.

Table 8.5   Dimensions of change in public employment regulation: Police, Sweden

Dimensions and characteristics	Pre-1990s	Early 2010s
1. Regulation of employment conditions		
Legal status	Employees with some privileges and duties	Employees
Collective regulations	Collective agreements	Collective agreements
Regulation of labour conflicts	Right to strike	No active right to strike due to executive powers
2. Personnel system		
Mode of advancement	Career-based	Front-line police: Career-based Back-office: Position-based for specific tasks (IT, Forensics, Management)
Openness	Closed	Front-line police: Closed Back-office: Opened for some special tasks
3. Personnel management		
Entry requirements	Formalized, low	Formalized, basic qualification for university or equivalent (*Folksscolen*)

Continued

Table 8.5 Continued

Dimensions and characteristics	Pre-1990s	Early 2010s
Recruitment	Special police training pathways	Special police training pathways Open for other disciplinary background in some specialised areas
Pay structure	Negotiation-based, centralised	Negotiation-based, agency level, individual
Evaluation and assessment	No	Individual level
Performance incentives	No	Few, higher ranks, collective primes on unit level
Opportunities for promotion	Seniority-based	Individualised, performance-based
Further education	No	Flexible, customised
4. Integration function of public employment regime		
Payment, social security	High	High
Employment security	High	High
Equal opportunity and treatment at the workplace	High	High
5. Specificity of public employment regime		
Difference to private sector employment regime	Low	Lowered

Finally, the emergence of second-class policing jobs in the United Kingdom and France should be mentioned. Characterized by fixed-term contracts, a lack of career prospects, and low wages, they serve either to compensate for the lack of numerical and financial flexibility of the established workforce as in the United Kingdom or to satisfy increasing demands on public security and police presence as is the case in France with the *adjoints de securité* (Mouhanna 2011). In both cases, a polarization of the police workforce can be observed. In the United Kingdom this is in line with the general alignment of the public service to private labour market employment conditions, whereas in France this precarious job category departs from the rather privileged and still distinct employment conditions in public employment.

Part IV
Summary and Conclusions

9
Summary and Integrated Comparison of Countries and Sectors

Introduction

As noted earlier, scholarly debates agree that during the last decades, public administration regimes have undergone substantial change. The question of whether and how these changes have affected public employment is at the core of this study, assuming that public employment in the past was characterized by distinct features historically enshrined in the civil servant status separating this type of employment from private sector employment. It was the 'Golden Age' of the modern nation-state, distinguished not only by territorial unity securing the rule of law and the establishment of democratic institutions, but also by willingness to intervene in market dynamics through a welfare state (Hurrelmann et al. 2007; Leibfried et al. 2015). The welfare state generated a substantial expansion of the public sector after the Second World War and established specific functions of public employment. In most OECD countries, the state became the largest employer (OECD 2009). Employment practices in the public sector created internal labour markets, high levels of job security, career progression based on seniority, and initial qualification for the whole range of the large and more heterogeneous public workforce. Moreover, the state aimed at being both a 'good' and 'model' employer for the private sector by setting high standards of public employment in terms of working conditions, job security, and integrating disadvantaged groups such as women, disabled persons, and migrants (Bach and Kessler 2007; Beaumont 1992).

From the 1970s onwards, these functions have been increasingly challenged by a transformation in the conception of the state and public policymaking. The paradigm shift towards monetarism and a 'lean and entrepreneurial state' in most Western countries – not least supported by OECD and EU policy scripts – resulted in welfare state retrenchment and a privatization of the public infrastructure (Obinger et al. 2010; Pierson 2001). The cost pressure on public budgets generated by, among others, the expansion of public employment and the so-called cost disease problem of service occupations (Baumol 1993) militated in favour of cost-cutting strategies in the public services. Moreover, public sector reforms motivated by NPM-related ideas have been introduced in order to ensure efficiency and effectivity within public administration (Kettl 1997; Hood 1991).

In the light of country-specific public administration systems clustering in different regimes and creating heterogeneous initial conditions for reform, this general transformation may take on different forms. One answer to how these systems vary in addressing the largely similar pressures mentioned above is the distinction between a primarily NPM-driven and a Neo-Weberian reform path of public administrations (Pollitt and Bouckaert 2011). This, however, might neglect potential heterogeneity *within* the Neo-Weberian reform path country cluster. Further open questions relate to how reform trajectories – be they administrative or direct HRM reforms – affect the size and specific aspects, as well as the different sectors of the remaining public employment (Derlien and Peters 2008b, pp. 7ff.). As noted earlier (see Chapters 2 and 3), we can assume that the scope of reforms in public employment regimes, irrespective of other factors, also depends on the degree of devolution of public responsibility. The design of our study tries to address these challenges by combining different levels of analysis. In order to account for possible variance within the Neo-Weberian reform trajectory, our analysis not only refers to OECD-wide macro comparisons but, by way of in-depth case studies, also investigates public employment change in three countries, German, France, and Sweden, representing three distinct administrative regimes in Western Europe assumed to follow a Neo-Weberian reform path. Additionally, the study focuses on three types of responsibility devolution represented by the sectors energy regulation, waste collection, and the police.

In the following, we summarize the general findings on the structure and change of public employment for the larger OECD set of countries (see Chapter 4) and for the country (see Chapter 5) and sector case studies (see Chapters 6–8), and compare the countries and sectors to the UK, which represents the original NPM-driven reform path and thus serves as a reference case. Comparing the countries with respect to direction and magnitude of change allows us to emphasize *commonalities in driving forces* for change and at the same time, regarding the case studies, to uncover *variance in the extent of public employment transformation across the countries* assumed to follow a Neo-Weberian reform path. Next we focus on employment change by sector across countries; this serves to identify *the role of responsibility devolution for the extent of change* and to relate sector-specific changes to country trends of public sector transformation. Thus, the analytical structure of the comparison in this summary is based on the comparative framework laid out in Chapter 3 (Table 3.1), while an assessment linking the observed change dynamics to broader discussions on transformations of the state, the role of moderating and mediating factors, and reform paths and institutional change will follow in the next chapter.

Direction and magnitude of change in public employment regimes

Changes in public employment regimes relate to size and costs, as well as to specific features of public employment. While there is manifold evidence for cross-country variety in the magnitude of these changes (Bordogna 2007; Derlien and Peters 2008a), the direction of change may seem relatively uniform. Comparative research has established early on that transformations of public employment have focused on downsizing the public workforce and reducing public employment expenditure on the one hand and an NPM-driven dismantling of the specificity and privileged nature of public employment on the other, put into effect via privatization, welfare state retrenchment, or NPM-related reforms (Cusack et al. 1989; Rothenbacher 1998). Challenges for these kinds of assessments are, however, the need to observe long-term trends, a comprehensive and comparable definition of the public workforce, and the availability of comparative data. These requirements are often mutually exclusive, since consistent definitions and availability of differentiated data over time often confines research to national statistics, which in turn complicates large-scale comparisons (Derlien and Peters 2008b, p. 15). Here, our study design seeks to strike a compromise between different types of data and comparisons.

In this section, we address the question of the extent to which the common challenges have led to similar reform trajectories and instigated similar changes of public employment. Drawing on both the larger OECD country comparison and the more specific country and sector case studies, the focus will be on the commonalities of structure and change, thus assessing the relative importance of the different drivers of change with respect to country trends. Based on the case studies of Germany, France, and Sweden, change in public employment will be addressed not only with respect to size and costs but also regarding qualitative aspects, the latter assessed by the dimensions and characteristics of public employment regulations and the ideal type heuristic of 'civil servant' versus 'service provider' as laid out in Chapters 2 and 3. Prior to this qualitative case-study-based evaluation, however, we will resume the analysis of macro-level developments regarding the *size and costs of public employment*, which helps to place the country and sector case studies and the UK reference case in the broader OECD context.

Interestingly, the OECD country comparison in Chapter 4 covering general government employment in 19 countries based on a new database (OECD 2009) supports neither the assumption of a more or less drastic cut in public personnel nor the alarmist notion of 'exploding' costs of public employment compensation. While prior studies exploring the development of overall public sector employment between the 1970s and mid-1990s indicated that the main trend is a decline after a long period of growth (Cusack et al. 1989; Rothenbacher 1998; OECD 2004, 2005), our analysis of the data for government employment in 2008 as compared to 1995 shows only minor, average reductions for common law countries and most civil law countries; Scandinavian civil law countries, which exhibit the largest public employment rates, even show a slight increase of employment in general government as a percentage of the labour force. At the same time, employment compensation expenditure (measured as a share of GDP) on average seems to have decreased, as has the government employment expenditure (measured as share of total government expenditure), again only with Scandinavian civil law countries marking an exception (see Chapter 4, Table 4.2). This may indicate that the majority of countries, after a period of employment cuts (at least for the period observed[1]), maintained a relatively stable level of public employment.

Moreover, although government employees' compensation expenditure appears to require a growing fraction of government budgets, many countries were able to contain or reduce government personnel expenditure, not least by controlling wage increases. However, as this macro trend assessment rests on highly aggregated data and is restricted to general government employment, specific dynamics by country and different sectors of public employment are not accounted for. This has called for the more nuanced country-specific investigations in Chapter 5.

Indeed, more specific accounts based on national statistical data (though with varying definitions of the public workforce) show a slightly different picture regarding the size of public employment for the countries included in the case studies. For Germany, a substantial decrease of the direct public workforce between 1991 and 2005 is reported, but then slowed down (Bosch 2013, p. 219), whereas France, which even increased public employment before 2003 (Kroos 2010), saw a reduction of the public workforce only after 2003, accelerated since 2007 by the 'one-for two-replacement rule' (Gautié 2013, p. 187). Even in Sweden, public employment as a share of total employment slightly declined from the 1990s onwards, followed until 2010 by stagnation on a still high level (Anxo 2013, p. 555).[2] A closer look at different sectors reveals that these national trends of decrease or stagnation do not apply equally across the board; there are not only sectors of public employment bearing higher shares of reduction due to their large size, such as education in France (Gautié 2013) or care services in Sweden (Anxo 2013), but also sectors which contribute less. According to our case studies, the latter especially holds for the police in Germany, France, and Sweden, which tend to be less affected by personnel cuts; moreover, the relatively small and newly established energy regulatory agencies in Germany, France, and Sweden have even been expanding personnel (see findings in Chapters 6, 7, and 8). So while in general the size and costs of public employment are still under pressure, cost containment policies seem to be more directed. These differences might not only reflect opportunities or limits in the discretion of personnel policies in the public sector – such as the 'two-for-one replacement' rule in case of retirement in France, thus circumventing violation of the high standards of job security in public employment – but also the devolution of public responsibilities. Where the state has given up both organizational and decision-making responsibility and has reduced its activity to the supervision of markets for former public utilities, cost reduction by personnel cuts is no longer an issue, as is the case in the newly established energy regulatory agencies staffed with highly qualified specialists. By contrast, sectors characterized by the devolution of only organizational responsibility, which implies direct or indirect market competition for services, are far more at risk of cuts in personnel and wages, as is the case for waste collection in this study.

Obviously, public employment changes occur not only with respect to the size but also with respect to *regulation of employment conditions and personnel policies*. As laid out in Chapter 3, ideal typical features of the civil servant type of employment are: authoritative employment regulation instead of contracts; loyalty requirements instead of the right to strike; pay and advancement according to grade and seniority instead of performance; and lifelong tenure instead of rules allowing for dismissal (see Chapter 3, Table 3.2). The extent to which these features have been changed are of special interest here. Taking into account that the traditional civil servant type of employment is highly legally entrenched, it is first of all noteworthy that basic structures, such as the state structure and the legal system in the three civil law countries under study, did not change during the observation period (see Chapter 5). *Nevertheless, a main finding of the case studies is that in all three countries, employment regulation and personnel policies for a majority of public employees changed in a way that moves public employment closer to the ideal type service provider and thus to the reference case UK, characterized by labour regulation based on private law, position-based recruitment, and performance-related pay and promotion* (see Figure 9.1). However, this shift occurs to a different extent in each country. First, it is noteworthy that in France and Sweden – where a majority of public employees shared, and still share, the same employment conditions – public employment as a whole has moved closer to the ideal type service provider, whereas in Germany, the distinction between the two large groups of civil servants (*Beamte*) and (other) public employees (*Tarifbeschäftigte*) continues to exist. Nevertheless, here too, both categories have moved towards the ideal type service provider. It can thus be summarized that even in countries with a Napoleonic, Germanic, or Scandinavian administrative tradition – which share a special role of the civil service based on the legal tradition of the state, and a civil law tradition – the specific and privileged civil servant status has been attenuated or

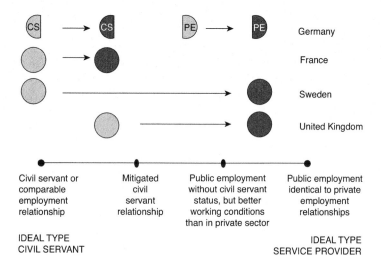

Figure 9.1   Varieties of public employment by country and national changes, 1980s–2010s

Note: Grey: early 1980s; dark grey: early 2010s.

CS: Civil servants (*Beamte*); PE: Public employees (*Tarifbeschäftigte*)

has lost importance. To put it the other way around: the respective historically inherited institutional and cultural frameworks that were assumed to erect high barriers against change in the civil service system as compared to the 'common law'-based Anglo-American administrative tradition have nevertheless allowed for a transformation of the employment category, which is usually seen as the 'backbone' of the state and state bureaucratic action.

A closer look reveals that in *Sweden* as early as 1965, core features of the traditional civil service system were called into question by the introduction of collective bargaining and the right to strike. This was followed by a series of adjustments to the general labour legislation, including co-determination at the workplace, to make the law applicable to both the private and public labour markets. A replacement of the rigid system of pay grades by a performance-oriented system of individual pay, as well as a decentralization of pay settlement allowing for more flexibility in pay-setting on the local level and within public organizations, completed the alignment of public and private employment regulation and policies from 1985 onwards. While the decentralization of administrative reforms during the 1980s was inspired by the idea of moving 'from authority culture to service culture' (quoted after Premfors 1991, p. 88), further reforms mainly had a cost-cutting notion and – apart from privatization and retrenchment of the public workforce – were geared towards increased competition in the provision of services (see Chapter 5; Anxo 2013). Consequently, regulation of employment conditions, personnel politics, and the personnel system of public employment in Sweden no longer show specificities, and thus public employment, still representing more than one-fourth of the workforce in Sweden, can be found in a position similar to the UK, albeit in the context of a much more employee-friendly environment (see Table 9.1).

Transformations of public employment in Germany and France started later, proceeded much more incrementally, and are still ongoing. Both countries neither questioned the civil servant status as the core employment category in public administration nor altered the more (France) or less (Germany) closed career system. Nevertheless, in these countries too, distinct features of the respective national public employment systems have been subject to change.

In *Germany*, debates questioning the efficiency and effectivity of public service provision as well as the duality of civil servants (*Beamte*) and other public employees (*Tarifbeschäftigte*) (the latter representing more than half of the public workforce) started as early as the 1970s. However, high legal barriers codified in the Basic Law against changing constitutive elements of the status of civil servants have been hindering more comprehensive reforms. While a reform in 1997 introducing performance bonuses brought only incremental change, a more substantive flexibilization of personnel policies and the personnel system was triggered by a politically induced structural reform of the German federal system. With the 2006 federal reform (*Föderalismusreform*), the 16 German *Länder*, employing more than half of the public workforce, have gained autonomy in regulating civil servants' salaries and pensions, the system of service classes, and the rules of advancement. Though the basic institutional guarantees for civil servants are still in place, this decentralization generated a formerly unknown differentiation, especially in remuneration for the majority of civil servants in Germany, and induced competition between different regional state employers for the best civil servants.

Over the course of this decentralization, employment conditions of public employees were also subject to change. The formerly close connection of employment regulation between civil servants and public employees, allowing for an alignment in pay structure, family-related salary components, seniority-based pay progression, and dismissal protection, has been loosened. In addition, central coordination of collective agreements for public employees on the regional state level broke off and, within the boundaries of framework agreements, paved the way for greater divergence in employment conditions. Finally, while the social partners did not agree on PRP, the introduction of a new low-wage bracket (to counteract privatization) and the expansion of fixed-term contracts at the *Länder* level – particularly prominent in the large education sector – indicate a further flexibilization of

Table 9.1 Public employment regime by country – characteristics and major changes

	Germany	France	Sweden	United Kingdom
Employment regulation				
Legal status	**Public employees (*Angestellte*): 63%; since 2005/06 single status for blue- and white-collar employees** Civil servants (*Beamte*): 37%	Civil servants (*fonctionnaires*): 83% **Public employees (*non-titulaires*): 17%** (new status group since 1984)	**Public employees: 99% (abolition of legal civil servant status in 1965)**	**Public employees: 89%** Core Civil Service: 11%
Collective regulations	CS: Legally formalized, decentralized (2009) PE: **Collective agreement, increasing decentralization**	Unilateral, centralized	**Collective agreement, decentralized**	Collective agreement, decentralized
Regulation of labour conflicts	CS: No right to strike PE: **Right to strike**	Right to strike	**Right to strike (since 1965)**	No active right to strike
Personnel policies				
Entry requirements and recruitment	CS: Legally formalized PE: **No formalization**	CS: Legally formalized access PE: Only minor formalization	Not formalized, no specific requirements	Not formalized, no specific requirements
Pay	CS: Salary brackets, based on length of service Performance-related pay elements (1997) PE: **Negotiated low-wage pay bands (2005)**	CS: Salary brackets, based on length of service; bonus based on function and individual performance (2009) PE: Unilateral	Negotiated base rate Performance-related pay elements (1985)	Negotiated base rate Performance-related pay elements (1980s)
Promotion	CS: Law-based promotion system, seniority, individual assessment (1997) PE: **Qualification-based promotion (2005/06)**	CS: Law-based promotion system, seniority, individual assessment (2007) PE: No opportunity for promotion	Position-based, not formalized **Performance-related promotion (1994)**	Position-based, not formalized Performance-related promotion (since 1980s)
Employment security	CS: Lifetime employment PE: **Strong job protection, increased use of fixed-term contracts (since 2002)**	CS: Lifetime employment PE: Limited job security, increased use of fixed-term contracts (mid-1990s)	**Open-ended contracts** (1965)	Open-ended contracts, increased use of fixed-term contracts (since 1980s)

Note: CS: Civil servants; PE: Public employees.

Bold = indicators for the ideal type service provider.

public employment. Although piecemeal, these changes have transformed the originally highly coordinated and uniform employment regulation in the still-small German public sector into a patchwork of regulations generating differences not only between civil servants and public employees but also within these groups depending on state level and on the financial situation of regional states (see Chapter 5; Briken et al. 2014). Whereas in the period of the 'Golden Age', alignment of employment conditions and regulation between civil servants and public employees promoted an attenuation of status differences in the public sector, the more recent developments rather reinforce the traditional duality (Keller and Seifert 2014). It is noteworthy, though, that this flexibilization went hand in hand with an attenuation of inequality with respect to gender, age, and family status. Not least due to the EU Equal Treatment Directive, the traditional male bias of the German civil service has been weakened, although vertical and horizontal gender segregation remain high (Rubery 2013, pp. 69ff.). Along the same line, seniority-based pay and advancement and family bonuses, at least for public employees, have been abolished (Keller 2008).

In *France,* transformations of the highly centralized and uniform public employment system – with the civil servant status (*fonctionnaire*) covering more than 80 per cent of the public workforce – started even later. First attenuations of distinct civil servant features occurred from the 1980s onwards, when trade unions were allowed to negotiate pay and the right to strike was confirmed for the whole public workforce, without, however, offsetting the government's unilateral regulatory power. Over the course of performance and quality management measures from the 1990s onwards, only moderate PRP elements – for example, merit-based allowances and bonuses, granted on a group rather than on an individual basis – were introduced. The decentralization acts (Acte I, 1982; Acte II, 2003) shifted regulatory powers to subgovernmental levels in terms of size and flexibility of public employment. The extension of the functional profile on the local level had ambiguous effects. On one hand, an increase in the local government staff and in the personnel costs induced an increase in public spending and the size of the French public sector in general (Kuhlmann 2011, pp. 320ff.). On the other hand, the local authorities used their new pockets of flexibility on the level of HRM and employed in increasing numbers employees on a fixed-term contract base, so-called *non-titulaire.* In sum, the French public employment system changed only moderately, but a friction between the central and the local public employment system can be observed, with the latter clearly attenuating the distinct civil servant features more extensively (Kroos 2010). This may be partly due to the resistance and discretion of long-standing bureaucrats socialized within the elite state training system and interested in upholding central control and established employment conditions. The rising fiscal pressure to reduce public employment expenditure set a more dynamic change in motion with the 'one-for-two replacement' rule introduced in 2007, and restrictions for wage increases in place since 2011. Although the latter allows exemptions for the lowest grades of employees, who are also sheltered by a minimum wage regulation, the more recent downsizing, wage control measures, and expansion of fixed-term contracts affect most weak labour market groups. Among these are low-skilled workers, women, and new entrants, who in the past profited from employment chances in the large public sector and the privileged and uniform features of the *fonctionnaire* status in France (see Chapter 5; Gautié 2013). Although changes still seem incremental and long-term effects remain unclear, they indicate that the specificity and model role of public employment in France becomes attenuated.

Thus, in all three countries the distinctiveness of public employment regulation has lost ground and public employment features, though to different degrees, show alignment to rules and regulations governing employment in the private sector. Table 9.1 summarizes the main characteristics and changes in public employment regulation in the four countries and highlights the introduction of elements representing a shift from the ideal type civil servant to the ideal type service provider, such as the right to strike (France), PRP elements and promotion (all countries), or the attenuation of employment security (all countries).

Downsizing of the public workforce and/or re-regulation of public employment as common features in all three countries suggest that the *driving forces* for these changes might be similar to the reference case UK, and that they have affected the transformation of public employment irrespective of the different administrative traditions within the three civil law tradition countries under study. Indeed *cost pressure* and *NPM ideology* in all countries provided a material and ideological background for these transformations.

However, a closer look uncovers important differences between Germany, France, and Sweden, denoting variance within the group of countries assumed to follow a uniform Neo-Weberian reform path. As the OECD comparison in Chapter 4 has established, national systems of administration are characterized by different degrees of openness to adopting NPM tools, which in turn also affects the public employment system. Our findings indicate that within the group of civil law countries, Scandinavian countries stand out by combining high levels of government employment with high levels of effectiveness and frequent use of NPM tools such as PRP. Based on the country case studies, a closer look at the development of public employment regulation in *Sweden* shows that the devolution of the traditional civil servant status already started in the 1960s, long before the emergence of the NPM paradigm. Moreover, the introduction of collective bargaining and the right to strike, as well as subsequent labour law adjustments, were mainly motivated by the goal of establishing equal rights for all workers, whether public or private. Nevertheless, in the light of the Swedish welfare model, the respective transformation of public employment from early on has also been informed by the idea of making effective use of public means, attributing the same paradigmatic relevance to efficiency as to equality and solidarity (Kettunen 2006, pp. 59f.). Most likely this early and specific entrenchment of efficiency considerations in combination with the practice of a cooperative administration with flat hierarchies (Lehmbruch 1991, p. 144) later on allowed for a pronounced openness to the NPM paradigm and stimulated a specific adaption of NPM tools (Anxo 2013, p. 550). The early transformation of the Swedish public employment system thus seems to follow a distinct path, at first informed by the specific norms of the Swedish welfare model and administrative system and only later on drawing on the NPM paradigm; and even then, developments were not only driven by (comparatively low) pressure on public budgets, but also by a distinct service and citizen orientation.

In *Germany*, in contrast, fiscal pressure enlarged by the costs of German unification from the 1990s onwards, and aggravated by restricted public revenues due to tax reforms since the early 2000s, constituted a strong driver for downsizing public employment and the privatization of public infrastructure. Cost concerns from the 2000s onwards also motivated changes – though less advanced and delayed in comparison to Sweden and the UK – in the regulation of public employment, which evolved mainly on the regional state level as a consequence of the 2006 federal system reform. Since the majority of the public workforce is employed on the regional and local state levels, fiscal pressure has been especially high here. Both offsetting the uniform civil servant pay scheme between central state levels and regional states as well as the strong coupling of pay-setting for civil servants and public employees provided regional states as employers with more autonomy in pay-setting and personnel policies. The effects and dynamics of these changes for the near future should not be underestimated since cost containment efforts regarding public employment are likely to stay on the regional states' agendas. Thus, expenditure for civil servants' public pensions (and probably the share of public expenses in GDP) will rise in the near future due to demographic change, while at the same time the most recent financial reform – the so-called debt brake (*Schuldenbremse*), incorporated into the German Basic Law since 2009 – compels the federal government and the *Länder* to eliminate their structural deficits by 2016 and 2020, respectively (Bosch 2013, p. 240).

In *France*, too, fiscal pressure has been a main driver for the reforms of public employment and has geared these mainly towards cost reduction. Efforts to change public service wage policy in order to curb public spending date back to the early 1980s; however, the downsizing of the public workforce and more pronounced cost reduction measures came into effect only in 2007 with the 'one-for-two replacement' rule and restrictions on wage increases. Given the relatively large size of the public sector, with a public employment share of more than 20 per cent, and the rising political pressure on France to comply with the EU criteria for fiscal consolidation of national budgets, the need for cost containment or reduction of public employment expenditure is likely to continue in France as well (Gautié 2013, pp. 177ff.).

While the role of fiscal pressure in transforming public employment in Germany and France is quite obvious, explicit reference to the NPM paradigm seems to be less pronounced, and the adoption of NPM tools reflects the specificities of the state structures and the administrative systems. In the unitary and highly centralized French state structure, administrative reforms have focused on decentralization, whereas in federal Germany, administrative reforms – the so-called New Steering Model (*Neues Steuerungsmodell*) – started on the local level and were inspired by local government modernization in the Netherlands rather than Anglo-American NPM ideas. Moreover, openness to, and adoption of, efficiency-oriented HRM tools (such as PRP) in the German and French public employment regimes still seems low and, unlike Sweden, basic structures of the public employment system such as the civil servant status and the closed career system have remained unaltered so far.

Thus, although we can observe a uniform direction of change, drivers for administrative and public employment reforms in the three countries under study vary: fiscal pressure worked as a strong driver only in Germany and France, and rather than taking up the original Anglo-American NPM design, all three countries developed specific reform framings. The way, and extent to which, transformations of public employment are informed by NPM ideas varies considerably, and changes in employment regulation reflect country-specific state structures, legal systems, and administrative cultures, as well as political constellations. Based on our comparative case study design, two basic reform trajectories can be distinguished. On the one hand, specific welfare norms in Sweden adhering to equality and efficiency eased an early abolition of the privileged civil servant status, and a low legal entrenchment and formalization of the administration, rather than the NPM paradigm as such, already from the 1970s onwards allowed for substantial reforms. On the other hand in Germany and France, high entrenchment of the civil servant status in the state structure so far has hindered far-reaching reforms. Moreover, in these two countries, contrary to Sweden, fiscal pressure on the national and regional state level enhanced the still limited – but nevertheless substantial – changes in public employment, which resulted in higher segmentation of the public workforce and tend to question the role of the state as a model employer. Whether and how these national trends are reflected in sector-specific re-regulation of employment is addressed in the next section.

Changes by country and sector

As argued in Chapters 2 and 3, the unravelling of state functions during the last decades has generated variation across public sectors in the extent to which these are exposed to the market. This also affects the public employment regime, which might be placed under pressure through enhanced competition on the labour market or on the markets for goods and services. Since the three sectors under study represent different degrees of responsibility devolution and market exposure, we have been able to examine if the form and degree of re-regulation of employment varies by sector.

Privatization of public infrastructure represents the most far-reaching devolution of state responsibility, as the state transfers organizational and decision-making responsibilities to private actors and in turn restricts itself to fostering and controlling the newly created markets. *Energy regulatory agencies* are an example of this new market regulation function of the state and provide a rare occasion for governments and administrations to create employment conditions unhindered by existing administrative traditions and employment regulations, so that these might be specifically open to NPM ideas. At the same time, the specialized task of market control requires highly educated personnel and confronts the state as employer with competition on the labour market due to the traditional public sector wage penalty in the higher wage brackets. This speaks in favour of a high flexibilization of traditional civil servant features of employment.

In the case of *waste collection on the municipal level*, the state only devolves organizational responsibility but retains both the political and the decision-making power. Here, the delivery of the respective services becomes competitive, and the state as employer is confronted with private providers that can draw on more flexible employment contracts, which in turn might put pressure on the relatively advantageous public employment conditions, including a low-wage premium.

In contrast to these constellations, core state functions such as public safety represent a case where the state retains all three modes of responsibility. In the *police forces*, changes to the employment regime are thus assumed not to be triggered by environmental changes, such as the need for new administrative units or competitive pressure, but rather follow the pathway and logic of administrative reform. Radical changes, however, are less probable due to a homogeneous and well-organized workforce vested with the civil servant status, and the importance of this group as voters.

In the following, we will first contrast the specificities of the employment regimes in the nine cases (threes sectors in three countries) by addressing the scope of sector-specific change across countries. We then assess observed differences with reference to the degree of responsibility devolution and market exposure. Finally, we resume to what extent sector-specific change is consistent with the general country trend and discuss exceptions from country trends.

If we look at the *scope of sector-specific change across countries*, we see that public employment in two sectors – energy regulation in the UK, Sweden, and France; and waste collection in the UK, Sweden, and Germany – exhibit substantial alignment to private sector employment regulation. In contrast, employment regulation in the police still tends to conform to the traditional civil servant type of employment in all countries apart from Sweden (see Figure 9.2). However, sector-cum-country constellations vary, as does the relationship of sector- and country-specific change, calling for a closer look at sector-specific change across countries (see also Table 9.2).

The *energy regulatory agencies* included in this study bear the typical features of national regulatory agencies in the utility sector which are set up to create and maintain fair competition after privatization. They have their own powers and responsibilities under public law and are separated from ministries in organizational terms, although they might share responsibilities with other public authorities. While the respective agencies for gas and electricity founded in the UK in the mid-1980s and consolidated into one institution in 2000 (Ofgem) can be seen as forerunners, France (2000), Sweden (2005), and Germany (2005) followed later, not least responding to EU legislation passed from the mid-1990s onwards demanding market liberalization for the former state monopolies in energy provision. All three agencies in the Neo-Weberian states hold a high degree of autonomy in employment regulation and personnel policies as compared to the regulations and policies governing the country-specific administration. At the

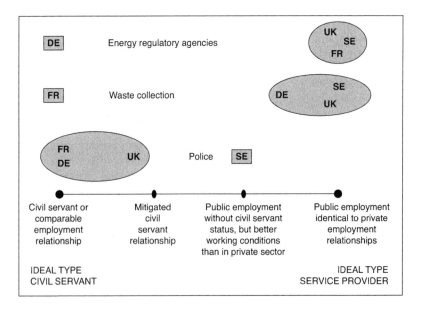

Figure 9.2   Varieties of public employment by sector, early 2010s

Note: DE: Germany; FR: France; SE: Sweden; UK: United Kingdom.

same time, they are characterized by specific features reflecting the national administrative culture.

As laid out in Chapter 6, we find strong indicators for flexible employment regulation, such as the use of open-ended contracts in the case of the Swedish *Energimarknadsinspektionen* (EI) (as opposed to tenured civil servant status as is the case in the German BNetzA) and fixed-term contracts in the French *Commission de Regulation de l'Energie* (CRE) for the majority of the employees. Even in the British Ofgem, where employment is formally accompanied by the civil servant status, a Civil Service Management Code (CSMC) introduced in 1996 allows for high autonomy of the HRM in recruitment, promotion, and even pay-setting (within a given pay and grading structure) of appropriate personnel. In all three cases, unilateral employment regulation characteristic of the traditional civil servant status is replaced by individual (and in the case of Sweden, also collective) bargaining. The highly qualified experts needed for the task of maintaining and controlling the energy markets are usually recruited from the external labour market, making internal training and recruitment a second-best choice. In France, the preferred recruitment of graduates from the *Grandes Écoles* provides for a specific elite recruitment and career track, but here – as well as in the case of Ofgem and EI – the skill profiles required are similar to those for private sector management, and expert positions and graduates of the *Grandes Écoles* are equally recruited by private employers. Finally, similar to the reference case Ofgem, pay and promotion in the Swedish and French agencies are performance-related and individually negotiated, although CRE in France also allows for reference to the wage index of the *'fonction publique'*. Systems of individual remuneration in the cases of Ofgem and EI reflect not only performance but also competitiveness with the private labour market as a way of retaining the highly skilled experts, whereas CRE, hampered in competitive pay due to budgetary constraints, tries to compensate by offering generous possibilities for further training. In contrast to this highly flexible agency employment, the German Federal Network Agency (*Bundesnetzagentur*) is still characterized by traditional forms of civil service employment and unilateral regulation. Performance orientation in personnel policies, in line with the general trend in the German civil service, is low. We will come back to this later.

Waste collection, being a long-standing municipal public infrastructure and a public sector granting employment security and a low-wage premium for a highly unionized workforce, has been subject to change in many European countries already from the 1980s onwards, amplified not least by EU liberalization policies. While political and decision-making responsibility rests with local public authorities, service provision has become competitive, either by direct competition through competitive bidding or virtual competition where public delivery is subject to benchmarking and cost comparisons. Consequently, the private share of service delivery has increased substantially in the cases under study, while at the same time the public workforce has declined. As detailed in Chapter 7, the remaining public services are confronted with high cost pressure, often negatively affecting wages as well as working conditions. Thus, employment in waste collection, not only in the UK but also in Germany and Sweden, shows high alignment to the private sector, whereas in France only minor changes can be observed.

In the UK, the waste collection sector is characterized by a frequent use of fixed-term employment and temporary agency work, and a lack of binding collective agreements, though coverage by collective bargaining is still relatively high. Additionally, protection of terms and conditions of employment for outsourced public services is weak. Alignment to private sector employment conditions is not least marked by the relevance of the Minimum Wage Act introduced in 1998, which limits downward trends in wage levels in both private and public service provision. In Germany, flexibilization of employment has mainly taken place in the area of packaging waste, triggered by a new regulation in 1991, which shifted responsibility for this service to the private market and introduced competitive bidding, thus reducing the public share to about 10 per cent. Since service contracts in this area are usually awarded for a limited time, employment too is highly flexibilized with a frequent use of fixed-term contracts and agency work, both in the public and the private sector. Employment and working conditions in household waste collection are generally more favourable because the public sector collective agreements are ensuring comparatively high employment security and pay. Nevertheless, employment regulation and working conditions in household waste collection have become more flexible and divergent as well, either by the abolition of seniority-related pay and tenure components for new entrants and the introduction of a new low-wage bracket, or by the dispensing of private law-based public companies in this area from compliance with public employment agreements. In Sweden, outsourcing of waste disposal is very common, enabled at the beginning of the 1990s by a law giving local councils autonomy in organizing service provision, staffing, and personnel policies. The private share in the sector amounted to 75 per cent in 2005, compared to roughly 50 per cent in the UK, Germany, and France. Differences in employment regulation and personnel policies between both sectors are not very pronounced since employment based on private law in both sectors is fully covered by collective agreements, setting relatively high standards for employment and working conditions. Regarding pay, general public sector frameworks on the national level define minimum standards and at the same time allow for high flexibility in wage settlements on the municipal level, including individual pay negotiation. As far as PRP components play a role, they are service- rather than efficiency-oriented. Thus, in contrast to the cost reduction notion in waste collection in the UK and Germany, flexibility in Sweden is rather employment-friendly and service-oriented.

Compared to energy regulation and waste disposal, employment regulation in *the police*, a core authoritative state function, has remained relatively stable. Only in Sweden, in line with the early and general abolishment of the civil servant status, was employment by contract introduced. Moreover, separate police pay regulations have been adapted to general public sector standards. In the UK, contractual employment of second-class police staff served to create some pockets of flexibility and reduction in personnel costs, while employment conditions of the majority of the police workforce did not change much. Similarly, in France and Germany, the civil servant status of police remained untouched. However, staff shortages and new forms of reporting and reviewing work performance have created an increased individual- and unit-related workload in all cases. At the same time, PRP components are of low importance and only the shift from seniority-based to performance-oriented criteria in career advancement indicates a sustainable attenuation of a core civil servant feature.

As these sector-specific results show, flexibilization of employment indeed varies primarily with the scope of responsibility devolution. Only where the state retains full responsibility for service provision, as is the case in the police as a core state function, have substantial features of traditional civil servant employment regulation been preserved. Devolution of organizational and/or decision-making responsibilities to private agents, however, creates *competition and exposes the state to labour or service market pressure*, thereby increasing the possibility of adaption of public employment regulation to market standards. This has been the case in newly set-up energy regulatory agencies, where the state surrenders both decision-making and organizational responsibilities to the private sector and, in three out of four cases under study, refrains from traditional civil servant features. Contrary to the general cost-cutting trend in public services, however, employment regulation and personnel policies are redesigned in this sector in order to cope with the traditional public sector high-wage disadvantage in hiring and retaining highly qualified experts who are needed for the task of fostering and controlling oligopolistic markets. Flexible contracts, PRP, and promotion rules, which are not (or only loosely) framed by the public sector wage scales and rigid career ladders, aim at competing with private employers for qualified experts. In waste collection, the devolution of organizational responsibility has generated competition between public and private providers of services and made labour costs a crucial factor in reframing public employment, traditionally characterized by a low-wage premium. As lean staffing, frequent use of fixed-term contracts, and low-wage brackets show, flexibilization in this sector is predominantly motivated by the aim of cost reduction.

However, coping with market pressures must not necessarily result in a far-reaching flexibilization of employment, as the two exceptions of the German *Bundesnetzagentur* (BNetzA) and the organization of waste collection in France

Table 9.2 Public employment regimes by sector – main characteristics

	Germany	France	Sweden	United Kingdom
Energy regulation	BNetzA	CRE	EI	Ofgem
Employment regulation	Civil servants (*Beamte*); lifetime employment	**Public employees; fixed-term contracts**	**Public employees; open-ended contracts**	**Public employees; open-ended contracts**
Personnel policies	Large internal labour market Fixed salary brackets	**Large external labour market (elite system) Flexible pay within budgetary constraints**	General labour market Individual performance-based components	General labour market **Individual performance-based components**
Waste collection				
Employment regulation	**Public employees; open-ended and fixed-term contracts, temporary agency work**	Civil servants; lifetime employment	**Public employees; open-ended contracts**	**Public employees; open-ended and fixed-term contracts, temporary agency work**
Personnel policies	**Dualization of employment security and pay levels**	High employment security; fixed salary brackets	Individual pay bargaining within fixed salary brackets	**Dualization of employment security and pay levels**
Police forces				
Employment regulation	Civil servants (*Beamte*); lifetime employment	Civil servants (*fonctionnaires*); lifetime employment **Increase in public employees; fixed-term contracts**	**Public employees; open-ended contracts, but very high job security**	Civil servants (*sworn officers*); open-ended contracts, but very high job security **Increase in public employees (civilians); open-ended contracts**
Personnel policies	Closed, internal labour market Fixed salary brackets	Closed, internal labour market Fixed salary brackets	**Extension to external labour market for specific tasks (high skilled)** Fixed salary brackets	**Large external labour market for public employees (civilians, high and low skilled)** Fixed salary brackets

Note: BNetzA: Bundesnetzagentur; CRE: Commission de régulation de l'énergie; EI: Energimarknadsinspektionen; Ofgem: Office of Gas and Electricity Markets; **Bold** = indicators for the ideal type service provider show. As we have seen earlier, in the case of the BNetzA, the civil servant status is maintained and, in contrast to the other cases under study, so far has not been subject to far-reaching change. The civil servant status implies lifetime employment, fixed pay schemes, and position-based advancement, characteristics which position BNetzA employment closer to the ideal type civil servant than the ideal type service provider. However, equally exposed to labour market competition for highly qualified experts, the agency has redesigned its recruitment and selection process in order to identify and hire applicants motivated to serve the public and interested in work-life balance rather than in high wages. Furthermore, an innovative HRM policy offers frequent changes of workplaces and tasks and a generous handling of flexible working time and part-time regulations. Finally, although bound to the civil servant career scheme, the large internal labour market of the BNetzA, which also hosts the regulatory authorities for telecommunication and the postal service, provides a broad range of career options and frequent chances of career advancement. Thus, within the framework of the legally defined civil servant status and fixed regulations for pay and promotion, personnel policies are nevertheless designed to create incentives for hiring and retaining a highly qualified workforce. This HRM strategy can be assessed as a functional equivalent for the employment flexibilization observed in the respective agencies in UK, Sweden, and France, which shows that the regulatory agencies face strong competition from the private sector for personnel in all four countries.

The exception observed in the French waste collection sector might rather represent a constellation where competition is less pronounced than in the other countries. Indeed, market pressure in waste collection in France so far seems to be limited, as the option to allow private firms to collect waste in the same places, as is the case in Paris, has not been taken up by many communities. This reluctance may be related to the fact that private providers are mainly seen as a backup, which helps to uphold a certain level of service provision in the case of (the more frequent) strikes on the side of public waste collection workers. Finally, the privatization option also indirectly serves to control wages and performance.

Thus, there are indeed sector-specific trends of change across countries, which can be explained by differences in the devolution of state responsibilities which typically take place on the sector level and do not cover all state activities. In order to assess the relevance of this trend for the unity of national public employment regimes and the state as employer, we have to examine *to what extent the observed sector-specific changes are consistent with the general country trends.*

As Figure 9.3 shows, we see a high consistency in the sector-specific move towards flexibilization with the general country trends in Sweden and the UK. In both countries, only employment in the police is still characterized by some features of the traditional status of civil servants, whereas

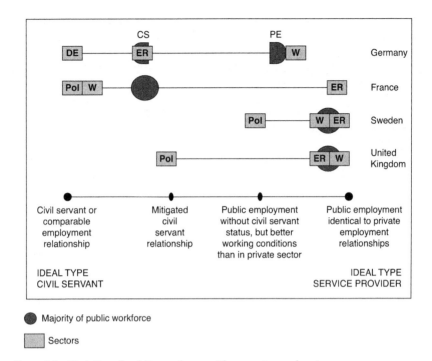

Figure 9.3   Varieties of public employment by country and sector

Note: CS: Civil servants (*Beamte*); PE: Public employees (*Tarifbeschäftigte*); Pol: Police; ER: Energy regulatory agencies; W: Waste collection.

employment in energy regulation agencies and waste collection is in line with the largely transformed country-specific public employment regime. France, too, exhibits a relatively high level of coherence, though at the other end of the spectrum with a public employment regime still maintaining core civil servant features. Here, employment conditions in the energy regulatory agency allowing for fixed-term employment, as well as for PRP, mark a stark contrast. This 'NPM-inspired island' becomes less puzzling when we take into account that the public sector in France is extended by a large share of state-owned enterprises (not only) in the energy market, whose management and higher positions serve as an attractive labour market for the highly qualified workforce of the energy regulatory agency. Rather than indicating a forerunner for the rest of the public sector, employment flexibilization in this sector seems to serve to retain a state elite workforce and allows for career trajectories typical for the graduates of the *Grandes Écoles* in the highly politicized French administration and economy. In Germany, the country trend is characterized by a duality of a more flexibilized employment regime for the public employees (*Tarifbeschäftigte*) and a relatively stable civil servant employment (*Beamte*). This duality is mirrored by the more flexible employment in waste collection and the more status-bound regulation in the other two sectors where the civil servant status still dominates.

Thus, sector-specific exceptions from country trends are most pronounced in France and can be traced back to a specific state-governed elite production and labour market rather than specificities of the sector or state responsibility devolution. The civil servant traits of police employment in the UK, in contrast, reflect that core state functions still restrict employment flexibilization, even in a country with a common law tradition and a strong NPM orientation of the public sector. This is not, or to a far lesser extent, the case in Sweden, where public employment has undergone the most profound change resulting from an early and consequent abolition of the civil servant status and civil servant privileges. In contrast to Germany, which is characterized by a reinforced dualistic public employment regime, public employment in Sweden is still comparatively homogeneous due to a pronounced policy of alignment of public and private sector employment.

To sum up, irrespective of commonalities in the direction of change characterized by a trend of alignment of public sector employment regulation towards the private sector, we can observe variance in the drivers of change, which cannot be reduced to cost pressure and NPM paradigm as common drivers. Moreover, we find high variance in the scope of public employment transformation within the group of countries assumed to follow a Neo-Weberian reform path, as well as variance of change by sector across countries. What follows from these findings for the assumptions regarding the convergence of public employment regimes, for factors accounting for the divergence of public employment regimes, and for the distinctiveness of public employment, will be addressed in the final chapter.

10
Conclusions and Outlook

Convergence of public employment regimes, or not?

According to most categorizations in macro-comparative political economy and public administration, the United Kingdom, France, Sweden, and Germany represent very different regimes. They all have established very specific variants of the *territorial state* securing the *rule of law*, upholding *democracy*, and *intervening in society and economy*, a country profile summarized with the acronym TRUDI (Leibfried and Zürn 2005). Sustaining these characteristics, the four countries realized high levels of wealth over the course of welfare state expansion after the Second World War, which was distributed among large segments of the population and generally offered agreeable living conditions to the vast majority of its citizens. The state provided many of the services supporting these conditions, and consequently, public employment grew into a major employment segment between the 1960s and the 1980s. However, due to the country-specific contexts in which these public employment regimes were embedded, they varied considerably across countries while exhibiting a substantial amount of homogeneity within countries. Our study has focused on one particular aspect of a more general transformation pattern of modern states, termed the 'unravelling of the state' (Leibfried et al. 2015), that is, developments in public employment regimes since the 1980s.

In their assessment of state transformation, Leibfried and Zürn (2005) suggest that this transformation is basically a shift in responsibility along two dimensions. On the territorial dimension, the nation-state loses sovereignty to both subnational and international levels of governance. On the organizational dimension, the state either transfers responsibility to private actors or expands its scope. These shifts in responsibility take different avenues in different policy areas, which results in an 'unravelling' of the homogeneous, almost monolithic appearance of the state prevailing during the 'Golden Age' of the welfare state. In this context, our research question has addressed the implications of changes in the way public (or 'normative') goods are provided for those individuals actually involved in providing the goods, that is, the public workforce.

We started our analysis from the observation that two major, and intertwined, driving forces have been challenging the established public sector employment regimes in advanced industrialized countries. The widening scope of state activity, along with the cost pressure inherent in services due to the lower potential of productivity growth in comparison to the industrial sector, progressively undermined the fundament of public finances. Partly in response to this challenge, monetarism and neo-liberalism replaced the Keynesian and welfarist consensus of the 'Golden Age' as the dominant ideology of state activity, first in the United Kingdom and the United States but soon spreading throughout the OECD world and beyond. New Public Management became the application of these ideas to the organization of public administration, aiming at its transformation into a service organization modelled upon the private sector. Given the similarity of problems facing governments and the identity of sources for ideas to confront these problems across the OECD world, the expectation of convergence is almost self-evident.

As discussed in Chapter 2, convergence can be studied at four different levels: discourse, decisions, operations, and results. Indeed, as amply documented in Chapters 5 to 8 and summarized in Chapter 9, all countries and all sectors studied have witnessed processes of convergence at the *discursive level*. Their public administrations have been subject to the same demands for cost reduction and efficiency gains, and the same cures have been proposed, including far-reaching changes in public employment regimes. Since the 1980s, no public administrative unit, no public agency, and no public enterprise had been shielded against scrutiny.

These examinations have not necessarily been consequential, however. At the *decisional level*, addressing actual changes in the legal foundation of public employment regimes, reforms since the 1980s have uniformly been motivated by cost reduction and efficiency gains. Nevertheless, the actual decisions have been heterogeneous and have increased variation in public employment regimes across countries and across sectors. Most notably, the United Kingdom and Sweden went much further in their alignment of public and private employment regimes than did France and Germany, as they downscaled or more or less dismissed the civil servant status, which originally was also a distinct element of their bureaucratic public administration. With respect to variation across sectors, trends are far less clear. In energy regulation, the scope ranges from an extension of the civil servant status to the newly established regulatory agency in Germany to fixed-term contracts in France, while Sweden and the United Kingdom offer open-ended contracts. In contrast, the employment regimes in the area of waste collection reflect competition in the service market. On the one hand, the United Kingdom, Sweden, and Germany have exposed their municipal waste collection systems to severe private competition. France, on the other hand, has established a dualist system in which private companies have only limited opportunities to compete against the public service providers which still employ civil servants. Finally, the police forces have experienced the least comprehensive challenges to their employment regime, although cost reduction, performance assessment, and efficiency evaluation of organizational units have become major issues on the reform agenda. Moreover, and perhaps more importantly, in some countries and sectors, new categories of public employees for administrative tasks have been introduced to various extents, thereby generating country-specific two-tier employment regimes. Thus, although the same issues have been raised across all countries and sectors analysed, and the same goals of reform have been articulated, the actions taken to attain these goals have not converged in any particular model of public employment regime.

At the *operational level* of actual practices, the heterogeneity of change dynamics is even larger. For example, the German energy regulation agency has been formally empowered to introduce performance-related pay schemes, but did not implement them in order not to distort an informal internal code of conduct. Employees in the French energy regulation agency, in contrast, cannot expect to obtain a permanent position, but may hope, with some reason, for a well-paid job in the mostly state-owned energy industry after their contract has expired. In general, the highly qualified employees are offered attractive working conditions. In different countries, agencies use different HRM practices to attract qualified personnel, ranging from competitive salaries to qualification opportunities to the status of a civil servant. In stark contrast to these conditions, competition from private service providers has challenged public waste collection systems. In general, we observe severe downward pressure on the quality of working conditions in the public sector, such as the introduction of new low-wage brackets in order to compete for tenders with the private sector or to prevent privatization, as is the case in Germany. Nevertheless, the relative shares of public and private providers and the employment conditions of those working for public providers vary considerably across countries. Turning to the police, although we observed rather few changes at the decisional level, this sector cannot be said to be an 'immovable object' (Pierson 1998) at the operational level. Given the exposure of this sector to the demands of efficiency gains, a variety of small adjustments below the level of regulatory change, but affecting the organization of work, have generated a substantial increase in diversity.

So, has there been convergence or not? One answer weighs down the heterogeneity of developments and emphasizes the general pattern of change: we observe strong pressures toward cost reduction and efficiency gains, and these pressures force all levels of public employment regulation to adjust in some way. According to this perspective, variation in detail actually only represents different starting points, different adjustment speeds, and different emphases, making all observed heterogeneity just variants of the same overarching theme. While this reading certainly captures an important dynamic, our analysis also suggests that this assessment alone falls short of providing an adequate understanding of the observed variation. Given the variety of transformations of the state, it also seems implausible that the framework conditions of reform are sufficiently similar in all policy areas to warrant the conclusion of a universal trend. From this perspective, local variation seems too large to accept the simple narrative of a universal trend. Despite the universal discourse of cost containment and efficiency gains promised by NPM, its impact on actual decisions has been limited, as discussed in Chapter 9, and operational changes have followed different, and in part contradictory trajectories that need a more fine-grained explanation.

Unravelling public services

In Chapter 2, we differentiated between moderating and mediating factors of change. With respect to the *moderating factors*, we discussed two sets of factors that are claimed in various research streams to impact on government activity and that are deemed responsible for variation in the way institutions are shaped and organized in different countries. One is the constitutional complexion of the state: constitutional rules generating and supporting veto players, such as federalism and consensual democracy, should restrain reform dynamics. The other factor is the administrative culture: in this regard, the resistance potential of administrators, the rule of law, and the lack of diversity of advice all militate against radical political reforms in general. We have argued that, if present, both factors should also be effective by moderating changes in public employment regimes.

Do these factors contribute to an explanation of the observed trajectories of public employment regimes? Disregarding detail, we have found a much more hesitant reform approach and severe resistance from stakeholders against the introduction of NPM in France and Germany than in the United Kingdom and Sweden. According to the reasoning offered in the previous paragraph, the unitary though decentralized political system in Sweden and the unitary and rather centralized system in the United Kingdom should be supportive of political change. Hence, these two countries are in line with expectations. However, using Mill's logic, we have to note that the similarities of the reform processes (or the lack thereof) in France, which has a unitary and centralized state structure, and in Germany, which is federalist and decentralized-coordinated, suggest that differences in the state structure cannot be regarded as sufficient conditions for explaining variation in transformations of public employment regimes. In regards to this factor, France is the puzzling case. Although the French Constitution yields much power to the central government, the government does not seem to engage in a proactive way in reform activities in the public employment regime.

In contrast to the state structure, the administrative culture draws the dividing line, which separates France and Germany from the United Kingdom and Sweden, much closer to the observed reform processes. The emphasis on the rule of law, the power of top-level administrators protected by the status of civil servant, and the rather closed system of political consultation, which characterize the public administration cultures of France and Germany, mitigate against reform activity in the public employment regime. This does not imply that the French and German public employment regimes are immovably locked into their specific paths. However, our analysis has shown that agents of reform needed to invest more 'energy' to pull the existing system into a different direction. Maintaining as much of the status quo as possible and making changes only at the margins after the pressure became too great were the two main pillars of defence.

The rough distinction between France and Germany on the one hand and the United Kingdom and Sweden on the other, however, should not induce us to underrate the differences between Sweden and the United Kingdom. Much to the contrary, although these two countries have moved far away from the traditional civil servant model of public employment, they have moved in rather different directions at different points in time. The early demise of the civil servant status in Sweden, effectuated during a hegemonic period of social democracy, resulted in a general upgrading of employee protection and worker rights and the alignment of private sector employment conditions to the high standard for public employees. In contrast, the British reforms were explicitly ideologically motivated and pushed through against fierce resistance from trade unions by the Conservative governments under Thatcher and Major. These reforms, inspired by the aims of reducing the role of the state in society as such, aligned public employment conditions to the much less employee-friendly ones prevalent in the private sector.

Turning to the *mediating factors* – that is, the implications of the extent of privatization of activities hitherto reserved for the state – we can distinguish three different configurations resulting from the type of responsibility that the public authorities have kept in hands. In Chapter 2, we argued that the new establishment of a regulatory agency allows a government to define the public employment regime according to its preferences. Indeed, as laid out in Chapter 6, employment conditions in the analysed regulatory agencies show substantial flexibility irrespective of the country-specific employment regimes. Although the privatization of energy provision as such is part of the state's response to cost pressures and neoliberal ideology, many of the actual departures in employment conditions from the civil service ideal type in these agencies may be better explained by competition with the private sector for qualified personnel instead of being viewed as a measure of NPM. We also expected that devolution of organizational responsibility, as in the case of municipal waste collection, which exposes public service provision itself to direct or indirect competition from private providers, pressured hitherto privileged public employment conditions. In line with this expectation, the results documented in Chapter 7 show that employment regulation in waste collection across countries has undergone quite substantial changes, which can generally be characterized by an alignment to the less favourable private sector employment conditions. Finally, preservation of the civil servant type of employment across countries in the police, where the state retains political, decision-making, and organizational responsibilities, laid out in Chapter 8, also speaks in favour of the importance of the proposed mediating factors for understanding variety in public employment regime change. However, as argued in the comparative assessment in Chapter 9, within these sector-specific trends we nevertheless find significant variation, which calls for even more fine-grained explanations. Regarding energy regulation, the extent to which the state as an employer has actually taken advantage of the potential for departure from the traditional civil service type of employment differs. The United Kingdom and Sweden have implemented a far-reaching alignment of the public employment regime with the private sector, thereby securing the attractiveness of public employment with respect to wages. Germany and France chose different paths following two contrasting logics. While the German agency set up a civil service regime in line with the tradition of sovereign state action, the French agency offered only fixed-term contracts to its externally recruited employees or relied on temporarily transferred civil servants from other government offices or agencies. The puzzling case in this context is Germany. The puzzle, however, can be solved by analysing the specific HRM strategies which allow for attracting and retaining the highly qualified workforce within the framework of the traditional civil service regime. In waste collection, commonalities in a flexibilized employment regime in the United Kingdom, Germany, and Sweden contrast with the preponderance of civil servant employment conditions in France, which are in line with the country's general resistance to change in overall public employment. Regarding the police, Sweden stands out as the only case where the civil servant status has been abolished, while all other countries, irrespective of the general country trend, uphold this status for this workforce. In the Swedish case, it seems to have been the upward adjustment of private sector employment conditions which facilitated the fundamental transformation of the public employment regime at an early stage.

Thus, variation in national public employment regimes can be traced back to both the moderating factors accounting for variation in the scope of change and the mediating factors responsible for internal differentiation of public employment regimes.

What are the implications of these processes for the hypothesis of an 'unravelling state' with respect to territorial and organizational change in TRUDI (Leibfried and Zürn 2005)? In their terms, we observe two 'macro trends', privatization and sub-nationalization, which affect the four countries and three sectors in different ways and to different degrees.

The impact of privatization on public employment regimes is observable at the most general level in the reversal of the relative position of the public and the private sector as a reference point of reform initiatives. The leading role of public employment conditions during the 'Golden Age' of the welfare state has been replaced by a hegemonic role of the private sector at the discursive level. At the decisional and the operational level, however, a variety of diverging practical solutions have been implemented. Typically, the employment regimes that evolved out of the process can be characterized as adjustments to the exigencies of both the sector-specific type of service provision and the sector-specific labour market conditions. Instead of resulting in an equally uniform new model, however, these adjustments took place within country-specific boundaries of change determined by the institutional conditions.

The impact of sub-nationalization on public employment regimes is particularly visible in a decentralization of employer tasks and a devolution of responsibility to regional or local levels of governance and to agencies in charge of specific state functions in all analysed countries. Gradually, the newly responsible agents of the employer role of the state developed their own solutions to the challenges which they faced, resulting in increasing divergence of employment conditions within hitherto uniform employment regimes, thus adding to territorial and functional diversity in public employment conditions.

Jointly, the two processes clearly point toward the existence of a process of 'unravelling' previously uniform public employment regimes, which undermines the notion of the state as employer in the singular. Depending on local, functional, and sectoral conditions, a multitude of sometimes small, sometimes large changes in the employment conditions of public employees have not only pulled real-world public employees away from the ideal type of the civil servant and pushed them towards the ideal type of the service provider, but have also increased the diversity of intermediate real types.

Reform paths and institutional change

In general, the results presented in this study are more in line with the divergence thesis than with the convergence thesis of public sector change. As argued in Chapter 2, however, there is a third intermediate position, suggesting that countries belonging to the same public employment regime might take similar steps towards reform. More specifically, our study has been informed by the distinction between an NPM reform path, prevalent in Anglo-American administrations, and a Neo-Weberian reform path, ascribed to Continental and Scandinavian administrations. In this juxtaposition, the latter is characterized by the attempt to protect the 'European Social Model' and the 'European administrative state' (Pollitt and Bouckaert 2011, p. 120) rather than to promote the withdrawal of the state in favour of private actors. Our country selection, including Germany, France, and Sweden as countries deemed to follow the NWS path and the United Kingdom as a reference case for the NPM reform path, allows us not only to contrast the two different reform paradigms but also to maximize variation within the Neo-Weberian countries as they represent different state structures, legal traditions, and administrative cultures.

As laid out in the summary comparison in Chapter 9, the latter group indeed shows a substantial variety in the scope of reform. Thus, Sweden and the United Kingdom, assumed to represent contrasting reform paradigms, show more similarity in the scope of reform than Sweden as compared to Germany and France. Public employment regulations in Sweden and the United Kingdom are characterized by a high alignment to employment in the private sector, as new forms of public management have been established in both countries. Distinct elements of the traditional civil service, such as lifelong tenure, were either abolished (Sweden) or restricted to a small workforce (United Kingdom), and seniority in pay and advancement was replaced by performance rules. Apart from this re-orientation in HRM, service orientation has also become a guiding principle of public administration in Sweden.

While this speaks in favour of placing Sweden on the NPM path, a substantial difference in the public sector reform trajectories between Sweden and the UK should be noted. In the United Kingdom, alignment of public employment to the private sector, in line with claiming a 'lean state', followed a 'low road' exposing the public workforce to the much less favourable working conditions of the private sector. In contrast, a general upgrading took place in Sweden, reinforcing rather than attenuating the role of the (welfare) state. Less favourable private sector working conditions were adjusted to the better standards in the public sector, and vice versa, as the relatively high wage levels and flexibility in wage regulation for the qualified public workforce show. Moreover, both countries differ not only in the public sector employment share and the quality of public employment but also with regard to the interpretation of service provision, which in Sweden is characterized by a citizen orientation rather than a consumer orientation. A strong focus on citizens' needs, as can be found in the Swedish police, the maintenance of decent working conditions, and an emphasis on the negotiation of reforms and employment regulation with strong unions, however, are more in line with the Neo-Weberian than the NPM reform path (Pollitt and Bouckaert 2011, pp. 118–19).

Thus, the Swedish reform trajectory takes on an intermediate position, exhibiting a 'high road' of NPM-inspired dismantling of traditional bureaucracy, while at the same time preserving favourable employment conditions in the public sector. This reform trajectory was not least facilitated by a low legal permeation of the administrative culture and an early and consensual emphasis on reconciling efficiency and solidarity by state activity. These features of public service provision are also guiding welfare reforms in the labour market in Scandinavian countries, which seek to combine flexibility and social security (Dingeldey 2009).

Germany and France, though sharing a civil law tradition with Sweden, in contrast, have undergone less far-reaching reform activities and have preserved favourable employment conditions in the public sector, thereby maintaining the traditional civil servant status for a core public workforce. In line with a highly legally permeated administrative culture, strong bureaucratic rules, and the presence of strong veto players, public sector reforms have rather unfolded through incremental changes. More specifically, institutional change in most instances has taken the form of layering, amending existing rules by new rules. In Germany, public sector transformation has been characterized by a lack of support for an early encompassing reform initiative in the 1970s and the absence of a general concept of 'modernization' of the public sector from 2000 onwards. While this reluctance to reform did not hinder the downsizing of the public workforce, it provided room for administrative reforms mainly on the local level with the so-called New Steering Model. Moreover, reforms of the civil service targeting pay regulations and working time were spurred rather indirectly by a structural reform of the federal system, devolving employer authority from the central state level to the *Länder* and generating a hitherto unknown differentiation in public sector pay and working time regulations for civil servants across the regional states, as well as a termination of coordination of pay raises between civil servants and public employees. In France, however, a top-down approach to administrative reform has been prevalent, although regional authorities also profited from decentralization of central state power. Apart from downsizing the public workforce by delayed and reduced replacement, re-regulation of public employment regulation so far has been limited. Only some seniority rules have been replaced by performance-related mechanisms, while the career-based system and prerogatives of the civil service remained untouched. However, in line with the layering pattern in administrative reforms of employment regulation in both countries, we observe personnel policies attempting to create pockets of flexibility without questioning the civil servant type of employment. While for a core workforce, irrespective of incremental adjustments in pay regulation and advancement, core elements of a distinct civil service are maintained, more far-reaching re-regulations – such as the introduction of a low-wage bracket in Germany for public employees, or fixed-term contracts for the group of *'non-titulaires'* in France – mainly affect new entrants or specific segments of the workforce, as has been shown in the sector case studies. These trends imply that, in Germany, the long-standing segmentation between civil servants and public employees becomes even more pronounced, as the latter group is more exposed to flexible employment conditions, and that in France, the originally inclusive public sector becomes dualized, as the *fonctionnaire* status no longer applies to the whole public workforce. Thus, incremental change nevertheless carries the potential of a more profound transformation of public employment regimes.

In light of these results, the assumption of not only contrasting NPM and Neo-Weberian reform paths but also of homogeneity within the group of Neo-Weberian States has to be refined. As the case of Sweden shows, we find the implementation of core NPM elements within an administrative culture which follows a civil law tradition. At the same time, public sector reforms and employment re-regulation in Sweden differ from Germany and France in scope and inclusiveness. Comparing administrative reform in Germany and France adds even more variety, as we can differentiate a more bottom-up reform trajectory in the former from a more top-down approach in the latter, both characterized by moderate attenuation of distinct public employment features which nevertheless generate substantial differentiation in public employment. Thus, irrespective of the scope and path of administrative reform, we can observe the unravelling of public employment regimes not only across countries but also within countries.

Public and private sector employment, or is there still a distinct public employment regime?

As argued in Chapter 2 and laid out in more detail in Chapter 4, change in public employment regimes has to be understood in a broader institutional context referring to the administrative regime and country-specific economic regulations. We not only discern distinct public employment regimes congruent with different politico-administrative regimes, but a cross-classification of the type of market economy and the type of public administration regime reveals even more 'structural fit' (Tepe et al. 2010). Thus, the distinctive nature of liberal market economies is fully congruent with the Anglo-American public administration regime based on common law and following the NPM reform path, whereas coordinated market economies can be observed in countries characterized by the administrative regimes based on a civil law tradition and deemed to follow a Neo-Weberian reform path. In the same vein, a cross-classification of administrative regimes and welfare regimes reveals an almost equally clear congruence of regime types (see Table 2.1 in Chapter 2 and Figure 4.2 in Chapter 4).

Although these observations leave the direction of influence open, we can assume that the institutional frameworks and regulation modes inherent to these constellations are rather stable and serve to channel changes in public employment regimes. Thus, the more general shift from the state as a model employer in the 'Golden Age' to the state as an employer seeking alignment of public employment conditions with the private sector should take on different forms, depending not only on the public employment regime but also on the respective private sector regime. Indeed, while we can observe a trend towards alignment of public and private sector employment conditions attenuating the distinctiveness of public employment in all countries, not only the extent but also the 'fabric' of this rapprochement varies. As discussed above, the 'low road' of adjusting public employment conditions to private sector conditions in the United Kingdom does not only imply the introduction of performance assessment and PRP. The United Kingdom reform trajectory is also characterized by a pronounced foundation in the liberal market economy, such as low employment security and restricted union power, which contrasts with the 'high road' in Sweden exhibiting more employee-friendly employment conditions and bilateral regulation involving strong unions, which are aspects distinctive for coordinated market economies. By the same token, adherence to the civil service type of employment and prerogatives of public employment in Germany and France might be seen as congruent with the coordinated market economy model. The dividing line with Sweden, the forerunner in public employment reform, in this case has to be drawn with respect to the administrative culture and the welfare regime.

At the same time, answers to the question of whether public employment is still distinctive must also take into account that private sector employment is not static, but rather has become more flexible and also more precarious during the last decades, especially in coordinated market economies and conservative welfare regimes. This tendency is revealed by high unemployment, increases in the share of low-wage work, and expansions of different types of non-standard work (Emmenegger et al. 2012). Thus, both in Germany and France, but also in the United Kingdom, employment in the public sector may still be perceived as providing better employment regulations and working conditions than comparable jobs in the private sector, although traditional privileges of the civil servant status such as tenure and seniority have become less pronounced. Indeed, the deregulation of labour markets in Germany, and to some extent also in France, has generated dualized employment. While this might indicate some alignment to liberal market economies, the more striking feature is that a core workforce tends to be shielded against downgrading of employment conditions both in the public and private sectors, while the costs of flexibilization of employment are borne by weaker labour market groups.

This trend also implies that, in all countries, the traditional role of the state as a 'good employer' providing favourable working conditions to the weaker labour market groups, and the model role with respect to the private sector, is fading. This may weaken the role of the democratic state with respect to equality and social integration and be more critical in countries with dualistic (Germany and France) and market-oriented (United Kingdom) labour market regimes than in countries such as Sweden with a more inclusive labour market (Gallie 2007).

Outlook

This study has attempted to capture the complexity and breadth of public sector reform trajectories and public employment change in Western countries using a multi-level approach. We not only addressed macro trends in size, costs, and reforms of public employment in OECD countries but also investigated more in-depth country- and sector-specific trends in selected Western European countries deemed to follow a Neo-Weberian reform path. Nevertheless, there are limits to this approach, and findings on the variety of change, too, suggest the need for further research.

As shown in the previous chapters, the sector comparison yielded interesting results about the impact of the extent of state responsibility devolution on the alignment of public sector employment to private sector conditions. This speaks in favour of a systematic sector-specific lens for public employment transformation. Since the sectors under study represent only part of the public service, investigations both within and across countries of other more important sectors (with regard to size), such as education or social services, might be fruitful.

Moreover, with the financial crisis and the aggravated budget crisis in many European countries, established forms of regulation of public employment are subject to new pressures. While some reactions to this pressure, such as further downsizing of the public workforce, wage freezes, and increase of fixed-term employment, are already visible, the more long-lasting impact remains to be seen. Indeed, resistance has grown to the dismantling of the public sector, which has been considered an 'essential element of the European Social Model' fostering economic growth and political stability (Vaughan-Whitehead 2013, p. 1). Unions and professional bodies representing the public workforce, as well as politicians and governments, protest against these developments, as shown by rising strike activities and the new tendency to re-municipalize public infrastructure (Wollmann and Marcou 2010; Hall 2012).

Finally, while focusing on the state as employer allows for the identification of re-regulation of public employment, this approach does not tell us how public employees themselves perceive administrative reforms entailing changes in work organization and emphasizing efficiency or citizens' or consumers' needs in public service provision. Since the state acts through its employees, and success in public sector reforms depends to a large extent on public employees' normative consent and active support in work practice, questions of public employees' motivation for, and perceptions of, public service provision and the changing role of the state as employer need further research (Gottschall et al. 2015).

The ongoing changes in public services also evoke basic tensions underlying public service provision in democratic states and market societies. Resources for public service provision are scarce and can only be increased with the support of the voters. At the same time, the potential for savings in public services is limited, as most of the public service provision relies heavily on human labour. Moreover, the quality of service and the quality of employment and service provision are highly entangled. Against this background, alignment of public employment to private sector employment might be limited and will remain a contested terrain.

Appendices

A.1 List of Statutory Regulations

European Union

Directive 2003/54/EC of the European Parliament and of the Council of 26 June 2003 concerning common rules for the internal market in electricity and repealing Directive 96/92/EC – Statements made with regard to decommissioning and waste management activities, Official Journal of the European Union, 15 July 2003, L 176, pp. 37–56

Directive 2003/55/EC of the European Parliament and of the Council of 26 June 2003 concerning common rules for the internal market in natural gas and repealing Directive 98/30/EC, Official Journal of the European Union, 15 July 2003, L 176, pp. 57–85

Germany

Allgemeines Eisenbahngesetz, AEG, 27. Dezember 1993, BGBl. I 1993: 2378, 2396; 1994: 2439

Arbeitnehmer-Entsendegesetz, AEntG, Gesetz über zwingende Arbeitsbedingungen für grenzüberschreitend entsandte und für regelmäßig im Inland beschäftigte Arbeitnehmer und Arbeitnehmerinnen, 20. April 2009, BGBl. I 2009: 799

Bayerisches Abfallwirtschaftsgesetz, BayAbfG, Gesetz zur Vermeidung, Verwertung und sonstigen Bewirtschaftung von Abfällen in Bayern, 9. August 1996, GVBl. 1996: 396

Beamtenrechtsrahmengesetz, BRRG, Rahmengesetz zur Vereinheitlichung des Beamtenrechts, 31. März 1999, BGBl. I 1999: 654

Beamtenstatusgesetz, BeamtStG, Gesetz zur Regelung des Statusrechts der Beamtinnen und Beamten in den Ländern, 17. Juni 2008, BGBl. I 2008: 1010

Berufskraftfahrer-Qualifikations-Gesetz, BKrFQG, Gesetz über die Grundqualifikation und Weiterbildung der Fahrer bestimmter Kraftfahrzeuge für den Güterkraft- oder Personenverkehr, 14. August 2006, BGBl. I 2006: 1958

Bundesbeamtengesetz, BBG, 5. Februar 2009, BGBl. I 2009: 160

Bundesbesoldungsgesetz, BBesG, 19. Juni 2009, BGBl. I 2009: 1434

Bundesdisziplinargesetz, BDG, 9. Juli 2001, BGBl. I 2001: 1510

Bundesgleichstellungsgesetz, BGleiG, Gesetz zur Durchsetzung der Gleichstellung von Frauen und Männern in der Bundesverwaltung und in den Gerichten des Bundes, 30. November 2001, BGBl. I 2001: 3234

Bundeslaufbahnverordnung, BLV, Verordnung über die Laufbahnen der Bundesbeamtinnen und Bundesbeamten, 12. Februar 2009, BGBl. 2009: 284

Bundesleistungsbesoldungsverordnung, BLBV, Verordnung des Bundes über leistungsbezogene Besoldungsinstrumente 23. Juli 2009, BGBl. I 2009: 2170

Bürgerliches Gesetzbuch, BGB, 2. Januar 2002, BGBl. I 2002: 42, 2909

Deutsche Gemeindeordnung, 20. Dezember 1945, RegBl. 1946: 5

Dienstrechtsneuordnungsgesetz, DNeuG, 5. Februar 2009, BGBl. I 2009: 160, 462

Energiewirtschaftsgesetz, EnWG, Gesetz über die Elektrizitäts- und Gasversorgung, 7. Juli 2005, BGBl. I 2005: 1970, berichtigt: 3621

Föderalismusreform, Gesetz zur Änderung des Grundgesetzes (Artikel 22, 23, 33, 52, 72, 73, 74, 74a, 75, 84, 85, 87c, 91a, 91b, 93, 98, 104a, 104b, 105, 107, 109, 125a, 125b, 125c, 143c), 2006, BGBl. I 2006: 2034

Gesetz zur Umsetzung europäischer Richtlinien zur Verwirklichung des Grundsatzes der Gleichbehandlung, EUGleichbUmsG, 14. August. 2006, BGBl. I 2006: 1897

Gleichstellungsdurchsetzungsgesetz, DGleiG, Gesetz zur Durchsetzung der Gleichstellung von Frauen und Männern, 30. November 2001, BGBl. I 2001: 3234

Grundgesetz, GG, Grundgesetz für die Bundesrepublik Deutschland, 23. Dezember 2014, BGBl. I 2014: 2438

Kreislaufwirtschaftsgesetz, KrWG, Gesetz zur Förderung der Kreislaufwirtschaft und Sicherung der umweltverträglichen Bewirtschaftung von Abfällen, 24. Februar 2012, BGBl. I 2012: 212

Preußisches Landrecht, Allgemeines Landrecht für die Preußischen Staaten, 1 Juni 1794

Reformgesetz, RefÖDG, Gesetz zur Reform des öffentlichen Dienstrechts, 24. Februar 1997, BGBl. I 1997: 322

Verpackungsverordnung, VerpackV, Verordnung über die Vermeidung und Verwertung von Verpackungsabfällen, 21. August 1998, BGBl. I 1998: 2379

Zweites Gesetz zur Vereinheitlichung und Neuregelung des Besoldungsrechts in Bund und Ländern, 2. BesVNG, 23. Mai 1975, BGBl. I 1975: 1173

France

Code du travail

Décret n° 45–2291 du 9 octobre 1945 portant règlement d'administration publique pour l'application de l'article 12 de l'ordonnance n° 45–2283 du 9 octobre 1945 relatif aux dispositions statutaires communes aux fonctionnaires appartenant aux corps et aux services auxquels destine l'école nationale d'administration

Décret n° 86–83 du 17 janvier 1986 relatif aux dispositions générales applicables aux agents contractuels de l'Etat pris pour l'application de l'article 7 de la loi n° 84–16 du 11 janvier 1984 portant dispositions statutaires relatives à la fonction publique de l'Etat

Décret n° 94–415 du 24 mai 1994 portant dispositions statutaires relatives aux personnels des administrations parisiennes

Décret no 94–732 du 24 août 1994 portant statut particulier du cadre d'emplois des agents de police municipale

Décret n° 2002–691 du 30 avril 2002 portant création du comité technique paritaire de la Commission de régulation de l'électricité

Décret n° 2008–1533 du 22 décembre 2008 relatif à la prime de fonctions et de résultats

Décret n° 2010–1402 du 12 novembre 2010 relatif à la situation de réorientation professionnelle des fonctionnaires de l'Etat

Décret n° 2010–761 du 7 juillet 2010 portant majoration de la rémunération des personnels civils et militaires de l'Etat, des personnels des collectivités territoriales et des établissements publics d'hospitalisation

Décret n° 2014–513 du 20 mai 2014 portant création d'un régime indemnitaire tenant compte des fonctions, des sujétions, de l'expertise et de l'engagement professionnel dans la fonction publique de l'Etat

Loi du 23 avril 1941 école national de police
Loi n° 46–2294 du 19 octobre 1946 relative au statut général des fonctionnaires
Loi n° 75–633 du 15 juillet 1975 relative à l'élimination des déchets et à la récupération des matériaux
Loi n° 82–213 du 2 mars 1982 relative aux droits et libertés des communes, des départements et des régions
Loi n° 83–8 du 7 janvier 1983 relative à la répartition de compétences entre les communes, les départements, les régions et l'Etat (loi Defferre)
Loi n° 83–634 du 13 juillet 1983 portant droits et obligations des fonctionnaires. Loi dite loi Le Pors
Loi n° 83–663 du 22 juillet 1983 complétant la loi n° 83–8 du 7 janvier 1983 relative à la répartition de compétences entre les communes, les départements, les régions et l'Etat (1)
Loi n° 84–16 du 11 janvier 1984 portant dispositions statutaires relatives à la fonction publique de l'Etat
Loi n° 84–53 du 26 janvier 1984 portant dispositions statutaires relatives à la fonction publique territoriale (1)
Loi n° 86–33 du 9 janvier 1986 portant dispositions statutaires relatives à la fonction publique hospitalière
Loi n° 95–73 du 21 janvier 1995 d'orientation et de programmation relative à la sécurité
Loi n° 97–940 du 16 octobre 1997 relative au développement d'activités pour l'emploi des jeunes (1)
Loi n° 2000–108 du 10 février 2000 relative à la modernisation et au développement du service public de l'électricité
Loi organique n° 2001–692 du 1 août 2001 relative aux lois de finances (LOLF)
Loi n° 2004–391 du 4 mai 2004 relative à la formation professionnelle tout au long de la vie et au dialogue social
Loi n° 2009–972 du 3 août 2009 relative à la mobilité et aux parcours professionnels dans la fonction publique
Loi n° 2011–267 du 14 mars 2011 d'orientation et de programmation pour la performance de la sécurité intérieure (1)
Loi n° 2012–347 du 12 mars 2012 relative à l'accès à l'emploi titulaire et à l'amélioration des conditions d'emploi des agents contractuels dans la fonction publique, à la lutte contre les discriminations et portant diverses dispositions relatives à la fonction publique
Loi organique n° 2014–125 du 14 février 2014 interdisant le cumul de fonctions exécutives locales avec le mandat de député ou de sénateur
Loi n° 2014–126 du 14 février 2014 interdisant le cumul de fonctions exécutives locales avec le mandat de représentant au Parlement européen

Sweden

Avfallsförordning (2001:1063)
Avfallsförordning (2011:927)
Förordning (2007:1118) med instruktion för Energimarknadsinspektionen
Kommunallag (1977:179)
Lag (1974:12) om anställningsskydd
Lag (1974:358) om facklig förtroendemans ställning på arbetsplatsen
Lag (1976:580) om medbestämmande i arbetslivet

Lag (1976:600) om offentlig anställning
Lag (1982:80) om anställningsskydd
Lag (1994:260) om offentlig anställning
Regeringens proposition 1977/78:34 om ändring i lagen (1976:600) om offentlig anställning
Regeringens proposition 1984/85:219 om den statliga personalpolitiken
Regeringsform, Kungörelse (1974:152) om beslutad ny regeringsform

United Kingdom

Civil Service Management Code
Civil Service Recruitment Principles
Civil Service Reward Principles
Code of Practice on Workforce Measures in Local Authority Service Contracts
Competition Act 1998 (1998 Chapter 41)
Electricity Act 1989 (1989 Chapter 29)
Employment Act 1980 (1980 Chapter 42)
Employment Act 1982 (1982 Chapter 46)
Employment Act 1988 (1988 Chapter 19)
Employment Act 1990 (1990 Chapter 38)
Employment Relations Act 2004 (2004 Chapter 24)
Employment Rights Act 1996 (1996 Chapter 18)
Energy Act 2004 (2004 Chapter 20)
Energy Act 2008 (2008 Chapter 32)
Energy Act 2010 (2010 Chapter 27)
Energy Act 2011 (2011 Chapter 16)
Energy Act 2013 (2013 Chapter 32)
Enterprise Act 2002 (2002 Chapter 40)
Environmental Protection Act 1990 (1990 Chapter 43)
Equality Act 2010 (2010 Chapter 15)
Gas Act 1986 (1986 Chapter 44)
Local Government Act 1988 (1988 Chapter 9)
Local Government Finance Act 1982 (1982 Chapter 32)
Metropolitan Police Act 1829 (1829 Chapter 44)
Municipal Corporations Act 1835 (5 & 6 Wm. IV, c.76)
National Minimum Wage Act 1998 (1998 Chapter 39)
Police Act 1964 (1964 Chapter 48)
Police Act 1996 (1996 Chapter 16)
Police Reform Act 2002 (2002 Chapter 30)
Race relations Act 1976 (1976 Chapter 74)
Sex Discrimination Act 1975 (1975 Chapter 65)
Trade Union Act 1984 (1984 Chapter 49)
Trade Union and Labour Relations (Consolidation) Act 1992 (1992: Chapter 52)
Trade Union Reform and Employment Rights Act 1993 (1993 Chapter 19)
Transfer of Undertakings (Protection of Employment) Regulations 1981 (1981 No. 1794)
Utilities Act 2000 (2000 Chapter 27)

A.2   Overview Expert Interviews (see Chapters 6, 7, and 8)

Sector	Country	n	Position	Place	Year
Energy	UK	1	HRM executive	London	2010
(n = 4)	DE	1	HRM executive	Bonn	2010
	FR	1	HRM executive	Paris	2010
	SE	1	HRM executive	Eskilstuna	2010
Waste	DE	8	HRM executives (4)	Five large cities	2010
(n=14)			Union representatives (4)	across Germany	
	FR	3	HRM executives	Three large cities across France	2010
	SE	3	HRM executives	Three large cities across Sweden	2010
Police	DE	11	HRM executives (5)	Five cities in	2009
(n=22)			Union representatives (3)	three different	and
			Equal opportunity officers (3)	*Länder*	2010
	FR	6	HRM executives (3)	Three cities in	2010
			Union representatives (3)	urban and rural areas	
	SE	5	HRM executives (3)	One large city	2009
			Union representatives (2)		

A.3   Cross-Country and Time-Series Data: Measurement Issues (see Chapter 4)

Measuring public employment in a comparative perspective is made extremely difficult by various methodological issues since comparative statistical sources tend to employ very different measurement concepts, and data are aggregated on different state levels (central, federal, local) or simply cover rather short periods of time (see, for example, Vaughan-Whitehead 2013 for country studies). In order to explore the dynamics between processes of downsizing and growing government employees' compensation expenditure, however, it is essential to use coherent data for both the cross-sectional and the time-series dimensions. Besides early attempts of collecting cross-national public employment figures by Rose et al. (1985), Cusack (1998) provides a full annual dataset on public employment in 21 OECD nations from 1960 to 1995. Drawing on OECD National Income Accounts (NIA), Cusack measured public employment as overall public sector employment. Unfortunately, due to methodological problems, the OECD discontinued reporting public employment in NIA after the mid-1990s. As this dataset is, in our view, still the most comprehensive attempt to provide comparative public employment data across OECD nations, we use it as a reference point for our own attempt to collect more current data on public administration employment.

Among international statistical sources, the World Bank, ILO, and the OECD provide comparative public employment data. The World Bank's (1999) 'Cross-

National Data on Government Employment & Wages' covers a range of 209 countries but contains no information on several core OECD countries. As it presents averaged employment data for two periods – 1990 to 1995 and 1996 to 2000 – the strength of the World Bank's (1999) dataset clearly lies in cross-sectional analyses. The ILO (2008) database on 'Public Sector Employment' offers cross-sectional time-series data for the majority of OECD countries. This dataset, however, is based on non-comparable measurement concepts across countries, which makes it virtually impossible to interpret cross-national variation in public employment. The OECD's (2002) 'Public Sector Pay and Employment Database' provides a public employment panel dataset covering 20 OECD nations between 1985 and 2000, which unfortunately is strongly unbalanced.

Due to its measurement inconsistencies, the OECD decided not to update this database any longer and is instead currently developing a new dataset, entitled 'Comparison of Employment in the Public Domain' (OECD 2007), which is consistent with the United Nation's System of National Accounts (SNA). In 2009 and 2011, the OECD published comprehensive reports on the state of the public sector in its member countries. These reports, entitled 'Government at a Glance', come with a complete list of indicators aiming to measure various aspects of state activity.

For the purpose of this chapter, we rely on the general government employment figures presented in these 'Government at a Glance' reports (OECD 2009, 2011). This measure of employment in general government covers employment at central and sub-central levels of government. The sub-central levels of government are comprised of state and local government, including regions, provinces, and municipalities (OECD 2011, p. 104).

The second measure, the costs of government employment, is taken from Table IV of the OECD's (2009) 'Classification of the Functions of Government' (COFOG). The COFOG provides information on government expenditure on government employees' compensation.

One should note that the expenditure measure and the measure of the size of general government employment do not need to fit perfectly. The two data sources – 'Government at a Glance' and COFOG – have not yet been harmonized by the OECD. Whereas in the 'Government at a Glance' approach, general government employees were counted and then allocated to different levels of government (local, regional, state), the COFOG approach begins with a measurement of overall government expenditure, which is then allocated to different functional categories of state activity, one of which is 'compensation of employees' (see also Parry 2007). Nevertheless, since we are not aware of any more precise cross-national measures, the indicators obtained from these two data sources provide the most consistent cross-sectional data in 19 OECD countries on government employees' compensation expenditure and the size of general government employment for two points in time (1995 and 2008). According to the OECD (2011, p. 104), there are a few cases in which employment in social security funds was not included under general government employment. Social security, however, 'represents a small number of employees' and is therefore of 'minor importance as a percentage of the total workforce' (OECD 2011, p. 104).

A.4 'Milestone' Events in the Introduction of Performance-Related Pay (see Chapter 4)

Country	Reform year	Type of reform	Source
Australia	1997	Performance-related pay	OECD (2005, p. 30) OECD Country Note Australia (2009, p. 2)
Austria		No performance-related pay	Lonti/Woods (2008, p. 96) OECD Country Note Austria (2009, p. 2)
Belgium		No performance-related pay	Lonti/Woods (2008, p. 96) OECD Country Note Belgium (2009, p. 2)
Canada	1964	Performance-related pay: Formal appraisals of performance and competence ('Senior Officers Pay Regulations', today 'Management Category Salary Administration Plan')	OECD (2005, p. 30, p. 94) OECD Country Note Canada (2009, p. 2)
Denmark	1987, 1997, 2002	Performance-related pay: Scheme for civil servants and for senior managers (1987), framework agreement concerning experiments with a new pay system (1997), collective agreement (2002)	OECD (2005, p. 30, pp. 98–104, p. 210) OECD Country Note Denmark (2009, p. 2)
Finland	1992	Performance-related pay ('State Employer's Salary and Wage Policy Programme')	OECD (2005, p.30, pp. 105–13, p. 211)
France	2004	Performance-related pay: Initially at director's level in six pilot ministries	OECD Country Note Finland (2009, p. 2) OECD (2005, p. 30, pp. 114–19, p. 212)
Germany	1997	Performance-related pay: Performance allowances and bonuses for outstanding special services, performance steps in the basic salary (*Reformgesetz*)	OECD Country Note France (2009, p. 2) OECD (2005, p. 30, pp. 120–5, p. 213) OECD Country Note Germany (2009, p. 2)
Ireland	1995, 2002	Performance-related pay	OECD (2005, p. 30) OECD Country Note Ireland (2009, p. 2)
Italy	1993	Performance-related pay: Law No. 29/1993	OECD (2005, p. 30, pp. 130–6, p. 215) OECD Country Note Italy (2009, p. 2)
Japan	1950	Performance-related pay: Diligence allowances	OECD (2005, p. 27) Lonti/Woods (2008, p. 96) OECD Country Note Japan (2009, p. 2)

Continued

Country	Reform year	Type of reform	Source
Netherlands	1989	Performance-related pay	OECD (2005, p. 30) OECD Country Note Netherlands (2009, p. 2)
Norway	1996	Performance-related pay	Public Management Department, Statskonsult, Norway (1999, p. 3) OECD Country Note Norway (2009, p. 2) Lonti and Woods (2008, p. 96)
Portugal		No performance-related pay	OECD Country Note Portugal (2009, p. 2)
Spain	1984	Performance-related pay: General position allowances, specific position allowances, productivity bonuses	OECD (2005, p. 30, p. 150, p. 218) OECD Country Note Spain (2009, p. 2)
Sweden	1989, 1994	Performance-related pay: System for individually differentiated pay at agency level (1989), full autonomy in employer policy matters to heads of agencies (1994)	OECD (2005, p. 30, pp. 153–8, p. 219) OECD Country Note Sweden (2009, p. 2)
Switzerland	2000	Performance-related pay: 'Law relating to Confederation staff'	OECD (2005, p. 30, pp. 159–64, p. 220)
United Kingdom	1985, 1996	Performance-related pay: Three-year experimental performance bonus scheme (1985), departments receive full delegation to develop terms and conditions for their staff (1996)	OECD Country Note Switzerland (2009, p. 2) OECD (2005, p. 30, pp. 165–73, p.221) OECD Country Note United Kingdom (2009, p. 2)
United States	1978, 1984, 1994, 2004	Performance-related pay: Merit pay system (for managers) ('Civil Service Reform Act') (1978), Performance management and recognition system (1984–1993), use of the guidelines of the Office of Personnel Management (1994), Departments of Homeland Security and Defense can develop their own pay systems, plans to shift to salary systems based on pay-for-performance (2004)	OECD (2005, pp. 28–30) OECD Country Note United States (2009, p. 2) Perry et al. (2009, p. 40)

Notes

1 Introduction

1. Normative goods are a specific subclass of public goods offered by Western nation-states characterized by the notion of TRUDI: peace and physical security, liberty and legal certainty, democratic self-determination, and economic growth and social welfare (Hurrelmann et al. 2007, p. 3).
2. Public employment comprises between 8 and 30 per cent of the national labour force (Oxley and Martin 1991, p. 168; OECD 2008; Derlien and Peters 2008, p. 7).

2 The Analytical Problem

1. See furthermore, most notably, Arts and Gelissen (2002), Bonoli (1997, 2003), Castles and Mitchell (1993), Castles and Obinger (2008), Esping-Andersen (1999), Gough (2001), Obinger and Wagschal (2001).
2. We do not elaborate on a further conception, New Public Governance, which currently seems to be more of a vision than an empirically saturated descriptive concept (Pollitt and Bouckaert 2011, p. 124). One of its most fervent proponents claims that New Public Governance is a new archetype of governance after New Public Management has ended the traditional bureaucratic public administration type, but is doomed to failure itself because of its unresponsive and undemocratic nature (Osborne 2006, p. 380). However, in the wider literature, the concept has not gained prominence.
3. Streeck and Thelen (2005b) identify a fifth mode, exhaustion, which is not a mode of change but of institutional death.

3 Research Design and Methods

1. German *Länder* are intermediate semi-sovereign state entities with broad autonomous competencies employing the majority of the public workforce.
2. More specific information on sampling and sector-specific sources of information are given in the respective chapters. In general, interviews with HR managers across all sectors served to identify how changes in employment regulation are reflected in HR strategies. Additionally, selective interviewing of union representatives and Equal Opportunity officers in some sectors and countries, who were involved in restructuring, helped to explore to what extend regulation of employment has been implemented. Citations from the interviews are anonymized and coded by sector: E for energy regulatory agencies, W for waste collection, P for police; by country: UK for United Kingdom/England and Wales, DE for Germany, FR for France, and SE for Sweden; and by number of expert interview. The interviews in the UK and Sweden were conducted in English, in France in French, and in Germany in German. Translations of quotations in Chapters 6, 7, and 8 have been made by the authors.

4   Public Employment Regimes in OECD Countries

1. Pollitt and Bouckaert (2011, p. 63) take a very different approach for measuring administrative traditions. They point out that the traditional classification of countries as having either a *Rechtsstaat* or a *public interest* tradition is becoming more and more outdated since many civil service systems contain elements of both traditions. Pollitt and Bouckaert (2011, p. 65) depart from this dichotomy by taking into account cultural differences between countries (Hofstede 2001). This data on cultural aspects, however, has been collected in private sector organizations, which limits the validity of these indicators in the context of public sector employment. Nevertheless, given that this data has not been collected for the public sector yet, and assuming that any actual bias will be in the same direction, it can be treated as a useful approximation for the purpose of a comparative analysis.

2. Before entering the MCA, all metric variables have been transformed into terciles.

3. The third dimension adds 10.77 per cent of total variance and the fourth dimension only 1.42 per cent of total variance. According to this pattern, the positioning on the first dimension is central for our interpretation, while the third and fourth dimensions are disregarded for the substantive interpretation (Clausen 1998, p. 24).

4. The term 'mixed' is used as an operational definition of the middle tercile of Lijphart's index measuring the state structure (federal/unitary dimension).

5. Identifying three distinct politico-administrative regimes, Tepe et al. (2010) find a high degree of institutional coherence between the coordination rules applying to the market economy model and those applying to the coordination of public employment, indicating the congruence of regulation in the public and private spheres of the political economy.

6. This conceptualization of the term 'regimes' implies that the institutional configuration distinguishing one regime from another is considered to be the result of long and cumulative historical processes.

7. The LIS data for the United Kingdom are incomplete in regards to core variables for this specific analysis.

8. The analysis is restricted to the period 2000–08 because of missing values.

9. This conclusion is certainly restricted empirically by the observation period at hand, since the UK, for example, experienced substantive reductions in public employment in the early 1980s.

10. Note that the analysis does not account for differences in the number of tasks that are allocated to the public sector.

11. In order to calculate changes in predicted probabilities, we employ the *prchange* command from the SPOST package by Long and Freese (2006).

5   A Comparison of Public Employment Regimes in Germany, France, Sweden, and the United Kingdom

1. With the devolution of Scotland, Wales, and Northern Ireland, the developments in these jurisdictions deviate from the those in England; most developments outlined here apply to England, Wales, and Scotland, whereas Northern Ireland has its own Civil Service (dating from 1921) and is not included here.

2. This far-reaching change is surprising for three reasons. First, as shown in the historical outline, the British Civil Service and administrative culture lacked any specifically 'managerialist' tradition (Wegrich 2009, p. 139). Second, while the UK has recently come to be seen as the prime example of radical public sector reforms, in the period before the 1980s it was considered to be 'amongst the most stable and least innovative [states] in the advanced industrial world' (Moran 2006, p. 31). Third, until the 1980s, the administrative and political culture and decision-making style in the UK was characterized as an informal, closed, and consensus-seeking 'club government', whereas in the last decades a governing style of low consensus and top-down implementation of public sector reforms has been created (Wegrich 2009, p. 146). In that sense, the Thatcherite reforms constituted a veritable breach with longstanding traditions.

3. However, the decline in public sector employment is slightly exaggerated due to reclassifications in the UK national accounts (especially regarding tertiary education).

4. Based on the catholic doctrine, this principle stipulates that the state should only be active where no other institution provides for specific tasks (von Bandemer and Hilbert 2005, p. 29).

5. For a detailed exposition of the structure of German public employment, see Derlien (2005, p. 15).

6. For salaried employees, the respective collective agreements were the *Bundes-Angestelltentarifvertrag*, BAT, and for workers, the *Manteltarifvertrag für Arbeiterinnen und Arbeiter des Bundes und der Länder* MTArb and *Bundesmanteltarif(vertrag) für Gemeinden*, BMT-G.

7. The aim of the law is to guarantee basic uniformity of the civil service and to ensure the mobility of civil servants (based on GG Art. 72). It entails rights and obligations in terms of GG Art. 74 Para. 1, and defines the nature, circumstances, legal form of reasoning, types, duration, and revocation of employment and dismissals, secondments, and transfers of civil servants. Moreover, it contains regulations concerning responsibilities and the consequences of noncompliance.

8. The regular weekly working time is: 40 hours in Bavaria, Berlin, Brandenburg, Bremen, Hamburg, Lower Saxony, Mecklenburg-Western Pomerania, Rhineland-Palatinate, Saarland, Saxony, Saxony-Anhalt; 41 hours for civil servants of the federal government, Baden-Württemberg, North Rhine-Westphalia, Schleswig-Holstein; and 42 hours in Hesse and Thuringia (DBB 2014).

9. The agreement applies to all federal states except the state of Hesse, which left TdL in 2004. Furthermore, Berlin was excluded from the employers association TdL in 1994 after it extended the privileged collective agreement for West Germany to East Berlin; Berlin was reintegrated into the TdL in 2013.

10. Indeed, the distinction between salaried employees and workers, established with the introduction of the Bismarckian social insurance system at the end of the 19th century, had imprinted strongly on social structure and class in pre-war German and post-war West German society (Kadritzke 1982).

11. Added to this, there are two other groups making up the sum of the public *sector*: (1) employees under specific labour law regulation working in the state-owned companies, and (2) the public administrations with employees under private labour law, like Social Security Funds. As we focus on changes in the public *service*, these groups are not considered in the following sections.

12. This system combines three elements: the president of the republic is elected by universal suffrage; he or she possesses substantial power; and a prime minister and ministers, legitimated by parliament and the people, who possess executive and governmental power, opposite to the president (Duverger 1980, p. 166). Even though the constitution did not give the president important *new* executive powers compared to the Fourth Republic, 'it did afford him an important new *power*' (Wright 1989, p.13, as cited in Elgie and Griggs 2000, p. 29), namely popular legitimacy.

13. An example is the emergence of statistics as a means of public policy guidance and implementation (Deroisières 2000; Ewald et al. 2009).

14. As Alexis de Tocqueville (1993/1866) had pointed out, this formal hierarchical structure (the intendant, the sub-delegate) was already known in the old regime, and was thus a pointer to an existing centralized system.

15. Crozier and Thoenig describe this complex entity as 'cross-regulation' (Crozier and Thoenig 1975, p. 11).

16. *Loi organique n° 2014–125 du 14 février 2014 interdisant le cumul de fonctions exécutives locales avec le mandat de député ou de sénateur* (Law to Prohibit the Concurrent Holding of Local Executive Offices and the Office of Member of Parliament); *Loi n° 2014–126 du 14 février 2014 interdisant le cumul de fonctions exécutives locales avec le mandat de représentant au Parlement européen* (Law to Prohibit the Concurrent Holding of Local Executive Offices and the Office of Member of the European Parliament).

17. The first was the *École de ponts et chausses* in 1747, followed by the *École du genie* in 1748, the *École d'Artillerie* in 1756, and the *École des mines* in 1783 (Rosanvallon 1990, p. 91).

18. However, as research shows, the republican idea of meritocracy, trying to ensure this through competitive exams, proved to be a social myth more than a reality (Bodiguel 1978; Bourdieu 1989).

19. *Décret n° 45–2291 du 9 octobre 1945*

20. A *corps* is defined as all civil servants subject to the same special status and having the same grades (*Loi n° 83–634 du 13 juillet 1983* Art. 13). For each *corps* exists a *statut particulier* that determines the modes of recruitment, career paths, and classifications within the *corps*. Furthermore, the *corps* is seen as the base for a specific public service identity (Siciliani 2008, p. 94).

21. In sum, four laws set up the rules and regulations for the public service. With the *loi n° 83–634 du 13 juillet 1983*, the rights and duties for all civil servants were defined; the *loi n° 84–16 du 11 janvier 1984* specified this for the FPE; the *loi n° 84–53 du 26 janvier 1984* for the FPT; and last not least, the *loi n° 86–33 du 9 janvier 1986* for the FPH.

22. *Loi n° 83–634 du 13 juillet 1983* Art 20ff.

23. *Acte I 1982–83s* abolished supervision by prefects and devolved executive powers from the prefect to the elected leaders of municipal, departmental, and regional councils.

24. *Loi organique n° 2001–692 du 1 août 2001 relative aux lois de finances*

25. *Décret n° 2008–1533 du 22 décembre 2008 relatif à la prime de fonctions et de résultats*

26. *Loi n° 2012–347 du 12 mars 2012 relative à l'accès à l'emploi titulaire et à l'amélioration des conditions d'emploi des agents contractuels dans la fonction publique, à la lutte contre les discriminations et portant diverses dispositions relatives à la fonction publique*

27. *Loi n° 2009–972 du 3 août 2009 relative à la mobilité et aux parcours professionnels dans la fonction publique*
28. The freeze has been reaffirmed by the Socialist President Francois Hollande. One hundred index points equal an annual pay of EUR 5556.35 (*Décret n° 2010–761 du 7 juillet 2010*). The minimum wage is equivalent to 280 index points.
29. *Décret n° 2014–513 du 20 mai 2014 portant création d'un régime indemnitaire tenant compte des fonctions, des sujétions, de l'expertise et de l'engagement professionnel dans la fonction publique de l'Etat*
30. The term 'Swedish Model' refers to a distinct welfare regime that grants encompassing social rights based on citizenship (Esping-Andersen 1990), embraces the idea of parity between capital and labour, and is based on the paradigm of a virtuous circle between 'efficiency, solidarity and equality' (Kettunen 2006, pp. 59–60).
31. We do not report these statistics in table form because of the lack of a formal differentiation between different types of employment or different categories of employees in the current Swedish public service.
32. The Swedish Police Service is made up of the National Police Board (*Rikspolisstyrelsen*, 2300 employees), the National Laboratory of Forensic Science (*Statens kriminaltekniska laboratorium*, 270 employees), and 20 separate geographical authorities (one for each county, jointly 25,200 employees) (Statistiska centralbyrån 2011, p. 24). About 20,000 of those employed by the counties are police officers.
33. Among the largest single agencies are: the Swedish Social Insurance Agency (*Försäkringskassan*, 12,100 employees), the Swedish Public Employment Service (*Arbetsförmedlingen*, 11,300 employees), the Swedish Tax Agency (*Skatteverket*, 9,900 employees), and the Swedish Transport Administration (*Trafikverket*, 6,000 employees) (Statistiska centralbyrån 2011, pp. 24ff.).
34. The full list of competencies includes health, regional development strategy (including tourism), transport (planning of regional public transport), regional economic support, and culture (European University Institute 2008, p. 292).
35. The areas of responsibility include care of the elderly, childcare, comprehensive schools and upper secondary schools, fire and rescue services, library and leisure facilities, local transport, planning permission, local planning, social benefits, water, and waste disposal (Arbetsgivarverket 2009a, p. 19).
36. Since the 1920s, the SAP established itself as Sweden's natural ruling party, and it continuously formed the government between 1932 and 1976.
37. However, this also consolidated the gender-based division of labour, as women were especially recruited into the care sector and seen as ideal employees for specific work tasks, particularly in the areas of healthcare, education, and childcare (Gonäs 1999). Thus, the high female labour force participation rate did not go hand in hand with equal pay, equal working time, or equal working conditions (Gornick and Jacobs 1998, p. 707; Jahn 2003, p. 116; Schunter-Kleemann 1992, pp. 274ff.). Nevertheless, high employment rates among mothers, long rather than short part-time, and a moderate gender pay gap, all promoted by public sector employment, distinguish female employment in Sweden from the United Kingdom and Germany (Eurostat 2015)
38. In order to provide the basis for the establishment of municipal institutions that were able to handle the rapidly increasing local government responsibilities, two territorial reforms taking effect in 1952 and 1974 reduced the number of municipalities drastically from about 2500 to less than 300 (Häggroth et al. 1999, pp. 11–16; Wollmann 2008, p. 266).

39. The principle of free collective bargaining between employers and salaried employees was also established in the local government sector (Ministry of the Budget 1978, p. 11).
40. Until 1988, the Ministry of Public Administration had been the driving force behind the reform efforts. Its Minister Bo Holmberg was increasingly criticized from within the SAP for 'too much talk and too little action', as well as his focus on democratic participation and decentralization.
41. Until the beginning of 1990s, the social democratic economic reform programme termed 'The Third Way' between neo-liberalism and Keynesianism had been quite successful, including measures to boost the economy, maintain full employment, and eliminate the budget deficit (Wilks 1996, p. 37).
42. An element of decentralized bargaining was introduced which established that 1 per cent of the pay bill of an agency had to be used for local negotiations (Andersson and Schager 1999, p. 246; Bender and Elliott 2003, p. 85). However, central government still decided on general pay raises for all grades (Murray 2000, p. 174).

6   Energy Regulatory Agencies

1. When analysing regulation, it has to be recognized that IRAs share regulatory functions with other public authorities (Jordana and Sancho 2004), most notably ministries and competition authorities. Grande and Hartenberger (2007), for example, have shown that utility regulation takes place in a tripolar governance structure, in which the strength of the poles – IRA, competition authority, ministry – can vary considerably between countries and sectors.
2. The interviews with HR managers took place in 2010 and lasted for 1.5 to 2.5 hours. They refer to the *Office of Gas and Electricity Markets* (Ofgem) in London, United Kingdom (interview code: EUK), the *Bundesnetzagentur* (BNetzA) in Bonn, Germany (interview code: EDE), the *Commission de Régulation de l'Énergie* (CRE) in Paris, France (interview code: EFR), and *Energimarknadsinspektionen* (EI) in Ekilstuna, Sweden (Interview code: ESE). Interviews in the UK, France, and Sweden were conducted in English, and in German in Germany. Two representatives of HRM participated in the interview at the BNetzA in Germany. Translations of interview passages from the German BNetzA cited in this chapter are by the authors. All information on HRM, if not noted otherwise, refers to the point in time of the interviews.
3. Non-ministerial government departments are one of the three main types of arm's-length organizations in the United Kingdom, the others being executive agencies and non-departmental public bodies (Cabinet Office 2010, pp. 9–12). For an overview of the British 'agency-jungle', see, for example, Verhey 2003.
4. The statutory powers and duties of Ofgem and its governing body – the Gas and Electricity Markets Authority (GEMA) – are laid down in the following acts: Gas Act 1986, Electricity Act 1989, Utilities Act 2000, Competition Act 1998, Enterprise Act 2002, and the Energy Acts 2004, 2008, 2010, 2011, and 2013.
5. Since then, employment figures have substantially increased (see Ofgem 2014, p. 67).
6. Although departments and agencies are also principally responsible for managing the Senior Civil Service (SCS), some of their terms and conditions such as pay and grading structures are still defined centrally by the Cabinet Office.

7. The RegTP took over the responsibilities of the former Federal Ministry of Post and Telecommunications and the Federal Office for Post and Telecommunications (Bundesnetzagentur 2009, p. 192). Therefore, its initial workforce consisted mainly of employees from the ministry and the federal office (Löhr 2006, p. 394).

8. Before the establishment of the BNetzA in 2005, Germany did not have a regulatory agency for the energy sector but relied on ex post oversight by the national competition authority (Eberlein 2005, p. 47).

9. From 2010 onwards, the energy regulation division of the BNetzA has been enlarged, not least due to new tasks in administrating the energy transition, such as the exit from nuclear and fossil energy and the promotion of renewable energy. By the end of 2014, the number of civil servants und employees had increased to 306 (email information by HR Manager of the Energy Regulatory Department in April 2015).

10. *Loi n° 84–16 du 11 janvier 1984* Art. 44–48 set out the guidelines for the secondment of *fonctionnaires*. *Agents contractuels* with contracts based on public law are a category of the so-called *agents non titulaires* of the *fonction publique de l'Etat*. Another category of the *agents non titulaires* is appointed on the basis of private law contracts. The guidelines for *agents contractuels* are set out by *Loi n° 84–16 du 11 janvier 1984* Art. 4, 6, and 7 and *Décret 86–83 du 17 janvier 1986*, which implements *Loi n° 84–16 du 11 janvier 1984* Article 7 and contains general provisions applicable to *agents non titulaires* on the state level.

11. These contracts specify the statutory provision under which the agent is recruited, the definition of the occupied post, the date of recruitment, the duration of the engagement, remuneration arrangements, and other conditions of employment of the agent, such as the working time (http://vosdroits.service-public.fr/F13117.xhtml, accessed 2 April 2015).

12. For comparison: while in 2012, the vast majority of the 1,922,306 employees of the ministries and the so-called *établissements publics administratifs* of the *fonction publique de l'État* were regular *fonctionnaires*, roughly 14.8 per cent were *agents non titulaires* (Ministère de la décentralisation et de la fonction publique 2014, p. 8).

13. The agency's legal basis is the *Förordning (2007:1118) med instruktion för Energimarknadsinspektionen.*

14. IRAs in Sweden apply a common HR strategy which operates through cooperation procedures, established by the Swedish Agency of Government Employers (*Arbetsgivarverket*), the member organization for government employers (Arbetsgivarverket 2009c).

15. Only the so-called 'Fast Stream Development Programme' (CSMC § 1.5) for graduates comprises a competitive centralized application and selection process. This programme, in which the participants run through different jobs within a department or agency and receive different forms of training, aims at developing future top Senior Civil Servants (Burnham and Pyper 2008, pp. 195–200).

16. The annual report from 2007 is the latest report in which these numbers have been published.

17. This code implemented ideas articulated in the 'Next Steps Programme 1988' and specified in two Government White Papers, 'The Civil Service: Continuity and Change' (1994) and 'The Civil Service: Taking Forward Continuity and Change' (1995).

18. The pay ranges were as follows: Band E – GBP 60,600 to GBP 82,000; Band D – GBP 41,200 to GBP 69,700; Band C – GBP 29,200 to GBP 45,700; Band B – GBP

22,100 to GBP 32,000; Band A – GBP 16,900 to GBP 25,000 (Ofgem 2010a). The base pay structure for the Senior Civil Service is centrally defined by the Cabinet Office, and most agencies use three core SCS pay bands. For 2010–11 the pay bands looked as follows: Pay Band 1 (Deputy Director) – GBP 58,200 to GBP 117,800; Pay Band 2 (Director) – GBP 82,900 to GBP 162,500; Pay Band 3 (Director General) – GBP 101,500 to GBP 208,100 (Cabinet Office 2010, p. 4ff.).

19. Consolidated increases are added to the monthly basic pay within a pay band and are pensionable. In contrast, non-consolidated payments are performance-related single bonuses that are not consolidated into basic pay, are not pensionable, and do not accrue additional expenditure. These single payments may, for example, 'also be used to reward those staff that are at the maximum of their pay range and are unable to receive any consolidated increases to their base pay' (HM Treasury 2009, p. 34).

20. Basic pay is supplemented, for example, by family allowance, allowances in specific cases, performance bonuses, or performance allowances, as set out in the Civil Servants' Remuneration Act.

21. This can be applied in each calendar year to 15 per cent of the civil servants that have not yet reached the final level of their pay grade.

22. The following section on the procedure of *lönesättande samtal* at EI is mainly based on an internal information document for the agency's employees.

23. 'We aim to attract, support, retain and motivate our staff by making sure that they have the skills and knowledge to perform their roles effectively and provide them with development opportunities to build a career. We offer a variety of formal training courses, on-the-job training, coaching and other development activities. There is also a comprehensive management development programme and support for further education and professional qualifications.' (http://www.ofgem.gov.uk/About%20us/Careers/Learn/Pages/Learn.aspx, accessed 6 April 2015).

24. The system has evoked much criticism (Wagner and Leppek 2009, p. 72). As Mayntz (1985, p. 167) has argued, even before the system was initiated, an appraisal that is conducted by the line manager inevitably contains subjective judgements that are likely to bring in unofficial criteria. Thus, in how far promotions are actually based on suitability, capability, and professional performance (criteria which, by the way, are generally hard to measure objectively), is an open question that can only be answered by detailed analyses of decisions on promotion.

25. On the general attractiveness of regulatory staff for the private sector companies, see Horn (1995, pp. 60f.).

26. Based on an explicit decision, it is also possible to provide *agents contractuels* with open-ended contracts after the end of the six-year period (*Loi n° 84–16 du 11 janvier 1984* Art. 4; *Décret n° 86–83 du 17 janvier 1986* Art. 6.). However, this option does not play an important role at CRE (Interview EFR).

27. For the CRE in 2013, a total female share of close to 50 per cent was reported. However, in the group of department heads, the female share was less than one-third (Commission de Régulation de l'Énergie 2014, pp. 20f.). In 2010, Ofgem reported a 43 per cent share of women in managerial grades and in Senior Civil Service a share of 35 per cent (Ofgem2010). Figures on staff of ethnic minority origin (20 per cent in 2010) and disabled persons (less than 1 per cent in 2010) are only available on a regular annual basis for Ofgem, but not for the other agencies under study (Ofgem 2010b).

7 Waste Collection

1. In the UK, the Environmental Protection Act 1990 (EPA) has redefined the fundamental structure of waste collection in England, Scotland, Wales, and Northern Ireland. In Germany, federal legislation – the *Kreislaufwirtschafts- und Abfallgesetz* – is implemented by the law of the state *Länder* (for example, in Bavaria the *Bayerisches Abfallwirtschaftsgesetz*). The Swedish regulation is laid down in the *Avfallsförordning* (2001:1063), and the French regulation in *Loi 75–633 du 15 juillet 1975*.

2. For example, in the waste collection in Germany, labour costs make up about 40 per cent of a contract's total costs, and pay in the public sector's collective agreement is more than twice as high as the minimum wage in this field (ver.di 2012, p. 7).

3. From February to June 2010, 11 interviews with HR managers of public waste collection organizations in Germany (n=5), France (n=3), and Sweden (n=3) were conducted. Additionally, three union representatives in Germany were interviewed. Interviews lasted from 1.5 to 2.5 hours. The cases were selected in order to represent the relevant competitive structures in the sector. Thus, in Germany, the cases entail public organizations that are closely controlled by the municipality (Interviews WDE1 and WDE2), as well as an independent public-law institution (*Anstalt/Körperschaft des öffentlichen Rechts*, Interviews WDE4 and WDE5) and a public company based on private law (Interview WDE3). Three of the five municipalities also provide the collection of packaging waste via subsidiary companies. In Sweden, all three cases are part of the municipal administration and are thus closely controlled by the municipality. In one case, the municipality decided for a regional division with a public organization in one part of the city and a private contractor in the other part (Interview WSE1). In France, a regional division of public and private providers is relevant in two cases (Interviews WFR1 and WFR3), whereas the city is the only service provider in the third case (Interview WFR2).

4. Employment Acts of 1980, 1982, 1988, 1990; Trade Union Act 1984; Trade Union Reform and Employment Rights Act 1993.

5. In contrast to the other countries, labour regulations in the United Kingdom do not comprise a positive right to strike, and collective agreements are generally neither binding nor legally enforceable (TULRCA 1992: Part IV, Chapter I). This reflects the tradition of a voluntaristic British system of industrial relations with the abstention of the state from direct intervention. Voluntarism has never been absolute and collective agreements were, and remain, unenforceable by law, but are 'binding in honour only' (Hyman 2001, p. 70).

6. Local Government Association, LGA 2012.

7. *Verordnung über die Vermeidung und Verwertung von Verpackungsabfällen* von 1991 (Packaging Waste Regulation of 1991).

8. The Association of Municipal Waste Disposal and Street Cleaning (*Verband Kommunaler Abfallwirtschaft und Stadtreinigung*, VKS), which is also associated with the VKA, reported 411 members with about 82,000 employees in 2007.

9. *Loi n° 83–634 du 13 juillet 1983 portant droits et obligations des fonctionnaires*. Employment regulation in Paris has its own rules, justified by the administrative and political specificity of the city of Paris, being both municipality and department. These rules, established by *Décret n° 94–415 du 24 mai 1994*, are sometimes inspired by the state civil service and sometimes by the local government service, or even by the medical sector.

10. *Convention Collective Nationale des Activités du Déchet* (CCNAD).
11. *Överenskommelse om Omställningsavtal* KOM-KL (Agreement on the Transition Contract).
12. Although no centralized recruitment criteria exist, legal regulations as well as collective agreements set requirements for the recruitment process, especially with regard to non-discrimination and equal treatment (Sex Discrimination Act 1975, Race Relations Act 1976, National Agreement on Pay and Conditions of Service 2005).
13. Subsidiarity is a principle of social organization that derives from the Catholic Church. It contains the idea of decentralization and holds that social affairs should be dealt with at the most immediate (or local) level. The principle is basic to the provision of services in the German welfare state, prioritizing not only decentralized provision of services but also, in the case of social services, provision by either the family or voluntary and non-profit organizations (Kaufmann 2007).
14. CCT was introduced for a large part of local public services by the Local Government Act 1988 and, at the same time, collective bargaining at national level was severed by the Employment Acts of 1980, 1982, 1988, 1990; Trade Union Act 1984; and Trade Union Reform and Employment Rights Act 1993.
15. Thirteen factors have been selected for the job evaluation: knowledge, initiative and independence, responsibility for people, mental skills, physical demands, responsibility for supervision/direction and coordination of employees, interpersonal and communication skills, mental demands, responsibility for financial resources, physical skills, emotional demands, responsibility for physical resources, and working conditions (NJC 4.9.9).
16. This is in contrast to the regulations for public employees of the *Länder*, where after a very short period, PRP was abolished (see Chapter 5).
17. *Adjoint technique de 2eme classe, Adjoint technique de 1ère classe, Adjoint technique principal de 2eme classe, Adjoint technique principal de 1ère classe* (CNFPT 2010b, p. 19).
18. CNNAD: *Valeur du point – indemnités 2015*
19. *Hududövereinkommelse om lön och almänna anställningsvillkor samt rekommendation om lokalt kollektivavtal* (HÖK, SKL 2010, SKL 2013).
20. The four *Länder* that so far have not enacted rules are Baden-Württemberg, Bavaria, Saxony, and Thuringia.
21. The entry level is the *Adjoint technique de 2ème classe*. The first career step is the *Adjoint technique de 1ère* classe (entry level for drivers), followed by the second career step as *Adjoint technique principal de 2ème classe*, and the final career step as *Adjoint technique de 1ère classe*.
22. 'L'employeur est tenu de procéder à un examen particulier de l'évolution de carrière des salariés dans la limite des besoins et des possibilités de l'entreprise' (CCNAD Art. 3-2-4).
23. As Colling reports, dismissals for redundancy were common, and '[e]mployees who would not or could not accept new workloads were initially counseled, but in the end many were disciplined and either encouraged to leave voluntarily or sacked. In building cleaning, ten of a total of eighty caretakers had faced some form of serious disciplinary action and the manager confided, "I've been involved in more disciplinary hearings in the last twelve months than in the previous ten years"' (Colling 1999, p. 142).

8 The Police

1. In most Western European countries, non-sovereign tasks such as in-house paperwork, property policing, or stationary traffic can be delegated to private providers. In some cases, sovereign rights are transferred to private providers by contract, ordinance, or law (such as *Beliehene* in Germany), or the sovereign rights are transferred to the private provider acting as if they are public police (like airport security). On the other hand, some police services can be bought by the public or are subject to a fee. In such cases 'the police retain their legal status and the access this provides to the legitimate use of physical, including deadly, force' (Ayling and Shearing 2008, p. 29).

2. This is reflected in public (media) representations and male police officers' perceptions of their job. Prominent points of reference are the idea of crime fighting and the exercise of physical force, two strongly gendered functions. Although women today are admitted in all Western European police forces, the professional or 'cop culture' is reported to entail 'doing masculinity' (Manning 2003; Behr 2000).

3. For the United Kingdom, see Loftus (2009); for Germany, see Künkel (2014); for France, see Fassin (2011); for Sweden, see Uhnoo (2015).

4. Information on the police in the UK refers to England and Wales and is based on document analysis and secondary literature.

5. These *corps* are listed in increasing hierarchical order: the *Corps de maîtrise et d'application* (Authority and Enforcement Corps), the *Corps de commandement et d'encadrement* (Command and Management Corps), and the *Corps de conception et de direction* (Conception and Direction Corps).

6. Interviews in France were conducted in French, in German in Germany, and in English in Sweden. Translation of the French and German interview quotes are by the authors. For cited interviews, the sector code for police is P, while the country codes are DE for Germany, FR for France, SE for Sweden, and UK for United Kingdom, followed by the number of the interview.

7. The police organization in Sweden is due to be reformed in 2015. In 2015, there will be one national headquarter and seven regional police areas (SOU 2012, p. 13, *En sammanhållen svensk polis*).

8. In this chapter, we focus on England and Wales.

9. All major police forces in Europe, as well as in the US, Canada, and Australia, routinely carry firearms. The exceptions are Britain, the Irish Republic, and New Zealand. In Norway, officers carry arms in their automobiles but not on their person. About 5 per cent of all police officers in England and Wales have the permission to carry guns (see BBC 2012).

10. Variations apply to the most senior ranks within the Greater London Metropolitan Police Service and within the City of London Police.

11. In terms of allotted shares to the police, the central government provides 51 per cent directly/an additional 29 per cent indirectly to local authorities; the remaining 20 per cent of funds are paid through the local police precept channelled to the police from local rates and community charges (Hunter 2003, p. 33). Chief constables are to decide how best to use those resources by, *inter alia*, setting staffing levels and the workforce mix; the Home Office does not interfere with staffing decisions.

12. Outsourcing included the impounding of vehicles, human resources, emergency call handling, and finance capabilities, as well as IT services. For an overview,

see the official guidelines of the National Audit Office and HM Chief Inspector of Constabulary (National Audit Office 2013).

13. The balanced scorecard (BSC) is a strategic performance management tool stemming from business and the private sector and has been extensively used since the 1990s. Generally, it consists of a semi-standard structured report, supported by design methods and automation tools that can be used by managers to keep track of the execution of activities by staff within their control and to monitor the consequences arising from these actions. The agreed characteristics that define a balanced scorecard are: the focus on the strategic agenda of the organization; the selection of a small number of data items to monitor; and a mix of financial and non-financial data items.

14. Since 2009, the budget and staff management of the *gendarmerie* are under the review of the Ministry of the Interior.

15. *Loi n° 97–940 du 16 octobre 1997 relative au développement d'activités pour l'emploi des jeunes.*

16. *Décret n° 94–732 du 24 août 1994 portant statut particulier du cadre d'emplois des agents de police municipale.*

17. *Loi n° 95–73 du 21 janvier 1995 d'orientation et de programmation relative à la sécurité.*

18. *Loi n° 2011–267 du 14 mars 2011 d'orientation et de programmation pour la performance de la sécurité intérieure.*

19. *Décret n° 2008–1533 du 22 décembre 2008 relatif à la prime de fonctions et de résultats.*

20. Even though statistics showed no real increase in overall crime rates, the number of threats, violations, and crimes against liberty increased. According to criminal sociology experts, this leads to a general feeling of insecurity in public space (Fritzell et al. 2010, p. 59).

21. Already in 1954, police training centres were founded in Malmö, Norrköping, Örebro, Gävle, and Luleå. According to Lord (1998), training for police officers was centralized even before local departments were transformed into a national force. By 1962, basic training consisted of 8 weeks of academy training and 12 weeks of job training, and an additional course of 21 weeks was offered for constables (Lord 1998).

22. This trend already started in the 1990s (see Chapter 5, Statskontoret 2010).

23. 'How to join the police force at a senior level through the direct entry scheme'. http://www.theguardian.com/public-leaders-network/2014/may/23/how-to-join-police-senior-jobs (accessed 22 March 2015).

24. Following public unrest in the 1960s, police schools broadened the curriculum and started to employ teaching practitioners, professionals, psychologists, political scientists, and sociologists (Schulte 1995).

25. Email communication by the authors with the Swedish National Police Academy on 8 February 2015.

26. Besides the field training in a police department, the Swedish recruits also work with a local social service agency and judicial agency, facilitating the cooperation among agencies and familiarizing the new officer with the functions and limitations of the other agencies. This exposure to public social problems is meant to develop a higher level of understanding and problem-solving skills (Ackerman 1996).

27. In 1978, against a background of chronic underpayment of police officers compared to the private sector employees and rapid rises in the cost of living,

the Edmund-Davies committee recommended a basic pay increase of up to 45 per cent for police constables. To ensure that their level of pay did not drop to unacceptable levels in the future, Edmund-Davies recommended that police pay should be annually uprated in accordance with an index of private sector non-manual worker pay. The government agreed to a 40 per cent phased increase in police earnings following the report, and the new PNB machinery applied a pay formula that linked changes in police pay rates to movements in the average earnings index (for all workers) for the preceding 12 months. This index was modified in 1984 when the underlying index of average earnings was substituted. In 1994, a new formula was introduced, relating police pay increases to non-manual settlements (Hunter 2003, p. 41). Since then, no major changes regarding the pay system were implemented.

28. The PNB is a United Kingdom non-departmental public body established by an Act of Parliament in 1980 to negotiate the pay and employment terms and conditions of the British police. It is funded by the Department for Work and Pensions, and the Office of Manpower Economics provides the Board with an independent Secretariat. The PNB consists of an independent chairman and deputy chairman, both appointed by the prime minister. They are to supply independent voices in all negotiations.

29. In detail, competence refers to professional competence and results, commitment to the job, relationships with the public and colleagues, and willingness to learn and adjust to new circumstances (see MPA 2002).

30. Currently, six *Länder* have implemented the two-tiered model: Bremen, Hesse, North Rhine-Westphalia, Saarland, Rhineland-Palatinate, and Lower Saxony.

31. The interviewee refers to a reform of age groups relevant for promotion, dating back to 1997 (the so-called *Dienstrechtsreform,* see Chapter 5).

32. At the same time, an increase of *non-titulaire (contractuels)* was projected to integrate specialized knowledge more easily without extending the number of civil servants (see increase of civilians between 2005 and 2010, Table 8.1).

33. For all changes, see Police Nationale 2004.

34. For the UK, see Cotton (2005) and Walker and Lewis (2012); for France, see Schneider (2014, p. 132); for Germany see Singelnstein (2013, pp. 4–5, 9); for Sweden, see Ramalingam (2012, p. 25).

35. See MET 2012.

36. According to UNISON police staff, over the course of the early 2010s, about 20 per cent of the workforce has been made redundant (UNISON 2015). Following the annual governmental reports, the number of sworn police officers made redundant from 2011 to 2012 is 2.9 per cent, as opposed to 4.9 per cent of losses in police staff (Home Office 2013, p. 4).

37. *Décret n° 2010–1402 du 12 novembre 2010 relatif à la situation de réorientation professionnelle des fonctionnaires de l'Etat.*

38. *Loi n° 2012–347 du 12 mars 2012 relative à l'accès à l'emploi titulaire et à l'amélioration des conditions d'emploi des agents contractuels dans la fonction publique, à la lutte contre les discriminations et portant diverses dispositions relatives à la fonction publique.*

39. There is strong evidence that police culture tends to encourage stereotypical, masculine values like aggression, physical activity, strong heterosexual orientations, paternalistic attitudes towards women, and prejudices against marginalized people and people of colour. Those values strengthen in-groups with exclusionary effects towards out-groups like women and ethnic minorities (Rabe-Hemp 2007; Silvestri et al. 2013; Fassin 2011; Loftus 2008).

40. We are not including disability-related policies. Such policies are systematically not of relevance when it comes to core police work due to the physical exigencies of the work. For the rest of the civilian police staff, the general policies of the public sector apply.
41. See *Gesetz zur Umsetzung europäischer Richtlinien zur Verwirklichung des Grundsatzes der Gleichbehandlung* (EUGleichbUmsG) (2006), BGBl. I: 1897, and *Gesetz zur Durchsetzung der Gleichstellung von Frauen und Männern (Gleichstellungsdurchsetzungsgesetz*, DGleiG) (2001), BGBl. I: 3234.
42. Findings from a study on women in the German police indicate that women are structurally under-evaluated when it comes to job assessments and thus are disadvantaged with respect to promotions (Tondorf and Jochmann-Döll 2013).

9 Summary and Integrated Comparison of Countries and Sectors

1. Whether these trends hold under conditions of aggravated pressure on public budgets and the financial crisis remains to be seen. First analyses reflecting these changes indicate substantial cutbacks in public employment and wages in several European countries (Vaughan-Whitehead 2013).
2. This is in line with the OECD data on government employment as percentage of the labour force, referred to in Chapter 4, that reports for Sweden a decrease between 1995 and 2008 – contrary to Denmark, Norway, and Finland (see Chapter 4, Table 4.2).

References

1 Introduction

Ashworth, Rachel and Tom Entwistle (2011) 'The Contingent Relationship between Public Management Reform and Public Service Work', in Paul Blyton, Edmund Heery, and Peter Turnbull (eds) *Reassessing the Employment Relationship*, Basingstoke: Palgrave Macmillan.

Bach, Stephen (2004) *Employment Relations in the Health Service*, London: Routledge.

Bach, Stephen and Lorenzo Bordogna (2011) 'Varieties of New Public Management or Alternative Models? The Reform of Public Service Employment Relations in Industrialized Democracies', *International Journal of Human Resource Management* 22, 2281–94.

Bach, Stephen and Lorenzo Bordogna (2013) 'Reframing Public Service Employment Relations: The Impact of Economic Crisis and the New EU Economic Governance', *European Journal of Industrial Relations* 19, 279–94.

Bach, Stephen and Ian Kessler (2007) 'HRM and New Public Management', in Peter Boxall, John Purcell, and Patrick Wright (eds) *The Oxford Handbook of Human Resource Management*, Oxford: Oxford University Press.

Bach, Stephen, Lorenzo Bordogna, Giuseppe Della Rocca, and David Winchester (eds) (1999) *Public Service Employment Relations in Europe: Transformation, Modernization or Inertia?* London: Routledge.

Baumol, William J. (1967) 'Macroeconomics of Unbalanced Growth: The Anatomy of Urban Crisis', *American Economic Review* 57, 415–26.

Bekke, Hans A.G.M. and Frits M. van der Meer (eds) (2000) *Civil Service Systems in Western Europe*, Cheltenham: Edward Elgar.

Christensen, Tom, Anne L. Fimreite, and Per Lægreid (2014) 'Joined-up Government for Welfare Administration Reform in Norway', *Public Organization Review* 14, 439–56.

Crouch, Colin (2005) *Capitalist Diversity and Change. Recombinant Governance and Institutional Entrepreneurs*, Oxford: Oxford University Press.

Cusack, Thomas R., Ton Notermans and Martin Rein (1989) 'Political-Economic Aspects of Public Employment', *European Journal of Political Research* 17, 471–500.

Demmke, Christoph and Timo Moilanen (2010) *Civil Services in the EU of 27. Reform Outcomes and the Future of the Civil Service*, Frankfurt am Main: Peter Lang.

Demmke, Christoph and Timo Moilanen (2013) *Government Transformation and the Future of Public Employment. The Impact of Restructuring on Status Development in the Central Administration of the EU*, Frankfurt am Main: Peter Lang.

Derlien, Hans-Ulrich and B Guy Peters (eds) (2008) *The State at Work*, 2 vol., Cheltenham: Edward Elgar.

Farnham, David and Sylvia Horton (eds) (1996) *Managing People in the Public Services*, Basingstoke: Macmillan.

Farnham, David, Sylvia Horton, John Barlow, and Annie Hondeghem (eds) (1996) *New Public Managers in Europe: Public Servants in Transition*, London: Macmillan.

Flora, Peter (ed.) (1986) *Growth to Limits. The Western European Welfare States Since World War II*, 3 vol., Berlin: de Gruyter.

Grimm, Dieter (2005) 'The Constitution in the Process of Denationalization', *Constellations* 12(4), 449–65.

Hammerschmid, Gerhard, Steven Van de Walle, Rhys Andrews, and Philippe Bezes (2015) *Public Administration Reforms in Europe: The View from the Top*, Cheltenham: Edward Elgar.

Hood, Christopher (1991) 'A Public Management for All Seasons?' *Public Administration* 69(1), 3–19.

Huber, Evelyne, Matthew Lange, Stephan Leibfried, Jonah D. Levy, Frank Nullmeier, and John D. Stephens (2015) 'Introduction: Transformations of the State', in Stephan Leibfried, Evelyne Huber, Matthew Lange, Jonah D. Levy, Frank Nullmeier, and John D. Stephens (eds) *The Oxford Handbook of Transformations of the State*, Oxford: Oxford University Press.

Hurrelmann, Achim, Stephan Leibried, Kerstin Martens, and Peter Mayer (eds) (2007) *Transforming the Golden-Age Nation State*, Basingstoke: Palgrave Macmillan.

Kaufmann, Franz-Xaver (2001) 'Towards a Theory of the Welfare State', in Stephan Leibfried (ed.) *Welfare State Futures*, Cambridge: Cambridge University Press.

Keller, Berndt (2010) *Arbeitspolitik im öffentlichen Dienst. Ein Überblick über Arbeitsmärkte und Arbeitsbeziehungen*, Berlin: Edition Sigma.

Leibfried, Stephan, Evelyne Huber, Matthew Lange, Jonah D. Levy, Frank Nullmeier, and John D. Stephens (eds) (2015) *The Oxford Handbook of Transformations of the State*, Oxford: Oxford University Press.

Leibfried, Stephan and Michael Zürn (eds) (2005) *Transformations of the State?* Cambridge: Cambridge University Press.

Levy, Jonah D. (ed.) (2006) *The State after Statism: New State Activities in the Age of Liberalization*, Cambridge, MA: Harvard University Press.

Levy, Jonah D., Stephan Leibfried, and Frank Nullmeier (2015) 'Changing Perspectives on the State', in Stephan Leibfried, Evelyne Huber, Matthew Lange, Jonah D. Levy, Frank Nullmeier, and John D. Stephens (eds) *The Oxford Handbook of Transformations of the State*, Oxford: Oxford University Press.

OECD (2008) *The State of the Public Service*, Paris: OECD.

OECD (2009) *Government at a Glance 2009*, Paris: OECD.

OECD (2010) *Public Administration after 'New Public Management'*, Paris: OECD.

OECD (2011) *Government at a Glance 2011*, Paris: OECD.

Oxley, Howard and John P. Martin (1991) 'Controlling Government Spending and Deficits Trends in the 1980s and Prospects for the 1990s', *OECD Economic Studies* 17(Autumn), 145–89.

Pierson, Paul (ed.) (2001) *The New Politics of the Welfare State*, Oxford: Oxford University Press.

Pollitt, Christopher and Geert Bouckaert (2011) *Public Management Reform: A Comparative Analysis. New Public Management, Governance, and the Neo-Weberian State*, 3rd ed., Oxford: Oxford University Press.

Raadschelders, Jos, Theo A.J. Toonen, and Frits M. Van der Meer (eds) (2007) *The Civil Service in the 21st Century. Comparative Perspectives*, Basingstoke: Palgrave-Macmillan.

Rose, Richard (ed.) (1985) *Public Employment in Western Nations*, Cambridge: Cambridge University Press.

Rothenbacher, Franz (1997) 'Public Sector Employment in Europe – Where Will the Decline End?' *EURODATA Newsletter* 6, 1–11.

Scharpf, Fritz W. (2000) 'The Viability of Advanced Welfare States in the International Economy: Vulnerabilities and Options', *Journal of European Public Policy* 7, 190–228.

Schneider, Volker, Simon Fink, and Marc Tenbrücken (2005) 'Buying Out the State: A Comparative Perspective on the Privatization of Infrastructures', *Comparative Political Studies* 38, 704–27.

Sørensen, Georg (2004) *The Transformation of the State: Beyond the Myth of Retreat*, Basingstoke: Palgrave Macmillan.

Streeck, Wolfgang and Kathleen Thelen (2005) 'Introduction: Institutional Change in Advanced Political Economies', in Wolfgang Streeck and Kathleen Thelen (eds) *Beyond Continuity. Institutional Change in Advanced Political Economies*, Oxford: Oxford University Press.

Suleiman, Ezra (2003) *Dismantling Democratic States*, Princeton: Princeton University Press.

Van der Meer, Frits M. (ed.) (2011) *Civil Service Systems in Western Europe*, 2nd ed., Cheltenham: Edward Elgar.

Vaughan-Whitehead, Daniel (ed.) (2013) *Public Sector Shock: The Impact of Policy Retrenchment in Europe*, Cheltenham: Edward Elgar.

Weber, Max (1949) *The Methodology of the Social Sciences*, Glencoe: The Free Press.

Zohlnhöfer, Reimut, Herbert Obinger, and Frieder Wolf (2008) 'Partisan Politics, Globalization, and the Determinants of Privatization Proceeds in Advanced Democracies (1990–2000)', *Governance* 21(1), 95–121.

2   The Analytical Problem

Ahmed, Amel (2013) *Democracy and the Politics of Electoral System Choice: Engineering Electoral Dominance*, Cambridge: Cambridge University Press.

Allen, Matthew (2004) 'The Varieties of Capitalism Paradigm: Not Enough Variety?', *Socio-Economic Review* 2(1), 87–108.

Amable, Bruno (2003) *The Diversity of Modern Capitalism*, Oxford: Oxford University Press.

Amable, Bruno (2009) 'Structural Reforms in Europe and the (In)Coherence of Institutions', *Oxford Review of Economic Policy* 25(1), 17–39.

Arts, Wil and John Gelissen (2002) 'Three Worlds of Welfare Capitalism or More? A State-of-the-Art Report', *Journal of European Social Policy* 12(2), 137–58.

Atzmüller, Roland and Christian Hermann (2004) 'Veränderung öffentlicher Beschäftigung im Prozess der Liberalisierung und Privatisierung. Rekommodifizierung von Arbeit und Herausbildung eines neoliberalen Arbeitsregimes', *Österreichische Zeitschrift für Soziologie* 29(4), 30–48.

Bach, Stephen and Giuseppe Della Rocca (2000) 'The Managment Strategies of Public Service Employers in Europe', *Industrial Relations Journal* 31(2), 82–96.

Bach, Stephen and Ian Kessler (2007) 'HRM and New Public Management', in Peter Boxall, John Purcell and Patrick Wright (eds) *The Oxford Handbook of Human Resource Management*, Oxford: Oxford University Press.

Bach, Stephen and Lorenzo Bordogna (2011) 'Varieties of New Public Management or Alternative Models? The Reform of Public Service Employment Relations in Industrialized Democracies', *International Journal of Human Resource Management* 22, 2281–94.

Baron, Reuben M. and David A. Kenny (1986) 'The Moderator-Mediator Variable Distinction in Social Psychological Research: Conceptual, Strategic, and Statistical Considerations', *Journal of Personality and Social Psychology* 51, 1173–82.

Barzelay, Michael and Raquel Gallego (2006) 'From "New Institutionalism" to "Institutional Processualism": Advancing Knowledge about Public Management Policy Change', *Governance* 19, 531–57.

Baumgartner, Frank R. and Bryan D. Jones (1993) *Agendas and Instability in American Politics*, Chicago: University of Chicago Press.

Baumol, William J. (1967) 'Macroeconomics of Unbalanced Growth: The Anatomy of Urban Crisis', *American Economic Review* 57, 415–26.

Baumol, William J. and William G. Bowen (1965) 'On the Performing Arts: The Anatomy of Their Economic Problems', *American Economic Review* 55, 495–502.

Beaumont, Phil B. (1992) *Public Sector Industrial Relations*, London: Routledge.

Bekke, Hans A.G.M. and Frits M. van der Meer (eds) (2000) *Civil Service Systems in Western Europe*, Cheltenham: Edward Elgar.

Bertelsmann Stiftung (2009) *Sustainable Governance in the OECD*, Gütersloh: Bertelsmann.

Bezès, Philippe and Martin Lodge (2007) 'Historical Legacies and Dynamics of Institutional Change in Civil Service Systems', in Jos Raadschelders, Theo A.J. Toonen and Frits M. Van der Meer (eds) *The Civil Service in the 21st Century. Comparative Perspectives*, Basingstoke: Palgrave-Macmillan.

Bordogna, Lorenzo (2007) *Industrial Relations in the Public Sector,* Dublin: European Foundation for the Improvement of Living and Working Conditions.

Briken, Kendra, Karin Gottschall, Sylvia Hils and Bernhard Kittel (2014) 'Wandel von Beschäftigung und Arbeitsbeziehungen im öffentlichen Dienst in Deutschland – zur Erosion einer sozialstaatlichen Vorbildrolle', *Zeitschrift für Sozialreform* 60(2), 123–48.

Brunnson, Nils (1989) *The Organisation of Hypocrisy: Talk, Decisions and Actions in Organisations*, Chichester: Wiley.

Campbell, John L. (2009) 'Institutional Reproduction and Change', in Glenn Morgan, John L. Campbell, Colin Crouch, Ove Kaj Pedersen and Richard Whitley (eds) *The Oxford Handbook of Comparative Institutional Analysis*, Oxford: Oxford University Press.

Capano, Giliberto (2009) 'Understanding Policy Change as an Epistemological and Theoretical Problem', *Journal of Comparative Policy Analysis* 11(1), 7–31.

Castles, Francis G. (1993) *Families of Nations. Patterns of Public Policy in Western Democracies*, Aldershot: Dartmouth.

Castles, Francis G. and Herbert Obinger (2008) 'Worlds, Families, Regimes: Country Clusters in European and OECD Area Public Policy', *West European Politics* 31, 321–44.

Chapman, Jeff and Grant Duncan (2007) 'Is There Now a New "New Zealand Model"?' *Public Management Review* 9(1), 1–25.

Christensen, Tom (2012) 'Global Ideas and Modern Public Sector Reforms: A Theoretical Elaboration and Empirical Discussion of a Neoinstitutionalist Theory', *American Review of Public Administration* 42, 635–53.

Christensen, Tom and Per Lægreid (2011) 'Complexity and Hybrid Public Administration – Theoretical and Empirical Challenges', *Public Organization Review* 11, 407–23.

Crouch, Colin (2005) *Capitalist Diversity and Change. Recombinant Governance and Institutional Entrepreneurs*, Oxford: Oxford University Press.

Crouch, Colin (2009) 'Typologies of Capitalism', in Bob Hancké (ed.) *Debating Varieties of Capitalism*, Oxford: Oxford University Press.

Crouch, Colin (2010) 'Complementarity', in Glenn Morgan, John L. Campbell, Colin Crouch, Ove Kaj Pedersen and Richard Whitley (eds) *The Oxford Handbook of Comparative Institutional Analysis*, Oxford: Oxford University Press.

Dahlström, Carl and Victor Lapuente (2010) 'Explaining Cross-Country Differences in Performance-Related Pay in the Public Sector', *Journal of Public Administration Research and Theory* 20, 577–600.

Demmke, Christoph and Timo Moilanen (2010) *Civil Services in the EU of 27. Reform Outcomes and the Future of the Civil Service*, Frankfurt am Main: Peter Lang.

DiMaggio, Paul (1997) 'Culture and Cognition', *Annual Review of Sociology* 23, 263–87.

Doeringer, Peter B. and Michael J. Piore (1971) *Internal Labor Markets and Manpower Analysis*, Lexington: Heath Lexington Books.

Duverger, Maurice (1951) *Les parties politiques*, Paris: Colin.

Economist, The (2010) 'Stop! The Size and Power of the State is Growing and Discontent is on the Rise', *The Economist* 23–28 January, 9–10.

Emmenegger, Patrick, Silja Häusermann, Bruno Palier and Martin Seeleib-Kaiser (eds) (2012) *The Age of Dualization. The Changing Face of Inequality in Deindustrializing Societies*, Oxford: Oxford University Press.

Esping-Andersen, Gøsta (1990) *The Three Worlds of Welfare Capitalism*, Cambridge: Polity Press.

Ferragina, Emanuele and Martin Seeleib-Kaiser (2011) 'Thematic Review: Welfare Regime Debate: Past, Present, Futures?', *Policy & Politics* 39, 583–611.

Flora, Peter (ed.) (1986) *Growth to Limits. The Western European Welfare States Since World War II*, 3 vol., Berlin: de Gruyter.

Gallie, Duncan (2007a) 'Production Regimes and the Quality of Employment in Europe', *Annual Review of Sociology* 33, 85–104.

Gallie, Duncan (2007b) 'Production Regimes, Employment Regimes, and the Quality of Work', in Duncan Gallie (ed.) *Employment Regimes and the Quality of Work*, Oxford: Oxford University Press.

Giordano, Raffaela, Domenico Depalo, Manuel Coutinho Pereira, Bruno Eugène, Evangelia Papapetrou, Javier J. Perez, Lukas Reiss and Mojca Roter (2011) *The Public Sector Pay Gap in a Selection of Euro Area Countries*, European Central Bank Working Paper Series 1406, Frankfurt am Main: European Central Bank.

Goodin, Robert E. (1996) *The Theory of Institutional Design*, Cambridge: Cambridge University Press.

Hall, Peter A. (1986) *Governing the Economy: The Politics of State Intervention in Britain and France*, Cambridge: Polity Press.

Hall, Peter A. and Daniel W. Gingerich (2009) 'Varieties of Capitalism and Institutional Complementarities in the Political Economy: An Empirical Analysis', *British Journal of Political Science* 39, 449–82.

Hall, Peter A. and David Soskice (eds) (2001) *Varieties of Capitalism. The Institutional Foundations of Comparative Advantage*, Cambridge: Cambridge University Press.

Hall, Peter A. and Kathleen Thelen (2009) 'Institutional Change in Varieties of Capitalism', *Socio-Economic Review* 7, 7–34.

Hermann, Christian and Jörg Flecker (eds) (2012) *Privatization of Public Services. Impacts for Employment, Working Conditions, and Service Quality in Europe*, New York: Routledge.

Hood, Christopher (1991) 'A Public Management for All Seasons?', *Public Administration* 69(1), 3–19.

Hood, Christopher (1995) 'The "New Public Management" in the 1980s: Variations on a Theme', *Accounting, Organizations and Society* 20(2–3), 93–109.

Hood, Christopher (2000) *The Art of the State: Culture, Rhetoric, and Public Management*, Oxford: Oxford University Press.

Horton, Sylvia and David Farnham (2000) 'Evaluating Human Resources Flexibilities: A Comparative Perspective', in David Farnham and Sylvia Horton (eds) *Human Resources Flexibilities in the Public Services: International Perspectives*, Basingstoke: Macmillan.

Huber, John D. and Charles R. Shipan (2002) *Deliberate Discretion? The Institutional Foundations of Bureaucratic Autonomy*, Cambridge: Cambridge University Press.

Jones, Bryan D. and Frank R. Baumgartner (2012) 'From There to Here: Punctuated Equilibrium to the General Punctuation Thesis to a Theory of Government Information Processing', *Policy Studies Journal* 40(1), 1–19.

Kalleberg, Arne L. and Aage B. Sørensen (1979) 'The Sociology of Labor Markets', *Annual Review of Sociology* 5, 351–79.

Kasza, Gregory J. (2002) 'The Illusion of Welfare "Regimes"', *Journal of Social Policy* 31, 271–87.

Katz, Richard S. (1980) *A Theory of Parties and Electoral Systems*, Baltimore: Johns Hopkins Press.

Kenworthy, Lane (2006) 'Institutional Coherence and Macroeconomic Performance', *Socio-Economic Review* 4, 69–91.

Kettl, Donald F. (1997) 'The Global Revolution in Public Management: Driving Themes, Missing Links', *Journal of Public Policy Analysis and Management* 16, 446–62.

Kettl, Donald F. (2000) *The Global Public Management Revolution: A Report on the Transformation of Government*, New York: The Brookings Institution.

Kickert, Walter J.M. and Frans-Bauke Van der Meer (2011) 'Small, Slow, and Gradual Reform: What can Historical Institutionalism Teach us?', *International Journal of Political Administration* 34, 475–85.

Kißler, Leo, René Lasserre and Marie-Hélène Pautrat (2006) *Öffentlicher Dienst und Personalmanagement. Zur Verwaltungsreform in Deutschland und Frankreich*, Frankfurt am Main: Campus.

Kittel, Bernhard and Herbert Obinger (2003) 'Political Parties, Institutions, and the Dynamics of Social Expenditures in Times of Austerity', *Journal of European Public Policy* 10(1), 20–45.

Kiwiet, D. Roderick and Matthew D. McCubbins (1991) *The Logic of Delegation. Congressional Parties and the Appropriation Process*, Chicago: University of Chicago Press.

Knill, Christoph (1999) 'Explaining Cross-National Variance in Administrative Reform: Autonomous versus Instrumental Bureaucracies', *Journal of Public Policy* 19(2), 113–39.

Knill, Christoph (2005) 'Introduction: Cross-National Policy Convergence: Concepts, Approaches and Explanatory Factors', *Journal of European Public Policy* 12, 764–74.

Krasner, Stephen (1982) 'Structural Causes and Regime Consequences: Regimes as Intervening Variables', *International Organization* 36(2), 185–205.

Kroos, Daniela and Karin Gottschall (2012) 'Dualization and Gender in Social Services. The Role of the State in Germany and France', in Patrick Emmenegger, Silja Häusermann, Bruno Palier and Martin Seeleib-Kaiser (eds) *The Age of Dualization. The Changing Face of Inequality in Deindustrializing Societies*, Oxford: Oxford University Press.

La Porta, Rafael, Florencio Lopez-de-Silanes and Andrei Shleifer (2008) 'The Economic Consequences of Legal Origins', *Journal of Economic Literature* 46, 285–332.

La Porta, Rafael, Florencio Lopez-de-Silanes, Andrei Shleifer and Robert W. Vishny (1998) 'Law and Finance', *Journal of Political Economy* 106, 1113–55.

Laver, Michael and Norman Schofield (1998) *Multiparty Government: The Politics of Coalition in Europe*, Ann Arbor: University of Michigan Press.

Laver, Michael and Kenneth A. Shepsle (eds) (1994) *Cabinet Ministers and Parliamentary Government*, Cambridge: Cambridge University Press.

Leibfried, Stephan, Evelyne Huber, Matthew Lange, Jonah D. Levy, Frank Nullmeier and John D. Stephens (eds) (2015) *The Oxford Handbook of Transformations of the State*, Oxford: Oxford University Press.

Leibfried, Stephan and Michael Zürn (eds) (2005) *Transformations of the State?*, Cambridge: Cambridge University Press.

Lijphart, Arend (1999) *Patterns of Democracy. Government Forms and Performance in Thirty-Six Countries*, New Haven: Yale University Press.

Lindner, Johannes (2003) 'Institutional Stability and Change: Two Sides of the Same Coin', *Journal of European Public Policy* 10, 912–35.

Lodge, Martin (2009) 'Administrative Patterns and National Politics', in B. Guy Peters and Jon Pierre (eds) *The Sage Handbook of Public Administration*, London: Sage.

MacCarthaigh, Muiris and Paul G. Roness (2012) 'Analyzing Longitudinal Continuity and Change in Public Sector Organizations', *International Journal of Public Administration* 35, 773–82.

Mahoney, James and Kathleen Thelen (2010) 'A Theory of Gradual Institutional Change', in James Mahoney and Kathleen Thelen (eds) *Explaining Institutional Change: Ambiguity, Agency, and Power*, Cambridge: Cambridge University Press.

Miller, Gary J. (2005) 'The Political Evolution of Principal-Agent Models', *Annual Review of Political Science* 8, 203–25.

Molina, Oscar and Martin Rhodes (2002) 'Corporatism: The Past, Present, and Future of a Concept', *Annual Review of Political Sciences* 2002, 305–31.

Morgan, E. Philip and James L. Perry (1988) 'Re-Orienting the Comparative Study of Civil Service Systems', *Review of Public Personnel Administration* 8, 84–95.

North, Douglass C. (1990) *Institutions, Institutional Change and Economic Performance*, Cambridge: Cambridge University Press.

Niskanen, William A., Jr. (1971) *Bureaucracy and Representative Government*, Chicago: Aldine.

Nullmeier, Frank and Franz-Xaver Kaufmann (2010) 'Post-War Welfare State Development', in Francis G. Castles, Stephan Leibfried, Jane Lewis, Herbert Obinger and Christopher Pierson (eds) *The Oxford Handbook of the Welfare State*, Oxford: Oxford University Press.

Obinger, Herbert, Stephan Leibfried and Francis G. Castles (eds) (2005) *Federalism and the Welfare State. New World and European Experiences*, Cambridge: Cambridge University Press.

Obinger, Herbert, Peter Starke, Julia Moser, Claudia Bogedan, Edith Gindulis and Stephan Leibfried (2010) *Transformations of the Welfare State. Small States, Big Lessons*, Oxford: Oxford University Press.

Obinger, Herbert and Uwe Wagschal (2010) 'Social Expenditure and Revenues', in Francis G. Castles, Stephan Leibfried, Jane Lewis, Herbert Obinger and Christopher Pierson (eds) *The Oxford Handbook of the Welfare State*, Oxford: Oxford University Press.

OECD (2008) *The State of the Public Service*, Paris: OECD.

OECD (2013) *Government at a Glance 2013*, Paris: OECD.

Osborne, David and Ted Gaebler (1991) *Reinventing Government. How the Entrepreneurial Spirit is Transforming the Public Sector*, Reading: Addison-Wesley.

Osborne, Stephen P. (2006) 'The New Public Governance?', *Public Management Review* 8, 377–87.

Page, Edward C. (1995) 'Administering Europe', in Jack Hayward and Edward C. Page (eds) *Governing the New Europe*, Cambridge: Polity Press.

Page, Stephen (2005) 'What's New about the New Public Management? Administrative Change in the Human Services', *Public Administration Review* 65, 713–27.

Painter, Martin and B. Guy Peters (2010) 'Administrative Tranditions in Comparative Perspective: Families, Groups and Hybrids', in Martin Painter and B. Guy Peters (eds) *Tradition and Public Administration*, Basingstoke: Palgrave-Macmillan.

Pierson, Paul (1994) *Dismantling the Welfare State? Reagan, Thatcher and the Politics of Retrenchment*, Cambridge: Cambridge University Press.

Pierson, Paul (ed.) (2001) *The New Politics of the Welfare State*, Oxford: Oxford University Press.

Pierson, Paul (2004) *Politics in Time. History, Institutions, and Social Analysis*, Princeton: Princeton University Press.

Piore, Michael J. and Suzanne Berger (1980) *Dualism and Discontinuity in Industrial Society*, Cambridge: Cambridge University Press.

Pollitt, Christopher (2001) 'Convergence. The Useful Myth?', *Public Management* 79, 933–47.

Pollitt, Christopher (2002) 'Clarifying Convergence. Striking Similarities and Durable Differences in Public Management Reform', *Public Management Review* 4(1), 471–92.

Pollitt, Christopher (2007) 'Convergence or Divergence: What Has Been Happening in Europe?', in Christopher Pollitt, Sandra Van Thiel and Vincent Homburg (eds) *New Public Management in Europe. Adaptation and Alternatives*, Basingstoke: Palgrave.

Pollitt, Christopher and Geert Bouckaert (2011) *Public Management Reform: A Comparative Analysis. New Public Management, Governance, and the Neo-Weberian State*, 3rd ed., Oxford: Oxford University Press.

Powell, Walter W. and Paul DiMaggio (eds) (1991) *The New Institutionalism in Organizational Analysis*, Chicago: University of Chicago Press.

Raadschelders, Jos C.N. and Mark R. Rutgers (1999) 'The Waxing and Waning of the State and its Study: Changes and Challenges in the Study of Public Administration', in Walter J.M. Kickert and Richard J. Stillman (eds) *The Modern State and its Study: New Administrative Science in a Changing Europe and United States*, Cheltenham: Edward Elgar.

Rothenbacher, Franz (1998) 'The Changing Public Sector in Europe: Social Structure, Income and Social Security', *EURODATA Newsletter* 8, 1–6.

Rubery, Jill (2013) 'Public Sector Adjustment and the Threat to Gender Equality', in Daniel Vaughan-Whitehead (ed.) *Public Sector Shock. The Impact of Polocy Retrenchment in Europe*, Cheltenham: Edward Elgar.

Rugge, Fabio (2007) 'Administrative Traditions in Western Europe', in B. Guy Peters and Jon Pierre (eds) *The Sage Handbook of Public Administration*, London: Sage.

Scharpf, Fritz W. (1988) 'The Joint-Decision Trap: Lessons from German Federalism and European Integration', *Public Administration* 66, 239–78.

Scharpf, Fritz W. (2006) 'The Joint-Decision Trap Revisited', *Journal of Common Market Studies* 44, 845–64.

Schneider, Volker, Simon Fink and Marc Tenbrücken (2005) 'Buying Out the State: A Comparative Perspective on the Privatization of Infrastructures', *Comparative Political Studies* 38, 704–27.

Schröder, Martin (2013) *Integrating Varieties of Capitalism and Welfare State Research. A Unified Typology of Capitalisms*, Basingstoke: Palgrave-Macmillan.

Scruggs, Lyle A. and James P. Allan (2008) 'Social Stratification and Welfare Regimes for the Twenty-First Century: Revisiting the Three Worlds of Welfare Capitalism', *World Politics* 60, 642–64.

Steinmo, Sven (2010) *The Evolution of Modern States: Sweden, Japan and the United States*, Cambridge: Cambridge University Press.

Streeck, Wolfgang and Kathleen Thelen (eds) (2005a) *Beyond Continuity: Institutional Change in Advanced Political Economies*, Oxford: Oxford University Press.

Streeck, Wolfgang and Kathleen Thelen (2005b) 'Introduction: Institutional Change in Advanced Political Economies', in Wolfgang Streeck and Kathleen Thelen (eds) *Beyond Continuity. Institutional Change in Advanced Political Economies*, Oxford: Oxford University Press.

Strøm, Kaare, Wolfgang C. Müller and Torbjörn Bergman (eds) (2003) *Delegation and Accountability in Parliamentary Democracies*, Oxford: Oxford University Press.

Suleiman, Ezra (2003) *Dismantling Democratic States*, Princeton: Princeton University Press.

Tepe, Markus, Karin Gottschall and Bernhard Kittel (2010) 'A Structural Fit Between States and Markets? Public Administration Regimes and Market Economy Models in the OECD', *Socio-Economic Review* 8, 653–84.

Tepe, Markus, Bernhard Kittel and Karin Gottschall (2015) 'The Competing State: Transformations of the Public/Private Sector Earnings Gap in Four Countries', in Heinz Rothgang and Steffen Schneider (eds) *State Transformations in OECD Countries: Dimensions, Driving Forces, and Trajectories*, Basingstoke: Palgrave-Macmillan.

Thelen, Kathleen (2012) 'Varieties of Capitalism: Trajectories of Liberalization and the New Politics of Social Solidarity', *Annual Review of Political Science* 15, 137–59.

Traxler, Franz (1999) 'The State in Industrial Relations: A Cross-National Analysis of Developments and Socio-Economic Effects', *European Journal of Political Research* 36, 55–85.

Tsebelis, George (2000) 'Veto Players and Institutional Analysis', *Governance* 13, 441–74.

Tsebelis, George (2002) *Veto Players: How Political Institutions Work*, Princeton: Princeton University Press.

Van der Heijden, Jeroen (2010) 'A Short History of Studying Incremental Institutional Change: Does Explaining Institutional Change Provide any New Explanations?', *Regulation & Governance* 4, 230–43.

Van der Heijden, Jeroen (2011) 'Institutional Layering: A Review of the Use of the Concept', *Politics* 31(1), 9–18.

Van der Heijden, Jeroen (2012) 'Different But Equally Plausible Narratives of Policy Transformation: A Plea for Theoretical Pluralism', *International Political Science Review* 34(1), 57–73.

Van der Meer, Frits M., Trui Steen and Anchrit Wille (2007) 'Western European Civil Service Systems: A Comparative Analysis', in Jos C.N. Raadschelders, Theo A.J. Toonen and Frits M. van der Meer (eds) *The Civil Service in the 21st Century. Comparative Perspectives*, Basingstoke: Palgrave-Macmillan.

Vaughan-Whitehead, Daniel (ed.) (2013) *Public Sector Shock. The Impact of Policy Retrenchment in Europe*, Cheltenham: Edward Elgar.

Weber, Max (1968) *Economy and Society. An Outline of Interpretive Sociology*, Berkeley: University of California Press.

Williamson, Oliver E. (1981) 'The Economics of Organization: The Transaction Cost Approach', *American Journal of Sociology* 87, 548–77.

Wise, Lois (1996) 'Internal Labor Markets', in Hans A.G.M. Bekke, James L. Perry and Theo A.J. Toonen (eds) *Civil Service Systems in Comparative Perspective*, Bloomington: Indiana University Press.

Zohlnhöfer, Reimut, Herbert Obinger and Frieder Wolf (2008) 'Partisan Politics, Globalization, and the Determinants of Privatization Proceeds in Advanced Democracies (1990–2000)', *Governance* 21(1), 95–121.
Zweigert, Konrad and Hein Kötz (1998) *An Introduction to Comparative Law*, 3rd ed., Oxford: Oxford University Press.

3   Research Design and Methods

Beach, Derek and Rasmus Brun Pedersen (2013) *Process-Tracing Methods. Foundations and Guidelines*, Ann Arbor: The University of Michigan Press.
Beck, Nathaniel and Jonathan N. Katz (2011) 'Modeling Dynamics in Time-Series-Cross-Section Political Economy Data', *Annual Review of Political Science* 14, 331–52.
Bergman, Max (ed.) (2008) *Advances in Mixed Methods Research. Theories and Applications*, London: Sage.
Blatter, Joachim K. and Markus Haverland (2012) *Designing Case Studies. Explanatory Approaches in Small-N Research*, Basingstoke: Palgrave.
Charlot, Jean (1994) *La politique en France*, Paris: Librairie generale française.
Collier, David, James Mahoney and Jason Seawright (2004) 'Claiming Too Much: Warnings about Selection Bias', in Henry E. Brady and David Collier (eds) *Rethinking Social Inquiry. Diverse Tools, Shared Standards*, Boulder: Rowman and Littlefield.
Ebbinghaus, Bernhard (2005) 'When Less Is More: Selection Problems in Large-N and Small-N Cross-National Comparisons ', *International Sociology* 20(2), 133–52.
Geddes, Barbara (1991) 'How the Cases You Choose Affect the Answers You Get: Selection Bias in Comparative Politics', in James A. Stimson (ed.) *Political Analysis*, vol. 2, Ann Arbor: University of Michigan Press.
George, Alexander L. and Andrew Bennett (2005) *Case Studies and Theory Development in the Social Sciences*, Cambridge, MA: MIT Press.
Gerring, John (2007) *Case Study Research. Principles and Practices*, Cambridge: Cambridge University Press.
Gomard, Bernhard (1961) 'Civil Law, Common Law and Scandinavian Law', *Scandinavian Studies in Law* 5, 27–38.
Häggroth, Sören, Kai Kronvall, Curt Riberdahl and Karin Rudebeck (1996) *Swedish Local Government. Tradition and Reform*, Stockholm: Swedish Institute.
Hall, Peter A. (2008) 'Systematic Process Analysis: When and How to Use It', *European Political Science* 7, 304–17.
Hoover, Kevin D. (2002) 'Econometrics and Reality', in Uskali Mäki (ed.) *Fact and Fiction in Economics. Models, Realism, and Social Construction*, Cambridge: Cambridge University Press.
Jackman, Robert W. (1985) 'Cross-National Statistical Reseach and the Study of Comparative Politics', *American Journal of Political Science* 29(1), 161–82.
Kasza, Gregory J. (2002) 'The Illusion of Welfare "Regimes"', *Journal of Social Policy* 31, 271–87.
Kersting, Norbert, Janice Caulfield, R. Andrew Nickson, Dele Olowu and Hellmut Wollmann (2009) *Local Governance Reform in Global Perspective*, Wiesbaden: VS Verlag für die Sozialwissenschaften.
King, Gary, Robert Keohane and Sidney Verba (1994) *Designing Social Inquiry. Scientific Inference in Qualitative Research*, Princeton: Princeton University Press.
Kingdom, John (2014) 'United Kingdom', in J.A. Chandler (ed.) *Comparative Public Administration*, 2nd ed., Abingdon: Routledge.

Kittel, Bernhard (2008) 'Statistical Narratives and the Properties of Macro-Level Variables: Labor Market Institutions and Employment Performance in Macrocomparative Research', in Alexander Hicks and Lane Kenworthy (eds) *Method and Substance in Macrocomparative Analysis*, Basingstoke: Palgrave Macmillan.

La Porta, Rafael, Florencio Lopez-de-Silanes and Andrei Shleifer (2008) 'The Economic Consequences of Legal Origins', *Journal of Economic Literature* 46, 285–332.

Lijphart, Arend (1971) 'Comparative Politics and the Comparative Method', *American Political Science Review* 65, 682–93.

Lijphart, Arend (1975) 'The Comparable-Cases Strategy in Comparative Research', *Comparative Political Studies* 8(2), 158–77.

Lodge, Martin (2009) 'Administrative Patterns and National Politics', in B. Guy Peters and Jon Pierre (eds) *The Sage Handbook of Public Administration*, London: Sage.

Mahoney, James and Dietrich Rueschemeyer (eds) (2003) *Comparative Historical Analysis in the Social Sciences*, Cambridge: Cambridge University Press.

Mahoney, Paul G. (2001) 'The Common Law and Economic Growth: Hayek Might Be Right', *Journal of Legal Studies* 30, 503–25.

Mill, John S. (1882) *A System of Logic, Ratiocinative and Inductive, Being a Connected View of the Principles of Evidence, and the Methods of Scientific Investigation*, New York: Harper & Brothers.

Page, Edward C. (1995) 'Administering Europe', in Jack Hayward and Edward C. Page (eds) *Governing the New Europe*, Cambridge: Polity Press.

Pierson, Paul (1994) *Dismantling the Welfare State? Reagan, Thatcher and the Politics of Retrenchment*, Cambridge: Cambridge University Press.

Raadschelders, Jos C.N. and Mark R. Rutgers (1999) 'The Waxing and Waning of the State and its Study: Changes and Challenges in the Study of Public Administration', in Walter J.M. Kickert and Richard J. Stillman (eds) *The Modern State and its Study: New Administrative Science in a Changing Europe and United States*, Cheltenham: Edward Elgar.

Rohlfing, Ingo (2012) *Case Studies and Causal Inference: An Integrative Framework*, Basingstoke: Palgrave.

Rosenberg, Alexander (2012) *Philosophy of Social Science*, 4th ed., Boulder: Westview Press.

Rudzio, Wolfgang (2011) *Das politische System der Bundesrepublik Deutschland*, 8th ed., Wiesbaden: VS Verlag für die Sozialwissenschaften.

Tashakkori, Abbas and Charles Teddlie (eds) (2002) *Handbook of Mixed Methods in Social and Behavioral Research*, London: Sage.

Tepe, Markus, Karin Gottschall and Bernhard Kittel (2010) 'A Structural Fit Between States and Markets? Public Administration Regimes and Market Economy Models in the OECD', *Socio-Economic Review* 8, 653–84.

Tepe, Markus, Bernhard Kittel and Karin Gottschall (2015) 'The Competing State: Transformations of the Public/Private Sector Earnings Gap in Four Countries', in Heinz Rothgang and Steffen Schneider (eds) *State Transformations in OECD Countries. Dimensions, Driving Forces, and Trajectories*, Basingstoke: Palgrave Macmillan.

Tilly, Charles (1984) *Big Structures, Large Processes, Huge Comparisons*, New York: Russell Sage Foundation.

4   Public Employment Regimes in OECD Countries

Afonso, António, Ludger Schuknecht and Vito Tanzi (2005) 'Public Sector Efficiency: An International Comparison', *Public Choice* 123(3–4), 321–47.

Alesina, Alberto, Silvia Ardagna and Francesco Trebbi (2006) *Who Adjusts And When? On The Political Economy Of Stabilizations, IMF Staff Papers* 53, http://scholar.harvard. edu/alesina/publications/who-Adjusts-And-When-Political-Economy-Stabilizations

Armingeon, Klaus, David Weisstanner, Sarah Engler, Panajotis Potolidis and Marlene Gerber (2012) *Comparative Political Data Set I 1960–2010*, Bern: Institute of Political Science, University of Bern.

Bach, Stephen (1999) 'Changing Public Service Employment Relations' in Stephen Bach, Lorenzo Bordogna, Giuseppe Della Rocca and David Winchester (eds) *Public Service Employment Relations in Europe: Transformation, Modernization or Inertia?*, London: Routledge.

Barlow, John, David Farnham, Sylvia Horton and F. F. Ridley (1996) 'Comparing Public Managers', in David Farnham, Sylvia Horton, John Barlow and Annie Hondeghem (eds) *New Public Managers in Europe: Public Servants in Transition*, London: Macmillan.

Baumol, William J. (1993) 'Health Care, Education and the Cost Disease – A Looming Crisis for Public Choice', *Public Choice* 77(1), 17–28.

Baumol, William J. and William G. Bowen (1966) *Performing Arts: The Economic Dilemma*, New York: 20th Century Fund.

Beck, Nathaniel, Johnathan Katz and Richard Tucker (1998) 'Taking Time Seriously: Time-Series-Cross-Section Analysis with a Binary Dependent Variable', *American Journal of Political Science* 42, 1260–88.

Blasius, Jorg and Michael Greenacre (2006) *Multiple Correspondence Analysis and Related Methods*, Boca-Raton: Chapman & Hall.

Bryson, Alex, Bernhard Ebbinghaus and Jelle Visser (2011) 'Introduction: Causes, Consequences and Cures of Union Decline', *European Journal of Industrial Relations* 17(2), 97–105.

Castles, Francis C. and Vance Merrill (1989) 'Towards a General Model of Public Policy Outcomes', *Journal of Theoretical Politics* 1, 177–212.

Christensen, Tom and Per Lægreid (2001) 'New Public Management: The Effects of Contractualism and Devolution on Political Control', *Public Management Review* 3(1), 73–94.

Clausen, Sten E. (1998) *Applied Correspondence Analysis*, London: SAGE University Paper.

Cusack, Thomas R. (1998) *Data on Public Employment and Wages for 21 OECD Countries*, Berlin: WZB.

Cusack, Thomas R., Ton Notermans and Martin Rein (1989) 'Political-Economic Aspects of Public Employment', *European Journal of Political Research* 17, 471–500.

Dahlström, Carl and Victor Lapuente (2010) 'Explaining Cross-Country Differences in Performance-Related Pay in the Public Sector', *Journal of Public Administration Research and Theory* 20, 577–600.

Ebbinghaus, Bernhard and Bernhard Kittel (2005) 'European Rigidity vs. American Flexibility? The Institutional Adaptability of Collective Bargaining', *Work and Occupations* 32(2), 163–95.

Ebbinghaus, Bernhard and Jelle Visser (1999) 'When Institutions Matter: Union Growth and Decline in Western Europe, 1950–1995', *European Sociological Review* 15(2), 135–58.

Ebbinghaus, Bernhard and Jelle Visser (2000) *Trade Unions in Western Europe since 1945*, London: Macmillan-Palgrave.

Esping-Andersen, Gøsta (1990) *The Three Worlds of Welfare Capitalism*, Cambridge: Polity Press.

Garand, James C., Catherine T. Parkhurst and Rusanne J. Seoud (1991) 'Bureaucrats, Policy Attitudes, and Political Behavior: Extension of the Bureau Voting Model of Government Growth', *Journal of Public Administration Research and Theory* 1(2), 177–212.

Georgellis, Yannis, Elisabetta Iossa and Vurain Tabvuma (2011) 'Crowding Out Intrinsic Motivation in the Public Sector', *Journal of Public Administration Research and Theory* 21, 473–93.

Giddens, Anthony (1994) *Beyond Left and Right: The Future of Radical Politics*, Cambridge: Polity Press.

Giger, Nathalie and Moira Nelson (2011) 'The Electoral Consequences of Welfare State Retrenchment: Blame Avoidance or Credit Claiming in the Era of Permanent Austerity?', *European Journal of Political Research* 50(1), 1–23.

Greenacre, Michael. J. (2006) 'From Simple to Multiple Correspondence Analysis', in Jorg Blasius and Michael Greenacre (eds) *Multiple Correspondence Analysis and Related Methods*, Boca-Raton: Chapman & Hall.

Hall, Peter and David Soskice (eds) (2001) *Varieties of Capitalism. The Institutional Foundations of Comparative Advantage*, Oxford: Oxford University Press.

Hicks, Alexander and Christopher Zorn (2005) 'Economic Globalization, the Macro Economy and Reversals of Welfare Expansion in Affluent Democracies, 1978–1994', *International Organization* 59, 631–62.

Hofstede, Geert (2001) *Culture's Consequences: Comparing Values, Behaviors, Institutions and Organizations Across Nations*, Thousand Oaks: Sage.

International Labour Organisation (2008) *LABORSTA: Public Sector Employment*, Geneva: ILO.

Jann, Werner (2011) 'Neues Steuerungsmodell', in Bernhard Blanke, Frank Nullmeier, Christoph Reichard and Göttrik Wewer (eds) *Handbuch zur Verwaltungsreform*, 4th ed., Wiesbaden: VS Verlag.

Keller, Bernd (1999) 'Germany: Negotiated Change, Modernization and the Challenge of Unification', in Stephen Bach, Lorenzo Bordogna, Giuseppe Della Rocca and David Winchester (eds) *Public Service Employment Relations in Europe: Transformation, Modernization or Inertia?*, London: Routledge.

Kittel, Bernhard and Herbert Obinger (2003) 'Political Parties, Institutions, and the Dynamics of Social Expenditure in Times of Austerity', *Journal of European Public Policy* 10(1), 25–45.

La Porta, Rafael, Florencio Lopez-de-Silanes and Andrei Shleifer (2008) 'The Economic Consequences of Legal Origin', *Journal of Economic Literature* 46, 285–332.

La Porta, Rafael, Florencio Lopez-de-Silanes, Andrei Shleifer and Robert W.Vishny (1998) 'Law and Finance', *Journal of Political Economy* 106, 1113–55.

Lijphart, Arend (1999) *Patterns of Democracy: Government Forms and Performance in Thirty-Six Countries*, New Haven: Yale University Press.

Long, J. Scott and Jeremy Freese. (2006) *Regression Models for Categorical Dependent Variables Using Stata*, College Station: Stata Press.

Lonti, Zsuzsanna and Matt Woods (2008) *Towards Government at a Glance: Identification of Core Data and Issues Related to Public Sector Efficiency*, OECD Working Papers on Public Governance No. 7, Paris: OECD.

Miller, Gary. J. (1992) *Managerial Dilemmas: The Political Economy of Hierarchy*, New York: Cambridge University Press.

Miller, Gary J. and Andrew B. Whitford (2002) 'Trust and Incentives in Principal Agent Negotiations: The "Insurance/Incentive Trade-off"', *Journal of Theoretical Politics* 14, 231–67.

OECD (2002) *Public Sector Pay and Employment Data*, Paris: OECD.

OECD (2004) *Public Sector Modernisation: Modernising Public Employment*, OECD Policy Brief, Paris: OECD.

OECD (2005) *Performance-Related Pay Policies for Government Employees*, Paris: OECD.

OECD (2007) *Towards Better Measurement of Government*, OECD Working Papers on Public Governance, vol. 1, Paris: OECD.

OECD (2009a) *COFOG Table IV: Expenditure by Function*, Paris: OECD.

OECD (2009b) *Government at a Glance 2009*, Paris: OECD.

OECD (2011) *Government at a Glance 2011*, Paris: OECD.

OECD (2012) *Public Sector Compensation in Times of Austerity*, Paris: OECD.

OECD Country Note Australia (2009) *Government at a Glance*, http://www.oecd.org/dataoecd/35/37/43925673.pdf

OECD Country Note Austria (2009) *Government at a Glance*, http://www.oecd.org/dataoecd/36/22/43925851.pdf

OECD Country Note Belgium (2009) *Government at a Glance*, http://www.oecd.org/dataoecd/5/6/44124870.pdf

OECD Country Note Canada (2009) *Government at a Glance*, http://www.oecd.org/dataoecd/33/35/43924690.pdf

OECD Country Note Denmark (2009) *Government at a Glance*, http://www.oecd.org/dataoecd/5/50/44124973.pdf

OECD Country Note Finland (2009a) *Government at a Glance*, http://www.oecd.org/dataoecd/35/39/43925746.pdf

OECD Country Note France (2009b) *Government at a Glance*, http://www.oecd.org/dataoecd/35/42/43925776.pdf

OECD Country Note Germany (2009) *Government at a Glance*, http://www.oecd.org/dataoecd/39/48/43933791.pdf

OECD Country Note Ireland (2009) *Government at a Glance*, http://www.oecd.org/dataoecd/46/38/44212694.pdf

OECD Country Note Italy (2005) *Government at a Glance*, http://www.oecd.org/dataoecd/35/43/43925786.pdf

OECD Country Note Japan (2009) *Government at a Glance*, http://www.oecd.org/dataoecd/36/20/43925814.pdf

OECD Country Note Netherlands (2009) *Government at a Glance*, http://www.oecd.org/dataoecd/36/21/43925832.pdf

OECD Country Note Norway (2009) *Government at a Glance*, http://www.oecd.org/dataoecd/35/41/43925766.pdf

OECD Country Note Portugal (2009) *Government at a Glance*, http://www.oecd.org/dataoecd/5/34/44125388.pdf

OECD Country Note Spain (2009) *Government at a Glance*, http://www.oecd.org/dataoecd/5/37/44125528.pdf

OECD Country Note Sweden (2009) *Government at a Glance*, http://www.oecd.org/dataoecd/35/40/43925756.pdf

OECD Country Note Switzerland (2009) *Government at a Glance*, http://www.oecd.org/dataoecd/5/61/44126473.pdf

OECD Country Note United Kingdom (2009) *Government at a Glance*, http://www.oecd.org/dataoecd/5/63/44126619.pdf

OECD Country Note: United States (2009) *Government at a Glance*, http://www.oecd.org/dataoecd/6/1/44126697.pdf

OECD Social Expenditure Database (SOCX) (2012) *Social Expenditure – Aggregated data*, Paris: OECD http://stats.oecd.org/Index.aspx?DataSetCode=SOCX_AGG

Painter, Martin and B. Guy Peters (eds) (2010) *Tradition and Public Administration*, Hampshire: Palgrave Macmillan.

Parry, Richard (2007) 'The Changing Cost of Government: Trends in the State Overhead Budget', in Francis G. Castles (ed.) *The Disappearing State?*, Cheltenham: Edward Elgar.

Pennings, Paul (1999) 'Explaining Variations in Public Employment', *International Journal of Comparative Sociology* 40(3), 332–50.

Perry, James L., Trent A. Eengbers and So Yun Jun (2009) 'So: Back to the Future? Performance-Related Pay, Empirical Research, and the Perils of Persistence', *Public Administration Review* 69(1), 39–51.

Peters, B. Guy and Jon Pierre (2001) 'Civil Servants and Politicians: The Changing Balance', in Guy B. Peters and Jon Pierre (eds) *Politicians, Bureaucrats and Administrative Reform*, London: Routledge.

Pierson, Paul (2000) 'Increasing Returns, Path Dependence, and the Study of Politics', *American Political Science Review* 94(2), 251–68.

Pierson, Paul (2001) 'Coping with Permanent Austerity: Welfare State Restructuring in Affluent Democracies', in Paul Pierson (ed.) *The New Politics of the Welfare State*, Oxford: Oxford University Press.

Pierson, Paul (2004) *Politics in Time. History, Institutions, and Social Analysis*, Princeton: Princeton University Press.

Pollitt, Christopher (1990) 'Performance Indicators: Root and Branch', in Martin Cave, Maurice Kogan and Robert Smith (eds) *Output and Performance Measurements in Government: The State of the Art*, London: Jessica Kingsley.

Pollitt, Christopher and Geert Bouckaert (2011) *Public Management Reform: A Comparative Analysis. New Public Management, Governance, and the Neo-Weberian State*, 3rd ed., Oxford: Oxford University Press.

Public Management Department, Statskonsult, Norway (2009) *Use of Performance Contracting in Norway*, http://www.oecd.org/dataoecd/11/41/1902765.pdf

Rose, Richard (1985) *Public Employment in Western Nations*, Cambridge: Cambridge University Press.

Rothenbacher, Franz (1997) 'Public Sector Employment in Europe – Where Will the Decline End?', *EURODATA Newsletter* 6, 1–11.

Rothenbacher, Franz (1998) 'The Changing Public Sector in Europe: Social Structure, Income and Social Security', *EURODATA Newsletter* 8, 1–6.

Schnapp, Kai-Uwe (2004) *Ministerialbürokratien in westlichen Demokratien. Eine vergleichende Analyse*, Opladen: Leske & Budrich.

SGI (2009) Sustainable Governance Indicators (SGI), http://www.sgi-network.org

Suleiman, Ezra (2003) *Dismantling Democratic States*, Princeton: Princeton University Press.

Tepe, Markus (2012) 'The Public/Private Sector Cleavage Revisited. The Impact of Government Employment on Political Attitudes and Behavior in Eleven West European Countries', *Public Administration* 90(1), 230–61.

Tepe, Markus (2015) 'In Public Servants We Trust? A Behavioral Experiment on Public Service Motivation and Trust among Students of Public Administration, Business Sciences and Law', *Public Management Review*, DOI: 10.1080/14719037.2015.1014396.

Tepe, Markus, Karin Gottschall and Bernhard Kittel (2010) 'A Structural Fit between States and Markets? Public Administration Regimes and Market Economy Models in the OECD', *Socio-Economic Review* 8, 653–84.

Tepe, Markus, Bernhard Kittel and Karin Gottschall (2015) 'The Competing State: Transformations of the Public/Private Sector Earnings Gap in Four Countries', in Heinz Rothgang and Steffen Schneider (eds) *State Transformations in OECD Countries. Dimensions, Driving Forces, and Trajectories*, Basingstoke: Palgrave Macmillan.

Tepe, Markus and Pieter Vanhuysse (2010) 'Who Cuts Back and When? The Politics of Delays in Social Expenditure Cutbacks, 1980–2005', *West European Politics* 33(6), 1214–40.

Thelen, Kathleen (2003) 'How Institutions Evolve: Insights from Comparative-Historical Analysis', in James Mahoney and Dietrich Rueschemeyer (eds) *Comparative Historical Analysis in the Social Sciences*, New York: Cambridge University Press.

Thompson, James (2007) 'Labor-Management Relations and Partnerships: Were They Reinvented?' in Guy B. Peters and Jon Pierre (eds) *The Handbook of Public Administration*, London: Sage.

Tufte, Edward (1978) *Political Control of the Economy*, Princeton: Princeton University Press.

Vandenabeele, Wouter (2008) 'Government Calling: Public Service Motivation as an Element in Selecting Government as an Employer of Choice', *Public Administration* 86, 1089–105.

Vaughan-Whitehead, Daniel (2013) *Public Sector Shock. The Impact of Policy Retrenchment in Europe*, Cheltenham: Edward Elgar.

Weaver, Kent (1986) 'The Politics of Blame Avoidance?', *Journal of Public Policy* 6, 371–98.

World Bank (1999) *Sector Employment & Wage Data by Country*. Washington, DC: World Bank.

World Bank (2011) *Worldwide Governance Indicators*, http://info.worldbank.org/governance/wgi/pdf/ge.pdf

5   A Comparison of Public Employment Regimes in Germany, France, Sweden, and the United Kingdom

Andersson, Patrik and Nils Henrik Schager (1999) 'The Reform of Pay Determination in the Swedish Public Sector', in Robert Elliott, Claudio Lucifora and Dominique Meurs (eds.) *Public Sector Pay Determination in the European Union*, Basingstoke: Macmillan.

Arbetsgivarpolitikutredningen (2002) *Den arbetsgivarpolitiska delegeringen i staten – en samlad utvärdering*, Stockholm: Fritze.

Arbetsgivarverket (2009a) *Central Government and Delegated Employer Responsibility – the Swedish Model*, Stockholm: Arbetsgivarverket.

Arbetsgivarverket (2009b) *SAGE – The Member Organization for Government Employers*, Stockholm: Arbetsgivarverket.

Archambault, Édith, Marie Gariazzo, Helmut K. Anheier and Lester M. Salamon (1999) 'France: From Jacobin Tradition to Decentralization', in Lester M. Salamon, Helmut K. Anheier, Regina List, Stefan Toepler, S. Wojciech Sokolowksi and Associates (eds.) *Global Civil Society: Dimensions of the Nonprofit Sector*, vol. 1, Baltimore: The Johns Hopkins Center for Civil Society Studies.

Åsard, Erik (1986) 'Industrial and Economic Democracy in Sweden: From Consensus to Confrontation', *European Journal of Political Research* 14, 207–19.

Audier, Florence, Maya Bacache, Pierre Courtioux and Jérôme Gautié (2012) *The Effects of Pay Reforms and Procurement Strategies on Wage and Employment Inequalities in France's Public Sector*, EWERC Working paper, Manchester: European Work and Employment Research Centre.

Auer, Astrid, Christoph Demmke and Robert Polet (1996) *Civil Services in the Europe of Fifteen: Current Situation and Prospects*, Maastricht: European Institute of Public Administration.

Bach, Stephen and Lorenzo Bordogna (2011) 'Varieties of New Public Management or Alternative Models? The Reform of Public Service Employment Relations in Industrialized Democracies', *International Journal of Human Resource Management* 22, 2281–94.

Bargain, Olivier and Blaise Melly (2008) *Public Sector Pay Gap in France: New Evidence Using Panel Data*, Discussion paper IZA DP No. 3427, Bonn: Institute for the Study of Labour.

Béduwé, Catherine and Jordis Planas (2002) *Educational Expansion and the Labour Market. Hausse d'éducation et marché du travail. Comparative Study Conducted in Five European Countries, France, Germany, Italy, Spain and the United Kingdom, with Reference to the United States. Final Report*, http://cordis.europa.eu/documents/documentlibrary/70595711EN6.pdf

Bender, Keith A. and Robert F. Elliott (2003) *Decentralised Pay Setting. A Study of the Outcomes of Collective Bargaining Reform in the Civil Service in Australia, Sweden and the UK*, Aldershot: Ashgate.

Benz, Arthur (1994) *Kooperative Verwaltung. Funktionen, Voraussetzungen und Folgen*, Baden-Baden: Nomos.

Bezès, Philippe (2001) 'Defensive versus Offensive Approaches to Administrative Reform in France (1988–97): The Leadership Dilemmas of French Prime Ministers', *Governance* 14, 99–132.

Bezès, Philippe (2009) *Reinventer l'Etat. Les reformes de l'administration francaise (1962–2008)*, Paris: Presses Universitaires de France.

Bezès, Philippe and Gilles Jeannot (2013) *Public Sector Reform in France: Views and Experiences from Senior Executives', Country Report as Part of the COCOPS Research Project. May 2013*, http://www.cocops.eu/wp-content/uploads/2013/06/France_WP3-Country-Report.pdf (accessed 20 July 2015).

Bodiguel, Jean-Luc (1978) *Les Anciens eleves de L'ENA*, Paris: Presses de la Fondation national des sciences politiques.

Bordogna, Lorenzo and Stefano Neri (2011) 'Convergence Towards an NPM Programme or Different Models? Public Service Employment Relations in Italy and France', *The International Journal of Human Resource Management* 22, 2311–30.

Bourdieu, Pierre (1989) *La Noblesse d'État. Grandes écoles et esprit de corps*, Paris: Les editions de minuit.

Boyne, George, Michael Poole and Glenville Jenkins (1999) 'Human Resource Management in the Public and Private Sectors: An Empirical Comparison', *Public Administration* 77, 407–20.

Brandes, Wolfgang and Friedrich Buttler (1990) *Der Staat als Arbeitgeber. Daten und Analysen zum öffentlichen Dienst in der Bundesrepublik*, Frankfurt am Main: Campus.

Briken, Kendra, Karin Gottschall, Sylvia Hils and Bernhard Kittel (2014), Wandel von Beschäftigung und Arbeitsbeziehungen im öffentlichen Dienst in Deutschland – zur Erosion einer sozialstaatlichen Vorbildrolle', in *Zeitschrift für Sozialreform* 60, 123–48.

Bull, Hans Peter (2006) *Vom Staatsdiener zum öffentlichen Dienstleister: zur Zukunft des Dienstrechts*, Berlin: Edition Sigma.

Burkitt, Brian and Philip Whyman (1994) 'Human Resource Management in the Public and Private Sectors: An Empirical Comparison', *The Political Quarterly* 65(3), 275–84.

Burnham, June (2000) 'Human Resources Flexibilities in France', in David Farnham and Sarah Horton (eds.) *Human Resources Flexibilities in the Public Services: International Perspectives*, Basingstoke: Macmillan.

Burnham, June and Sylvia Horton (2013) *Public Management in the United Kingdom. A New Introduction*, Basingstoke: Palgrave Macmillan.

Chevallier Jacques (1996) 'Public Administration in Statist France', *Public Administration Review* 56(1), 67–74.

Clark, David (2002) 'Neoliberalism and Public Service Reform: Canada in Comparative Perspective', *Canadian Journal of Political Science/Revue canadienne de science politique* 35, 771–93.

Cole, Alistair (1999) 'The Service Public Under Stress', *West European Politics* 22(4), 166–84.

Cole, Alistair (2006) 'Decentralization in France: Central Steering, Capacity Building and Identity Construction', *French Politics* 4(1), 31–57.

Cole, Alistair (2010) 'State Reform in France: From Public Service to Public Management?', *Perspectives on European Politics and Society* 11, 343–57.

Cole, Alistair (2014) 'Not Saying, Not Doing: Convergences, Contingencies and Causal Mechanisms of State Reform and Decentralisation in Hollande´s France', *French Politics* 12(2), 104–35.

Cole, Alistair and Glyn Jones (2005) 'Reshaping the State: Administrative Reform and New Public Management in France', *Governance* 18, 567–88.

Corbett, Anne (2010) 'Public Management Policymaking in France: Legislating the Organic Law on Laws of Finance (LOLF), 1998–2001', *Governance* 23, 225–49.

Crozier, Michel and Jean-Claude Thoenig (1975) 'La régulationdes systèmes organisés complexes. Le cas du système de décision politico-administratif local en France', *Revue Francaise de Sociologie* 16(1), 3–32.

Czerwick, Edwin (2007) *Die Ökonomisierung des öffentlichen Dienstes: Dienstrechtsreformen und Beschäftigungsstrukturen seit 1991*, Wiesbaden: VS Verlag für Sozialwissenschaften.

de Tocqueville, Alexis (1993 [1866]) *L'ancien régime et la Révolution*, Paris: Garnier-Flammarion.

Demmke, Christoph (2011) 'Die Reform der öffentlichen Dienste im internationalen Vergleich', in Rainer Koch, Peter Conrad and Wolfgang H. Lorig (eds.) *New Public Service. Öffentlicher Dienst als Motor der Staats- und Verwaltungsmodernisierung*, 2nd ed., Wiesbaden: Gabler.

Derlien, Hans-Ulrich (2005) 'German Public Administration: Weberian Despite "Modernization"', in Krishna K. Tummala (ed.) *Comparative Bureaucratic Systems*, Lanham: Lexington Books.

Derlien, Hans-Ulrich (2008) 'The German Public Service: Between Tradition and Transformation', in Hans-Ulrich Derlien and Guy Peters (eds.) *The State at Work, Volume 1. Public Sector Employment in Ten Western Countries*, Cheltenham: Edward Elgar.

Deroisières, Alain (2000) *La politique des grands nombres: histoire de la raison statistique*, Paris: La Découverte.

Destatis (2015) Beschäftigte nach Art des Dienst- oder Arbeitsvertragsverhältnisses, https://www.destatis.de/DE/ZahlenFakten/GesellschaftStaat/Oeffentliche FinanzenSteuern/OeffentlicherDienst/Personal/Tabellen/Beschaeftigungsart.html (accessed 15 March 2015).

Deutscher Beamtenbund und Tarifunion (DBB) (2014) Arbeitszeit, http://www.dbb. de/themen/themenartikel/a/arbeitszeit.html (accessed 19 January 2015).

Deutscher Beamtenbund und Tarifunion (DBB) (2015) Entgelttabellen und Beamtenbesoldung, http://www.dbb.de/service/entgelttabellen-und-beamtenbesol-dung.html (accessed 10 April 2015).

Di Luzio, Gaia (2002) *Verwaltungsreform und Reorganisation der Geschlechterbeziehungen*, Frankfurt am Main: Campus.

Duverger, Maurice (1974) *La Monarchie républicaine: ou comment les démocraties se donnent des rois*, Paris: Laffont.

Duverger, Maurice (1980) 'A New Political System Model: Semi-Presidential Government', *European Journal of Political Research* 8(2), 165–87.

Edwards, Arthur and Peter Hupe (2000) 'France: A Strong State, Towards A Stronger Local Democracy?', in Harry Daeman and Linze Schaap (eds.) *Citizen and City: Developments in Fifteen Local Democracies in Europe*, Delft: Eburon.

Ehn, Peter (2011) *I statens tjänst – en roll med många bottnar*, Stockholm: Kompetensrådet för utveckling i staten.

Ehn, Peter, Magnus Isberg, Claes Linde and Gunnar Wallin (2003) 'Swedish Bureaucracy in an Era of Change', *Governance* 16, 429–58.

Ekonomifakta (2014) Privat och offentlig sysselsättning; http://www.ekonomifakta.se/sv/Fakta/Arbetsmarknad/Sysselsattning/Privat-och-offentlig-sysselsattning/ (accessed 30 March 2015).

Elgie, Robert and Steven Griggs (2000) *French Politics: Debates and Controversies*, Abingdon: Routledge.

Esping-Andersen, Gøsta (1990) *The Three Worlds of Welfare Capitalism*, Cambridge: Polity Press.

European Foundation for the Improvement of Living and Working Conditions (EUROFOUND) (2007) *Industrial Relations in the Public Sector Report*, http://eurofound.europa.eu/sites/default/files/ef_files/docs/eiro/tn0611028s/tn0611028s.pdf

European University Institute (2008) *Study on the Division of Powers between the European Union, the Member States, and Regional and Local Authorities*, Brussels: Committee of the Regions.

Eurostat (2015) Gender Pay Gap Statistics, http://ec.europa.eu/eurostat/statistics-explained/index.php/Gender_pay_gap_statistics (accessed 10 April 2015).

Ewald, François, Christian Gollier and Nicolas de Sadeleer (2009) *Le Principe de précaution*, Paris: Presses Universitaire de France.

Farnham, David and Sylvia Horton (eds.) (1996) *Managing People in the Public Services*, Basingstoke: Macmillan.

Ferner, Anthony (1994) 'The State as Employer', in Richard Hyman and Anthony Ferner (eds.) *New Frontiers in European Industrial Relations*, Oxford: Blackwell.

Forest, Virginie (2008) 'Performance-Related Pay and Work Motivation: Theoretical and Empirical Perspectives for the French Civil Service', *International Review of Administrative Sciences* 74, 325–39.

Förvaltningspolitiska kommissionen (1997) *I medborgarnas tjänst – en samlad förvaltningspolitik för staten*, Stockholm: Fritze.

Gautié, Jérôme (2013) 'France: "The Public Service under Pressure"', in Daniel Vaughan-Whitehead (ed.) *Public Sector Shock. The Impact of Policy Retrenchment in Europe*, Cheltenham: Edward Elgar.

Godin, Emmanuel and Tony Chafer (eds.) (2005) *The French Exception*, Oxford: Berghahn Books.

Goetz, Klaus H. (2000) 'The Development and Current Features of the German Civil Service System', in Hans A.G.M. Bekke and Frits M. van der Meer (eds.) *Civil Service Systems in Western Europe*, Cheltenham and Northampton: Elgar.

Gonäs, Lena (1999) 'Die 90er Jahre: Das Jahrzehnt des Rückzugs? Männer und Frauen auf dem schwedischen Arbeitsmarkt', in Claudius Riegler and Olaf Schneider (eds.) *Schweden im Wandel – Entwicklungen, Probleme, Perspektiven*, Berlin: Verlag A. Spitz.

Gornick, Janet C. and Jerry A. Jacobs (1998) 'Gender, the Welfare State, and Public Employment: A Comparative Study of Seven Industrialized Countries', *American Sociological Review* 63, 688–710.

Gottschall, Karin (2009) 'Der Staat und seine Diener: Metamorphosen eines wohlfahrtsstaatlichen Beschäftigungsmodells', in Herbert Obinger and Elmar Rieger (eds.) *Wohlfahrtsstaatlichkeit in entwickelten Demokratien: Herausforderungen, Reformen und Perspektiven*, Frankfurt am Main: Campus Verlag.

Grémion, Pierre (1976) *Le pouvoir peripherique: Bureaucrates et notable dans le système politique francais*, Paris: Le Seuil.

Grimshaw, Damian (2013) 'Austerity, Privatization and Levelling Down. Public Sector Reforms in the United Kingdom', in David Vaughan-Whitehead (ed.) *Public Sector Shock. The Impact of Policy Retrenchment in Europe*, Cheltenham: Edward Elgar.

Günther, Hellmuth (2010) 'Gesetzgebungskompetenzen für das Beamtenrecht, Kodifikationen des allgemeinen Beamtenrechts – Vom Kaiserreich bis zur Bundesrepublic nach der Föderalismusreform', *Zeitschrift für Beamtenrecht* 1–2, 1–21.

Gustafsson, Lennart and Arne Svensson (1999) *Public Sector Reform in Sweden*, Malmö: Liber Ekonomi.

Häggroth, Sören, Kai Kronvall, Curt Riberdahl and Karin Rudebeck (1999) *Swedish Local Government. Traditions and Reforms*, 3rd rev. ed., Stockholm: The Swedish Institute.

Haug, Ralph (2004) 'The History of Industrial Democracy in Sweden: Industrial Revolution to 1980', *International Journal of Management* 21, 7–15.

Hebeler, Timo (2008) *Verwaltungspersonal. Eine rechts- und verwaltungswissenschaftliche Strukturierung*, Baden-Baden: Nomos.

Hils, Sylvia and Sebastian Streb (2010) *Vom Staatsdiener zum Dienstleister? Veränderungen öffentlicher Beschäftigungssysteme in Deutschland, Grossbritannien, Frankreich und Schweden*, TranState Working Paper 111, Bremen: CRC 597 Collaborative Research Centre 597 – Transformations of the State, University of Bremen.

Hood, Christopher (1991) 'A Public Management for All Seasons?', *Public Administration* 69(1), 3–19.

Hood, Christopher (1995) 'The "New Public Management" in the 1980s: Variations on a Theme', *Accounting, Organizations and Society* 20(2–3), 93–109.

Hustedt, Thurid and Jan Tiessen (2006) *Central Government Coordination in Denmark, Germany and Sweden – An Institutional Policy Perspective*, Potsdam: Universitätsverlag Potsdam.

Innenministerium des Landes Nordrhein-Westfalen (ed.) (2003) *Zukunft des öffentlichen Dienstes – öffentlicher Dienst der Zukunft. Bericht der von der Landesregierung Nordrhein-Westfalen eingesetzten Regierungskommission*, Düsseldorf.

Jacobsson, Bengt and Göran Sundström (2009) 'Between Autonomy and Control: Transformation of the Swedish Administrative Model', in Paul G. Roness and Harald Sætren (eds.) *Change and Continuity in Public Sector Organizations – Essays in Honour of Per Lægreid*, Bergen: Fagbokforlaget.

Jahn, Detlef (2003) 'Das politische System Schwedens', in Wolfgang Ismayr (ed.) *Die politischen Systeme Westeuropas*, 3rd ed., Opladen: Leske + Budrich.

Jann, Werner (2000) 'Verwaltungskulturen im internationalen Vergleich. Ein Überblick über den Stand der empirischen Forschung', *Die Verwaltung* 33, 325–49.

Jarvis, Richard (2002) *The UK Experience of Public Administration Reform. Current Good Practices and New Developments in Public Service Management,* London: Commonwealth Secretariat.

Jeannot, Gilles (2003) 'The "Service Project" Experience in the French Civil Service', *International Journal of Public Sector Management* 16, 459–67.

Jeannot, Gilles (2006) 'Diffusing Values or Adjusting Practices? A Review of Research on French Public Utilities', *International Journal of Public Sector Management* 19, 598–608.

Jörges-Süß, Katharina (2007) *Leistungsbezogene Bezahlung in der Öffentlichen Verwaltung. Eine neoinstitutionalistisch-historische Analyse,* München: Rainer Hampp.

Kadritzke, Ulf (1982) 'Angestellte als Lohnarbeiter. Ein kritischer Nachruf auf die deutsche Kragenline', in Gert Schmidt, Hans-Joachim Braczyk and Jost von dem Knesebeck (eds.) *Materialien zur Industriesoziologie, Supplement 24 of Kölner Zeitschrift für Soziologie und Sozialpsychologie,* Opladen: Westdeutscher Verlag, 219–49.

Kananen, Johannes (2014) *The Nordic Welfare State in Three Eras: From Emancipation to Discipline,* Farnhem: Ashgate.

Keller, Berndt (2006) 'Aktuelle Entwicklungen der Beschäftigungsbeziehungen im öffentlichen Dienst', *Die Verwaltung* 39, 79–99.

Keller, Berndt (2008) 'Wandel der Arbeitsbeziehungen im öffentlichen Dienst: Entwicklungen und Perspektiven', in: Reinhold Sackmann, Bernadette Jonda and Maria Reinhold (eds.), *Demographie als Herausforderung für den öffentlichen Sektor,* Wiesbaden: VS Verlag für die Sozialwissenschaften.

Keller, Berndt (2010) *Arbeitspolitik im öffentlichen Dienst. Ein Überblick über Arbeitsmärkte und Arbeitsbeziehungen,* Berlin: Edition Sigma.

Keller, Berndt and Hartmut Seifert (2014) 'Atypische Beschäftigungsverhältnisse im Öffentlichen Dienst', *WSI-Mitteilungen* 8/2014, 1–12.

Kersting, Norbert, Janice Caulfield, R. Andrew Nickson, Dele Olowu and Hellmut Wollmann (2009) *Local Governance Reform in Global Perspective,* Wiesbaden: VS Verlag für die Sozialwissenschaften.

Kettunen, Pauli (2006) 'The Power of International Comparison. A Perspective on the Making and the Challenging of the Nordic Welfare State', in Niels F. Christiansen, Klaus Peteresen, Nils Edling and Per Haave (eds.) *The Nordic Model of Welfare. A Historical Reappraisal,* Copenhagen: Tusculanum Press.

Kickert, Walter J. M. (ed.) (1997) *Public Management and Administrative Reform in Western Europe,* Cheltenham: Edward Elgar.

Knill, Christoph (1999) 'Explaining Cross-National Variance in Administrative Reform: Autonomous versus Instrumental Bureaucracies', *Journal of Public Policy* 19(2), 113–39.

Koch, Rainer (2008) *Strategischer Wandels des Managements öffentlicher Dienste,* Wiesbaden: Gabler Edition Wissenschaft.

Koetter, Matthias (2010) 'Rechtsstaat and Rechtsstaatlichkeit in Germany', in Matthias Koetter and Gunnar Folke Schuppert (eds.) *Understandings of the Rule of Law in various Legal Orders of the World,* Rule of Law Working Paper Series Nr. 1, Berlin.

Kommittén angående den arbetsgivarpolitiska delegeringen (1997) *Arbetsgivarpolitik i staten – för kompetens och resultat,* Stockholm: Fritze.

Kroos, Daniela (2010) *Warum hat 'Marianne' so viele Diener? Zum Wachstum des französischen öffentlichen Dienstes entgegen internationaler Trends,* TranState Working Paper 115, Bremen: CRC 597 Collaborative Research Centre 597 – Transformations of the State, University of Bremen.

Kuhlmann, Sabine (2011) 'Decentralization in France: The "Jacobin" State Stuck between Continuity and Transformation', *Croatian and Comparative Public Administration* 11, 311–36.

Kuhlmann, Sabine, Jörg Bogumil and Stephan Grohs (2008) 'Evaluating Administrative Modernization in German Local Governments: Success or Failure of the "New Steering Model"?', *Public Administration Review* 68, 851–63.

Kuhlmann, Sabine and Manfred Röber (2004) 'Civil Service in Germany: Characteristics of Public Employment and Modernization of Public Personnel Management' at the Conference *Modernization of State and Administration in Europe: A France-Germany Comparison, 14–15 May 2004*, presentation, Bordeaux: Goethe-Institut.

Kuhlmann, Sabine and Hellmut Wollmann (2010) *Verwaltung in Europa. Verwaltungssysteme und -reformen in vergleichender Perspektive*, manuscript, Hagen: FernUniversität Hagen.

Lecheler, Helmut (2007) 'Die Auswirkungen der Föderalismusreform auf die Statusrechte der Beamten', *Zeitschrift für Beamtenrecht* 55(1–2), 18–23.

Lehmbruch, Gerhard (1991) 'The Organization of Society, Administrative Strategies, and Policy Networks. Elements of a Developmental Theory of Interest Systems', in Roland M. Czada and Adrienne Windhoff-Héritier (eds.) *Political Choice. Institutions, Rules, and the Limits of Rationality*, Frankfurt am Main: Campus Verlag.

Leyland, Peter (2012) *The Constitution of the United Kingdom. A Contextual Analysis*, Oxford: Hart.

Lorig, Wolfgang H. (2011) 'Das Laufbahnwesen nach der Föderalismusreform – Auf dem Weg zu größerer Flexibilisierung und erhöhter Disponierbarkeit?', in Rainer Koch, Peter Conrad and Wolfgang H. Lorig (eds.) *New Public Service. Öffentlicher Dienst als Motor der Staats- und Verwaltungsmodernisierung*, 2nd ed., Wiesbaden: Gabler.

Lorse, Jürgen (2007) 'Aktuelle tarif- und dienstrechtliche Reformüberlegungen im öffentlichen Dienst – eine Zwischenbilanz', *Zeitschrift für Beamtenrecht* 55(1/2), 24–35.

Lovecy, Jill (1999) 'The End of French Exceptionalism?', *West European Politics* 22, 205–24.

Lucifora, Claudio and Dominique Meurs (2006) 'The Public Sector Pay Gap in France, Great Britain and Italy', *Review of Income and Wealth* 52(1), 43–59.

Mayntz, Renate (1985) *Soziologie der öffentlichen Verwaltung*, 3rd ed., Heidelberg: C.F. Müller Juristischer Verlag.

McLaughlin, Kate and Stephen P. Osborne (2002) 'Current Trends and Future Prospects of Public Management. A Guide', in Kate McLaughlin, Stephen P. Osborne and Ewan Ferlie (eds.) *New Public Management. Current Trends and Future Prospects*, London: Routledge.

Mehde, Veith (2011) 'Arbeitsbeziehungen im Rahmen der Modernisierung von Staat und Verwaltung', in Rainer Koch, Peter Conrad & Wolfgang H. Lorig (eds.) *New Public Service. Öffentlicher Dienst als Motor der Staats- und Verwaltungsmodernisierung*, Wiesbaden: Gabler Verlag.

Meunier, Sophie (2000) 'The French Exception', *Foreign Affairs* 4, 104–16.

Ministère de la décentralisation et de la fonction publique (2014) *Rapport annuel sur l'état de la fonction publique. Politiques et pratiques de ressources humaines. Faits et chiffres*, http://www.fonction-publique.gouv.fr/files/files/statistiques/rapports_annuels/2014/pdf/RA_2014_opti.pdf (accessed 20 July 2015).

Ministère du Budget, des Comptes Publics et de la Fonction Publique (2008) *Rapport annuel sur l'état dela fonction publique – Faits et chiffres 2007–2008*, Paris: La Documentation Francaise.

Ministry of the Budget (1978) *Public Employment in Sweden. Procedures for Determining Conditions of Work and Employment in the Public Service*, Stockholm: LiberFörlag.

Moran, Michael (2006) 'The Transformation of the British State: From Club Government to State-Administered High Modernism', in Jonah D. Levy (ed.) *The State after Statism: New State Activities in the Age of Liberalization*, Cambridge, MA: Harvard University Press.

Morgan, Philip and Nigel Allington (2003) 'Private Sector "Good", Public Sector "Bad"? Transformation or Transition in the UK Public Sector?', *Scientific Journal of Administrative Development* 1, 22–53.

Mossé, Philippe and Robert Tchobanian (1999) 'France: The Restructuring of Employment Relations in the Public Services', in Stephen Bach, Lorenzo Bordogna, Giuseppe Della Rocca and David Winchester (eds.) *Public Service Employment Relations in Europe: Transformation, Modernization or Inertia?*, London: Routledge.

Murray, Richard (2000) 'Human Resources Management in Swedish Central Government', in David Farnham and Sarah Horton (eds.) *Human Resources Flexibilities in the Public Services: International Perspectives*, Basingstoke: Macmillan.

Naschold, Frieder (1996) *New Frontiers in Public Sector Management: Trends and Issues in State and Local Government in Europe*, Berlin: de Gruyter.

Négrier, Emmanuel (1999) 'The Changing Role of French Local Government', *West European Politics* 22(4), 120–40.

OECD (2005) *Performance-Related Pay Policies for Government Employees*, Paris: OECD.

OECD (2012) *Human Resources Management Country Profiles, United Kingdom*, Paris: OECD.

OECD (2011) *Government at a Glance 2011*, Paris: OECD.

Office for National Statistics (2014) Public Sector Employment, Q3 2014, http://www.ons.gov.uk/ons/publications/re-reference-tables.html?edition=tcm%3A77–335609 (accessed 10 April 2015).

Osborne, Stephen P. and Kate McLaughlin (2008) 'The Study of Public Management in Great Britain. Public Service Delivery and Its Management', in W. J. M. Kickert (ed.) *Routledge Studies in Public Management, Vol. 2, the Study of Public Management in Europe and the US. A Competitive Analysis of National Distinctiveness*, London: Routledge.

Page, Edward (2010) 'Has the Whitehall Model Survived?', *International Review of Administrative Sciences* 76, 407–23.

Parliamentary Auditors (1995) *Statlig Personalpolitik, Report 1993–15–12*, Stockholm.

Parry, Richard (1985) 'Britain. Stable Aggregates, Changing Composition', in Richard Rose (ed.) *Public Employment in Western Nations*, Cambridge: Cambridge University Press.

Parry, Richard (2011) 'The United Kingdom Civil Service. A Devolving System', in Andrew Massey (ed.) *International Handbook on Civil Service Systems*, Cheltenham: Edward Elgar.

Peters, B. Guy (1985) 'Sweden: The Explosion of Public Employment', in Richard Rose (ed.) *Public Employment in Western Nations*, Cambridge: Cambridge University Press.

Peters, B. Guy (2008) 'The Napoleonic Tradition', *International Journal of Public Sector Management* 21(2), 118–32.

Petersson, Olof (1994) *Swedish Government and Politics*, Stockholm: Fritzes.

Pierre, Jon (2001) 'Parallel Paths? Administrative Reform, Public Policy and Politico-Bureaucratic Relationships in Sweden', in B. Guy Peters and Jon Pierre (eds.) *Politicians, Bureaucrats and Administrative Reform*, London: Routledge.

Pierre, Jon (2003) 'When the Bottom Line Is the Bottom Line: Public Sector Reform in Sweden', in Joachim Jens Hesse, Christopher Hood and Guy B. Peters (eds.) *Paradoxes in Public Sector Reform: An International Comparison*, Berlin: Duncker & Humblot.

Pierre, Jon (2010) 'Administrative Reform in Sweden: The Resilience of Administrative Tradition?', in Martin Painter and B. Guy Peters (eds.) *Tradition and Public Administration*, Basingstoke: Palgrave.

Pochard, Marcel (2011) *Les 100 Mots de la Foction Publique*, Paris: Presses Universitaires de France.

Pollitt, Christopher and Geert Bouckaert (2011) *Public Management Reform: A Comparative Analysis. New Public Management, Governance, and the Neo-Weberian State*, 3rd ed., Oxford: Oxford University Press.

Pontusson, Jonas (1992) 'At the End of the Third Road: Swedish Social Democracy in Crisis', *Politics & Society* 20, 305–32.

Premfors, Rune (1991) 'The "Swedish Model" and Public Sector Reform', *West European Politics* 14, 83–95.

Premfors, Rune (1998) 'Reshaping the Democratic State: Swedish Experiences in a Comparative Perspective', *Public Administration* 76(Spring), 141–59.

Prowse, Peter and Julie Prowse (2007) 'Is There Still a Public Sector Model of Employment Relations in the United Kingdom?', *International Journal of Public Sector Management* 20, 48–62.

Röber, Manfred and Elke Löffler (2000) 'Germany: the Limitations of Flexibility Reforms', in David Farnham and Sylvia Horton (eds.) *Human Resources Flexibilities in the Public Services. International Perspectives*, Basingstoke: Macmillan.

Rosanvallon, Pierre (1990) *L' Etat en France de 1789 à nos jours*, Paris: Le Seuil.

Rouban, Luc (2007) 'Public Management and Politics: Senior Bureaucrats in France', *Public Administration* 85, 473–501.

Rouban, Luc (2008a) 'Reform without Doctrine: Public Management in France', *International Journal of Public Sector Management* 21(2), 133–49.

Rouban, Luc (2008b) 'The French Paradox: A Huge but Fragmented Public Service', in Hans-Ulrich Derlien and B. Guy Peters (eds.) *The State at Work, Volume 1: Public Sector Employment in Ten Western Countries*, Cheltenham: Edward Elgar.

Schalauske, Jan and Sebastian Streb (2008), '"Wettbewerbsmodernisierung" im Wohlfahrtsstaat: Die Reorganisation öffentlicher Infrastrukturdienstleistungen in Schweden', in Hans-Jürgen Bieling, Christina Deckwirth and Stefan Schmalz (eds.) *Liberalisierung und Privatisierung in Europa: Die Reorganisation der öffentlichen Infrastruktur in der Europäischen Union*, Münster: Westfälisches Dampfboot.

Schmidt, Klaus-Dieter and Richard Rose (1985) 'Germany: The Expansion of an Active State', in Richard Rose (ed.) *Public Employment in Western Nations*, Cambridge: Cambridge University Press.

Schröter, Eckhard (2001) 'A Solid Rock in Rough Seas? Institutional Change and Continuity in the German Federal Bureaucracy', in B. Guy Peters and Jon Pierre (eds.) *Politicians, Bureaucrats and Administrative Reform*, London: Routledge.

Schunter-Kleemann, Susanne (ed.) (1992) *Herrenhaus Europa – Geschlechterverhältnisse im Wohlfahrtsstaat*, Berlin: Edition Sigma.

Siciliani, Jean-Ludovic (2008) *Livre Blanc sur l'avenir de la fonction publique. Faire des services publics et la fonction publique des atouts pour la France*, Paris: La Documentation française.

Siewert, Beate and Thilo Wendler (2005) 'Die Klassifizierung von Kommunen – ein Ansatz zur Vergleichbarkeit deutscher Städte und Gemeinden', in Statistisches

Bundesamt (ed.) *Wirtschaft und Statistik 08/2005*, Wiesbaden: Statistisches Bundesamt.

Smith, Bo and Christine Lidbury (1996) 'Human Resource Management Reforms in the Swedish State Sector', in OECD (ed.) *Integrating People Management into Public Service Reform*, Paris: OECD.

Statistics Sweden (2008) *Public Finances in Sweden 2008*, Örebro: Statistics Sweden.

Statistisches Bundesamt (2000) *Finanzen und Steuern: Personal des öffentlichen Dienstes 1999*, Wiesbaden: Statistisches Bundesamt.

Statistisches Bundesamt (2010) *Finanzen und Steuern: Personal des öffentlichen Dienstes 2009*, Wiesbaden: Statistisches Bundesamt.

Statistisches Bundesamt (2012) *Finanzen und Steuern: Personal des öffentlichen Dienstes 2011*, Wiesbaden: Statistisches Bundesamt.

Statistiska centralbyrån (2011) *Löner och sysselsättning inom statlig sektor 2010*.

Statistiska centralbyrån (2014) Sysselsatta inom offentlig sektor (statlig-, landstings-, primärkommunal-, kyrkokommunal- samt övrig sektor) efter sektor och kön. År 1992 – 2013, http://www.statistikdatabasen.scb.se/pxweb/sv/ssd/START__AM__AM0104__AM0104C/Statlig12g/?rxid=b1fd2726–1175–4a3d-ac6b-620d7d16f7bd (accessed 30 March 2015).

Studienkommission (1973) *Reform des Öffentlichen Dienstrechts. Vorschläge aus dem Bericht der Studienkommission*, Baden-Baden: Nomos.

Sveriges Kommuner och Landsting (SKL) (2015) Om SKL, http://skl.se/tjanster/omskl.409.html (accessed 10 April 2015).

Swedish Association of Local Authorities and Regions (2009) *The Swedish Association of Local Authorities and Regions (SALAR) – A Presentation*, Stockholm.

Swedish Ministry of Finance (1995) *The Public Sector Labour Market in Sweden. A Presentation*, Stockholm: Swedish Ministry of Finance.

Thoenig, Jean-Claude (2005) 'Territorial Administration And Political Control: Decentralisation in France', *Public Administration* 83, 685–708.

Tümmers, Hans J. (2006) *Das politische System Frankreichs. Eine Einführung*, München: C.H. Beck.

Vimont, Claude and Geneviève Gontier (1965) 'Une enquête sur les femmes fonctionnaires', *Population* 20(1), 21–52.

Von Bandemer, Stephan and Josef Hilbert (2005) 'Vom aktivierenden zum expandieren Staat', in Bernhard Blanke, Frank Nullmeier, Christoph Reichard and Göttrik Wewer (eds.) *Handbuch zur Verwaltungsreform*, Wiesbaden.

Von Otter, Casten (1994) 'Reform Strategies in the Swedish Public Sector', in Frieder Naschold and Marga Pröhl (eds.) *Produktivität öffentlicher Dienstleistungen*, Gütersloh: Bertelsmann-Stiftung.

Von Otter, Casten (1996) '"Creative Destruction" of the Public Sector? Approaching Welfare Markets in Sweden', in Frieder Naschold and Casten von Otter (eds.) *Public Sector Transformation. Rethinking Markets and Hierarchies in Government*, Amsterdam: Benjamins.

Von Otter, Casten (1999) 'Öffentlicher Sektor im Wohlfahrtsstaat', in Claudius Riegler and Olaf Schneider (eds.) *Schweden im Wandel – Entwicklungen, Probleme, Perspektiven*, Berlin: Berlin-Verlag Spitz.

Wegrich, Kai (2009) 'Public Management Reform in the United Kingdom. Great Leaps, Small Steps and Policies as Their Own Cause', in Shaun F. Goldfinch and Joe L. Wallis (eds.) *International Handbook of Public Management Reform*, Cheltenham: Edward Elgar.

Wilks, Stuart (1996) 'Sweden', in Norman Flynn and Franz Strehl (eds.) *Public Sector Management in Europe*, London: Prentice-Hall.

Winchester, David and Stephen Bach (1999) 'Britain. The Transformation of Public Service Employment Relations', in Stephen Bach, Lorenzo Bordogna, Giuseppe Della Rocca and David Winchester (eds.) (1999) *Public Service Employment Relations in Europe: Transformation, Modernization or Inertia?*, London: Routledge.

Wise, Lois Recascino (1993) 'Whither Solidarity? Transitions in Swedish Public-Sector Policy', *British Journal of Industrial Relations* 31(1), 75–95.

Wolff, Heinrich Amadeus (2009) 'Die Reformpolitik der kleinen Schritte. Zum Erlass des Gesetzes zur Neuordnung und Modernisierung des Bundesdienstrechts (Dinestrechtsneuordnungsgesetz, DNeuG)', *Zeitschrift für Beamtenrecht*(3), 73–79.

Wollmann, Hellmut (1996) 'Institutionenbildung in Ostdeutschland: Neubau, Umbau und "schöpferische Zerstörung"', in Max Kaase, Andreas Eisen, Oscar W. Gabriel and Oskar Niedermayer (eds.) *Politisches System*, Opladen: Leske+Budrich.

Wollmann, Hellmut (2008) Comparing Local Government Reforms in England, Sweden, France and Germany, http://www.wuestenrot-stiftung.de/download/local-government (accessed 10 April 2015).

Yates, Jacqueline (2000) 'Sweden', in J. A. Chandler (ed.) *Comparative Public Administration*, London: Routledge.

6   Energy Regulatory Agencies

Andersson, Patrik and Nils H. Schager (1999) 'The Reform of Pay Determination in the Swedish Public Sector', in Robert Elliott, Claudio Lucifora and Dominique Meurs (eds.) *Public Sector Pay Determination in the European Union*, Basingstoke: Macmillan.

Arbetsgivarverket (2009a) *Central Government and Delegated Employer Responsibility – the Swedish Model*, Stockholm: Arbetsgivarverket.

Arbetsgivarverket (2009b) *Chef i staten. Din roll som arbetsgivare*, Stockholm: Arbetsgivarverket.

Arbetsgivarverket (2009c) *SAGE – The Member Organization for Government Employers*, Stockholm: Arbetsgivarverket.

Arbetsgivarverket (2009d) *Working as a Government Employee in Sweden – Benefits and Terms of Employment*, Stockholm: Arbetsgivarverket.

Bach, Stephen (2009) *Industrial Relations in the Public Sector – United Kingdom*, http://www.eurofound.europa.eu/eiro/studies/tn0611028s/uk0611029q.htm (accessed 20 July 2015).

Bertelsmann Stiftung (ed.) (2004) *Leistungssteigerung und Fortschritt im öffentlichen Bereich: Organisationskultur und Wettbewerb*, Gütersloh: Bertelsmann.

Bossaert, Danielle, Christoph Demmke, Koen Nomden, Robert Polet and Astrid Auer (2001) *Der öffentliche Dienst im Europa der Fünfzehn. Trends und neue Entwicklungen*, Maastricht: European Institute of Public Administration.

Bower, John (2003) *Why Ofgem?*, https://www.ofgem.gov.uk/ofgem-publications/37510/4858-oxford-instituteenergystudies.pdf (accessed 20 July 2015).

Bundesnetzagentur (2009) *Annual Report 2008*, Bonn: Federal Network Agency for Electricity, Gas, Telecommunications, Post and Railway.

Burnham, Jane and Robert Pyper (2008) *Britain's Modernised Civil Service*, Basingstoke: Palgrave Macmillan.

Cabinet Office (2006) *Civil Service Reward Principles*, http://www.civilservice.gov.uk/Assets/CivilServiceReward_tcm6–35261.pdf

Cabinet Office (2010) *Senior Civil Service. HR Practitioner's Guide to SCS Reward, Benefits & Recruitment for 2010–11*, London.

Cameron, Peter D. (2007) *Competition in Energy Markets: Law and Regulation in the European Union*, 2nd ed., New York: Oxford University Press.

Civil Service Commission (2011) *Chairing Competitions – A Guide to the Approach of the Civil Service Commission*, London.

Cole, Gerald A. (2002) *Personnel and Human Resource Management*, 5th ed., London: Thomson.

Commission de Régulation de l'Électricité (2001) *Rapport d' Activité Juin 2001*, Paris.

Commission de Régulation de l'Énergie (2003) *Activity Report 2003*, Paris.

Commission de Régulation de l'Énergie (2006) *Activity Report June 2006*, Paris.

Commission de Régulation de l'Énergie (2007) *Activity Report June 2007*, Paris.

Commission de Régulation de l'Énergie (2008) *Activity Report June 2008*, Paris.

Commission de Régulation de l'Énergie (2009) *Activity Report 2009*, Paris.

Commission de Régulation de l'Energie (2011) *Activity Report 2011*, Paris.

Commission de Régulation de l'Energie (2014) *Activity Report 2013*, Paris.

Conseil d'État (2001) *Rapport Public 2001: Jurisprudence et avis de 2000 – Les autorités administratives indépendantes*, Paris.

Cross, Eugene D. (1996) *Electric Utility Regulation in the European Union: A Country by Country Guide*, London: Wiley.

Eberlein, Burkhard (2005) 'Configurations of Economic Regulation in the European Union: the Case of Electricity in Comparative Perspective', *Current Politics and Economics of Europe* 16, 37–62.

Eising, Rainer (2000) *Liberalisierung und Europäisierung: die regulative Reform der Elektrizitätsversorgung in Großbritanien, der Europäischen Gemeinschaft und der Bundesrepublik Deutschland*, Opladen: Leske + Budrich.

Eising, Rainer (2002) 'Policy Learning in Embedded Negotiations: Explaining EU Electricity Liberalization', *International Organization* 56(1), 85–120.

Elgie, Robert (2006) 'Why Do Governments Delegate Authority to Quasi-Autonomous Agencies? The Case of Independent Administrative Authorities in France', *Governance: An International Journal of Policy and Administration* 19, 207–27.

Energimarknadsinspektionen (2015) Arbeta hos oss, http://www.energimarknadsinspektionen.se/sv/Om-oss/arbeta-hos-oss/ (accessed 8 April 2015).

Energimarknadsinspektionen (2009) *Årsrapport 2008*, Eskilstuna: Energimarknadsinspektionen.

Energimarknadsinspektionen (2010) *Årsredovisning 2009*, Eskilstuna: Energimarknadsinspektionen.

Energimarknadsinspektionen (2014) *Årsredovisning 2013*, Eskilstuna: Energimarknadsinspektionen.

Genoud, Christophe and Matthias Finger (2004) 'Electricity Regulation in Europe', in Dominique Finon and Atle Midttun (eds.) *Reshaping European Gas and Electricity Industries*, Oxford: Elsevier.

Grande, Edgar (1997) 'Vom produzierenden zum regulierenden Staat: Möglichkeiten und Grenzen von Regulierung bei Privatisierung', in Klaus König and Angelika Benz (eds.) *Privatisierung und staatliche Regulierung*, Baden-Baden: Nomos.

Grande, Edgar and Burkhard Eberlein (2000) 'Der Aufstieg des Regulierungsstaates im Infrastrukturbereich: Zur Transformation der politischen Ökonomie der Bundesrepublik Deutschland', in Roland Czada and Hellmut Wollmann (eds.) *Von der Bonner zur Berliner Republik: 10 Jahre Deutsche Einheit*, Opladen: Westdeutscher Verlag.

Grande, Edgar and Ute Hartenberger (2007) 'Regulatory Governance im europäischen Mehrebenensystem', in Ingeborg Tömmel (ed.) *Die Europäische Union: Governance und Policy Making*, Wiesbaden: VS Verlag für die Sozialwissenschaften.

Héritier, Adrienne (2001) 'Market Integration and Social Cohesion: The Politics of Public Services in European Regulation', *Journal of European Public Policy* 8, 825–52.

HM Treasury (2009) *Civil Service Pay Guidance 2010–2011*, London.

Horn, Murray J. (1995) *The Political Economy of Public Administration. Institutional Choice in the Public Sector*, Cambridge: Cambridge University Press.

Horton, Sylvia (1996) 'The Civil Service', in David Farnham and Sylvia Horton (eds.) *Managing People in the Public Services*, Basingstoke: Macmillan.

International Energy Agency (2001) *Regulatory Institutions in Liberalised Electricity Markets*, Paris: OECD.

Jordana, Jacint and David Sancho (2004) 'Regulatory Designs, Institutional Constellations and the Study of Regulatory State', in Jacint Jordana and David Levi-Faur (eds.) *The Politics of Regulation. Institutions and Regulatory Reforms for the Age of Governance*, Cheltenham: Edward Elgar.

Jorion, Benoît (1998) *Les autorités administratives indépendantes*, Paris: La Documentation francaise.

Kirkpatrick, Ian and Kim Hoque (2005) 'The Decentralisation of Employment Relations in the British Public Sector', *Industrial Relations Journal* 36(2), 100–20.

Löhr, Franziska A. (2006) *Bundesbehörden zwischen Privatisierungsgebot und Infrastrukturauftrag. zur demokratischen Legitimation der Regulierung durch die Bundesnetzagentur in den Bereichen Telekommunikation und Post*. Baden-Baden: Nomos.

Mahoney, James and Kathleen Thelen (2010) 'A Theory of Gradual Institutional Change', in James Mahoney and Kathleen Thelen (eds.) *Explaining Institutional Change: Ambiguity, Agency, and Power*, Cambridge: Cambridge University Press.

Majone, Giandomenico (1994) 'The Rise of the Regulatory State in Europe', *West European Politics* 17, 77–101.

Majone, Giandomenico (ed.) (1996) *Regulating Europe*, London: Routledge.

Majone, Giandomenico (1997) 'From the Positive to the Regulatory State: Causes and Consequences of Changes on the Mode of Governance', *Journal of Public Policy* 17, 139–68.

Marsden, David (2004) 'The Role of Performance-Related Pay in Renegotiating the 'Effort Bargain': the Case of the British Public Service', *Industrial and Labor Relations Review* 57, 350–70.

Mayntz, Renate (1985) *Soziologie der öffentlichen Verwaltung*, 3rd ed., Heidelberg: C.F. Juristischer Verlag Müller.

McGowan, Francis (ed.) (1996) *European Energy Policies in a Changing Environment*, Heidelberg: Physica.

Ministère de la décentralisation et de la fonction publique (2014) *Fonction publique. Chiffres-clés*. Paris.

Moran, Michael (2002) 'Review Article: Understanding the Regulatory State', *British Journal of Political Science* 32, 391–413.

OECD (2001) *Public Sector – An Employer of Choice?*, Paris: OECD.

OECD (2005) *Performance-Related Pay Policies for Government Employees*, Paris: OECD.

OECD (2008) *The State of the Public Service*, Paris: OECD.

Ofgem (2007) *Performance Management for New Starters*, London: Ofgem.

Ofgem (2009) *Gender Equality Scheme*. London: Ofgem.

Ofgem (2010a) *Annual Report and Accounts 2009–10*, London: Ofgem.

Ofgem (2010b) *Ofgem Organisational Chart as at 30th June 2010*, London: Ofgem.

Ofgem (2014) *Annual Report and Accounts 2013–14*, London: Ofgem.

Otto, Kai-Andreas (2007) *Civil Service Salary System in Germany and Recent Reform Trends*. Conference on Civil Service Systems in Europe, Bucharest, *25 April 2007*, conference paper, http://www.oecd.org/countries/romania/38655690.pdf

Pollitt, Christopher, Karen Bathgate, Janice Caulfield and Amanda Smullen (2001) 'Agency Fever? Analysis of an International Policy Fashion', *Journal of Comparative Policy Analysis* 3, 271–90.

Prowse, Peter and Julie Prowse (2007) 'Is There Still a Public Sector Model of Employment Relations in the United Kingdom?', *International Journal of Public Sector Management* 20, 48–62.

Rouban, Luc (2008) 'The French Paradox: A Huge but Fragmented Public Service', in Hans-Ulrich Derlien and B Guy Peters (eds.) *The State at Work, Volume 1: Public Sector Employment in Ten Western Countries*, Cheltenham: Edward Elgar.

Rubery, Jill (2013) 'Public Sector Adjustment and the Threat to Gender Equality', in Daniel Vaughan-Whitehead (ed.) *Public Sector Shock. The Impact of Policy Retrenchment in Europe*, Cheltenham: Edward Elgar.

Schmidt, Christian (2005) ,Von der RegTP zur Bundesnetzagentur: Der organisationsrechtliche Rahmen der neuen Regulierungsbehörde', *Die Öffentliche Verwaltung* 24, 1025–32.

Schmidt, Susanne (1998) 'Commission Activism: Subsuming Telecommunications and Electricity under European Competition Law', *Journal of European Public Policy* 5(1), 169–84.

Schneider, Volker, Simon Fink and Marc Tenbrücken (2005) 'Buying Out the State: A Comparative Perspective on the Privatization of Infrastructures', *Comparative Political Studies* 38, 704–27.

Schön, Josef (2009) *Das neue Dienstrecht der Bundesbeamten. Die wichtigsten Neuregelungen verständlich erläutert*, Regensburg: Walhalla Fachverlag.

Stern, Jon (2000) 'Electricity and Telecommunications Regulatory Institutions in Small and Developing Countries', *Utilities Policy* 9, 131–57.

Süsskind, Bettina (2010) *Die autorités administratives indépendantes. Eine Untersuchung über den Wandel des französischen Einheitsstaates*, Baden-Baden: Nomos.

Swedish Ministry of Finance (1995) *The Public Sector Labour Market in Sweden. A Presentation*, Stockholm.

Thatcher, Mark (2002) 'Delegation to Independent Regulatory Agencies: Pressures, Functions and Contextual Mediation', *West European Politics* 25, 125–47.

Thatcher, Mark (2007) *Internationalisation and Economic Institutions: Comparing European Experiences*, Oxford: Oxford University Press.

Thurley, Djuna (2010) *Civil Service Compensation Scheme*, London.

Verhey, Luc (2003) 'British Agencies: Surveying the Quango State', in Luc Verhey and Tom Zwart (eds.) *Agencies in European and Comparative Perspective*, Antwerp: Intersentia.

Vincent, Catherine (2008) Industrial Relations in the Public Sector – France, http://www.eurofound.europa.eu/eiro/studies/tn0611028s/fr0611029q.htm (accessed 18 March 2011).

Wagner, Fritjof and Sabine Leppek (2009) *Beamtenrecht*, Heidelberg: Verlagsgruppe Hüthig-Jehle-Rehm.

Wilks, Stuart (1996) 'Sweden', in Norman Flynn and Franz Strehl (eds.) *Public Sector Management in Europe*, London: Prentice Hall.

Winchester, David and Stephen Bach (1999) 'Britain. The Transformation of Public Service Employment Relations', in Stephen Bach, Lorenzo Bordogna, Giuseppe Della Rocca and David Winchester (eds.) *Public Service Employment Relations in Europe: Transformation, Modernization or Inertia?*, London: Routledge.

Zohlnhöfer, Reimut, Herbert Obinger and Frieder Wolf (2008) 'Partisan Politics, Globalization, and the Determinants of Privatization Proceeds in Advanced Democracies (1990–2000)', *Governance* 21(1), 95–121.

7   Waste Collection

Ambrosius, Gerold (2008) 'Konzeptionen öffentlicher Dienstleistungen in Europa', *WSI Mitteilungen* 10/2008, 527–33.

Auer, Astrid, Christoph Demmke and Robert Polet (1997) *Der öffentliche Dienst im Europa der Fünfzehn: Lage und Perspektiven*, Maastricht: European Institut of Public Administration.

Avfall Sverige (2007) *Insamling och behandling av hushållsavfall. Former och utförande samt ekonomiska effekter på avfallsavgifterna*, Malmö: Avfall Sverige.

Bach, Stephen (1999) 'Europe. Changing Public Service Employment Relations', in Stephen Bach, Lorenzo Bordogna, Giuseppe Della Rocca and David Winchester (eds.) *Public Service Employment Relations in Europe: Transformation, Modernization or Inertia?*, London: Routledge.

Bach, Stephen and David Winchester (2003) 'Individualism and Collectivism in Industrial Relations', in Paul Edwards (ed.) *Industrial Relations: Theory and Practice*, vol. 2, Malden: Blackwell.

Bäck, Henry and Torbjörn Larsson (2008) *Den svenska politiken*, Stockholm: Liber.

BMAS, Bundesministerium für Arbeit und Soziales (2015) *Verzeichnis der für allgemeinverbindlich erklärten Tarifverträge*, Berlin: BMAS.

Bossaert, Danielle, Christoph Demmke, Koen Nomden, Robert Polet and Astrid Auer (eds.) (2001) *Der öffentliche Dienst im Europa der Fünfzehn: Trends und neue Entwicklungen*, Maastricht: European Institute of Public Administration.

Brandes, Wolfgang and Friedrich Buttler (1990) *Der Staat als Arbeitgeber. Daten und Analysen zum öffentlichen Dienst in der Bundesrepublik*, Frankfurt am Main: Campus.

Bremeier, Wolfram, Hans Brinckmann and Werner Kilian (2006) *Public Governance kommunaler Unternehmen: Vorschläge zur politischen Steuerung ausgegliederter Aufgaben auf der Grundlage einer empirischen Erhebung*, Düsseldorf: Hans-Böckler-Stiftung.

Brunk, Thomas and Michael Wahman (2009) Sweden: Collective Bargaining and Continuous Vocational Training. European Observatory of Working Life, http://eurofound.europa.eu/observatories/eurwork/comparative-information/national-contributions/sweden/sweden-collective-bargaining-and-continuous-vocational-training (accessed 9 April 2015).

Bryntse, Karin and Carsten Greve (2002) 'Competitive Contracting for Public Services: A Comparison of Policies and Implementations in Denmark and Sweden', *International Public Management Review* 3(1), 1–21.

Bundesministerium des Innern (2006) *Der öffentliche Dienst in Deutschland*, Berlin: Bundesministerium des Innern.

Burnham, June (2000) 'Human Resources Flexibilities in France', in David Farnham and Sarah Horton (eds.) *Human Resources Flexibilities in the Public Services: International Perspectives*, Basingstoke: Palgrave Macmillan.

Cabinet Office (2010) *Machinery of Governmment Changes: Best Practice Handbook,* https://www.gov.uk/government/uploads/system/uploads/attachment_data/file/61287/moghandbook.pdf

Christensen, Tom and Per Laegreid (2003) 'Transforming Governance in the New Millenium', in Tom Christensen and Per Laegreid (eds.) *New Public Management. The Transformation of Ideas and Practice,* Aldershot: Ashgate.

CNFPT (2010a) *Guide des Métiers Territoriaux,* Paris: CNFPT.

CNFPT (2010b) *Guide Practique fonction Publique Territoriale,* Paris: CNFPT.

Colling, Trevor (1999) 'Tendering and Outsourcing : Working in the Contract State?', in Susan Corby and Geoff White (eds.) *Employee Relations in the Public Services. Themes and Issues,* London: Routledge.

Crouch, Colin (2003) 'The State: Economic Management and Incomes Policy', in Paul Edwards (ed.) *Industrial Relations. Theory and Practice,* vol. 2, Oxford: Blackwell.

Czerwick, Edwin (2007) *Die Ökonomisierung des öffentlichen Dienstes: Dienstrechtsreformen und Beschäftigungsstrukturen seit 1991,* Wiesbaden: VS Verlag für Sozialwissenschaften.

Davies, Steve (2003) *European Waste Managment: Background to a Discussion on EWCs. A PSIRU Report for EPSU,* http://www.psiru.org/reports/european-waste-management-background-discussion-ewcs (accessed 20 July 2015).

Deutscher Gewerkschaftsbund (DGB) (2007) *Der große Ausverkauf oder: Rekommunalisierung versus Privatisierung. Dokumentation der Tagung des DGB Region Frankfurt-Rhein-Main am 3. Juli 2007,* Frankfurt am Main: DGB Region Frankfurt-Rhein-Main.

Dijkgraaf, Elbert, Govert Gijsbers, Dirk Maier and Franz von der Zee (2009) *Investing in the Future of Jobs and Skills. Scenarios, Implications and Options in Anticipation of Future Skills and Knowledge Needs. Sector Report Electricity, Gas, Water and Waste,* http://eurofound.europa.eu/sites/default/files/ef_files/pubdocs/2009/561/en/1/EF09561EN.pdf

Dijkgraaf, Elbert and Raymond H. J. M. Gradus (2008) *The Waste Market: Institutional Developments in Europe,* Dordrecht: Springer Science + Business Media B.V.

Diskrimineringsombudsmannen (2009) *Pay Surveys – Provisions and Outcomes,* Stockholm.

Domberger, Simon and Paul Jensen (1997) 'Contracting Out by the Public Sector. Theory, Evidence, Prospects', *Public Investment* 13(4), 67–75.

Dörring, Werner and Jürgen Kutzki (eds.) (2007) *TVöD-Kommentar Arbeitsrecht für den öffentlichen Dienst,* Berlin: Springer-Verlag.

Edeling, Thomas, Erhard Stölting and Dieter Wagner (2004) *Öffentliche Unternehmen zwischen Privatwirtschaft und öffentlicher Verwaltung. Eine empirische Studie im Feld kommunaler Versorgungsunternehmen,* Wiesbaden: VS Verlag für Sozialwissenschaften.

Eriksson, Kurt (2010) *The Swedish Rules on Negotioation and Mediation – A Brief Summary,* Stockholm: Medlingsinstitutet.

European Commission (2001) *Employment Effects of Waste Management Policies,* Brussels: European Commission.

European Commission (2009) *Electricity, Gas, Water and Waste. Comprehensive Sectoral Analysis of Emerging Competences and Economic Activities in the European Union,* Brussels: European Commission.

European Foundation for the Improvement of Living and Working Conditions (EUROFOUND) (2007) *Industrial Relations in the Public Sector,* Dublin: EUROFOUND.

Ferner, Anthony (1994) 'The State as Employer', in Richard Hyman and Anthony Ferner (eds.) *New Frontiers in European Industrial Relations*, Oxford: Blackwell.

Fulton, Lionel (2013) Collective Bargaining, http://www.worker-participation.eu/ National-Industrial-Relations/Countries/United-Kingdom/Collective-Bargaining (accessed 10 April 2015).

Hafkamp, Wim (2002) 'Comparison of National Solid Waste Regimes in Trajectories of Change', in Nicolas Buclet (ed.) *Municipal Waste Management in Europe. European Policy between Harmonisation and Subsidiarity*, Dordrecht: Kluwer.

Hall, David (2006) *Waste Management Companies in Europe: A Report Commissioned by the European Federation of Public Service Unions (EPSU)*, http://www.epsu.org/IMG/ pdf/EN_PSIRU_waste_management_in_EU_Feb_06.pdf

Hall, David (2010) *Waste Management Companies in Europe: Framework, Trends and Issues*, http://www.psiru.org/reports/waste-management-europe-framework-trends- and-issues (accessed 20 July 2015).

Health and Safety Executive (2004) *Mapping Health and Safety Standards in the UK Waste Industry*, Norwich.

Hemmer, Dagmar, Andreas Höferl and Bela M. Hollos (2003) *Privatisierung und Liberalisierung öffentlicher Dienstleistungen in der EU-15: Abfallwirtschaft*, Wien: Österreichische Gesellschaft für Politikberatung und Politikentwicklung.

Hood, Christopher (1991) 'A Public Management for all Seasons?', *Public Administration* 69(1), 3–19.

Horton, Sylvia (2000) 'Human Resources Flexibilities in UK Public Services', in David Farnham and Sylvia Horton (eds.) *Human Resources Flexibilities in the Public Services: International Perspectives*, Basingstoke: Palgrave Macmillan.

Horton, Sylvia and David Farnham (2000) 'Evaluating Human Resources Flexibilities: A Comparative Perspective', in David Farnham and Sarah Horton (eds.) *Human Resources Flexibilities in the Public Services: International Perspectives*, Basingstoke: Palgrave Macmillan.

Hyman, Richard (2001) *Understanding European Trade Unionism: Between Market, Class and Society*, London: Sage.

Income Data Services (IDS) (2003) *Recruitment and Retention, Pay Levels and the Use of Agency Workers in Local Government*, London.

Kaufmann, Franz X. (2007) 'Welfare State, Social Policy', in George Ritzer (ed.) *The Blackwell Encyclopaedia of Sociology*, vol. 9, Oxford: John Wiley and Sons Ltd.

Keller, Berndt (2008) *Einführung in die Arbeitspolitik. Arbeitsbeziehungen und Arbeitsmarkt in sozialwissenschaftlicher Perspektive*, 7nd ed., München: Oldenbourg Verlag München.

Kerr, Allan and Mike Radford (1994) 'TUPE or not TUPE: Competitive Tendering and the Transfer Laws', *Public Money and Management* 14(4), 37–45.

Kirkpatrick, Ian and Kim Hoque (2005) 'The Decentralisation of Employment Relations in the British Public Sector', *Industrial Relations Journal* 36(2), 100–20.

Kullander, Mats (2009) *Sweden: Industrial Relations Profile*, https://eurofound.europa. eu/sites/default/files/ef_files/eiro/country/sweden.pdf

L'Agence de l'Environnement et de la Maîtrise de l'Energie (ADEME) (2009) *La collecte des déchets par le service public en France. Résultats Année 2005*, Angers: L'Agence de l'Environnement et de la Maîtrise de l'Energie.

Linde, Peter and Beatrix Jansen (2009) *Beschäftigte im öffentlichen Dienst. Grundlagen des Arbeitsverhältnisses*, Heidelberg: Decker.

Local Government Association (LGA) (2012) Green Book: National Agreement on Pay and Conditions of Service for Local Government Services, http://www.local.gov.uk/ workforce/-/journal_content/56/10180/3510601/ARTICLE (accessed 10 April 2015).

Local Government Association (LGA) (2013) *Local Government Earnings Survey 2010/11*, London.

Local Government Employers (LGE) (2004) *2004 Single Status Local Pay Reviews Survey Report*, London.

Local Government Employers (LGE) (2006) *LGE Survey of Pay Structure Development*, London: KLM Press.

Mendroch, Erich (2008) 'Abfallwirtschaft', in Torsten Brandt, Thorsten Schulten, Gabriele Sterkel and Jörg Wiedemuth (eds.) *Europa im Ausverkauf. Liberalisierung und Privatisierung öffentlicher Dienstleistungen und ihre Folgen für die Tarifpolitik*, Hamburg: VSA-Verlag.

Montin, Stig (1993) *Swedish Local Government in Transition: A Matter of Rationality and Legitimacy*, Örebro: University of Örebro.

Morgan, Phillip and Nigel Allington (2003) 'Private Sector "Good", Public Sector "Bad"? Transformation or Transition in the UK Public Sector', *Scientific Journal of Administrative Development* 1, 22–53.

Mossé, Phillippe and Robert Tchobanian (1999) 'France. The Restructuring of Employment Relations in the Public Services', in Stephen Bach, Lorenzo Bordogna, Giuseppe Della Rocca and David Winchester (eds.) *Public Service Employment Relations in Europe: Transformation, Modernization or Inertia?*, London: Routledge.

NJC, National Joint Council for Local Government Services (2005) '*National Agreement on Pay and Concitions of Service*', London.

Nullmeier, Frank (2005) 'Wettbewerb und Konkurrenz', in Bernhard Blanke, Stephan von Bandemer, Frank Nullmeier and Göttrik Wewer (eds.) *Handbuch zur Verwaltungsreform*, Wiesbaden: VS Verlag für Sozialwissenschaften.

OECD (2004) *Trends in Human Resources Management Policies in OECD Countries: An Analysis of the Results of the OECD Survey in Strategic Human Resources Management*, Paris: OECD.

Page, Edward C. and Vincent Wright (eds.) (2007) *From the Active to the Enabling State: The Changing Role of Top Officials in European Nations*, Basingstoke: Palgrave Macmillan.

Perkins, Stephen J. and Geoff White (2010) 'Modernising Pay in the UK Public Services: Trends and Implications', *Human Resource Management Journal* 20, 244–57.

Sachdev, Sanjiv (2001) *Contracting Culture: From CCT to PPPs. The Private Provision of Public Services and Its Impact on Employment Relations*, Kingston: Unison.

Sengenberger, Werner (1987) *Struktur und Funktionsweise von Arbeitsmärkten. Die Bundesrepublik Deutschland im internationalen Vergleich*, Frankfurt am Main: Campus.

Sveriges Kommuner och Landsting (SKL) (2006) *Employer Perspectives on Local Authorities and County Councils*, Stockholm: Swedish Association of Local Authorities and Regions.

Sveriges Kommuner och Landsting (SKL) (2010) *Huvudöverenskommelse om lön och allmänna anställningsvillkor samt rekommendation om lokalt kollektivavtal HÖK 10*, Stockholm: Sveriges Kommuner och Landsting.

Sveriges Kommuner och Landsting (SKL) (2013) *Huvudöverenskommelse om lön och allmänna anställningsvillkor samt rekommendation om lokalt kollektivavtal HÖK 13*, Stockholm: Sveriges Kommuner och Landsting.

Szymanski, Stefan (1996) 'The Impact of Compulsory Competitive Tendering on Refuse Collection Services', *Fiscal Studies* 17(3), 1–20.

Tepe, Markus and Daniela Kroos (2010) 'Lukrativer Staatsdienst? Lohndifferenzen zwischen öffentlichem Dienst und Privatwirtschaft', *WSI Mitteilungen* 01/2010, 3–10.

Unison (2003) *Unison Guide Best Value Code of Practice on Worforce Matters in Local Authority Service Contracts in England*, London: Unison.

United Nations (UN) (2006) *United Kingdom Public Administration Country Profile*, New York.

Vereinte Dienstleistungsgewerkschaft (ver.di) (2012) *Tariflandschaft und Tarifbindung der Abfallwirtschaft in Deutschland*, Berlin: ver.di.

White, Geoff (1999) 'The Remuneration of Public Servants: Fair Pay or New Pay?', in Susan Corby and Geoff White (eds.) *Employee Relations in the Public Services. Themes and Issues*, London: Routledge.

White, Geoff and Barry Hutchinson (1996) 'Local Government', in David Farnham and Sylvia Horton (eds.) *Managing People in the Public Services*, Basingstoke: Palgrave Macmillan.

Winchester, David and Stephen Bach (1999) 'Britain. The Transformation of Public Service Employment Relations', in Stephen Bach, Lorenzo Bordogna, Giuseppe Della Rocca and David Winchester (eds.) *Public Service Employment Relations in Europe: Transformation, Modernization or Inertia?*, London: Routledge.

Wollmann, Hellmut (2004) 'Local Government Reforms in Great Britain, Sweden, Germany and France: Between Multi-Function and Single Purpose Organisations', *Local Government Studies* 20, 639–65.

Wollmann, Hellmut (2006) 'Staatsorganisation zwischen Territorial- und Funktionalprinzip im Ländervergleich – Varianten der Institutionalisierung auf der dezentral-lokalen Ebene', in Jörg Bogumil, Werner Jann and Frank Nullmeier (eds.) *Politik und Verwaltung*, Wiesbaden: VS Verlag für Sozialwissenschaften.

Wollmann, Hellmut (2008) Comparing Local Government Reforms in England, Sweden, France and Germany, http://www.wuestenrot-stiftung.de/download/local-government (accessed 10 April 2015).

8   The Police

Ackerman, Thomas H. (1996) *An Examination of the Selection and Training of Police Commissioners and Patrol Officer Recruits of the Swedish National Police Force, Master's Thesis*, Ann Arbor: Michigan State University.

Andersson, Thomas and Stefan Tengblad (2009) 'When Complexity Meets Culture: New Public Management and the Swedish Police', *Qualitative Research in Accounting & Management* 6(1/2), 41–56.

Audit Commission (1996) *Streetwise. Effective Foot Patrol*, London: HSMO.

Auffenberg, Jennie and Bernhard Kittel (2015) *Negotiating Reforms in the Public Services: Trajectories of New Public Management Reforms in the French and Swedish Police Forces*, TranState Working Papers, Bremen: Collaborative Research Centre 597, University Bremen.

Ayling, Julie and Clifford Shearing (2008) 'Taking Care of Business: Public Police as Commercial Security Vendors', *Criminology and Criminal Justice* 8(1), 27–50.

BBC (2012) Why British Police Don't Have Guns, http://www.bbc.co.uk/news/magazine-19641398 (accessed 20 February 2015).

Becker Harold K. and Eijon O. Hjellemo (1976) *Justice in Modern Sweden. A Description of the Components of the Swedish Criminal Justice System*, Springfield: Charles C. Thomas.

Behr, Raphael (2000) *Cop Culture – Der Alltag des Gewaltmonopols*, Wiesbaden: VS Verlag für die Sozialwissenschaften.

Briken, Kendra (2014) 'Ein vertriebswirtschaftlichtes Gewaltmonopol? New Police Management im europäischen Vergleich', *Kriminologisches Journal* 4, 213–31.

Brodeur, Jean P. (2010) *The Policing Web*, Oxford: Oxford University Press.

Carson, David (2009) 'Mentoring for Women in Policing in the UK', *International Journal of Evidence Based Coaching and Mentoring*, Special Issue 3, 51–63.

Cayrel, Laurent and Olivier Diederichs (2010) *Rapport sur le rôle et le positionnement des polices municipals*, http://www.interieur.gouv.fr/Publications/Rapports-de-l-IGA/Securite/Role-et-positionnement-des-polices-municipales (accessed 20 July 2015).

Cotton, Judith (2005) *Police Complaints and Discipline England and Wales, 12 Months to March 2004*, http://webarchive.nationalarchives.gov.uk/20110218135832/rds. homeoffice.gov.uk/rds/pdfs04/hosb1704.pdf (accessed 20 July 2015).

Dahlgren, Johanna (2007) *Kvinnor i polistjänst. Föreningen Kamraterna, Svenska Polisförbundet och kvinnors inträde i polisyrket 1957–1971*, Umeå: Skrifter från Institutionen för historiska studier, Genusforskarskolan, Umeå universitet.

Die Zeit (2014) Der Polizei fehlen Migranten, http://www.zeit.de/gesellschaft/2014–09/polizei-migrantion-studie (accessed 17 March 2015).

Eick, Volker (2011) 'Policing "Below the State" in Germany', in Laura Huey and Luis A. Fernandez (eds) *Rethinking Policing and Justice. Exploring Alternatives to Law*, New York: Routledge.

Elefalk, Kjell (2001) 'The Balanced Scorecard of the Swedish Police Service: 7000 Officers in Total Quality Management Project, *Total Quality Management* 12, 958–66.

Fassin, Didier (2011) *La Force de l'Ordre. Une anthropologie de la police des quartiers*, Paris: Seuil.

Fritzell, Johan, Jennie Bacchus Hertzman, Olof Bäckman, Ida Borg, Tommy Ferrarini and Kenneth Nelson (2010) *Growing Inequality and Its Impact in Sweden*, http://gini-research.org/system/uploads/451/original/Sweden.pdf?1370090633

Funk, Albrecht (1986) *Polizei und Rechtsstaat. Frankfurt: Entstehungsgeschichte der preußischen Polizei 1848–1914*, Frankfurt: Campus.

Furuhagen, Björn (2004) *Ordning på stan: Polisen i Stockholm 1848–1917*, Eslöv: Symposion.

Furuhagen, Björn (2009) *Från fjärdingsman till närpolis – en kortfattad svensk polishistoria*, Växjö: Växjö Universitet.

Fyfe, Nicolas R. (2013) 'Complex Transition and Uncertain Trajectories. Reflections on Recent Developments in Police Professionalism', *Journal of Workplace Learning* 25, 407–20.

Gash, Tom (2008) *The New Bill: Modernising the Police Workforce*, London: Institute for Public Policy Research.

Grahame, Allen (2001) *Police Service Strength: England and Wales, 31 March 1977 to 30 September 2000*, London: House of Commons Library.

Grande, Edgar (1997) 'Vom produzierenden zum regulierenden Staat: Möglichkeiten und Grenzen von Regulierung bei Privatisierung', in Klaus König and Angelika Benz (eds.) *Privatisierung und staatliche Regulierung*, Baden-Baden: Nomos.

Groß, Hermann (2008) 'Deutsche Länderpolizeien', *Aus Politik und Zeitgeschichte* 48, 20–22.

Gurr, Robert Ted, Peter N. Grabowsky and Richard C. Hula (1977) *The Politics of Crime and Conflict: A Comparative History of Four Cities*, London: Sage.

Haselow, Reinhard and Guido P. Kissmann (2003) 'Ausbildungs- und Sozialisationsprozesse der Polizei seit 1949' in Hans-Juergen Lange (ed.) *Die Polizei der Gesellschaft*, Opladen: Westdeutscher Verlag.

Her Majesty's Inspectorate of Constabulary (HMIC) (1999) *Police Integrity: Securing and Maintaining Public Confidence. National Report*, http://www.justiceinspectorates. gov.uk/hmic/media/police-integrity-19990601.pdf (accessed 20 July 2015).

Her Majesty's Inspectorate of Constabulary (HMIC) (2014) *Policing in Austerity: Meeting the Challenge*, London: Home Office.

Hills, Alice (2009) 'The Possibility of Transnational Policing', *Policing and Society* 19, 300–17.

Holdaway, Simon (1996) *The Racialisation of British Policing*, Basingstoke: Palgrave Macmillan.

Home Office (eds) (2001) *Policing a New Century*, London: HMSO.

Home Office (2013) Police Workforce: England and Wales, 31 March 2013, https:// www.gov.uk/government/publications/police-workforce-england-and-wales-31 -march-2013/police-workforce-england-and-wales-31-march-2013 (accessed 15 March 2015).

Home Office (2015) Police Workforce, England and Wales, 30 September 2014: data tables, https://www.gov.uk/government/statistics/police-workforce-england-and-wales-30-september-2014-data-tables (accessed 20 February 2015).

Horton, Christine (1995) *Policing in France*, London: Policy Studies Institute.

Hunold, Daniela, Daniela Klimke; Rafael Behr and Rüdiger Lautmann (2010) *Fremde als Ordnungshüter? Die Polizei in der Zuwanderungsgesellschaft Deutschland*, Wiesbaden: VS Verlag für die Sozialwissenschaften.

Hunter, Laurie (2003) 'Police Pay and Bargaining in the UK, 1978–2000', *British Journal of Industrial Relations* 41(1), 29–52.

IMK, Innenministerkonferenz (2011) *Zertifizierung von Unternehmen im privaten Sicherheitsgewerbe. Zwischenbericht*, http://www.innenministerkonferenz.de/IMK/ DE/termine/to-beschluesse/11–12–09/Anlage07–1-1.pdf?__blob=publicationFile &v=2 (accessed 20 July 2015).

Ivarsson Westerberg, Anders (2004) *Papperspolisen: den ökande administrationen i moderna organisationer*, Dissertation, Stockholm: Handelshögskolan.

Johnston, Les (1992) 'British Policing in the Nineties: Free Market and Strong State?', *International Criminal Justice Review* 2(1), 1–18.

Jones, Trevor and Jim Newburn (1998) *Private Security and Public Policing*, Oxford: Clarendon Press.

Karp, Staffan and Henric Stenmark (2011) 'Learning to Be a Police Officer. Tradition and Change in the Training and Professional Lives of Police Officers', *Police Practice and Research: An International Journal* 12(1), 4–15.

Knöbl, Wolfgang (1998) *Polizei und Herrschaft im Modernisierungsprozeß, Staatenbildung und innere Sicherheit in Preußen, England und Amerika 1700–1914*, Frankfurt am Main: Campus.

Körlin, Jenny, Pia Svedberg and Kristina Alexanderson (2006) *Sjukfrånvaro bland kvinnor och män anställda inom polisen (Sickness absence among women and men in the Police)*, Sektionen för personskadeprevention, Institutionen för klinisk neurovetenskap, Solna: Karolinska Institutet.

Kroos, Daniela, Sylvia Hils and Sebastian Streb (2011) 'Public Employment between Markets and Institutions. Competition and Its Impact on Public Personnel Policies', *Industrielle Beziehungen*, 18(1–2), 39–59.

Künkel, Jenny (2014) 'Cop Culture Reloaded? Wandel und Persistenzen schut- zpolizeilicher Macht', *KrimJ* 46, 264–83.

Lange, Hans J. and Jean-Claude Schenck (2004) *Polizei im kooperativen Staat. Verwaltungsreform und Neues Steuerungsmodell in der Sicherheitsverwaltung*, Wiesbaden: VS Verlag für die Sozialwissenschaften.

Loader, Ian (2000) 'Plural Policing and Democratic Governance', *Social Legal Studies* 9, 323–45.

Loader, Ian and Neil Walker (2001) 'Policing as a Public Good: Reconstituting the Connection between Policing and the State', *Theoretical Criminology* 5(1), 9–35.

Loftus, Bethan (2008) 'Dominant Culture Interrupted. Recognition, Resentment and the Politics of Change in an English Police Force', *British Journal of Criminology* 48, 756–77.

Loftus, Bethan (2009) *Police Culture in a Changing World*, Oxford: Oxford University Press.

Lord, Vivian B. (1998) 'Swedish Police Selection and Training: Issues from a Comparative Perspective', *Policing: An International Journal of Police Strategies & Management* 21, 280–92.

Loubet del Bayle, Jean-Louis (2010) 'Le syndicalisme policier français', *Cahiers de la sécurité* 13(Juillet–Septembre 2010), 159–71.

Macpherson of Cluny, Sir William (1999) *The Stephen Lawrence Inquiry*, London: HMSO.

Manning, Peter (2003) *Policing Contingencies*, Chicago: University of Chicago Press.

Mawby, Rob and Alan Wright (2005) Police Accountability in the United Kingdom, Written for the Commonwealth Human Rights Initiative. January 2005, http://www.humanrightsinitiative.org/programs/aj/police/res_mat/police_accountability_in_uk.pdf (accessed 20 July 2015).

Metropolitan Police (MET) (2012) *Information Request Form*, http://www.met.police.uk/foi/pdfs/disclosure_2012/april_2012/2011040002218.pdf (accessed 20 July 2015).

Metropolitan Police Authority (MPA) (2002) Police Negotiating Board (PNB) agreement on police pay and conditions, http://policeauthority.org/metropolitan/committees/x-hr/2002/020725/11/index.html, date accessed 19 February 2015.

Ministère de la fonction publique (2011) *Rapport annuel sur l'état de la fonction publique 2010–2011. Politiques et pratiques de ressources humaines; Faits et chiffres*, Paris: La Documentation Française.

Ministère de la fonction publique (2012) *Rapport annuel sur l'état de la fonction publique 2011–2012. Politiques et pratiques de ressources humaines; Faits et chiffres*, Paris: La Documentation Française.

Ministère de la fonction publique et de la réforme de l'état (2004) *Fonction publique: Faits et chiffres 2003*, Paris: La Documentation Française.

Ministère de la réforme de l'état, de la décentralisation et de la fonction publique (2012) *Rapport annuel sur l'état de la fonction publique. Édition 2012. Politiques et pratiques de ressources humaines; Faits et chiffres*, Paris: La Documentation Française.

Ministère du budget, des comptes publics et de la fonction publique (2007) *Rapport annuel sur l'état de la fonction publique. Volume 1: Faits et chiffres 2006–2007*, Paris: La Documentation Française.

Ministère du budget, des comptes publics et de la fonction publique (2008) *Rapport annuel sur l'état de la fonction publique. Volume 1: Faits et chiffres 2007–2008,* Paris: La Documentation Française.

Ministère du budget, des comptes publics, de la fonction publique et de la réforme de l'état (2009) *Rapport annuel sur l'état de la fonction publique. Volume 1: Faits et chiffres 2008–2009*, Paris: La Documentation Française.

Matelly, Jean-Hugues and Christian Mouhanna (2007) *Police: des chiffres et des doutes*, Paris: Michalon.

Metcalfe, Beverly (2004) 'New Police Management, Performance and Accountability', in Mike Dent, John Chandler and Jim Barry (eds) *Questioning the New Public Management*, Aldershot: Ashgate.

Monjardet, Dominique (1996) *Ce que fait la police. Sociologie da la force public*, Paris: La Découverte.

Mouhanna, Christian (2009) 'Is the Police Moving from Community Policing to Wholesale Order Maintenance?', in Laurent Mucchielli (ed.) *The Security Mania. France 2010*, Paris: Carceral Notebooks.

Mouhanna, Christian (2011) *La Police contre les citoyens?*, Nimes: Champs Social.

Nasreen, Bibi, Michelle Clegg and Rachel Pinto (2005) *Police Service Strength: England and Wales, 31 March 2005*, London: Home Office.

National Audit Office (2013) *Private Sector Partnering in the Police Service*, http://www.nao.org.uk/wp-content/uploads/2013/07/10127_Private-sector-partnering-in-the-police-service_NEW.pdf (accessed 20 July 2015).

National Police Board (NPB) (eds) (2005) *A Presentation of the Swedish Police Service*, Stockholm: NPB.

Nyzell, Stefan (2014) 'The Policeman as a Worker – or Not? International Impulses and National Developments within the Swedish Police, ca. 1850–1940', *Nordisk politiforskning* 2, 149–65.

OECD (2012) *Public Governance Reviews: France: An International Perspective on the General Review of Public Policies*, OECD: Paris.

Pagon, Milan, Bojana Virjent-Novak, Melita Djuric and Branko Lobnikar (1996) European Systems of Police Education and Training, https://www.ncjrs.gov/policing/eur551.htm (accessed 2 April 2015).

Peterson, Abby and Sara Uhnoo (2012) 'Trials of Loyalty: Ethnic Minority Police Officers as "Outsiders" within a Greedy Institution', *European Journal of Criminology* 9, 354–69.

Police Nationale (2004) *Protocole d'Accord. Sur réforme des corps et carrières de la police nationale*, http://www.policefr.com/basepn/public/reforme.pdf (accessed 20 July 2015).

Polisförbundet (2008) ATA/Polis – Ligger det någon sanning bakom myterna? http://www.diva-portal.org/smash/get/diva2:278791/FULLTEXT01.pdf (accessed 22 March 2015).

Polisförbundet (2010) ATA/Polis– arbetstidsavtal för Polisen. Utgåva 3 – 2010-01-01, http://www.polisforbundet.se/lokala_avtal/ATA_Polis_popularversion%20 3_20101001.pdf (accessed 22 March 2015).

Polisförbundet (2013) In English, http://www.polisforbundet.se/in-english/ (accessed 22 March 2015).

Polismyndigheten (2015) *Polisens årsredovisning 2014*, Polisen: Stockholm.

Pütter, Norbert and Martina Kant (2000) 'Ehrenamtliche PolizeihelferInnen. Polizeidienste, Sicherheitswachten und Sicherheitspartner', *Bürgerrechte & Polizei/CILIP* 66(2), 16–30.

Rabe-Hemp, Cara (2007) 'Survival in an "all boys club": Policewomen and Their Fight for Acceptance', *Policing: An International Journal of Police Strategies and Management* 31, 251–70.

Ramalingam, Vidhya (2012) *Impact of Counter-Terrorism on Communities: Sweden Background Report*, London: Institute for Strategic Dialogue.

Regge, Felix (2013) *Migranten im Polizeidienst: Motivation und Hemmnisse von Bewerbern*. München: Grin Verlag GmbH.

Reiner, Robert (2000) *The Politics of the Police*, 3rd ed., Oxford: Oxford University Press.

Rikspolisstyrelsen (2010) *Antal anställda vid polisen 1997–2007, fördelat på personalkategori, per myndighet*, http://www.polisen.se/Global/www och Intrapolis/Statistik/01

Polisen nationellt/Personalstatistik/Antal_anstallda_1997_till_2007.pdf (accessed 18 June 2013).

Rikspolistyrelsen (1973) *Svensk polis – tidskrift för Sveriges polisväsende*, Stockholm: Inrikesdepartementet.

Rikspolisstyrelsen (2011) *Polisens årsredovisning 2010*, Stockholm: Rikspolisstyrelsen.

Rikspolisstyrelsen (2013) *Antal anställda per myndighet den 31 december 1999–2012*, http://www.polisen.se/Global/www och Intrapolis/Statistik/01 Polisen nationellt/ Personalstatistik/Antal anställda per personalkategori 1999–2012.pdf (accessed 18 June 2013).

Ritsert, Rolf (2011) *Wirkungsorientierte Steuerung bei der Polizei. Vortrag im Rahmen des 11. Speyerer Forum Haushalts- und Rechnungswesen 2011. Steuerungswirkungen des Neuen Haushalts- und Rechnungswesen*, http://www.dhv-speyer.de/muehlenkamp/ Weiterbildung/Speyerer%20Forum%202011%20f%C3%BCr%20Netz/Herr%20 Prof.%20Ritsert.pdf (accessed 20 July 2015).

Roché, Sebastian (2005) *Police de Proximité. Nos politiques de sécurité*, Paris: Seuil.

Rolandsson, Bertil (2015) 'Partnerships with the Police – Logics and Strategies of Justification', *Qualitative Research in Organizations and Management: An International Journal* 10(1), 2–20.

Scarman, Lord J. (1981) *The Brixton Disorders, 10–12th April, 1981*, London: HMSO.

Schneider, Cathy L. (2014) *Police Power and Race Riots: Urban Unrest in Paris and New York*. Philadelphia: University of Pennsylvania Press.

Schulte, Martin (1995) 'Gefahrenabwehr durch private Sicherheitskräfte im Lichte des staatlichen Gewaltmonopols', *Deutsches Verwaltungsblatt* 1995, 130–35.

Sigurdsson, Jenny and Amardeep Dhani (2010) *Police Service Strength: England and Wales, 31 March 2010*, London: Home Office.

Silvestri, Marisa, Stephen Tong and Jennifer Brown (2013) 'Gender and Police Leadership: Time for a Paradigm Shift?', *International Journal of Police Science & Management* 15(1), 61–73.

Singelnstein, Tobias (2013) *Strafverfahren gegen Polizisten wegen Körperverletzung im Amt*, Freiburg: ms.

Skills for Justice UK (SFJUK) (2013) New Police Promotion Plan Moves Closer, http://www. sfjuk.com/new-police-promotion-plan-moves-closer/ (accessed 25 February 2015).

Smith, David J. and Jeremy Gray (1985) *Police and People in London. The PSI Report*, Aldershot: Gower.

SPS (2008) *A Presentation of The Swedish Police Service, The Swedish Police Service – SPS*, https://www.polisen.se/PageFiles/329361/Polis-presentation_eng%5B1%5D.pdf (accessed 20 July 2015).

Statistisches Bundesamt (1982) *Fachserie 14 Reihe 6 – Steuern und Finanzen: Personal des öffentlichen Dienstes 30. Juni 1980*, Wiesbaden: Statistisches Bundesamt.

Statistisches Bundesamt (1987) *Fachserie 14 Reihe 6 – Steuern und Finanzen: Personal des öffentlichen Dienstes 1985*, Wiesbaden: Statistisches Bundesamt.

Statistisches Bundesamt (1997) *Fachserie 14 Reihe 6 – Steuern und Finanzen: Personal des öffentlichen Dienstes 1995*, Wiesbaden: Statistisches Bundesamt.

Statistisches Bundesamt (2007) *Fachserie 14 Reihe 6 – Steuern und Finanzen: Personal des öffentlichen Dienstes 2005*, Wiesbaden: Statistisches Bundesamt.

Statistisches Bundesamt (2011) *Fachserie 14 Reihe 6 – Steuern und Finanzen: Personal des öffentlichen Dienstes 2010*, Wiesbaden: Statistisches Bundesamt.

Statistisches Bundesamt (2014) *Fachserie 14 Reihe 6 – Steuern und Finanzen: Personal des öffentlichen Dienstes 2013*, Wiesbaden: Statistisches Bundesamt.

Statens Ofentliga Utrendigna (2012) *En sammanhållen svensk polis*. Stockholm: Fritzes.

Statskontoret (2010) One from Several: The Benefits of Mono-Agencies. Summary of the Publication När flera blir en – om nyttan med enmyndigheter, http://www.statskontoret.se/in-english/publications/2010/one-from-several-the-benefits-of-mono-agencies/ (accessed 22 March 2015).

Stockholm County Police (SCP) (eds) (2009) *A Presentation*, Stockholm: SCP.

Stokke, Torgeir A. and Christer Thörnqvist (2001) 'Strikes and Collective Bargaining in the Nordic Countries', *European Journal of Industrial Relations* 7, 245–67.

Swedish National Police Board (2012) *The Swedish Police – an Introduction*, Stockholm.

Tondorf, Karin and Andrea Jochmann-Döll (2013) *Nach Leistung, Eignung und Befähigung? Beurteilungen von Frauen und Männern im Polizeivollzugsdienst, Arbeitspapier 276*, Düsseldorf: Hans-Böckler-Stiftung.

Uhnoo, Sara (2015) 'Within "the Tin Bubble": The Police and Ethnic Minorities in Sweden', *Policing and Society: An International Journal of Research and Policy* 25, 129–49.

UNISON (2015) Cut crime not police staff, http://www.unison.org.uk/at-work/police-and-justice-staff/key-issues/cut-crime-not-police-staff/home/ (accessed 9 April 2015).

Wakefield, Alison (2003) *Selling Security: The Private Policing of Public Space*, Cullompton, Devon: Willan Publishing.

Wakefield, Alison and Jenny Fleming (2009) *The SAGE Dictionary of Policing*, London: Sage.

Walker, Peter and Paul Lewis (2012) Ian Tomlinson Death: Simon Harwood Cleared of Manslaughter, *The Guardian*, July 19, http://www.theguardian.com/uk/2012/jul/19/simon-harwood-not-guilty-ian-tomlinson (accessed 2 April 2015).

Weiland, Agneta (1995) *Swedish National Police College: Sörentorp 1970–95*, Sweden.

Westmarland, Louise (2001) *Gender and Policing: Sex Power and Police Culture*, Devon: Willan Publishers.

White, Michael D. and Gipsy Escobar (2008) 'Making Good Cops in the Twenty-First Century: Emerging Issues for the Effective Recruitment, Selection and Training of Police in the United States and Abroad' *International Review of Law Computers & Technology* 22(1–2), 119–34.

Wilz, Sylvia M. (2005) '"Nicht genügend kann davor gewarnt werden..." – Männer und Frauen bei der Polizei: Fakten und Diskurse', in Jens-Rainer Ahrens, Maja Apelt and Christiane Bender (eds) *Frauen im Militär. Empirische Befunde und Perspektiven zur Integration von Frauen in die Streitkräfte*, Wiesbaden: VS Verlag für Sozialwissenschaften.

9   Summary and Integrated Comparison of Countries and Sectors

Anxo, Dominique (2013) 'Early Fiscal Consolidation and Negotiated Flexibility in Sweden: A Fair Way out of the Crisis?', in Daniel Vaughan-Whitehead (ed.) *Public Sector Shock. The Impact of Policy Retrenchment in Europe*, Cheltenham: Edward Elgar.

Bach, Stephen and Ian Kessler (2007) 'HRM and New Public Management', in Peter Boxall, John Purcell and Patrick Wright (eds.) *The Oxford Handbook of Human Resource Management*, Oxford: Oxford University Press.

Baumol, William J. (1993) 'Health Care, Education and the Cost Disease – A Looming Crisis for Public Choice', *Public Choice* 77(1), 17–28.

Beaumont, Phil B. (1992) *Public Sector Industrial Relations*, London: Routledge.

Bordogna, Lorenzo (2007) *Industrial Relations in the Public Sector,* Dublin: European Foundation for the Improvement of Living and Working Conditions.

Bosch, Gerhard (2013) 'Public Sector Adjustments in Germany: From Cooperative to Competitive Federalism', in Daniel Vaughan-Whitehead (ed.) *Public Sector Shock. The Impact of Policy Retrenchment in Europe,* Cheltenham: Edward Elgar.

Briken, Kendra, Karin Gottschall, Sylvia Hils and Bernhard Kittel (2014) 'Wandel von Beschäftigung und Arbeitsbeziehungen im öffentlichen Dienst in Deutschland – zur Erosion einer sozialstaatlichen Vorbildrolle', *Zeitschrift für Sozialreform* 60(2), 123–48.

Cusack, Thomas R., Ton Notermans and Martin Rein (1989) 'Political-Economic Aspects of Public Employment', *European Journal of Political Research* 17, 471–500.

Derlien, Hans-Ulrich and B. Guy Peters (eds.) (2008a) *The State at Work,* 2 vol., Cheltenham: Edward Elgar.

Derlien, Hans-Ulrich and B. Guy Peters (2008b) 'Introduction: The State at Work', in Hans-Ulrich Derlien and B. Guy Peters (eds.) *The State at Work, Volume 1. Public Sector Employment in Ten Western Countries,* Cheltenham: Edward Elgar.

Gautié, Jérôme (2013) 'France: "The Public Service Under Pressure"', in Daniel Vaughan-Whitehead (ed.) *Public Sector Shock. The Impact of Policy Retrenchment in Europe,* Cheltenham: Edward Elgar.

Hood, Christopher (1991) 'A Public Management for All Seasons?', *Public Administration* 69(1), 3–19.

Hurrelmann, Achim, Stephan Leibried, Kerstin Martens and Peter Mayer (eds.) (2007) *Transforming the Golden-Age Nation State,* Basingstoke: Palgrave Macmillan.

Keller, Berndt (2008) 'Wandel der Arbeitsbeziehungen im öffentlichen Dienst: Entwicklungen und Perspektiven', in: Reinhold Sackmann, Bernadette Jonda and Maria Reinhold (eds.), *Demographie als Herausforderung für den öffentlichen Sektor,* Wiesbaden: VS-Verlag für die Sozialwissenschaften.

Keller, Berndt and Hartmut Seifert (2014) 'Atypische Beschäftigungsverhältnisse im Öffentlichen Dienst', *WSI-Mitteilungen* 8/2014, 1–12.

Kettl, Donald F. (1997) 'The Global Revolution in Public Management: Driving Themes, Missing Links', *Journal of Public Policy Analysis and Management* 16, 446–62.

Kettunen, Pauli (2006) 'The Power of International Comparison. A Perspective on the Making and the Challenging of the Nordic Welfare State', in Niels F. Christiansen, Klaus Peteresen, Nils Edling and Per Haave (eds.) *The Nordic Model of Welfare. A Historical Reappraisal,* Copenhagen: Tusculanum Press.

Kroos, Daniela (2010) *Warum hat 'Marianne' so viele Diener? Zum Wachstum des französischen öffentlichen Dienstes entgegen internationaler Trends,* TranState Working Paper 115, Bremen: CRC 597 Collaborative Research Centre 597 – Transformations of the State, University of Bremen.

Kuhlmann, Sabine (2011) 'Decentralization in France: The "Jacobin" State Stuck between Continuity and Transformation', *Croatian and Comparative Public Administration* 11, 311–36.

Lehmbruch, Gerhard (1991) 'The Organization of Society, Administrative Strategies, and Policy Networks. Elements of a Developmental Theory of Interest Systems', in Roland M. Czada and Adrienne Windhoff-Héritier (eds.) *Political Choice. Institutions, Rules, and the Limits of Rationality,* Frankfurt am Main: Campus Verlag.

Leibfried, Stephan, Evelyne Huber, Matthew Lange, Jonah D. Levy, Frank Nullmeier and John D. Stephens (eds.) (2015) *The Oxford Handbook of Transformations of the State,* Oxford: Oxford University Press.

Obinger, Herbert, Peter Starke, Julia Moser, Claudia Bogedan, Edith Gindulis and Stephan Leibfried (2010) *Transformations of the Welfare State. Small States, Big Lessons*, Oxford: Oxford University Press.

OECD (2004) *Public Sector Modernisation: Modernising Public Employment*, Paris: OECD.

OECD (2005) *Performance-Related Pay Policies for Government Employees*, Paris: OECD.

OECD (2009) *Government at a Glance 2009*, Paris: OECD.

Pierson, Paul (ed.) (2001) *The New Politics of the Welfare State*, Oxford: Oxford University Press.

Pollitt, Christopher and Geert Bouckaert (2011) *Public Management Reform: A Comparative Analysis. New Public Management, Governance, and the Neo-Weberian State*, 3rd ed., Oxford: Oxford University Press.

Premfors, Rune (1991) 'The "Swedish Model" and Public Sector Reform', *West European Politics* 14, 83–95.

Rothenbacher, Franz (1998) 'The Changing Public Sector in Europe: Social Structure, Income and Social Security', *EURODATA Newsletter* 8, 1–6.

Vaughan-Whitehead, Daniel (ed.) (2013) *Public Sector Shock: The Impact of Policy Retrenchment in Europe*, Cheltenham: Edward Elgar.

10 Conclusions and Outlook

Dingeldey, Irene (2009) 'Changing Forms of Governance as Welfare State Restructuring. Activating Labour Market Policies in Denmark, the UK and Germany', in Dingeldey, Irene and Heinz Rothgang (eds.) *Governance of Welfare State Reform. A Cross National and Cross Sectoral Comparison of Policy and Politics*, Cheltenham: Edward Elgar.

Emmenegger, Patrick, Silja Häusermann, Bruno Palier and Martin Seeleib-Kaiser (eds.) *The Age of Dualization: The Changing Face of Inequality in Deindustrializing Societies*, Oxford: Oxford University Press.

Gallie, Duncan (2007) 'Regimes, Employment Regimes, and the Quality of Work', in Duncan Gallie (ed.) *Employment Regimes and the Quality of Work*, Oxford: Oxford University Press.

Gottschall, Karin; Andreas Häberle, Jan-Ocko Heuer and Sylvia Hils (2015) *Weder Staatsdiener noch Dienstleister. Selbstverständnis öffentlich Beschäftigter in Deutschland*, TranState Working Paper 187, Bremen: CRC 597 Collaborative Research Centre 597 – Transformations of the State, University of Bremen.

Hall, David (2012) *Re-Municipalising Municipal Services in Europe. A Report Commissioned by EPSU to Public Services International Research Unit (PSIRU), May 2012*, Greenwich: PSIRU.

Leibfried, Stephan and Michael Zürn (eds.) (2005) *Transformations of the State?*, Cambridge: Cambridge University Press.

Leibfried, Stephan, Evelyne Huber, Matthew Lange, Jonah D. Levy, Frank Nullmeier and John D. Stephens (eds.) (2015) *The Oxford Handbook of Transformations of the State*, Oxford: Oxford University Press.

Pierson, Paul (1998) 'Irresistible Forces, Immovable Objects: Post-Industrial Welfare States Confront Permanent Austerity', *Journal of European Public Policy* 5, 539–60.

Pollitt, Christopher and Geert Bouckaert (2011) *Public Management Reform: A Comparative Analysis. New Public Management, Governance, and the Neo-Weberian State*, 3rd ed., Oxford: Oxford University Press.

Tepe, Markus, Karin Gottschall and Bernhard Kittel (2010) 'A Structural Fit between States and Markets? Public Administration Regimes and Market Economy Models in the OECD', *Socio-Economic Review* 8, 653–84.

Vaughan-Whitehead, Daniel (2013) *Public Sector Shock: The Impact of Policy Retrenchment in Europe*, Cheltenham: Edward Elgar.

Wollmann, Hellmut and Gérard Marcou (eds.) (2010) *The Provision of Public Services in Europe: Between State, Local Government and Market*, Cheltenham: Edward Elgar.

Index

CPSIA information can be obtained
at www.ICGtesting.com
Printed in the USA
LVOW04*1518210916

505617LV00021B/324/P